DISNEY INFINITY

WRITTEN BY
MICHAEL KNIGHT & MICHAEL SEARLE

MARVEL
SUPER HEROES

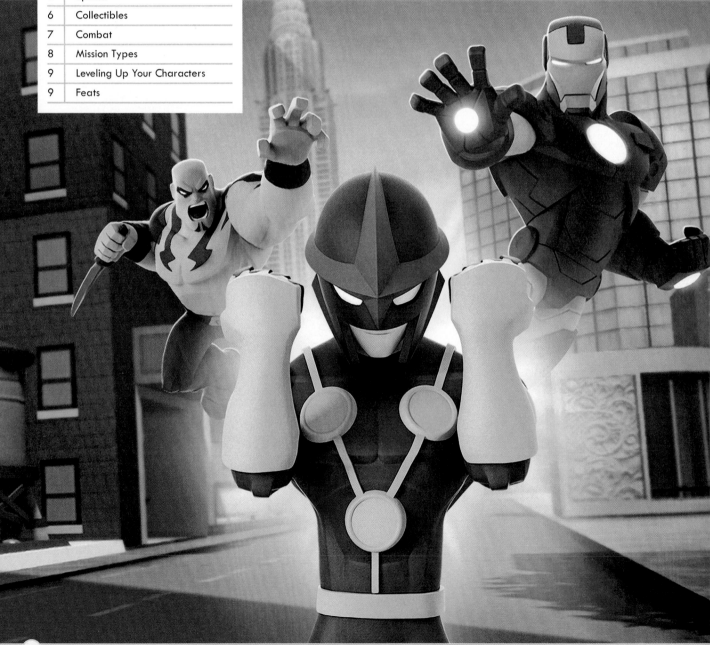

GAME BASICS

YOUR SCREEN

1 **Character Portrait:** A picture of the hero currently in use.

2 **Blue Sparks:** You accumulate these from breaking open blue capsules and as rewards at the end of a mission. Spend them in the Toy Store on cool toys and accessories.

3 **Level:** The number shows your current level, and the bar displays your progress toward the next level.

4 **Objective Marker:** A mission marker that pinpoints distance and location for your next objective.

5 **Mini-Map:** A radar map showing the direction you're facing. Various points of interest display on the map, such as objectives as yellow dots and challenges as green dots.

6 **Targeting Circle:** This is where you are pointing. Very important for ranged combat and locking on to targets.

7 **Your Hero:** In this case, Thor, the God of Thunder. He's a flyer, so he can float above the city streets.

MOVEMENT

——BASIC MOTION——

There are a large number of characters to play in the game, and fortunately they all move in a similar fashion. You use one stick to move and the other to look around, and you use the same buttons to jump, block, dodge, and activate abilities; however, each hero from a Play Set is unique and has his or her own special abilities and methods of attack. They do all share a few common movements that are essential for navigation and platforming.

——JUMPING——

The first common technique is the double jump, and while it is easy to do, there is more to it than merely pressing a button twice. Double jumps will allow you to jump higher, but they can also allow you to jump longer. If you wait until you begin to fall on the first part of your jump, and then press the jump button for the second time, you will extend the distance you cover, allowing you to jump across far ledges and buildings. In each Play Set, jump platforms are set up to launch characters up to predefined landing spots. For those characters without flying, using jump platforms is essential to reach rooftops and other high platforms. If you have Super Jump, holding the jump button sends you sky high. If you don't begin with Super Jump, check your skill tree for it and, if you have it, unlock your Super Jump ability when you want to increase your vertical leap.

CLIMBING

Most of the platforming in the game will include plenty of climbing. The skill is easy to perform, but it can be tricky to know where you can actually climb. Look for railings along climbable edges; usually these railings are yellow or blue. Once you are hanging, there are a lot of options including jumping up or over to another grapple point, jumping down or off the structure, or following the hand hold to maneuver around the edge. Other objects, such as poles, can also be climbed. If a hero has Wall Crawl, he or she can climb straight up a surface, regardless of edges or railings.

BLOCK/DODGE

All heroes have the ability to move in a quick fashion—rolling, flipping, hopping—which can be used for defense or offense. A dodge is a great way to avoid an attack (by holding block and pressing the control stick in the direction you want to dodge) and to maneuver into a better position, such as behind an enemy for a sneak attack. If you don't touch the control stick and press the block button, you defend in place and decrease the damage from melee attacks.

FLYING

Some heroes have the ability to fly. In *hover mode*, the left control stick is used to move left/ right/ forward/ backwards, the jump button moves up, and right control stick moves the camera. In *flight mode* (i.e., with the left trigger down), the left control stick does barrel rolls (left/right) and the right control stick steers (up/down/left/right). Don't worry about falling; you can't be hurt. When you want to land, you can continue full speed into the ground and perform an Air Attack, or you can use your block button to suddenly stop flying and drop to the ground. Some characters might not be able to fly, but they can Web Swing, which, once you know how to sling yourself along, can be almost as good.

VEHICLES

GROUND AND FLYING

All vehicles move by using one stick to steer and the other to look around, and they all use the triggers to accelerate and brake/reverse. Ground vehicles, like the S.H.I.E.L.D. Motorcycle, will get you from point A to point B quicker than running it, and with vehicles you have limited jumping and shooting abilities to clear obstacles. However, if you're a character who relies on your feet to get around, you really want a flying vehicle as soon as possible. Certain missions require that you reach rooftops or high platforms, and though you have jump platforms to help you reach any location, it's much easier to navigate the 3D space once you acquire that flying vehicle.

DRIFTING

Drifting is the process of holding both triggers while driving into a turn or even a circle. This maneuver is great for getting around corners when you are at top seeds, but more importantly it builds up the turbo meter. More turbo means more speed. Drift in any race or situation where you need to store up that potential boost.

TURBO

There is a meter under your vehicle that indicates how many bars of turbo you have. When you do a stunt or drift, the meter in one bar will fill until it is yellow, which means you can activate that boost. After one bar is yellow, the next gauge will start to fill and continue the process. Once all segments of the meter are yellow, you are wasting an effort to build turbo and should use a boost as soon as possible. Turbo activation is a simple flick of the control stick and your vehicle will shoot flames showing you are boosting. Obviously, it can be dangerous to boost at a turn, but a drift can help control that speed. A turbo assist is great any time you are in a straightaway, a close race to the finish, or when you want to hit a ramp at top speed to maximize your air time for stunts or tricks.

GAME BASICS

CHARACTERS

POWER DISCS

MARVEL'S THE AVENGERS

SPIDER-MAN

GUARDIANS OF THE GALAXY

TOY BOX

TOY BOX COLLECTION

ACHIEVEMENTS

STUNT/TRICKS

Probably the coolest thing about vehicles, besides high-speed driving, is the tricks you can pull off. After leaping in the air, pushing the right stick up, down, left, or right will trigger front or back flips, spins, or barrel rolls. Doing two of the same motion while in the air is considered a double trick. However, if you push in two different directions, the stunt is considered a combo and earns more points. If you get enough height and speed, it is possible to pull off a triple combo for really big points on courses like the ice stunt park. The key to chaining moves is to immediately flip the control stick when you are airborne and quickly press another direction as that move completes to perform the next trick.

SPARKS

BLUE SPARKS

Sparks usually come from capsules; break open a capsule and Sparks spill out. You may have to run through them to capture them all because they only last for a limited time. Blue Sparks are your form of currency. Take all the blue Sparks you capture and spend those blue Sparks in the Toy Store on various cool toys and accessories. You are also rewarded blue Sparks at the completion of each mission.

GREEN SPARKS

Green Sparks are for health regeneration. As your character takes damage, your health bar decreases; green Sparks fill your health bar back up.

ORANGE SPARKS

Orange Sparks give you experience. Just like defeating foes and gaining experience through the orange Sparks they drop, orange capsules give you experience Sparks, only there are usually more orange Sparks in a capsule than even a modest enemy encounter.

PURPLE SPARKS

Collecting purple Sparks adds to your special ability bar. Depending on your character and your skills, you may have more than one section on your special ability bar, and these purple Sparks fill the bar up so you can use your really powerful abilities.

COLLECTIBLES

CROSSOVER COINS

Each Play Set has two Crossover Characters, which can only be unlocked after you find all ten Crossover Coins belonging to that character. These spinning Crossover Coins will be spread throughout the Play Set—on street corners, high up on rooftops, or hidden under platforms, for example. After you unlock a Crossover Character, you will receive three unique side missions designed specially for that character. For example, if you discover all ten Crossover Coins for Iron Man in the Guardians of the Galaxy Play Set, Iron Man will become available to undertake three side missions that rely on flight and his particular fighting skills to complete.

Game Basics

GAME BASICS

CHARACTERS

POWER DISCS

MARVEL'S THE AVENGERS

SPIDER-MAN

GUARDIANS OF THE GALAXY

TOY BOX

TOY BOX COLLECTION

ACHIEVEMENTS

Crossover Characters		
CROSSOVER HERO	COIN COLOR	PLAY SET UNLOCKED IN
Nova	Blue	Avengers, Guardians of the Galaxy
Rocket Raccoon	Yellow	Avengers
Iron Man	Red	Spider-Man, Guardians of the Galaxy
Hulk	Green	Spider-Man

BONUS BOXES

There are five different Bonus Box types in each Play Set, and collecting all twenty of a Bonus Box type accomplishes a feat. The Bonus Box types are as follows: Tech (Avengers, Guardians of the Galaxy Play Sets only), Web Swing (Spider-Man Play Set only), Wall Crawl, Flight, Super Jump, and Maximum Strength. Each Bonus Box type requires you to use that ability to discover each associated cube. For example, a Tech hero can use certain Tech stations to unlock a hidden Tech Bonus Box, a Wall Crawl hero will have to crawl up a building face to retrieve a Wall Crawl cube, Flight Bonus Boxes are high up in the sky, Super Jump Bonus Boxes can only be reached with a big leap, and Maximum Strength Bonus Boxes, though near street level, may require a crushing blow to reveal them from their surroundings.

NOTE

Keep in mind, though, that you can only see a Bonus Box if you have the associated skill; otherwise, the Bonus Box will be faded out and nearly invisible to you. Someone like the Hulk will initially be able to see Maximum Strength Bonus Boxes, but won't be able to see Flight or Tech Bonus Boxes. If you upgrade to Hulk's Superhuman Leap ability, you will be able to see Super Jump Bonus Boxes, and if you upgrade to his Crushing Climb ability you will be able to see Wall Crawl Bonus Boxes.

COMBAT

MELEE

All heroes have melee skills, though some like Hulk, Venom, and Drax are more skilled in hand-to-hand combat than others. In melee, one punch or kick may be fine, but you usually want to string together a combo of melee attacks to inflict maximum damage on a foe. Many enemies will fall down after taking some damage, but that doesn't mean they are defeated. A lot of them can be hit while they are down or trying to get up, so make sure to finish off a single enemy. Quickly switching from enemy to enemy is a good tactic when you are surrounded, but it is always a good idea to reduce the number of foes you face as soon as possible.

RANGED

Heroes like Hawkeye, Nova, and Star-Lord have ranged attacks that can deal damage far away from the potential danger of melee combat. Ranged attacks will generally shoot at the closest target; however, when you need precision, you can enter a zoomed-in mode where you can place the aiming cursor over what you want to hit. When your ranged fire is locked on an enemy like this, you can still run and gun, allowing you to move quickly while unloading ranged damage on a single target. It's also a good technique for destroying obstacles.

AREA-EFFECT

Certain heroes have area-effect attacks that will damage multiple enemies that are close together. Area-effect comes in two forms: personal area-effects, such as Thor's Lightning Strike, which surrounds the hero with damage, or ranged area-effects, such as Hawkeye's Rain of Arrows, which deals out damage to all enemies in the area surrounding the point of attack. All heroes have the ability to perform an Air Attack, which is useful when surrounded by enemies as it lifts your character out of danger for a second and delivers an attack to the enemies immediately nearby.

SPECIAL MOVES

Every hero has different special moves that make them unique in combat. Depending on the mission and enemy encounters, you may want a quicker hero like Iron Fist, or a well-rounded hero like Spider-Man, or a ranged specialist like Rocket Raccoon. Your main special ability is powered by purple Sparks. Once you trigger it, such as Thor's Lighting Strike, your special ability bar depletes and you'll need more purple Sparks to power it back up. Get to know your heroes and what they can do. When you receive a mission that requires stealth, call on Black Widow, but a mission with hordes of Frost Giants pinning you down might benefit from Cap's Shield Assault.

BLOCKING

On the opposite end of the combat spectrum is the defensive ability to block with a simple button press. Most attacks can be blocked, and while this doesn't get you any closer to defeating your enemy, the maneuver can set your enemy up to drop its guard. By blocking or absorbing an attack, it can create an opening for you to counter or avoid getting knocked down. If you aren't sure what to do in a battle, especially when faced with a powerful foe, fall back on the block and plan your next move. Keep in mind, too, that certain attacks can break blocks and deliver potent counterattacks. For example, Hulk's Sonic Clap Combo breaks an opponent's block and juggles them into the air for a Sonic Clap Attack.

MISSION TYPES

Mission givers send you on your missions. A blue exclamation mark floats over a mission giver's head if he or she has a mission to discuss with you. If there's a question mark over the mission giver's head, it means you are already on a mission for that character. Mission givers also send out a blue beacon that can be seen from far away. Once you embark on a mission, yellow objective markers will guide you from task to task. When you get near to an objective, yellow arrows will help you identify tasks. If you see a green beacon, it notes the location of a challenge; these will unlock throughout the game as you complete various missions and tasks. Remember that some missions only become available after completing other tasks, unlocking specific conditions, or getting to certain points in the game.

> **NOTE**
>
> Your Mission Log is a useful tool for keeping track of your missions. At any point, you can see your Active Missions, Available Missions, and Completed Missions. You also have an option to guide you to a specific mission giver, which will display a yellow objective marker that you can follow right to the mission in question.

MAIN MISSIONS

Play Sets come with a variety of fun missions, and your main missions drive the main story forward.

These are your primary quests where you will encounter many familiar characters from the Play Set's world. All of the main missions combine to tell a complete tale from start to finish, although the story can have several branching elements. To finish the Play Set's story, you will have to complete all main missions.

SIDE MISSIONS

Side missions are usually optional tasks that can be done to enhance the journey. Beyond the obvious joy of completing them, there are often rewards that make it well worth your time to go through each one. These missions can be as quick as a single task or more involved like your main missions.

CHALLENGES

Challenges are unlocked as you complete certain missions or achieve at least the Bronze goal on previous challenges. They give off a green beacon, but the beacon will not appear if you are using a hero who cannot enter the challenge. Most challenges are meant for all heroes in that Play Set, but some are specific to heroes, such as Iron Man's Fight or Flight challenge. Each challenge has three goal levels: Bronze, Silver, and Gold. Rewards are handed out based on your level of success and follow the same reward levels: 75 blue Sparks for Bronze, 325 blue Sparks for Silver, and 825 blue Sparks for Gold.

LEVELING UP YOUR CHARACTERS

As your characters collect orange Sparks, they earn experience and, when they have enough, they level up. Every time they level up, they also earn Skill Points that they can spend in the Skill Tree. You can get to the Skill Tree from the pause menu. Each character's Skill Tree is different. It consists of skills that can affect health, speed, melee combat, ranged combat, the speed at which Power Discs recharge, and a unique Special Move. This move must be unlocked in the Skill Tree and can then be upgraded. For most characters, you want to get your special move as quickly as possible. Depending on your character, you may choose to focus on melee or ranged attacks.

> **NOTE**
>
> Characters can advance up to level 20. However, you will not have enough Skill Points to purchase every single skill. Therefore, you have to be careful what you pick. When you reach level 10 and then again at level 20, you can respend your Skill Points. However, this is a one-time event for each time, so you still have to be careful.

The Skill Tree is called such because you can't just pick any skill you want. You have to follow the branches of the tree to get to some skills, purchasing others along the way. Therefore, look at all the skills and find out which you really want and begin spending Skill Points to get to them. When looking at a Skill Tree, you may notice that some of the skills have laurels around them. These are skills that the game designers recommend and are very useful for that specific character. Try to include those in your acquired skills.

> **NOTE**
>
> Check out the Characters chapter to learn all about each of the skills on the Skill Trees for each of the Marvel characters. If you look at the included Skill Tree for each character, you can see the skills highlighted that the game testers found most useful. This can serve as a guide if you are not sure what skills you want to get.

FEATS

Feats are tasks you complete during your missions for accomplishments in combat, collection, or even hero-specific deeds. Their difficulty can be easy (Beginning Bonus: Collect a Bonus Box in the Avengers Play Set), medium (Damage Control: Deliver 16 civilians to heat generators), or hard (Un-De-Feat-Able: Complete all feats). They can be specific to a hero (Thor's Green Thunder, which requires Thor attack Hulk), or completely fun and random (Road Trip: Ride a motorcycle as Captain America for 5 kilometers). Working on challenges, feats, and collecting Bonus Boxes will complete even more feats for you, as many center around these three areas. You will have a great time playing through the Play Set missions—and you'll have an even better time if you try to complete the feats along the way!

> **NOTE**
>
> See the last page in each Play Set chapter for the complete rundown on that Play Set's feats.

GAME BASICS

CHARACTERS

POWER DISCS

MARVEL'S THE AVENGERS

SPIDER-MAN

GUARDIANS OF THE GALAXY

TOY BOX

TOY BOX COLLECTION

ACHIEVEMENTS

CHARACTERS

MARVEL'S THE AVENGERS

Take flight to pulse blast your foes with Iron Man's Stark Tech armor.

SPECIAL ABILITIES
- Flying
- Tech
- Repulsor Blasts
- Mini Missiles
- Shields
- Crossover Character

SKILL TREE

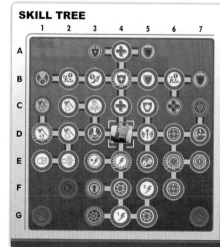

IRON MAN

	SKILL	DESCRIPTION	COST
	Skills		
B3	Acceleration Upgrade – Level 1	Increases Iron Man's running speed.	1
D2	Damage Increase 1	Increases the damage of Iron Man's combo attack. (Tap attack button.)	2
C2	Damage Increase 2	Increases the damage of Iron Man's combo attack. (Tap attack button.)	4
B1	Full Thrusters	Increases the Speed of Iron Man's flight. (Hold the jump button to hover, hold Left Trigger while hovering for free flight.)	3
E2	Grapple Mines	Deploys a grapple mine (hold attack button) that detonates on contact with an opponent, breaking their block. Can be fired for defense against an incoming attack by continuing to hold the attack button to deploy more mines. Mines will detonate upon releasing the attack button.	2
C4	Health Boost 1	Increases Iron Man's maximum health.	1
A4	Health Boost 2	Increases Iron Man's maximum health.	3
B6	Helping Hand	Decreases the amount of health needed to revive another Character or sidekick.	2
D5	Mid-Air Recovery	Allows the Character to recover in mid-air by tapping the jump button.	1
E4	Missile Barrage	Iron Man's Special Move (tap special move button). Stand in place and shoot a barrage of missiles that will seek out opponents within a certain range.	2
E5	Paired Pulse Bolts	Allows Iron Man to shoot Pulse Bolts (Tap ranged attack button) from both hands.	3
C3	Pavement Pounder	Increases the damage and area affected by Iron Man's Air Assault. (Tap jump button, then tap attack button.)	2
F3	Power Disc Recharge Upgrade 1	Increases the rate at which the Power Disc meter fills.	3
F2	Power Disc Recharge Upgrade 2	Increases the rate at which the Power Disc meter fills.	5
E6	Power Pulse Bolts	Iron Man can charge up his Pulse Bolt by holding the ranged attack button for a more powerful firing blast.	2
D7	Pulse Bolt Blitz	Increases the Pulse Bolt's rate of fire (Tap ranged attack button.)	3
E7	Quick Charge	Reduces the time it takes to charge up the Pulse Bolts. (Hold ranged attack button.)	4
D6	Ranged Attack Upgrade 1	Increases the damage of Iron Man's Pulse Bolt attack. (Tap ranged attack button.)	2
F6	Ranged Attack Upgrade 2	Increases the damage of Iron Man's Pulse Bolt attack. (Tap ranged attack button.)	4
B4	Regenerating Shields	Shields that must be depleted before Iron Man's health is affected. These shields regenerate over time.	2
A3	Regenerative Powers	Increases the rate that the shields regenerate.	5
C5	Repel	Repel an attacking opponent. Tap the defend button just before an attack. Requires skilled timing.	3
E1	Repulsor Blossom Attack	After detonating a grapple mine, release the attack button and then tap it again to perform a spinning attack that damages surrounding opponents.	4
G1	Respender 1	At level 10, allows you to completely respend all of your skill points. Use it wisely, though. Once purchased, it will be permanently used.	0
G7	Respender 2	At level 20, allows you to completely respend all of your skill points. Use it wisely, though. Once purchased, it will be permanently used.	0
B5	Shield Surge 1	Increases the amount of damage the shield can stop.	3
B7	Shield Surge 2	Increases the amount of damage the shield can stop.	5
A5	Shield Surge 3	Increases the amount of damage the shield can stop.	6
G5	Special Move Bonus 2	Increases the damage caused by the Missile Barrage. (Tap special move button.)	4
F4	Special Move Bonus 1	Increases the damage caused by the Missile Barrage. (Tap special move button.)	2
G3	Special Move Mega Bonus	Increases the damage caused by the Missile Barrage. (Tap special move button.)	6
G4	Special Move Meter Upgrade 1	Adds a portion to the Special Move meter. When filled, the Character can activate a Special Move.	3
F5	Special Move Meter Upgrade 2	Adds a portion to the Special Move meter. When filled, the Character can activate a Special Move.	5
E3	Speedy Meter Upgrade	Increases the rate at which the Special Move meter fills when Power Pickups are obtained.	4
D1	Stark's Strong Finish	Adds a new finishing move to Iron Man's combo attack. (Tap attack button.)	4
D3	Street Spike	Allows the Character to slam a carried object into the ground by tapping the attack button.	1
C1	Super Damage Increase	Increases the damage of Iron Man's combo attack. (Tap attack button.)	6
C6	Super Health Boost	Maximizes Iron Man's health.	5
B2	Team Player	Decreases the amount of time it takes to revive another Character or sidekick.	2
C7	Ultra Ranged Attack Upgrade	Increases the damage of Iron Man's Pulse Bolt attack. (Tap ranged attack button.)	6

THOR

Thor uses his cosmic hammer of thunder and his immortal strength to vanquish his foes.

SPECIAL ABILITIES

- Flying
- Maximum Strength
- Mjolnir
- Lightning

SKILL TREE

Skills			
	SKILL	**DESCRIPTION**	**COST**
D3	Damage Increase 1	Increases the damage of Thor's combo attack. (Tap attack button.)	1
C1	Damage Increase 2	Increases the damage of Thor's combo attack. (Tap attack button.)	4
A4	Gusting Winds – Level 1	Increases Thor's running speed.	2
E2	Hammer Down	Increases the damage and range of Thor's Air Assault. (Tap jump button, then tap attack button.)	2
C4	Health Boost 1	Increases Thor's maximum health.	1
B4	Health Boost 2	Increases Thor's maximum health.	3
A6	Health Boost 3	Increases Thor's maximum health.	5
B6	Health Boost 4	Increases Thor's maximum health.	6
C3	Heavy Hammer	A combo (hold attack button) that breaks an opponent's block and juggles them into the air for a final attack with Mjolnir.	2
A5	Helping Hand	Decreases the amount of health needed to revive another Character or sidekick.	2
B5	Helping Hand Upgrade	Decreases the amount of health needed to revive another Character or sidekick.	4
E4	Lightning Strike	Thor's Special Move (tap special move button). Summons lightning to Mjolnir, creating a destructive area of lightning around Thor.	2
D5	Mid-Air Recovery	Allows the Character to recover in mid-air by tapping the jump button.	1
C5	Mjolnir Flight Upgrade	Increases the Speed of Thor's flight. (Hold the jump button to hover, hold left trigger while hovering for free flight.)	3
D6	Mjolnir Lightning Charge	Mjolnir can now be charged with lightning (hold ranged attack button) that will arc to enemies as the hammer flies past.	2
D7	Mjolnir Lightning Charge Upgrade	Decreases the time it takes to charge Mjolnir (hold ranged attack button) with lightning.	5
F3	Power Disc Recharge Upgrade 1	Increases the rate at which the Power Disc meter fills.	3
F2	Power Disc Recharge Upgrade 2	Increases the rate at which the Power Disc meter fills.	5
E6	Ranged Attack Upgrade 1	Increases the damage of Thor's Mjolnir Throw attacks. (Tap ranged attack button.)	2
C6	Ranged Attack Upgrade 2	Increases the damage of Thor's Mjolnir Throw attacks. (Tap ranged attack button.)	4
D2	Repel	Repel an attacking opponent. Tap the defend button just before an attack. Requires skilled timing.	3
G1	Respender 1	At level 10, allows you to completely respend all of your skill points. Use it wisely, though. Once purchased, it will be permanently used.	0
G7	Respender 2	At level 20, allows you to completely respend all of your skill points. Use it wisely, though. Once purchased, it will be permanently used.	0
F4	Special Move Bonus 1	Increases the damage caused by Thor's Lightning Strike. (Tap special move button.)	2
F5	Special Move Bonus 2	Increases the damage caused by Thor's Lightning Strike. (Tap special move button.)	4
G5	Special Move Mega Bonus	Increases the damage caused by Thor's Lightning Strike. (Tap special move button.)	6
G4	Special Move Meter Upgrade 1	Adds a portion to the Special Move meter. When filled, the Character can activate a Special Move.	3
G3	Special Move Meter Upgrade 2	Adds a portion to the Special Move meter. When filled, the Character can activate a Special Move.	5
E5	Speedy Meter Upgrade	Increases the rate at which the Special Move meter fills when Power Pickups are obtained.	4
E3	Street Spike	Allows the Character to slam a carried object into the ground by tapping the attack button.	1
E7	Summon Mjolnir	This upgrade allows Thor to call Mjolnir back (Tap ranged attack button) before it has finished the attack.	6
E1	Super Damage Increase	Increases the damage of Thor's combo attack. (Tap attack button.)	6
B2	Super Health Boost	Maximizes Thor's maximum health.	6
A3	Team Player	Decreases the amount of time it takes to revive another Character or sidekick.	2
B3	Team Player Upgrade	Decreases the amount of time it takes to revive another Character or sidekick.	4
D1	Thor's Strong Finish	Adds an additional attack to Thor's combo attack. (Tap attack button.)	4
C2	Thunder Shake	Heavy strike with Mjolnir (hold attack, then release and tap attack early) to send opponent flying. Requires skilled timing.	4
C7	Ultra Ranged Attack Upgrade	Increases the damage of Thor's Mjolnir Throw attacks. (Tap ranged attack button.)	6

GAME BASICS

CHARACTERS

POWER DISCS

MARVEL'S THE AVENGERS

SPIDER-MAN

GUARDIANS OF THE GALAXY

TOY BOX

TOY BOX COLLECTION

ACHIEVEMENTS

BLACK WIDOW

A covert ops expert, Black Widow uses invisibility and stingers to complete her stealth missions.

SPECIAL ABILITIES
- Super Jump
- Tech
- Widow's Bite Stingers
- Widow's Veil S.H.I.E.L.D. tech

SKILL TREE

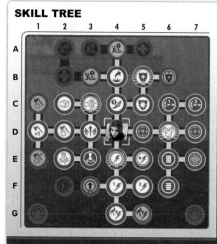

Skills			
SKILL		**DESCRIPTION**	**COST**
E2	Air Assault Upgrade	Increases the damage and area of effect of Black Widow's Air Assault. (Tap jump button, then tap attack button.)	3
D2	Damage Increase 1	Increases the damage of Black Widow's combo attack. (Tap attack button.)	2
C1	Damage Increase 2	Increases the damage of Black Widow's combo attack. (Tap attack button.)	4
D6	Double Trouble	This allows Black Widow to shoot with a pistol in each hand. (Tap ranged attack button.)	3
C6	Fire Power Upgrade – Level 1	Increases the rate of fire of Black Widow's pistols. (Tap ranged attack button.)	4
C7	Fire Power Upgrade – Level 2	Increases the rate of fire of Black Widow's pistols. (Tap ranged attack button.)	6
C2	Flying Kick	After firing a stinger, release the attack button and then tap the attack button to perform a flying kick that sends opponents flying.	4
A5	Health Boost	Increases Black Widow's maximum health.	3
A4	Helping Hand	Decreases the amount of health needed to revive another Character or sidekick.	2
A3	Helping Hand Upgrade	Decreases the amount of health needed to revive another Character or sidekick.	4
B4	Jumping Spider	This unlocks Black Widow's Super Jump ability. (Hold jump button.)	1
D3	Mid-Air Recovery	Allows the Character to recover in mid-air by tapping the jump button.	1
F3	Power Disc Recharge Upgrade 1	Increases the rate at which the Power Disc meter fills.	3
F2	Power Disc Recharge Upgrade 2	Increases the rate at which the Power Disc meter fills.	5
B5	Protective S.H.I.E.L.D.	Protective shields that must be penetrated before Black Widow's health is damaged. Regenerates over time.	3
D5	Ranged Attack Upgrade 1	Increases the damage of Black Widow's pistols. (Tap ranged attack button).	1
D7	Ranged Attack Upgrade 2	Increases the damage of Black Widow's pistols. (Tap ranged attack button).	4
C5	Repel	Repel an attacking opponent. Tap the defend button just before an attack. Requires skilled timing.	3
G1	Respender 1	At level 10, allows you to completely respend all of your skill points. Use it wisely, though. Once purchased, it will be permanently used.	0
G7	Respender 2	At level 20, allows you to completely respend all of your skill points. Use it wisely, though. Once purchased, it will be permanently used.	0
C4	Romanoff Rush	Increases Black Widow's running speed.	1
B6	Shield Strength	Increases the rate that the shield regenerates.	6
F4	Special Move Meter Upgrade 1	Adds a portion to the Special Move meter. When filled, the Character can activate a Special Move.	3
F5	Special Move Meter Upgrade 2	Adds a portion to the Special Move meter. When filled, the Character can activate a Special Move.	5
E5	Speedy Meter Upgrade	Increases the rate at which the Special Move meter fills when Power Pickups are obtained.	4
E3	Street Spike	Allows the Character to slam a carried object into the ground by tapping the attack button.	1
D1	Strong Finish	Adds a new finished move to the Character's combo attack. (Tap attack button)	4
E1	Super Damage Increase	Increases the damage of Black Widow's combo attack. (Tap attack button).	6
B2	Super Health Boost	Increases Black Widow's maximum health.	5
B3	Team Player	Decreases the amount of time it takes to revive another Character or sidekick.	2
A2	Team Player Upgrade	Decreases the amount of time it takes to revive another Character or sidekick.	4
E7	Ultra Ranged Attack Upgrade	Increases the damage of Black Widow's pistols. (Tap ranged attack button).	6
E6	Weapon Upgrade – Level 1	Increases the number of shots that can be fired (tap ranged fire button) before pausing to reload.	3
F6	Weapon Upgrade – Level 2	Increases the number of shots that can be fired (tap ranged fire button) before pausing to reload.	5
C3	Widow's Sting	Fire a stinger (hold attack button) at an opponent, shocking them and breaking their block. Electricity from the stinger will arc to nearby enemies.	2
E4	Widow's Veil	Black Widow's Special Move (tap special move button). She becomes cloaked via S.H.I.E.L.D. tech accessible from her gauntlets.	2
G4	Widow's Veil Upgrade – Level 1	Increases the duration Widow's Veil (tap special move button) will stay active.	4
G5	Widow's Veil Upgrade – Level 2	Increases the duration Widow's Veil (tap special move button) will stay active.	6

CAPTAIN AMERICA

Captain America courageously meets evil head on with the help of his indestructible combat shield.

SPECIAL ABILITIES

- Cap's Shield
- Super Jump

SKILL TREE

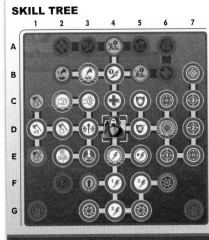

GAME BASICS

CHARACTERS

POWER DISCS

MARVEL'S THE AVENGERS

SPIDER-MAN

GUARDIANS OF THE GALAXY

TOY BOX

TOY BOX COLLECTION

ACHIEVEMENTS

		Skills	
	SKILL	**DESCRIPTION**	**COST**
E4	Cap's Shield Assault	Captain America's Special Move (tap special move button). Cap throws his shield, which makes a wide spiral pattern as it slowly returns to him, damaging opponents and obstacles in its wake.	2
D2	Damage Increase 1	Increases the damage of Captain America's combo attack. (Tap attack button).	2
C1	Damage Increase 2	Increases the damage of Captain America's combo attack. (Tap attack button).	4
C2	Flying the Colors	Throw Cap's shield after starting Vibranium Vengeance (hold attack, then release and tap attack early) to send the opponent flying. Requires skilled timing.	4
C4	Health Boost 1	Increases Captain America's maximum health.	1
B6	Health Boost 2	Increases Captain America's maximum health.	3
B5	Helping Hand	Decreases the amount of health needed to revive another Character or sidekick.	2
A6	Helping Hand Upgrade	Decreases the amount of health needed to revive another Character or sidekick.	4
D3	Mid-Air Recovery	Allows the Character to recover in mid-air by tapping the jump button.	1
F3	Power Disc Recharge Upgrade 1	Increases the rate at which the Power Disc meter fills.	3
F2	Power Disc Recharge Upgrade 2	Increases the rate at which the Power Disc meter fills.	5
C6	Ranged Attack Upgrade 1	Increases the damage of Cap's Shield Strike. (Hold ranged attack button).	2
E7	Ranged Attack Upgrade 2	Increases the damage of Cap's Shield Strike. (Hold ranged attack button).	4
C5	Repel	Repel an attacking opponent. Tap the defend button just before an attack. Requires skilled timing.	3
G1	Respender 1	At level 10, allows you to completely respend all of your skill points. Use it wisely, though. Once purchased, it will be permanently used.	0
G7	Respender 2	At level 20, allows you to completely respend all of your skill points. Use it wisely, though. Once purchased, it will be permanently used.	0
D6	Shield Strike	Charges Cap's ranged attack (hold ranged attack button) to deliver more damage and ricochet between targets.	2
E6	Shield Strike Upgrade – Level 1	Allows Cap's shield to ricochet among more targets when it's charged. (Hold ranged attack button).	3
D7	Shield Strike Upgrade – Level 2	Allows Cap's shield to ricochet among more targets when it's charged. (Hold ranged attack button).	4
C7	Shield Strike Upgrade – Level 3	Allows Cap's shield to ricochet among more targets when it's charged. (Hold ranged attack button).	5
G3	Special Move Bonus 1	Increases the damage of Cap's Shield Assault. (Tap special move button).	2
G5	Special Move Bonus 2	Increases the damage of Cap's Shield Assault. (Tap special move button).	4
F6	Special Move Mega Bonus	This increases the damage of Cap's Shield Assault. (Tap special move button).	6
F4	Special Move Meter Upgrade 1	Adds a portion to the Special Move meter. When filled, the Character can activate a Special Move.	3
G4	Special Move Meter Upgrade 2	Adds a portion to the Special Move meter. When filled, the Character can activate a Special Move.	5
F5	Special Move Meter Upgrade 3	Adds a portion to the Special Move meter. When filled, the Character can activate a Special Move.	6
E5	Speedy Meter Upgrade	Increases the rate at which the Special Move meter fills when Power Pickups are obtained.	4
E3	Street Spike	Allows the Character to slam a carried object into the ground by tapping the attack button.	1
D1	Strong Finish	Adds a new finishing move to Captain America's combo attack. (Tap attack button.)	4
E1	Super Damage Increase	Increases the damage of Captain America's combo attack. (Tap attack button.)	6
A2	Super Health Boost	Increases Captain America's maximum health.	5
B3	Super Soldier Jump – Level 1	Unlocks Captain America's Super Jump ability. (Hold jump button.)	1
B2	Super Soldier Jump – Level 2	Increases the strength of the Super Soldier Jump. (Hold jump button.)	3
B4	Super Soldier Speed – Level 1	Increases Captain America's running speed.	1
A3	Super Soldier Speed – Level 2	Increases Captain America's running speed.	3
E2	Super Soldier Strike Upgrade	Increases the damage and area effect of Captain America's Air Assault. (Tap jump button, then tap attack button.)	2
A4	Team Player	Decreases the amount of time it takes to revive another Character or sidekick.	2
A5	Team Player Upgrade	Decreases the amount of time it takes to revive another Character or sidekick.	4
B7	Ultra Ranged Attack Upgrade	Increases the damage of Cap's Shield Strike. (Hold ranged attack button.)	6
D5	Vibranium Defense	While blocking (hold defend button while standing still), Cap can ricochet certain ranged attacks.	1
C3	Vibranium Vengeance	A combo (hold attack button) that breaks an opponent's block, juggling them into the air to be finished by Cap's shield.	2

HAWKEYE

A master archer from close or afar, Hawkeye never misses a target.

SPECIAL ABILITIES

- Hawkeye's Bow
- Super Jump
- Tech

SKILL TREE

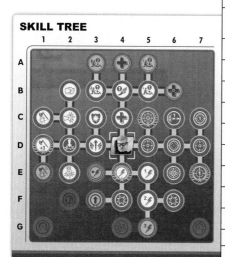

		Skills	
	SKILL	**DESCRIPTION**	**COST**
B2	Arrow Assault	After performing the Bow Block Breaker, release the attack button, and then tap the attack button to fire a powerful arrow that repels an opponent.	4
D1	Barton's Blast	Adds an additional move to Hawkeye's ground attack. (Tap attack button.)	4
C2	Bow Block Breaker	A swift strike with the bow (hold attack button) that allows Hawkeye to break an opponent's block.	2
C1	Damage Increase 1	Increases the damage of Hawkeye's combo attack. (Tap attack button.)	3
D6	Energy Shot – Level 1	Hawkeye can now charge his arrow (Hold ranged attack button) for increased damage.	2
C7	Energy Shot – Level 2	Decreases the time needed to charge an arrow. (Hold ranged attack button.)	5
E7	Exploding Arrows	Arrows fired from Hawkeye's standard bow attack (tap ranged attack button) now explode on impact, doing damage to nearby areas.	6
C6	Fire Away	Increases the rate of fire for Hawkeye's standard bow attacks. (Tap ranged attack button.)	4
E2	Hawk's Dive	Increases the damage of Hawkeye's Air Assault. (Tap jump button, then tap attack button.)	3
C4	Health Boost 1	Increases Hawkeye's maximum health.	1
A4	Health Boost 2	Increases Hawkeye's maximum health.	3
B5	Helping Hand	Decreases the amount of health needed to revive another Character or sidekick.	2
A5	Helping Hand Upgrade	Decreases the amount of health needed to revive another Character or sidekick.	4
D3	Mid-Air Recovery	Allows the Character to recover in mid-air by tapping the jump button.	1
C5	Open Fire	Firing an arrow (tap ranged fire button) results in spread fire that damages all enemies in the area of the shot.	4
F3	Power Disc Recharge Upgrade 1	Increases the rate at which the Power Disc meter fills.	3
F2	Power Disc Recharge Upgrade 2	Increases the rate at which the Power Disc meter fills.	3
E4	Rain of Arrows	Hawkeye's Special Move (tap special move button). Hawkeye fires a flurry of arrows into the air, which land in the area ahead of him, detonating and causing damage to anything hit.	2
D5	Ranged Attack Upgrade 1	Increases the damage of Hawkeye's Bow attacks. (Tap ranged attack button.)	1
D7	Ranged Attack Upgrade 2	Increases the damage of Hawkeye's Bow attacks. (Tap ranged attack button.)	4
C3	Repel	Repel an attacking opponent. Tap the defend button just before an attack. Requires skilled timing.	3
G1	Respender 1	At level 10, allows you to completely respend all of your skill points. Use it wisely, though. Once purchased, it will be permanently used.	0
G7	Respender 2	At level 20, allows you to completely respend all of your skill points. Use it wisely, though. Once purchased, it will be permanently used.	0
F4	Special Move Bonus 1	Increases the damage caused by Hawkeye's Special Move. (Tap special move button.)	2
F6	Special Move Bonus 2	Increases the damage caused by Hawkeye's Special Move. (Tap special move button.)	4
G4	Special Move Mega Bonus	Increases the damage caused by Hawkeye's Special Move. (Tap special move button.)	6
E5	Special Move Meter Upgrade 1	Adds a portion to the Special Move meter. When filled, the Character can activate a Special Move.	3
F5	Special Move Meter Upgrade 2	Adds a portion to the Special Move meter. When filled, the Character can activate a Special Move.	5
G5	Special Move Meter Upgrade 3	Adds a portion to the Special Move meter. When filled, the Character can activate a Special Move.	6
E3	Speedy Meter Upgrade	Increases the rate at which the Special Move meter fills when Power Pickups are obtained.	4
D2	Street Spike	Allows the Character to slam a carried object into the ground by tapping the attack button.	1
E1	Super Damage Increase	Increases the damage of Hawkeye's combo attack. (Tap attack button.)	5
B6	Super Health Boost	Increases Hawkeye's maximum health.	5
B4	Swift as an Arrow	Increases Hawkeye's running speed.	1
B3	Team Player	Decreases the amount of time it takes to revive another Character or sidekick.	2
A3	Team Player Upgrade	Decreases the amount of time it takes to revive another Character or sidekick.	4
E6	Ultra Ranged Attack Upgrade	Increases the damage of Hawkeye's Bow attacks. (Tap ranged attack button.)	6

HULK

Let Hulk smash your enemies with his unstoppable super strength.

SPECIAL ABILITIES

- Maximum Strength
- Regenerative Health
- Super Jump
- Wall Crawl
- Crossover Character

SKILL TREE

	1	2	3	4	5	6	7
A							
B							
C							
D							
E							
F							
G							

	Skills		
	SKILL	**DESCRIPTION**	**COST**
C6	Crushing Climb	Climb walls by jumping into them.	3
D2	Damage Increase 1	Increases the destructive power of Hulk's combo attack. (Tap attack button.)	2
C1	Damage Increase 2	Increases the destructive power of Hulk's combo attack. (Tap attack button.)	4
E7	Dash and Smash	Finish Hulk's Rampaging Rush with a powerful smash attack by releasing the ranged attack button.	5
G4	Destructive Distance	Increases the damage of Hulk's Raging Roar! (Tap special move button.)	3
C4	Health Boost 1	Increases Hulk's maximum health.	1
A3	Health Boost 2	Increases Hulk's maximum health.	3
A4	Helping Hand	Decreases the amount of health needed to revive another Character or sidekick.	2
A5	Hulk's Healing Factor – Level 1	Allows Hulk to regenerate health over time.	4
A6	Hulk's Healing Factor – Level 2	Maximizes the rate of Hulk's Healing Factor.	6
D3	Mid-Air Recovery	Allows the Character to recover in mid-air by tapping the jump button.	1
C2	Power Attack	While performing the Sonic Clap Combo, release the attack button before jumping and then tap the attack button to perform a powerful attack that repels an opponent.	4
F3	Power Disc Recharge Upgrade 1	Increases the rate at which the Power Disc meter fills.	3
F2	Power Disc Recharge Upgrade 2	Increases the rate at which the Power Disc meter fills.	5
E4	Raging Roar!	Hulk's most powerful move! Increase in size and let loose with a powerful roar that will send enemies flying in every direction by pressing the special move button.	2
D7	Rampaging Rush	Unlocks Hulk's powerful running charge. (Hold the ranged attack button.)	3
D6	Ranged Attack Upgrade 1	Increases the damage caused by Hulk's Charge attack. (Tap ranged attack button.)	2
C7	Ranged Attack Upgrade 2	Increases the damage caused by Hulk's Charge attack. (Tap ranged attack button.)	4
E2	Repel	Repel an attacking opponent. Tap the defend button just before an attack. Requires skilled timing.	3
G1	Respender 1	At level 10, allows you to completely respend all of your skill points. Use it wisely, though. Once purchased, it will be permanently used.	0
G7	Respender 2	At level 20, allows you to completely respend all of your skill points. Use it wisely, though. Once purchased, it will be permanently used.	0
B4	Savage Speed – Level 1	Increases Hulk's running speed.	1
A2	Savage Speed – Level 2	Increases Hulk's running speed.	3
C3	Sonic Clap Combo	A combo that breaks an opponent's block and juggles them into the air for a Sonic Clap Attack. (Hold attack button.)	2
F4	Special Move Bonus 1	Increases the damage of Hulk's Raging Roar! (Tap special move button.)	2
F6	Special Move Bonus 2	Increases the damage of Hulk's Raging Roar! (Tap special move button.)	4
G3	Special Move Mega Bonus	Increases the damage of Hulk's Raging Roar! (Tap special move button.)	6
F5	Special Move Meter Upgrade 1	Adds a portion to the Special Move meter. When filled, the Character can activate a Special Move.	3
G5	Special Move Meter Upgrade 2	Adds a portion to the Special Move meter. When filled, the Character can activate a Special Move.	5
E3	Speedy Meter Upgrade	Increases the rate at which the Special Move meter fills when Power Pickups are obtained.	4
E5	Street Shaker	Increases the power and range of Hulk's Air Assault. (Tap jump button, then tap attack button.)	2
D5	Street Spike	Allows the Character to slam a carried object into the ground by tapping the attack button.	1
D1	Strong Finish	Adds a new finishing move to Hulk's combo attack. (Tap attack button.)	4
E1	Super Damage Increase	Increases the destructive power of Hulk's combo attack. (Tap attack button.)	6
B2	Super Health Boost	Increases Hulk's maximum health.	5
C5	Superhuman Leap	Hold jump button to perform a Superhuman Leap.	1
B5	Superhuman Leap Upgrade – Level 1	Increases the power of Hulk's Superhuman Leap. (Hold jump button.)	3
B6	Superhuman Leap Upgrade – Level 2	Maximizes the power of Hulk's Superhuman Leap. (Hold jump button.)	5
B3	Team Player	Decreases the amount of time it takes to revive another Character or sidekick.	2
E6	Ultra Ranged Attack Upgrade	Increases the damage caused by Hulk's Charge attack. (Tap ranged attack button.)	6

SPIDER-MAN

SPIDER-MAN

> Use Spidey's wall climbing and web slinging powers to put your enemies in sticky situations.

SPECIAL ABILITIES

- Spidey Sense
- Super Jump
- Wall Crawl
- Web Swinger

SKILL TREE

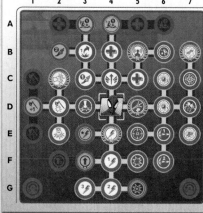

	Skills		
	SKILL	**DESCRIPTION**	**COST**
C2	Block Breaker Combo	A counter attack maneuver (hold attack button) that allows Spider-Man to break an opponent's block.	2
D2	Damage Increase 1	Increases the damage of Spider-Man's combo attack. (Tap attack button.)	2
C1	Damage Increase 2	Increases the damage of Spider-Man's combo attack. (Tap attack button.)	4
D7	Dual Web Bolt	Allows Spider-Man to shoot Web Bolts (tap ranged attack button) from both hands.	3
B4	Health Boost 1	Increases Spider-Man's maximum health.	1
C5	Health Boost 2	Increases Spider-Man's maximum health.	2
A5	Health Boost 3	Increases Spider-Man's maximum health.	4
A4	Helping Hand	Decreases the amount of health needed to revive another Character or sidekick.	2
A6	Helping Hand Upgrade	Decreases the amount of health needed to revive another Character or sidekick.	4
C4	Mid-Air Recovery	Allows the Character to recover in mid-air by tapping the jump button.	1
F3	Power Disc Recharge Upgrade 1	Increases the rate at which the Power Disc meter fills.	3
F2	Power Disc Recharge Upgrade 2	Increases the rate at which the Power Disc meter fills.	5
E5	Ranged Attack Upgrade	Increases the damage of Spider-Man's Web Bolt and Web Line attacks. (Tap ranged attack button.)	2
E6	Rapid Fire – Level 1	Increases the rate of fire of Spider-Man's Web Bolts. (Tap ranged attack button.)	3
F6	Rapid Fire – Level 2	Increases the rate of fire of Spider-Man's Web Bolts. (Tap ranged attack button.)	5
G1	Respender 1	At level 10, allows you to completely respend all of your skill points. Use it wisely, though. Once purchased, it will be permanently used.	0
G7	Respender 2	At level 20, allows you to completely respend all of your skill points. Use it wisely, though. Once purchased, it will be permanently used.	0
F5	Special Move Bonus	Increases the damage of Spider-Man's Web Barrage. (Tap special move button.)	2
G5	Special Move Mega Bonus	Increases the damage of Spider-Man's Web Barrage. (Tap special move button.)	4
F4	Special Move Meter Upgrade 1	Adds a portion to the Special Move meter. When filled, the Character can activate a Special Move.	3
G4	Special Move Meter Upgrade 2	Adds a portion to the Special Move meter. When filled, the Character can activate a Special Move.	5
G3	Special Move Meter Upgrade 3	Adds a portion to the Special Move meter. When filled, the Character can activate a Special Move.	6
E3	Speedy Meter Upgrade	Increases the rate at which the Special Move meter fills when Power Pickups are obtained.	4
B3	Spider Jump Upgrade	Increases the speed, distance, and height of Spider-Man's Super Jump. (Hold jump button.)	2
E2	Spider Pound Upgrade	Increases the damage and area of effect for Spider-Man's Air Assault. (Tap jump button, then tap attack.)	2
B5	Spidey Sense	Increases Spider-Man's ability to sense and repel enemies, and increases alert time. Reveals hidden items on your radar.	4
C3	Spidey Speed – Level 1	Increases Spider-Man's running speed.	1
B2	Spidey Speed – Level 2	Increases Spider-Man's running speed.	3
D3	Street Spike	Allows the Character to slam a carried object into the ground by tapping the attack button.	1
D1	Strong Finish	Adds a new finished move to Spider-Man's Melee Combo attack. (Tap attack button.)	4
E1	Super Damage Increase	Increases the damage of Spider-Man's combo attack. (Tap attack button.)	6
A2	Super Health Boost	Increases Spider-Man's maximum health.	5
A3	Team Player	Decreases the amount of time it takes to revive another Character or sidekick.	2
C7	Ultra Ranged Attack Upgrade	Increases the damage of Spider-Man's Web Bolt and Web Line attacks. (Tap ranged attack button.)	4
E4	Web Barrage	Allows Spidey to perform an amazing jump and web attack combo to stun multiple enemies in an area. His most powerful move! (Tap special move button.)	2
D5	Web Line	Allows Spider-Man to use a Web Bolt attack (hold ranged attack button) to capture an enemy. Release ranged attack button to pull in the enemy.	1
E7	Web Line Flurry	Adds the ability to attack an enemy with a flurry of strikes (tap attack button) after a Web Line attack (hold ranged attack button).	4
B7	Web Line Strike	Adds a powerful strike (hold attack button) to the aftermath of a Web Line attack (hold special move button).	6
B6	Web Sling Upgrade	Allows Spider-Man to travel farther and higher with his Web Swing. (During a Double Jump or Super Jump, press and hold the jump button again to Web Swing.)	5
D6	Web Stun – Level 1	Increases the duration of Spider-Man's web stuns.	2
C6	Web Stun – Level 2	Increases the duration of Spider-Man's web stuns.	4

NOVA

Nova's cosmic speed and power blasts are perfect complements to achieve fast victories.

SPECIAL ABILITIES
- Energy Blasts
- Flier
- Crossover Character

SKILL TREE

Skills			
	SKILL	**DESCRIPTION**	**COST**
C2	Air Assault Upgrade	Increases the range and damage of Nova's Air Assault. (Tap jump button, then tap attack button.)	2
D6	Charged Energy Blasts	Increases the power of Nova's energy blast attack. (Hold ranged attack button.)	2
D2	Damage Increase	Increases the damage of Nova's combo attack. (Tap attack button.)	2
C6	Dual Energy Blasts	Allows Nova to fire Energy Blasts (tap ranged attack button) from both hands.	3
E7	Energy Charge – Level 1	Decreases the time it takes to charge Nova's Energy Blast. (Hold ranged attack button.)	4
D7	Energy Charge – Level 2	Decreases the time it takes to charge Nova's Energy Blast. (Hold ranged attack button.)	6
C5	Fast Blast	Allows Nova to fire his Energy Blasts (tap ranged attack button) at a faster rate.	3
B4	Flight Speed – Level 1	Increases Nova's flight speed. (Hold the jump button to hover, hold left trigger while hovering for free flight.)	1
B6	Flight Speed – Level 2	Maximizes Nova's flight speed. (Hold the jump button to hover, hold left trigger while hovering for free flight.)	3
F4	Healing Upgrade – Level 1	Using Nova's Special Move increases his health. (Tap special move button.)	3
G4	Healing Upgrade – Level 2	Using Nova's Special Move increases his health. (Tap special move button.)	5
G3	Healing Upgrade – Level 3	Using Nova's Special Move increases his health. (Tap special move button.)	6
C4	Health Boost	Increases Nova's maximum health.	1
A3	Health Boost 2	Increases Nova's maximum health.	3
A4	Helping Hand	Decreases the amount of health needed to revive another Character or sidekick.	2
A5	Helping Hand Upgrade	Decreases the amount of health needed to revive another Character or sidekick.	4
D3	Mid-Air Recovery	Allows the Character to recover in mid-air by tapping the jump button.	1
E4	Nova Core	Nova's most powerful move! Nova's energy lifts opponents into the air and sends them flying! (Tap special move button.)	2
D1	Nova Force Block Breaker Combo	A combo (hold attack button) that allows Nova to lift an enemy into the air, breaking its block, and then kicking it away.	2
B1	Power Attack	When Performing a Block Breaker Combo, release the attack button early and then tap it again to perform a powerful rush attack that sends an opponent away. Requires skilled timing.	4
F3	Power Disc Recharge Upgrade 1	Increases the rate at which the Power Disc meter fills.	3
F2	Power Disc Recharge Upgrade 2	Increases the rate at which the Power Disc meter fills.	5
D5	Ranged Attack Upgrade 1	Increases the damage of Nova's Energy Blasts. (Tap ranged attack button.)	1
E6	Ranged Attack Upgrade 2	Increases the damage of Nova's Energy Blasts. (Tap ranged attack button.)	4
G1	Respender 1	At level 10, allows you to completely respend all of your skill points. Use it wisely, though. Once purchased, it will be permanently used.	0
G7	Respender 2	At level 20, allows you to completely respend all of your skill points. Use it wisely, though. Once purchased, it will be permanently used.	0
B5	Run Speed	Increases Nova's running speed.	1
E3	Special Move Bonus 1	Increases the damage caused by Nova's Special Move. (Tap special move button.)	2
F6	Special Move Bonus 2	Increases the damage caused by Nova's Special Move. (Tap special move button.)	4
E1	Special Move Mega Bonus	Increases the damage caused by Nova's Special Move. (Tap special move button.)	6
E5	Special Move Meter Upgrade 1	Adds a portion to the Special Move meter. When filled, the Character can activate a Special Move.	3
F5	Special Move Meter Upgrade 2	Adds a portion to the Special Move meter. When filled, the Character can activate a Special Move.	5
G5	Special Move Meter Upgrade 3	Adds a portion to the Special Move meter. When filled, the Character can activate a Special Move.	6
E2	Speedy Meter Upgrade	Increases the rate at which the Special Move meter fills when Power Pickups are obtained.	4
C3	Street Spike	Allows the Character to slam a carried object into the ground by tapping the attack button.	1
C1	Super Damage Increase	Increases the damage of Nova's combo attack. (Tap attack button.)	4
B7	Super Health Boost	Increases Nova's maximum health.	5
B3	Team Player	Decreases the amount of time it takes to revive another Character or sidekick.	2
B2	Team Player Upgrade	Decreases the amount of time it takes to revive another Character or sidekick.	4
C7	Ultra Ranged Attack Upgrade	Increases the damage of Nova's Energy Blasts. (Tap ranged attack button.)	6

IRON FIST

With his super-charged martial arts skills, Iron Fist is a master of combat action.

SPECIAL ABILITIES
- Chi
- Maximum Strength
- Super Jump
- The Iron Fist

SKILL TREE

Skills			
	SKILL	**DESCRIPTION**	**COST**
C3	Air Assault Upgrade	Increases the range and damage caused by Iron Fist's Air Assault. (Tap jump button, then tap attack button.)	3
D2	Block Breaker Combo	A three-part maneuver (hold attack button) that allows Iron Fist to break an opponent's block and send them away.	2
D6	Chi State	Striking an enemy with a fully charged Iron Fist Attack (hold ranged attack button) will put Iron Fist into a special state where all attacks are powered up for a limited time.	2
C7	Chi State – Upgrade 1	Increases the duration of the Chi State after landing a fully charged Iron Fist Attack. (Hold ranged attack button.)	5
B7	Chi State – Upgrade 2	Increases the duration of the Chi State after landing a fully charged Iron Fist Attack. (Hold ranged attack button.)	6
C2	Chi Strength	Maximizes Iron Fist's strength.	4
C1	Chi Strike Kick	When performing a Block Breaker Combo, release the attack button early and then tap it again to perform a powerful kick attack that sends an opponent away. Requires skilled timing.	4
C6	Healing Aura	Allows Iron Fist to heal heroes around him while blocking. (Hold defend button.)	4
C5	Healing Block	Allows Iron Fist to heal himself while blocking. (Hold defend button.)	2
A3	Health Boost	Increases Iron Fist's maximum health.	3
E1	Heightened Awareness	Increases Iron Fist's ability to sense and repel enemies, and increases the alert time. Reveals hidden items on the radar.	5
A4	Helping Hand	Decreases the amount of health needed to revive another Character or sidekick.	2
D5	Iron Fist Attack	Allows Iron Fist to charge up his ranged attack (hold ranged attack button) and increase its damage.	1
E6	Iron Fist Attack Upgrade	Reduces the time required to charge Iron Fist's ranged attack. (Hold ranged attack button.)	4
C4	Mid-Air Recovery	Allows the Character to recover in mid-air by tapping the jump button.	1
F3	Power Disc Recharge Upgrade 1	Increases the rate at which the Power Disc meter fills.	3
F2	Power Disc Recharge Upgrade 2	Increases the rate at which the Power Disc meter fills.	5
E5	Ranged Attack Upgrade 1	Increases the damage of Iron Fist Attack. (Tap ranged attack button.)	2
D7	Ranged Attack Upgrade 2	Increases the damage of Iron Fist Attack. (Tap ranged attack button.)	4
E2	Repel	Repel an attacking opponent. Tap the defend button just before an attack. Requires skilled timing. Repelling enemies replenishes Iron Fist's Special Move meter.	3
G1	Respender 1	At level 10, allows you to completely respend all of your skill points. Use it wisely, though. Once purchased, it will be permanently used.	0
G7	Respender 2	At level 20, allows you to completely respend all of your skill points. Use it wisely, though. Once purchased, it will be permanently used.	0
B4	Run Speed - Upgrade 1	Increases Iron Fist's running speed.	1
B6	Run Speed - Upgrade 2	Increases Iron Fist's running speed.	3
E4	Shou-Lao the Undying	Unlocks Iron Fist's Special Move (tap special move button)! Iron Fist unleashes the Dragon Shou-Lao, dealing damage to anyone in its path.	2
F4	Special Move Bonus 1	Increases the damage of Shou-Lao the Undying. (Tap special move button.)	2
G5	Special Move Bonus 2	Increases the damage of Shou-Lao the Undying. (Tap special move button.)	4
F6	Special Move Mega Bonus	Increases the damage of Shou-Lao the Undying. (Tap special move button.)	6
G4	Special Move Meter Upgrade 1	Adds a portion to the Special Move meter. When filled, the Character can activate a Special Move.	3
G3	Special Move Meter Upgrade 2	Adds a portion to the Special Move meter. When filled, the Character can activate a Special Move.	5
F5	Special Move Meter Upgrade 3	Adds a portion to the Special Move meter. When filled, the Character can activate a Special Move.	6
E3	Speedy Meter Upgrade	Increases the rate at which the Special Move meter fills when Power Pickups are obtained.	4
D3	Street Spike	Allows the Character to slam a carried object into the ground by tapping the attack button.	1
D1	Strong Finish	Adds an additional attack to Iron Fist's ground combo attack. (Tap attack button.)	4
A5	Super Health Boost	Increases Iron Fist's maximum health.	5
B5	Super Jump	Unlocks Iron Fist's ability to Super Jump. (Hold jump button.)	2
B3	Team Player	Decreases the amount of time it takes to revive another Character or sidekick.	2
B2	Team Player Upgrade	Decreases the amount of time it takes to revive another Character or sidekick.	4
E7	Ultra Ranged Attack Upgrade	Increases the damage of the Iron Fist Attack. (Tap ranged attack button.)	6

NICK FURY

Use Nick Fury to spy on crime with his tactical S.H.I.E.L.D. tech abilities.

SPECIAL ABILITIES

- Cloaking
- Martial Arts
- Shields
- S.H.I.E.L.D. Pistols
- Tech

SKILL TREE

	Skills		
	SKILL	**DESCRIPTION**	**COST**
B3	Air Assault Damage Upgrade	Increases the damage caused by Nick Fury's Air Assault. (Tap jump button, then tap attack button.)	2
G3	Armed Life Model Decoy	Allows Nick Fury's Life Model Decoy to automatically target and fire at nearby enemies. (Tap special move button.)	6
D1	Block Breaker Combo	A three-part maneuver (hold attack button) that allows Nick to break an enemy's block and send them away.	2
B1	Charged Shot	When performing a Block Breaker Combo, release the attack button early and then tap it again to perform a powerful ranged attack that sends an opponent away. Requires skilled timing.	4
C2	Damage Increase 1	Increases the damage of Nick Fury's combo attack. (Tap attack button.)	2
F2	Damage Increase 2	Increases the damage of Nick Fury's combo attack. (Tap attack button.)	4
D5	Double Trouble	Allows Nick Fury to fire with two pistols. (Tap ranged fire button.)	1
D7	Explosive Shells	S.H.I.E.L.D. Pistols (tap ranged attack button) are loaded with explosive rounds that cause more damage.	5
B4	Feet of Fury	Increases Nick Fury's running speed.	1
C5	Furious Fire – Level 1	Increases the firing rate of S.H.I.E.L.D. Pistols. (Tap ranged attack button.)	3
C7	Furious Fire – Level 2	Increases the firing rate of S.H.I.E.L.D. Pistols. (Tap ranged attack button.)	5
B6	Health Boost	Increases Nick Fury's maximum health.	2
B5	Helping Hand	Decreases the amount of health needed to revive another Character or sidekick.	2
A5	Helping Hand Upgrade	Decreases the amount of health needed to revive another Character or sidekick.	4
E4	Life Model Decoy	S.H.I.E.L.D. Tech allowing Nick Fury to turn invisible and generate a temporary decoy to draw enemy fire. (Tap special move button.)	2
E3	Life Model Decoy Duration Upgrade 1	Increases the duration of Nick Fury's Life Model Decoy. (Tap special move button.)	3
F3	Life Model Decoy Duration Upgrade 2	Increases the duration of Nick Fury's Life Model Decoy. (Tap special move button.)	5
C4	Mid-Air Recovery	Allows the Character to recover in mid-air by tapping the jump button.	1
F5	Power Disc Recharge Upgrade 1	Increases the rate at which the Power Disc meter fills.	3
F6	Power Disc Recharge Upgrade 2	Increases the rate at which the Power Disc meter fills.	5
D6	Ranged Attack Upgrade 1	Increases the damage of Nick Fury's automatic pistol attacks. (Tap ranged attack button.)	2
C6	Ranged Attack Upgrade 2	Increases the damage of Nick Fury's automatic pistol attacks. (Tap ranged attack button.)	4
D2	Repel	Repel an attacking opponent. Tap the defend button just before attack. Requires skilled timing.	3
G1	Respender 1	At level 10, allows you to completely respend all of your skill points. Use it wisely, though. Once purchased, it will be permanently used.	0
G7	Respender 2	At level 20, allows you to completely respend all of your skill points. Use it wisely, though. Once purchased, it will be permanently used.	0
D3	S.H.I.E.L.D. Defense Tech	Unlocks Nick Fury's regenerating protective shields.	1
E1	S.H.I.E.L.D. Defense Tech Upgrade	Increases the speed at which Nick Fury's shields regenerate.	5
E2	Shield Surge	Increases the protective power of Nick Fury's shields.	3
E5	Shots Fired – Level 1	Increases the number of shots Nick Fury can fire before needing to reload. (Tap ranged attack button.)	2
E6	Shots Fired – Level 2	Increases the number of shots Nick Fury can fire before needing to reload. (Tap ranged attack button.)	4
G4	Special Move Meter Upgrade 1	Adds a portion to the Special Move meter. When filled, the Character can activate a Special Move.	3
G5	Special Move Meter Upgrade 2	Adds a portion to the Special Move meter. When filled, the Character can activate a Special Move.	5
F4	Speedy Meter Upgrade	Increases the rate at which the Special Move meter fills when Power Pickups are obtained.	4
C3	Street Spike	Allows the Character to slam a carried object into the ground by tapping the attack button.	1
C1	Strong Finish	Adds an additional attack to Nick Fury's melee combo attack. (Tap attack button.)	4
B2	Super Damage Increase	Increases the damage of Nick Fury's combo attack. (Tap attack button.)	6
A6	Super Health Boost	Increases Nick Fury's maximum health.	4
A4	Team Player	Decreases the amount of time it takes to revive another Character or sidekick.	2
A3	Team Player Upgrade	Decreases the amount of time it takes to revive another Character or sidekick.	4
E7	Ultra Ranged Attack Upgrade	Increases the damage of Nick Fury's automatic pistol attacks. (Tap ranged attack button.)	6

GAME BASICS

CHARACTERS

POWER DISCS

MARVEL'S THE AVENGERS

SPIDER-MAN

GUARDIANS OF THE GALAXY

TOY BOX

TOY BOX COLLECTION

ACHIEVEMENTS

VENOM

Strike fear into your enemies with Venom's evil symbiote-slinging web powers.

SPECIAL ABILITIES

- Maximum Strength
- Regenerative Health
- Super Jump
- Wall Crawl
- Web Swing
- Villain

SKILL TREE

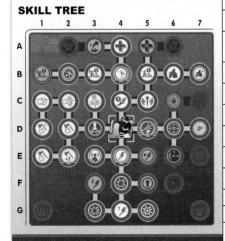

Skills			
	SKILL	**DESCRIPTION**	**COST**
D2	Damage Increase 1	Increases the damage of Venom's combo attack. (Tap attack button.)	2
E1	Damage Increase 2	Increases the damage of Venom's combo attack. (Tap attack button.)	4
A4	Health Boost	Increases Venom's maximum health.	2
B6	Health Regeneration – Level 1	Unlocks regenerating health.	3
B7	Health Regeneration – Level 2	Increases the rate at which Venom recovers.	6
B5	Helping Hand	Decreases the amount of health needed to revive another Character or sidekick.	2
A6	Helping Hand Upgrade	Decreases the amount of health needed to revive another Character or sidekick.	4
G5	Special Move Mega Bonus	Increases the damage of Venom's Symbiote Storm. (Tap special move button.)	6
C5	Mid-Air Recovery	Allows the Character to recover in mid-air by tapping the jump button.	1
F5	Power Disc Recharge Upgrade 1	Increases the rate at which the Power Disc meter fills.	3
F6	Power Disc Recharge Upgrade 2	Increases the rate at which the Power Disc meter fills.	5
D6	Ranged Attack Upgrade 1	Increases the damage of Venom's Web Bolt and Symbiote Line attacks. (Tap ranged attack button.)	2
E7	Ranged Attack Upgrade 2	Increases the damage of Venom's Web Bolt and Symbiote Line attacks. (Tap ranged attack button.)	4
E6	Rapid Fire	Venom can shoot Symbiote Bolts faster. (Tap ranged attack button.)	3
G1	Respender 1	At level 10, allows you to completely respend all of your skill points. Use it wisely, though. Once purchased, it will be permanently used.	0
G7	Respender 2	At level 20, allows you to completely respend all of your skill points. Use it wisely, though. Once purchased, it will be permanently used.	0
C3	Sinister Slam	Increases the damage of Venom's Air Assault. (Tap jump button, then tap attack button.)	2
F4	Special Move Bonus 1	Increases the damage of Venom's Symbiote Storm. (Tap special move button.)	2
G3	Special Move Bonus 2	Increases the damage of Venom's Symbiote Storm. (Tap special move button.)	4
G4	Special Move Meter Upgrade 1	Adds a portion to the Special Move meter. When filled, the Character can activate a Special Move.	3
F3	Special Move Meter Upgrade 2	Adds a portion to the Special Move meter. When filled, the Character can activate a Special Move.	5
E5	Speedy Meter Upgrade	Increases the rate at which the Special Move meter fills when Power Pickups are obtained.	4
D3	Street Spike	Allows the Character to slam a carried object into the ground by tapping the attack button.	1
E2	Strong Finish	Adds an additional attack to Venom's Melee Combo attack. (Tap attack button.)	4
D1	Super Damage Increase	Increases the damage of Venom's combo attack. (Tap attack button.)	6
A5	Super Health Boost	Increases Venom's maximum health.	4
A3	Super Jump Upgrade	Increases the distance and height of Venom's Super Jump. (Hold jump button.)	2
D5	Symbiote Line	Venom's Web Line attack (hold ranged attack button) can bind and pull enemies.	1
D7	Symbiote Line Combo	Complete Venom's Symbiote Line attack (hold ranged attack button) with a powerful finishing move (hold attack button).	4
C1	Symbiote Send Attack	After performing a Symbiote Uppercut, release the attack button, and then tap the attack button again to perform a powerful attack that sends an opponent away!	4
E4	Symbiote Storm	Venom's most powerful attack. Unleash an onslaught of symbiote tendrils. (Tap special move button.)	2
C2	Symbiote Uppercut	An uppercut (hold attack button) that allows Venom to break an opponent's block.	2
B3	Team Player	Decreases the amount of time it takes to revive another Character or sidekick.	2
B1	Team Player Upgrade	Decreases the amount of time it takes to revive another Character or sidekick.	4
C7	Ultra Ranged Attack Upgrade	Increases the damage of Venom's Web Bolt and Symbiote Line attacks. (Tap ranged attack button.)	6
E3	Venom Sense	Increases Venom's ability to sense and repel enemies, and increases the alert time. Reveals hidden items on your radar.	4
C4	Venom Speed – Level 1	Increases Venom's running speed.	1
A2	Venom Speed – Level 2	Increases Venom's running speed.	3
B2	Web Sling Upgrade	Allows Venom to travel farther and higher with his Web Swing. (During a Double Jump or Super Jump, press and hold the jump button again to Web Swing.)	4
C6	Web Stun Upgrade	Enemies remain stunned longer.	3
B4	Web Swing	Unlocks Venom's ability to Web Swing. (During a Double Jump or Super Jump, press and hold the jump button again to Web Swing.) Who says Spider-Man gets to have all the fun?	1

GUARDIANS OF THE GALAXY

STAR-LORD

Use Star-Lord's ranged gadget attacks and tactical powers for cosmic adventures.

SPECIAL ABILITIES
- Elemental Guns
- Super Jump
- Tech

SKILL TREE

Skills		
SKILL	**DESCRIPTION**	**COST**
D1 Damage Increase	Increases the damage of Star-Lord's combo attack. (Tap attack button.)	2
D5 Double Trouble	Allows Star-Lord to attack with two Elemental Guns. (Tap ranged attack button.)	1
C6 Fired Up – Level 1	Increases the rate of fire of Star-Lord's Elemental Guns. (Tap ranged attack button.)	3
C7 Fired Up – Level 2	Increases the rate of fire of Star-Lord's Elemental Guns. (Tap ranged attack button.)	5
C1 Hadron Enforcer	Unleashes the power of Star-Lord's Hadron Enforcer. Release the attack button and tap the attack button to perform a powerful attack that repels an opponent.	4
C4 Health Boost 1	Increases Star-Lord's maximum health.	1
A4 Health Boost 2	Increases Star-Lord's maximum health.	3
B5 Helping Hand	Decreases the amount of health needed to revive another Character or sidekick.	2
B6 Helping Hand Upgrade	Decreases the amount of health needed to revive another Character or sidekick.	4
A5 Leaps and Bounds	Increases the speed, distance, and height of Star-Lord's Super Jump. (Hold jump button.)	5
D3 Mid-Air Recovery	Allows the Character to recover in mid-air by tapping the jump button.	1
E4 Plasma Assault	Unlocks Star-Lord's Special Move (tap special move button)! Places Plasma Turrets that fire continuously at targets.	2
E2 Plasma Blast	Gives Star-Lord's Plasma Turret more health.	5
F3 Power Disc Recharge Upgrade 1	Increases the rate at which the Power Disc meter fills.	3
F2 Power Disc Recharge Upgrade 2	Increases the rate at which the Power Disc meter fills.	5
C5 Ranged Attack Upgrade 1	Increases the damage of Star-Lord's Elemental Gun. (Tap ranged attack button.)	2
E6 Ranged Attack Upgrade 2	Increases the damage of Star-Lord's Elemental Gun. (Tap ranged attack button.)	4
G1 Respender 1	At level 10, allows you to completely respend all of your skill points. Use it wisely, though. Once purchased, it will be permanently used.	0
G7 Respender 2	At level 20, allows you to completely respend all of your skill points. Use it wisely, though. Once purchased, it will be permanently used.	0
B7 Round Trip Target	Upgrades the ammunition in Star-Lord's Elemental Gun (tap range attack button) to rounds that seek opponents.	6
B4 Run for Your Lives	Increases Star-Lord's running speed.	1
C3 Shock Mine	Deploy a Shock Mine (hold attack button) that detonates on contact with an opponent, breaking its block. Can be used defensively by firing it (hold attack button) until ready to detonate (release attack button).	2
D6 Shots Fired – Level 1	Increases the number of shots Star-Lord can fire from his Elemental Gun. (Tap ranged attack button) before reloading.	2
E7 Shots Fired – Level 2	Increases the number of shots Star-Lord can fire from his Elemental Gun (Tap ranged attack button) before reloading.	4
F4 Special Move Bonus 1	Increases the damage of Star-Lord's Plasma Turret. (Tap special move button.)	2
F5 Special Move Bonus 2	Increases the damage of Star-Lord's Plasma Turret. (Tap special move button.)	4
G3 Special Move Mega Bonus	Increases the damage of Star-Lord's Plasma Turret. (Tap special move button.)	6
E5 Special Move Meter Upgrade 1	Adds a portion to the Special Move meter. When filled, the Character can activate a Special Move.	3
F6 Special Move Meter Upgrade 2	Adds a portion to the Special Move meter. When filled, the Character can activate a Special Move.	5
E3 Speedy Meter Upgrade	Increases the rate at which the Special Move meter fills when Power Pickups are obtained.	4
E1 Star-Lord Strike	Increases the damage and area of effect of Star-Lord's Air Assault. (Tap jump button, then tap attack button.)	2
D2 Street Spike	Allows the Character to slam a carried object into the ground by tapping the attack button.	1
C2 Super Damage Increase	Increases the damage of Star-Lord's combo attack. (Tap attack button.)	4
A3 Super Health Boost	Increases Star-Lord's maximum health.	6
B3 Team Player	Decreases the amount of time it takes to revive another Character or sidekick.	2
B2 Team Player Upgrade	Decreases the amount of time it takes to revive another Character or sidekick.	4
G4 Turret Clip – Level 1	Increases the number of shots Star-Lord's Turret can fire before reloading. (Tap special move button.)	3
G5 Turret Clip – Level 2	Increases the number of shots Star-Lord's Turret can fire before reloading. (Tap special move button.)	6
D7 Ultra Ranged Attack Upgrade	Increases the damage of Star-Lord's Elemental Gun. (Tap ranged attack button.)	6

GAMORA

Use a Super Hero martial artist to ward off enemies with her keen sword-fighting skills.

SPECIAL ABILITIES
- Super Jump
- Sword and Guns

SKILL TREE

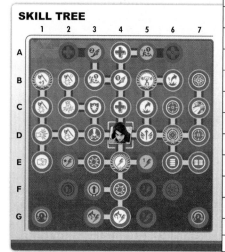

	Skills		
	SKILL	**DESCRIPTION**	**COST**
E6	Big Shot – Level 1	Increases the number of shots Gamora can fire from her rifle (tap ranged attack button) before reloading.	2
E7	Big Shot – Level 2	Maximizes the number of shots Gamora can fire from her rifle (tap ranged attack button) before reloading.	4
C5	Bound and Determined – Level 1	Unlocks Gamora's Super Jump ability. (Hold jump button.)	1
B6	Bound and Determined – Level 2	Increases the speed, distance, and height of Gamora's Super Jump ability. (Hold jump button.)	4
D2	Damage Increase 1	Increases the damage of Gamora's combo attack. (Tap attack button.)	2
C1	Damage Increase 2	Increases the damage of Gamora's combo attack. (Tap attack button.)	4
C2	Gamora's Fury	Increases the damage and range of Gamora's Air Assault. (Tap jump button, then tap attack button.)	2
C4	Health Boost 1	Increases Gamora's maximum health.	1
A4	Health Boost 2	Increases Gamora's maximum health.	2
A2	Health Boost 3	Increases Gamora's maximum health.	4
A5	Helping Hand	Decreases the amount of health needed to revive another Character or sidekick.	2
G4	In a Blur – Level 1	Increases the duration of Gamora's speed boost.	2
G3	In a Blur – Level 2	Increases the duration of Gamora's speed boost.	4
B4	Like the Wind – Level 1	Increases Gamora's running speed.	1
A3	Like the Wind – Level 2	Increases Gamora's running speed.	3
C7	Loaded Shot	Gamora's rifles (tap ranged attack button) fire more projectiles when charged.	3
D5	Mid-Air Recovery	Allows the Character to recover in mid-air by tapping the jump button.	1
B5	Most Dangerous Woman in the World	Increases Gamora's strength, allowing her to pick up enormous objects.	3
F3	Power Disc Recharge Upgrade 1	Increases the rate at which the Power Disc meter fills.	3
F2	Power Disc Recharge Upgrade 2	Increases the rate at which the Power Disc meter fills.	5
E4	Power Trip	Unlocks Gamora's Special Move (tap special move button)! Gamora runs faster and has a powerful dash attack (tap attack button) that breaks blocks and deals high damage.	2
D7	Ranged Attack Upgrade 1	Increases the damage of Gamora's rifle attacks. (Tap ranged attack button.)	2
C6	Ranged Attack Upgrade 2	Increases the damage of Gamora's rifle attacks. (Tap ranged attack button.)	4
C3	Repel	Repel an attacking opponent. Tap the defend button just before attack. Requires skilled timing.	3
G1	Respender 1	At level 10, allows you to completely respend all of your skill points. Use it wisely, though. Once purchased, it will be permanently used.	0
G7	Respender 2	At level 20, allows you to completely respend all of your skill points. Use it wisely, though. Once purchased, it will be permanently used.	0
D6	Seeker Blast	Charge's Gamora's rifles (hold ranged attack button) to increase their damage and number of projectiles.	1
F4	Special Move Bonus 1	Increases the damage of Gamora's Special Move. (Tap special move button.)	2
E3	Special Move Bonus 2	Increases the damage of Gamora's Special Move. (Tap special move button.)	4
F6	Special Move Mega Bonus	Increases the damage of Gamora's Special Move (Tap special move button.)	6
E5	Special Move Meter Upgrade 1	Adds a portion to the Special Move meter. When filled, the Character can activate a Special Move.	3
F5	Special Move Meter Upgrade 2	Adds a portion to the Special Move meter. When filled, the Character can activate a Special Move.	5
G5	Special Move Meter Upgrade 3	Adds a portion to the Special Move meter. When filled, the Character can activate a Special Move.	6
E2	Speedy Meter Upgrade	Increases the rate at which the Special Move meter fills when Power Pickups are obtained.	4
E1	Spinning Slash	After performing a Sword Uppercut, release the attack button, then tap the attack button again to perform a powerful repelling attack.	4
D3	Street Spike	Allows the Character to slam a carried object into the ground by tapping the attack button.	1
B1	Strong Finish	Adds a new finishing move to Gamora's ground attack. (Tap attack button.)	4
B2	Super Damage Increase	Increases the damage of Gamora's combo attack. (Tap attack button.)	6
A6	Super Health Boost	Increases Gamora's maximum health.	5
D1	Sword Uppercut	An upward swing of Gamora's sword (hold attack button) will break an opponent's block and send them flying.	2
B3	Team Player	Decreases the amount of time it takes to revive another Character or sidekick.	2
B7	Ultra Ranged Attack Upgrade	Increases the damage of Gamora's rifle attacks. (Tap ranged attack button.)	6

ROCKET RACCOON

Take on enemies with heavy ranged explosive powers for tactical action.

SPECIAL ABILITIES

- Hadron Gun
- Quantum Cannons
- Super Jump
- Tech
- Crossover Character

SKILL TREE

Skills			
	SKILL	DESCRIPTION	COST
E4	Big Guns	This unlocks Rocket's Special Move (tap special move button)! Rocket unleashes a flurry of shots using his gun.	2
E5	Cannon Fodder – Level 1	Increases the clip size for Rocket's Quantum Cannon. (Tap ranged attack button.)	2
F6	Cannon Fodder – Level 2	Increases the clip size for Rocket's Quantum Cannon. (Tap ranged attack button.)	4
E7	Cannonade	Increases the rate of fire of the Quantum Cannon. (Tap ranged attack button.)	4
D5	Double Whammy	Allows Rocket to wield two Quantum Cannons. (Tap ranged attack button.)	1
E1	Go Boom	Deploy a series of unblockable grenades. (Hold attack button.)	4
A5	Health Boost	Increases Rocket Raccoon's maximum health.	2
A4	Helping Hand	Decreases the amount of health needed to revive another Character or sidekick.	2
B5	Helping Hand Upgrade	Decreases the amount of health needed to revive another Character or sidekick.	4
C4	Mid-Air Recovery	Allows the Character to recover in mid-air by tapping the jump button.	1
F3	Power Disc Recharge Upgrade 1	Increases the rate at which the Power Disc meter fills.	3
F2	Power Disc Recharge Upgrade 2	Increases the rate at which the Power Disc meter fills.	5
D6	Ranged Attack Upgrade 1	Increases the damage of Rocket's Quantum Cannon attacks. (Tap ranged attack button.)	2
C6	Ranged Attack Upgrade 2	Increases the damage of Rocket's Quantum Cannon attacks. (Tap ranged attack button.)	4
D1	Repel	Repel an attacking opponent. Tap the defend button just before attack. Requires skilled timing.	3
G1	Respender 1	At level 10, allows you to completely respend all of your skill points. Use it wisely, though. Once purchased, it will be permanently used.	0
G7	Respender 2	At level 20, allows you to completely respend all of your skill points. Use it wisely, though. Once purchased, it will be permanently used.	0
D7	Rock It	Allows Rocket to charge his Quantum Cannon (hold ranged attack button) for increased damage.	4
C3	Rocket Blast	Unlock's Rocket's Super Jump ability. (Hold jump button.)	1
B2	Rocket Blast Upgrade	Increases the speed, distance, and height of Rocket's Super Jump. (Hold jump button.)	5
B4	Rocket Run	Maximizes Rocket's running speed.	1
D2	Rocky Road	Increases the range and damage of Rocket's Air Assault. (Tap jump button, then tap attack button.)	3
F5	Special Move Bonus 1	Increases the damage of Rocket's gun. (Tap special move button.)	2
G3	Special Move Bonus 2	Increases the damage of Rocket's gun. (Tap special move button.)	4
E2	Special Move Mega Bonus	Increases the damage of Rocket's gun. (Tap special move button.)	6
F4	Special Move Meter Upgrade 1	Adds a portion to the Special Move meter. When filled, the Character can activate a Special Move.	3
G4	Special Move Meter Upgrade 2	Adds a portion to the Special Move meter. When filled, the Character can activate a Special Move.	5
G5	Special Move Meter Upgrade 3	Adds a portion to the Special Move meter. When filled, the Character can activate a Special Move.	6
E3	Speedy Meter Upgrade	Increases the rate at which the Special Move meter fills when Power Pickups are obtained.	4
D3	Street Spike	Allows the Character to slam a carried object into the ground by tapping the attack button.	1
C1	Super Damage Increase	Increase the damage of Rocket's combo attack. (Tap attack button.)	3
C2	Super Health Boost	Maximizes Rocket's health.	4
C7	Taking Charge – Level 1	Reduces the time it takes to charge Rocket's Quantum Cannon. (Hold ranged attack button.)	5
C5	Taking Charge – Level 2	Reduces the time it takes to charge Rocket's Quantum Cannon. (Hold ranged attack button.)	6
B3	Team Player	Decreases the amount of time it takes to revive another Character or sidekick.	2
A3	Team Player Upgrade	Decreases the amount of time it takes to revive another Character or sidekick.	4
E6	Ultra Ranged Attack Upgrade	Increases the damage of Rocket's Quantum Cannon attacks. (Tap ranged attack button.)	6

DRAX

Super-charge your adventures with Drax, the intergalactic destroyer.

SPECIAL ABILITIES

- Destroyer Mode
- Health Regeneration
- Maximum Strength
- Super Jump
- Wall Crawl

SKILL TREE

	1	2	3	4	5	6	7
A							
B							
C							
D							
E							
F							
G							

Skills

	SKILL	DESCRIPTION	COST
C2	Concussive Blast	Increases the damage and range of Drax's Air Assault. (Tap jump button, then tap attack button.)	2
D2	Damage Increase 1	Increases the damage of Drax's combo attack. (Tap attack button.)	2
E2	Damage Increase 2	Increases the damage of Drax's combo attack. (Tap attack button.)	4
G5	Destroyer Duration – Level 1	Increases the amount of time Drax can stay in Destroyer Mode. (Tap special move button.)	3
F6	Destroyer Duration – Level 2	Increases the amount of time Drax can stay in Destroyer Mode. (Tap special move button.)	5
D1	Drax Attack	Adds an additional move to Drax's ground attack. (Tap attack button.)	4
E4	Drax the Destroyer	Unleash Drax's rage with his Special Move (tap special move button)! His strength and attack speed increase for a limited time.	2
C4	Health Boost 1	Increases Drax's maximum health.	1
A4	Health Boost 2	Increases Drax's maximum health.	3
A3	Helping Hand	Decreases the amount of health needed to revive another Character or sidekick.	2
B5	Jumping Drax – Level 1	Unlocks Drax's Super Jump ability. (Hold jump button.)	2
A6	Jumping Drax – Level 2	Increases the speed, distance, and height of Drax's Super Jump. (Hold jump button.)	5
C7	Lunge Lizard	Allows Drax to finish his running charge with a lunging attack by releasing the ranged attack button.	4
D3	Mid-Air Recovery	Allows the Character to recover in mid-air by tapping the jump button.	1
F3	Power Disc Recharge Upgrade 1	Increases the rate at which the Power Disc meter fills.	3
F2	Power Disc Recharge Upgrade 2	Increases the rate at which the Power Disc meter fills.	5
E1	Power Kick	When performing Uppercut Flurry, release attack button and then tap attack button again to perform a powerful kick that repels an opponent. Requires skilled timing.	4
D7	Ranged Attack Upgrade 1	Increases the damage of Drax's charging attack. (Tap ranged attack button.)	2
B7	Ranged Attack Upgrade 2	Increases the damage of Drax's charging attack. (Tap ranged attack button.)	4
B4	Renewable Energy	Unlocks regenerating health.	3
A5	Renewable Energy Upgrade	Increases the rate at which Drax's health regenerates.	6
E7	Repel	Repel an attacking opponent. Tap the defend button just before attack. Requires skilled timing.	3
G1	Respender 1	At level 10, allows you to completely respend all of your skill points. Use it wisely, though. Once purchased, it will be permanently used.	0
G7	Respender 2	At level 20, allows you to completely respend all of your skill points. Use it wisely, though. Once purchased, it will be permanently used.	0
D5	Running Rampant	Maximizes Drax's running speed.	1
F4	Special Move Bonus 1	Increases the damage of Drax's Destroyer Mode. (Tap special move button.)	2
F5	Special Move Bonus 2	Increases the damage of Drax's Destroyer Mode. (Tap special move button.)	4
E6	Special Move Mega Bonus	Increases the damage of Drax's Destroyer Mode. (Tap special move button.)	6
G4	Special Move Meter Upgrade 1	Adds a portion to the Special Move meter. When filled, the Character can activate a Special Move.	3
G3	Special Move Meter Upgrade 2	Adds a portion to the Special Move meter. When filled, the Character can activate a Special Move.	5
E5	Speedy Meter Upgrade	Increases the rate at which the Special Move meter fills when Power Pickups are obtained.	4
C3	Street Spike	Allows the Character to slam a carried object into the ground by tapping the attack button.	1
C6	Strength of the Destroyer	Increases Drax's strength, allowing him to pick up enormous objects.	3
D6	Super Charge	Allows Drax to perform a sustained running charge. (Hold ranged attack button.)	2
C1	Super Damage Increase	Increases the damage of Drax's combo attack. (Tap attack button.)	6
B2	Super Health Boost	Increases Drax's maximum health.	5
B3	Team Player	Decreases the amount of time it takes to revive another Character or sidekick.	2
B6	Ultra Ranged Attack Upgrade	Increases the damage of Drax's charging attack. (Tap ranged attack button.)	6
E3	Uppercut Flurry	A combo (hold attack button) that breaks an opponent's block, juggles him into the air, and finishes him off with a flurry of attacks.	2
C5	Warrior Wall Crawl	Gives Drax the ability to Wall Crawl using his knives.	1

GROOT

Skills			
	SKILL	**DESCRIPTION**	**COST**
G5	Bark Regrowth	Allows Groot to regenerate his Bark Shield by entering a blocking state (hold defend button). As long as some of the Bark Shield remains, it will regenerate while blocking. Once it is completely depleted, it can be regrown again with his Special Move. (Tap special move button.)	6
C2	Bough Breaker	Groot can break an opponent's block by swinging his arms upward. (Hold attack button.)	2
B1	Branching Out	After performing a Bough Breaker, release the attack button and then tap the attack button again to perform a powerful attack that repels an opponent.	4
C5	Climbing Vines	Gives Groot the ability to Wall Crawl.	1
D2	Damage Increase 1	Increases the damage of Groot's combo attack. (Tap attack button.)	2
C1	Damage Increase 2	Increases the damage of Groot's combo attack. (Tap attack button.)	4
C4	Health Boost 1	Increases Groot's maximum health.	1
B3	Health Boost 2	Increases Groot's maximum health.	2
B5	Health Boost 3	Increases Groot's maximum health.	3
B6	Health Boost 4	Increases Groot's maximum health.	4
A4	Helping Hand	Decreases the amount of health needed to revive another Character or sidekick.	2
A5	Helping Hand Upgrade	Decreases the amount of health needed to revive another Character or sidekick.	4
E4	I am Groot!	This unlocks Groot's Special Move (tap special move button)! Groot grows and performs a series of close-range attacks. Upon completion, he returns to his original size.	2
C6	Make Like a Tree	Increases Groot's running speed.	2
D3	Mid-Air Recovery	Allows the Character to recover in mid-air by tapping the jump button.	1
F3	Power Disc Recharge Upgrade 1	Increases the rate at which the Power Disc meter fills.	3
F2	Power Disc Recharge Upgrade 2	Increases the rate at which the Power Disc meter fills.	5
D6	Ranged Attack Upgrade 1	Increases the damage of Groot's burrowing arm attacks. (Tap ranged attack button.)	2
C7	Ranged Attack Upgrade 2	Increases the damage of Groot's burrowing arm attacks. (Tap ranged attack button.)	4
C3	Repel	Repel an attacking opponent. Tap the defend button just before attack. Requires skilled timing.	3
G1	Respender 1	At level 10, allows you to completely respend all of your skill points. Use it wisely, though. Once purchased, it will be permanently used.	0
G7	Respender 2	At level 20, allows you to completely respend all of your skill points. Use it wisely, though. Once purchased, it will be permanently used.	0
D7	Root for Groot	Hold ranged attack button to spawn multiple arms that seek out targets in a cone in front of Groot.	4
E5	Shrub Drub	Increases the damage and area of Groot's Air Assault. (Tap jump button, then tap attack button.)	2
F5	Special Move Bonus 1	Increases the damage of Groot's Special Move. (Tap special move button.)	3
G3	Special Move Bonus 2	Increases the damage of Groot's Special Move. (Tap special move button.)	4
E2	Special Move Mega Bonus	Increases the damage of Groot's Special Move. (Tap special move button.)	6
F4	Special Move Meter Upgrade 1	Adds a portion to the Special Move meter. When filled, the Character can activate a Special Move.	3
F6	Special Move Meter Upgrade 2	Adds a portion to the Special Move meter. When filled, the Character can activate a Special Move.	5
E6	Special Move Meter Upgrade 3	Adds a portion to the Special Move meter. When filled, the Character can activate a Special Move.	6
E3	Speedy Meter Upgrade	Increases the rate at which the Special Move meter fills when Power Pickups are obtained.	4
D5	Street Spike	Allows the Character to slam a carried object into the ground by tapping the attack button.	1
D1	Strong Finish	Provides an additional upgrade to Groot's ground attack. (Tap the attack button.)	4
E1	Super Damage Increase	Increases the damage of Groot's combo attack. (Tap attack button.)	6
A3	Super Health Boost	Increases Groot's maximum health.	5
B4	Team Player	Decreases the amount of time it takes to revive another Character or sidekick.	2
B2	Team Player Upgrade	Decreases the amount of time it takes to revive another Character or sidekick.	4
G4	Tough Bark	Allows Groot to grow a temporary bark shield while he performs his Special Move. (Tap special move button.)	3
E7	Ultra Ranged Attack Upgrade	Increases the damage of Groot's burrowing arm attacks. (Tap ranged attack button.)	6

Villains beware of Groot's crushing strength and heavy-duty defense.

SPECIAL ABILITIES

- Healing
- Maximum Strength
- Wall Crawl

SKILL TREE

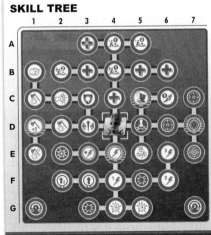

GAME BASICS

CHARACTERS

POWER DISCS

MARVEL'S THE AVENGERS

SPIDER-MAN

GUARDIANS OF THE GALAXY

TOY BOX

TOY BOX COLLECTION

ACHIEVEMENTS

POWER DISCS

Disney Infinity: Marvel Super Heroes Play Sets and Toy Box Worlds can be modified or customized through the use of Power Discs. These interactive discs are placed on the Disney Infinity base to power up characters, grant unique abilities, customize the world, and provide exclusive toys. There are two distinct types of Power Discs: a circular disc and a hexagonal-shaped disc. Circular Power Discs grant your character special power-ups that can be used in the Play Sets as well as in the Toy Box. Hexagonal Power Discs, on the other hand, unlock special gadgets, vehicles or mounts, and themes to help you personalize the Toy Box even more.

Power Discs are sold in blind packs of two, and it is a mystery which ones you will receive. Furthermore, some Power Discs are rare (having a lower chance to be in each pack)—they have an orange border around them to designate their rarity. The mystery of what is in each blind pack makes Power Discs very collectible and provides a great opportunity for people to swap them and try to collect them all.

> **NOTE**
>
> There are 40 Power Discs released in Wave 1. These are all covered in this chapter. In addition, there will be 40 Power Discs released in Wave 2. Be sure to collect them all.

DISC TYPES

ABILITIES: CIRCULAR POWER DISCS

Usage: Placed underneath the character on the Disney Infinity base.

The circular Power Discs provide some very powerful abilities to your characters. They can be used in both the Play Sets as well as the Toy Box Worlds. Up to two circular Power Discs can be placed under each character. These Power Discs can be divided into three different categories based on the type of ability they provide—events, costumes, and team-ups. Event discs allow characters to use a powerful type of attack after a warm-up period. Costumes change the look of a specific character and can also give an improved ability to all characters who use it. Team-ups bring in an AI-controlled character to help your character defeat nearby enemies for a limited amount of time. When these discs are placed under a character, an icon will appear under that character's stats to show you what abilities are now equipped. For events and team-ups, a yellow circle will fill around the icon to show you when the ability is ready to be used.

TOYS: HEXAGONAL POWER DISCS

Usage: Placed on the hexagonal slot on the Disney Infinity base.

Toy discs are hexagonal discs that unlock gadgets, weapons, vehicles, and more in the Toy Box Worlds. However, these toys will only appear when the hexagonal disc is on the Disney Infinity base. Remove the disc from the base and the unlocked item goes away.

CUSTOMIZATION: HEXAGONAL POWER DISCS

Usage: Placed on the hexagonal slot on the Disney Infinity base.

These discs provide numerous ways to personalize the atmosphere of the Toy Box Worlds. Customization discs come in two different types— one that alters the Sky Theme and another that changes the Toy Box World's textures. Changing the Sky Theme alters the sky background as well as the music to match the theme of the disc. The texture disc changes the land and terrain to create a new visual theme. While there are Sky Theme and texture discs that share a common theme, you can mix and match any sky with any texture to create your own Toy Box Worlds. Once you have used these discs to change the sky and textures, you can remove them from the base and use other hexagonal disks on the base.

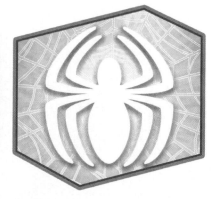

POWER DISCS

⭐ ABILITIES: CIRCULAR POWER DISCS

S.H.I.E.L.D. HELICARRIER STRIKE

Got it? ☑

Marvel's The Avengers
Category: Event
Rarity: Common

A S.H.I.E.L.D. airstrike can turn the tide of any battle. After this event is ready, you can call in a missile strike from the sky to attack enemies in a targeted area in front of your character.

IRON PATRIOT

Got it? ☑

Iron Man
Category: Marvel Team-Up
Rarity: Common

When the chips are down, Rhodey's there to lend an iron hand. After this ability charges up, you can activate it to bring Iron Patriot to help you defeat the enemies.

SORCERER SUPREME

Got it? ☑

Doctor Strange
Category: Event
Rarity: Common

Summon the assistance of Doctor Stephen Strange. When activated, a magical barrier appears around your character and acts as a shield against damage.

ANT-MAN

Got it? ☑

Marvel's The Avengers
Category: Marvel Team-Up
Rarity: Common

An assist from Ant-Man is no small request. Get his help for a limited amount of time.

INFINITY GAUNTLET

Got it? ☑

Marvel's Guardians of the Galaxy
Category: Event
Rarity: Rare

Become the envy of Thanos when you wield this powerful object. A shield appears around your character and it becomes invulnerable for a period of time. In addition, damage is inflicted on enemies in the area around your character.

WHITE TIGER

Got it? ☑

Spider-Man
Category: Marvel Team-Up
Rarity: Common

White Tiger is ready to lend her powerful clawed hands. Bring her in to help fight off foes.

GAME BASICS
CHARACTERS
POWER DISCS
MARVEL'S THE AVENGERS
SPIDER-MAN
GUARDIANS OF THE GALAXY
TOY BOX
TOY BOX COLLECTION
ACHIEVEMENTS

WINTER SOLDIER

Got it? ✓

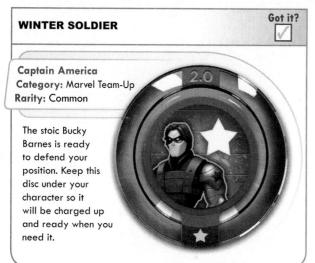

Captain America
Category: Marvel Team-Up
Rarity: Common

The stoic Bucky Barnes is ready to defend your position. Keep this disc under your character so it will be charged up and ready when you need it.

GAMMA RAYS

Got it? ✓

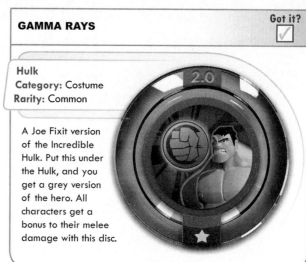

Hulk
Category: Costume
Rarity: Common

A Joe Fixit version of the Incredible Hulk. Put this under the Hulk, and you get a grey version of the hero. All characters get a bonus to their melee damage with this disc.

YONDU

Got it? ✓

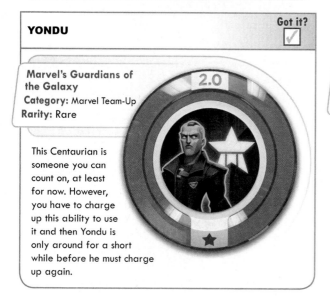

Marvel's Guardians of the Galaxy
Category: Marvel Team-Up
Rarity: Rare

This Centaurian is someone you can count on, at least for now. However, you have to charge up this ability to use it and then Yondu is only around for a short while before he must charge up again.

THE IMMORTAL IRON FIST

Got it? ✓

Iron Fist
Category: Costume
Rarity: Common

Danny Rand in his sleek white costume. Use Iron Fist to get the change in outfit. This disc provides a healing bonus for all characters who use it.

ALIEN SYMBIOTE

Got it? ✓

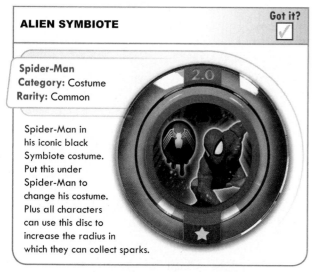

Spider-Man
Category: Costume
Rarity: Common

Spider-Man in his iconic black Symbiote costume. Put this under Spider-Man to change his costume. Plus all characters can use this disc to increase the radius in which they can collect sparks.

SENTINEL OF LIBERTY

Got it? ✓

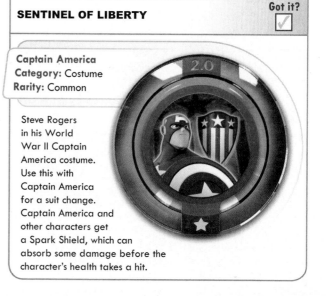

Captain America
Category: Costume
Rarity: Common

Steve Rogers in his World War II Captain America costume. Use this with Captain America for a suit change. Captain America and other characters get a Spark Shield, which can absorb some damage before the character's health takes a hit.

SPACE ARMOR

Got it? ☑

Gamora
Category: Costume
Rarity: Common

Gamora in her protective spacesuit armor. This disc gives characters some additional protection from damage as the armor protects them. Gamora, though, is the only one who gets a new costume.

STARK ARC REACTOR

Got it? ☑

Iron Man
Category: Costume
Rarity: Common

A shiny new upgraded suit from the *Iron Man* films. If you put this under Iron Man, he will change into his Mark 42 armor. However, every character gets a bonus to damage inflicted by ranged attacks.

TOYS: HEXAGONAL POWER DISCS

SPIDER GLIDER

Got it? ☑

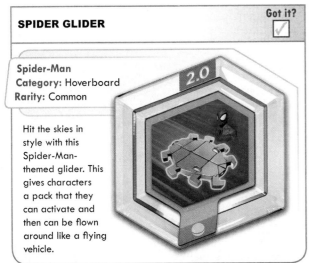

Spider-Man
Category: Hoverboard
Rarity: Common

Hit the skies in style with this Spider-Man-themed glider. This gives characters a pack that they can activate and then can be flown around like a flying vehicle.

CLOAK OF LEVITATION

Got it? ☑

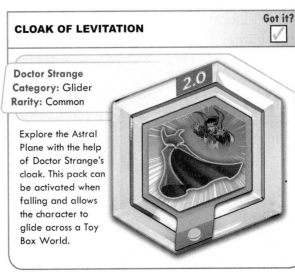

Doctor Strange
Category: Glider
Rarity: Common

Explore the Astral Plane with the help of Doctor Strange's cloak. This pack can be activated when falling and allows the character to glide across a Toy Box World.

JACK O-LANTERN'S GLIDER

Got it? ☑

Spider-Man
Category: Hoverboard
Rarity: Common

Don't wait for Halloween to enjoy this powerful flying contraption. It acts like a pack, but when activated, you can use it like a flying vehicle.

FALCON'S WINGS

Got it? ☑

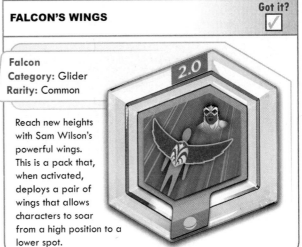

Falcon
Category: Glider
Rarity: Common

Reach new heights with Sam Wilson's powerful wings. This is a pack that, when activated, deploys a pair of wings that allows characters to soar from a high position to a lower spot.

GAME BASICS

CHARACTERS

POWER DISCS

MARVEL'S THE AVENGERS

SPIDER-MAN

GUARDIANS OF THE GALAXY

TOY BOX

TOY BOX COLLECTION

ACHIEVEMENTS

GHOST RIDER'S CHAIN WHIP

Got it? ✓

Ghost Rider
Category: Weapon
Rarity: Rare

The Spirit of Vengeance's weapon of choice. This weapon can attack enemies at a distance in front of the character using it.

S.H.I.E.L.D. CONTAINMENT TRUCK

Got it? ✓

Marvel's The Avengers
Category: Vehicle
Rarity: Common

When you can't call "The Cavalry," call in the firepower of this vehicle. As with all vehicles, press the item select button to bring up a selection screen where you can choose which weapons to use on this truck.

BLACK PANTHER'S VIBRANIUM KNIVES

Got it? ✓

Black Panther
Category: Weapon
Rarity: Common

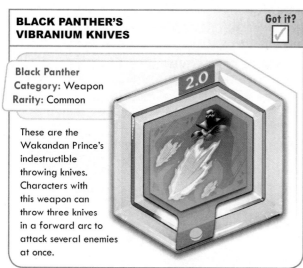

These are the Wakandan Prince's indestructible throwing knives. Characters with this weapon can throw three knives in a forward arc to attack several enemies at once.

LOLA

Got it? ✓

Marvel's Agents of S.H.I.E.L.D..
Category: Vehicle
Rarity: Common

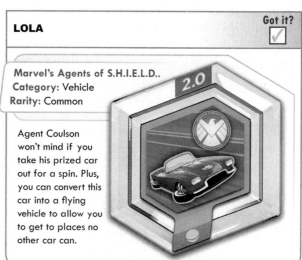

Agent Coulson won't mind if you take his prized car out for a spin. Plus, you can convert this car into a flying vehicle to allow you to get to places no other car can.

ODIN'S HORSE

Got it? ✓

Thor
Category: Mount
Rarity: Common

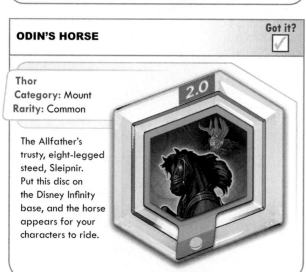

The Allfather's trusty, eight-legged steed, Sleipnir. Put this disc on the Disney Infinity base, and the horse appears for your characters to ride.

SPIDER-BUGGY

Got it? ✓

Spider-Man
Category: Vehicle
Rarity: Common

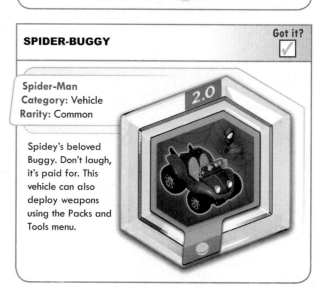

Spidey's beloved Buggy. Don't laugh, it's paid for. This vehicle can also deploy weapons using the Packs and Tools menu.

SPIDER-CYCLE

Got it? ☑

Spider-Man
Category: Motorcycle
Rarity: Rare

Tired of wall crawling? Rev the engines of this sweet street machine. Like vehicles, this motorcycle has weapons that can be deployed.

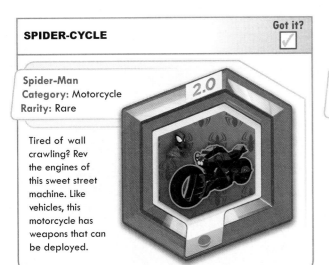

THE AVENJET

Got it? ☑

Marvel's The Avengers
Category: Flying Vehicle
Rarity: Common

The Avengers' signature plane, fueled and ready for action. While this plane has machine guns as the default weapon, you can change to three other types of weapons by pressing the Packs and Tools button and choosing what you want.

HYDRA MOTORCYCLE

Got it? ☑

Captain America
Category: Motorcycle
Rarity: Common

Race to bring order to a chaotic world. Hail Hydra! Don't forget the weapons.

SPIDER-COPTER

Got it? ☑

Spider-Man
Category: Flying Vehicle
Rarity: Common

It's Spider-Man's awesome helicopter! Green Goblin will never see it coming. You don't have to be Spider-Man to fly this. Just place the disc on the Disney Infinity base and get ready to take off.

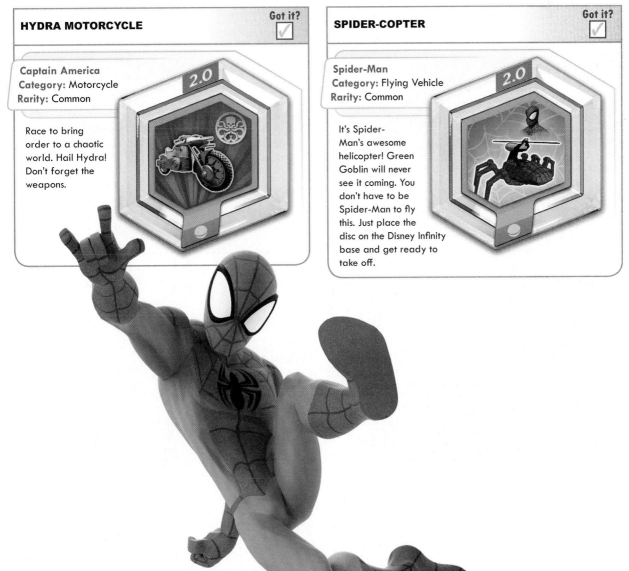

GAME BASICS

CHARACTERS

POWER DISCS

MARVEL'S THE AVENGERS

SPIDER-MAN

GUARDIANS OF THE GALAXY

TOY BOX

TOY BOX COLLECTION

ACHIEVEMENTS

CUSTOMIZING: HEXAGONAL POWER DISCS

STARK TECH

Got it? ☑

Iron Man
Category: Terrain Theme
Rarity: Common

Fill your Toy Box with surfaces and objects inspired by Stark Industries tech. Just place this on the Disney Infinity base and this disc will do the rest.

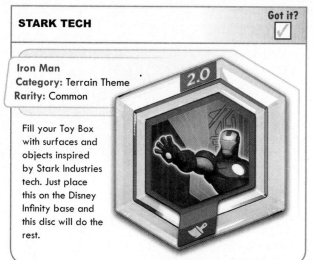

VIEW FROM THE SUIT

Got it? ☑

Iron Man
Category: Sky Theme
Rarity: Common

See the world around you as Tony Stark does when you add this sky to your Toy Box.

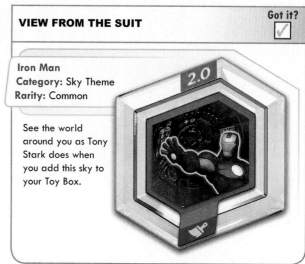

SPIDEY'S STREETS

Got it? ☑

Spider-Man
Category: Terrain Theme
Rarity: Common

Use this disc to change the surfaces and objects in your Toy Box to a theme inspired by Spider-Man's suit.

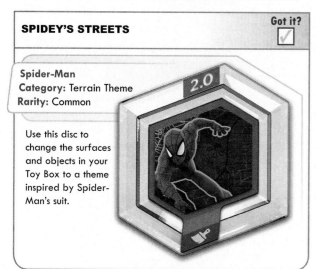

SPIDEY SKY

Got it? ☑

Spider-Man
Category: Sky Theme
Rarity: Common

Fill your sky with spiderwebs with this Spider-Man-themed sky.

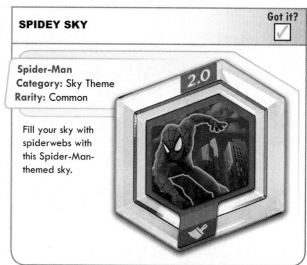

WORLD WAR HULK

Got it? ☑

Hulk
Category: Terrain Theme
Rarity: Common

This disc creates heavily damaged surfaces and objects inspired by a Hulk rampage.

WORLD WAR HULK SKY

Got it? ☑

Hulk
Category: Sky Theme
Rarity: Common

Turn the overhead atmosphere to green with this Hulk-themed sky.

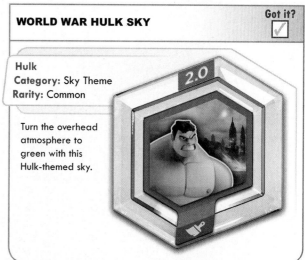

STAR-LORD'S GALAXY

Got it? ✓

Marvel's Guardians of the Galaxy
Category: Terrain Theme
Rarity: Common

Use this disc and get galactic surfaces and objects from *Guardians of the Galaxy*.

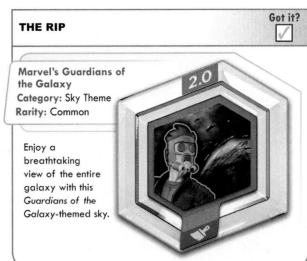

THE RIP

Got it? ✓

Marvel's Guardians of the Galaxy
Category: Sky Theme
Rarity: Common

Enjoy a breathtaking view of the entire galaxy with this *Guardians of the Galaxy*-themed sky.

DINOSAUR WORLD

Got it? ✓

Dinosaur World
Category: Terrain Theme
Rarity: Common

Prehistoric jungle surfaces and objects from the Marvel Universe fill your Toy Box when you use this disc.

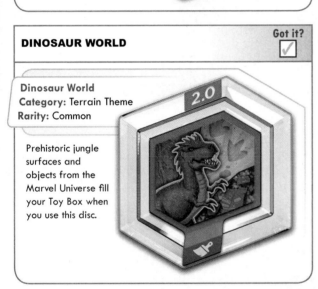

FORGOTTEN SKIES

Got it? ✓

Dinosaur World
Category: Sky Theme
Rarity: Common

You'll feel like you're looking upward through a prehistoric jungle canopy when you add this sky to your Toy Box.

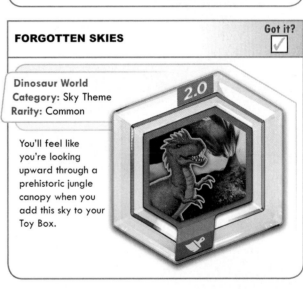

GROOT'S ROOTS

Got it? ✓

Marvel's Guardians of the Galaxy
Category: Terrain Theme
Rarity: Common

Fill your Toy Box with surfaces and objects inspired by Groot from *Guardians of the Galaxy*.

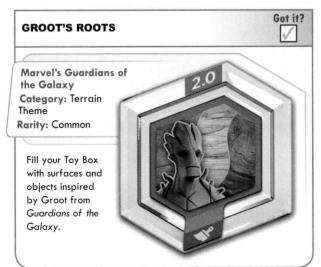

GROOT'S VIEW

Got it? ✓

Marvel's Guardians of the Galaxy
Category: Sky Theme
Rarity: Common

Give your Toy Box a tree branch twist when you add this sky, inspired by Groot from *Guardians of the Galaxy*.

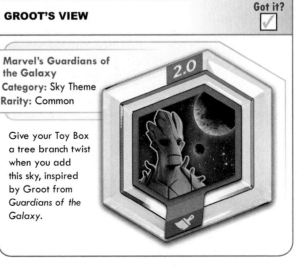

GAME BASICS

CHARACTERS

POWER DISCS

MARVEL'S THE AVENGERS

SPIDER-MAN

GUARDIANS OF THE GALAXY

TOY BOX

TOY BOX COLLECTION

ACHIEVEMENTS

MARVEL'S THE AVENGERS

MARVEL'S THE AVENGERS PLAY SET

INSIDE AVENGERS TOWER

AVENGERS TOWER (PART 1)

COLD OPENING

RECOMMENDED HERO: IRON MAN

Mission Giver: JARVIS
Type: Combat
Rewards: 75 Blue Sparks

The Avengers begin their first mission thawing out inside Avengers Tower. Loki has sent a furious ice storm against Manhattan and Frost Giants have taken up residence in the facility. They apparently desire something in the lab, and it's your job to fire up those boot jets and take a torch to their plans. Before you leave the first area, though, you may want to check for blue Sparks up the stairs and encased in the ice blocks scattered about the room.

> **NOTE**
>
> You can choose any Marvel Character from this Play Set and be successful on these missions. Each hero is special and much of the fun is replaying through the missions with different heroes, leveling up and unlocking their special abilities as you go. However, there are some spots in each mission where a particular hero may be better suited to overcome an obstacle or a particular hero's skills may allow you to proceed through a mission easier. And sometimes we just thought it was cool to have a particular hero on a mission, like Captain America battling in an A.I.M. Weapon Factory. With that in mind, we've chosen a Recommended Hero for each mission to maximize your superhero potential.

AVENGERS TOWER (PART 2)

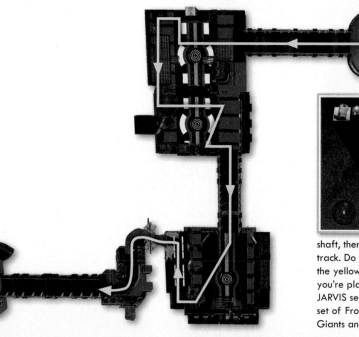

Break through the ice block in front of the elevator entrance. Jump up into the elevator shaft, then perform an Air Attack to jolt the elevator car down the track. Do it a second time to reach the bottom. Jump up and grab the yellow ledge, then jump again to exit the elevator shaft. If you're playing with Iron Man, you can simply fly up and out. JARVIS seals the next room and instructs you to neutralize the first set of Frost Giants. Practice your melee attacks on the three Frost Giants and scoop up the green capsules if you need some healing.

When you pass through the shimmering blue security screen across the exit, the security system turns on. Bypass the three lasers by jumping over the first, ducking under the second, and jumping over the third. With Iron Man, you can hover a little above the first laser and then fly full speed through to the other side and avoid laser burn.

In the next room, practice your blocking against the Frost Giants. When a Frost Giant's fist ices up and it rears back to punch, block so you don't take heavy damage. After you defeat the Frost Giants on the bottom level, head up the stairs and beat up on the remaining Frost Giant. A hole blasts through the nearby wall once you obliterate that last Frost Giant.

Navigate through the empty control room and blast the ice blocks in the far corner. Follow the tunnel down to the next Avengers Tower corridor.

AVENGERS TOWER (PART 3)

In the next room, jump off the broken platform and defend against the Frost Giants who tunnel through the far wall. Practice your Alternate Attack against these Giants; in the case of Iron Man, use his Pulse Bolts at range to blast the Frost Giants before they can reach you.

NOTE

Congratulations! You should gain enough experience to level up in this room or the next. After you receive the notification, go to the main menu and select "Skill Tree." Spend your skill point on one of the highlighted skills to improve your hero. Iron Man, for example, can choose from four skills: Health Boost, Mid-Air Recovery, Missile Barrage, and Street Spike. Though he will definitely want Missile Barrage soon, you probably want to give Iron Man Health Boost now to increase his life during a fight and set up Iron Man's skill tree to now be adjacent to another unique skill—Regenerating Shields.

If you try and exit through the security screen, a wall of lasers barricades the way. You can't get through until you hack the access panel on the platform to the right of the exit. Smash through the debris in the corridor, or jump/fly over it to reach the next room.

Your combat moves will be tested in this next room. You have to battle through a dozen Frost Giants, while making sure not to get surrounded or fall in the large hole ripped in the floor. Either mistake will cost you your life. At the end of the fight, fly up to the exit on the upper platform (non-flyers will have to climb up the blue pole, cross the catwalk, and make a jump).

Beat up on the next set of Frost Giants in the corridor. JARVIS opens a new door after you defeat them, but this one too is guarded by security measures. Jump or fly over the first laser beams, duck under the second, and jump/fly over the third. Alternatively, you can use the access panel in the corridor to shut off the third lasers.

Exit the next room through the ventilation shaft to your right. If you go to the left, you can smash into a side area for extra Sparks. Follow the ventilation shaft until you run into three ice blocks shielding the way. Smash them and you reach the lab.

You realize that the Frost Giants have stolen the Arc Reactor in the lab's central power core. Fly down to the Arc Reactor platform. If you don't have a flying hero, use the rails along the wall to your right to slide down to the platform. Once you reach the platform and stand on the highlighted square, a force field envelopes the energy bursting out from the power core, trapping you in with a swarm of Frost Giants.

Concentrate on staying alive and destroying Frost Giants one by one. Despite JARVIS's warnings, the power core will not explode. Be careful not to get surrounded and take heavy damage from multiple Giant attacks, or get knocked into the power core, which is instant goodbye. If you need a breather, run around the core in a circle and collect green capsules to heal back up into fighting shape. Capsules will spawn over time, so keep circling if you need more. Eventually, you will defeat all the Giants and can stabilize the power core at the main control panel. A few Frost Giants manage to escape through a large tunnel. Follow them to a ladder that leads out onto the streets of Manhattan and your next adventure.

 Feat Complete: **Tower Power**
Feat Complete: **Getting Your Feat Wet**

THE STREETS OF MANHATTAN

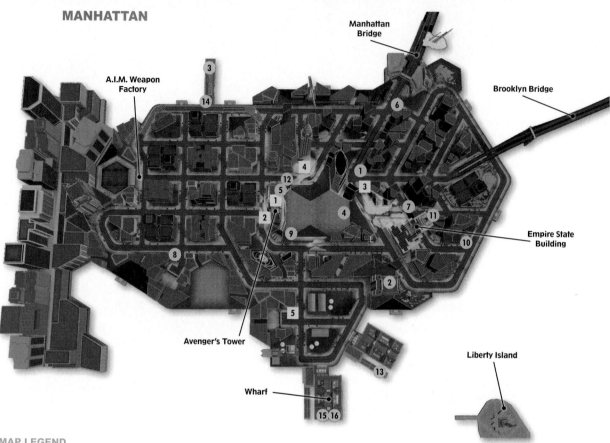

MANHATTAN

Manhattan Bridge

A.I.M. Weapon Factory

Brooklyn Bridge

Empire State Building

Avenger's Tower

Liberty Island

Wharf

MAP LEGEND

MISSION GIVERS	CHALLENGES			
1 JARVIS	1 Hulk Smash!	5 Vs. Mode: Avengers Tower	9 Tread Dead	13 Super Jump Race
2 Nick Fury	2 Fight or Flight	6 A Shot at Glory	10 High Flier	14 Splash Landing
3 Wasp	3 Vs. Mode: Docks	7 Quick Pace Race	11 Skyward Score	15 Thrills and Chills
4 Captain Marvel	4 Vs. Mode: Park	8 Route to Victory	12 Flight Targets	16 So Much Ice, So Little Time
5 Sif				

SHEER WHEEL POWER

RECOMMENDED HERO: BLACK WIDOW

Mission Giver: Nick Fury
Type: Collect
Reward: 100 Blue Sparks, S.H.I.E.L.D. Motorcycle

Sliding a manhole cover aside, you climb up onto a Manhattan street. Nick Fury contacts you with an offer to help him with Loki's Frost Giants across the city. To sweeten the deal, he includes an incentive to join him: Hop on the S.H.I.E.L.D. Motorcycle parked on the nearby corner, drive it to Fury, and he'll let you keep the wheels for yourself. It's a good deal, and becomes a great deal as you upgrade to even better vehicles later in the game and can spawn vehicles at any time at the S.H.I.E.L.D. transportation request stations about the city. Also, don't miss the Rocket Raccoon and Nova Crossover Coins spinning behind Nick Fury.

ENEMIES

SMALL FROST GIANT

The most common ice foe in the Avengers Play Set. Easy to take out, but watch out for its icy fists that can land a teeth-chattering blow.

MEDIUM FROST GIANT

A step up from its smaller cousins, the medium variety Frost Giant lasts longer in combat, and some will summon more Frost Giants into the fray if you let them.

SHIELDED FROST GIANT

This Frost Giant's shields can reduce melee blows and protect against ranged attacks. Add a spear to its arsenal and you have trouble.

LARGE FROST GIANT

The most serious of Frost Giants has two fearsome attacks: a hand clap that sends out an icy wave that freezes solid anyone caught in its wake, and ice boulders it can throw long distances. Oh yeah, and it takes a whole lot of damage to bring it down.

SECURITY DRONE

Invented by M.O.D.O.K., these flying surveillance devices have also been equipped with energy blasts that will roast you to a crisp if you're slow.

ENERGY CRISIS

RECOMMENDED HERO: THOR

Mission Giver: JARVIS
Type: Combat
Rewards: 150 Blue Sparks

JARVIS lets you know that power needs to be restored to Avengers Tower, and the only way to do that is by activating the emergency power overrides in the area surrounding the Tower. If you have a hero like Thor, it's a quick aerial jaunt to each location. If you can't fly, hop on your new S.H.I.E.L.D. Motorcycle to race to Avengers Tower.

The first power override station rests a few blocks away at the back of an alley between the buildings adjacent to the Empire State Building. Because you are in tight quarters in the alley, try to take out the spawning Frost Giants quickly, before they can swarm you. If you're having problems, fly up out of harm's way and reposition at the front of the alley or perform an Air Attack for area-effect damage. Press the IN button to activate the first of the override stations.

SINGLE POWER DISCS

Even a single Power Disc can give your hero that extra boost offensively or defensively to win the day, or imbue your hero with an extra ability he or she might not possess. You may want to add White Tiger as an ally with the Marvel Team-Up: White Tiger disc, or attach the Alien Symbiote disc to your hero and widen his collection radius. If you're lucky enough to gain one of the rare Power Discs, such as the uber-powerful Infinity Gauntlet, it's a no-brainer to stack it with your hero. The only down side for some Power Discs like that is that they need time to recharge in between uses.

You can find the second power override station a couple of blocks away. When you arrive, Frost Giants spawn in the area and converge. Don't let them get the jump on you. Pull back from the machine and hurl Mjolnir at each one until they explode into ice fragments. If you've upgraded Thor's skills to Mjolnir Lightning Charge, your ranged attacks will splinter the Frost Giants handily, and even Thor's Lightning Strike area-effect special ability can take down the enemies quickly. Use the IN button on the power override station to activate it, then move on to the final one.

The third power override station is outside the building adjacent to Avengers Tower. More Frost Giants spawn around this machine, and this time a stronger type of Frost Giant takes the battlefield. This type of Frost Giant can spawn new Frost Giants by sending out a blast of ice that travels along the ground and spews out a new Giant at the end of its icy path. Avoid going toe-to-toe with this new foe; rather, slam it from the side or behind to take it out before the stronger Frost Giant can land a powerful blow. Once you defeat them all, press the IN button and activate the third power override station to complete the mission and turn the Avengers Tower lights on.

New Challenge Available: Quick Pace Race

SIDE MISSION

ON THE GRID

RECOMMENDED HERO: IRON MAN

Mission Giver: JARVIS	**Rewards:** 250 Blue Sparks, Tony Stark's Sports Car
Type: Combat	

Fly atop Avengers Tower, or if you're hoofing it, use the elevator to reach the top. Speak with JARVIS through the rooftop control panel, and he will hand you a mission to activate six generators across the city to help the citizens stay warm.

 Feat Complete: Bird's Eye View

Fly down to the first generator on the rooftop on one of the buildings a few blocks from the Tower. Press the IN button to turn the sector's power grid back online. Zip across town to the second generator and activate the machine after dealing with the spawning Frost Giants. The third generator takes you out on the docks, where it's an easier flip once you reach it.

HERO TIP: BLACK WIDOW

Black Widow can use her Widow's Veil ability to slip past Frost Giants and activate generators without excessive combat.

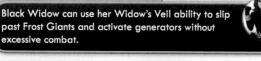
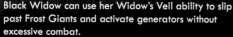

Look for the fourth generator across the water and atop the building near the bridge. Use the IN button to activate the fourth generator and clear out before Frost Giants catch wind of you. Fly directly toward the Empire State Building and zip behind it to find the fifth generator atop the roof of a smaller building overshadowed by two larger buildings. Battle through the Frost Giants protecting the generator to activate it. Go around the building and fly over to the warehouse district for the final generator. Press the last IN button to activate the sixth generator and bring power back to the whole city.

BACKING UP S.H.I.E.L.D.

 Feat Complete: Power Up

STREET SWEEPER

RECOMMENDED HERO: CAPTAIN AMERICA

Mission Giver: Nick Fury
Type: Combat
Rewards: 150 Blue Sparks

Frost Giants have clogged up the streets with ice blockades, and S.H.I.E.L.D. troops can't get through. The Avengers have been tasked with clearing a path through the blockades, and Cap with his sweeping Shield Assault is the best soldier for the job. When you get close to the ice blockades, throw Cap's shield and it will chip away at the ice while damaging any Frost Giants in its arc. Now that's doing double duty!

 Feat Complete: Break the Ice

You can find the first blockade past the Avengers Tower, through the park, and up the next block. Destroy the first set of ice barriers and move on to the second set where Frost Giants spawn to guard the ice. Destroy the Giants before smashing the ice, and then wind through the streets splintering ice and Giants' skulls. When you reach the bridge, Fury alerts you that the streets are finally clear of threats and S.H.I.E.L.D. can move in.

 New Challenge Available: High Flier

BRIDGE MAY BE ICY

RECOMMENDED HERO: HAWKEYE

Mission Giver: Nick Fury
Type: Combat
Rewards: 250 Blue Sparks

HERO TIP: HULK

Any hero who likes hand-to-hand like the Hulk can pick up a Frost Giant and heave them off the side of the bridge.

On this next mission, Nick Fury informs you that a busload of civilians is trapped on the bridge by marauding Frost Giants. You want an Avenger with a strong ranged attack for this battle, such as Hawkeye with Rain of Arrows or Open Fire, which gives him plenty of firepower to do the trick.

Jump on your S.H.I.E.L.D. Motorcycle and zoom over to the bridge. Approach the bridge with caution as Frost Giants will begin spawning and charging down at you. Always focus on the closest one and pick it off before it gets into melee range. When groups attack, rely on an area-effect attack like Hawkeye's Open Fire. Backpedal if you need more space to plant arrows in your foes.

Make your way up the bridge and avoid the falling debris and eroding pavement. Destroy the ice barriers as you go, and perform an Air Strike on the slab of concrete in front of the bus to smash it down and fill in a hole in the road. Once you break all the ice trapping the bus and defeat a new group of spawning Frost Giants, the bus will slowly begin rolling down the broken bridge road.

Escort the bus down the road. As Frost Giants appear, pick them off at range, and if a group collects in one spot, use an area-effect ability like Hawkeye's Rain of Arrows to punish them. Avoid the holes in the road as you blow up the ice barricades that slow down the bus.

Don't let the Frost Giants pound away on the bus. Keep clearing ice blockades and Frost Giants until the bus rolls past the stone arch leading into Manhattan. Fury will alert you when the civilians are safe and your mission is complete.

SHAKING THE WASP'S NEST

RECOMMENDED HERO: HULK

Mission Giver: Wasp
Type: Combat
Rewards: 250 Blue Sparks, Wasp

Wasp's apartment building has been encased in ice. Normally, that wouldn't be a big deal, since so is the rest of Manhattan; however, a horde of Frost Giants are assaulting the building too. Even that wouldn't be too bad, but large Frost Giants have been added to the mix, and they are a serious challenge. Large Frost Giants can throw spears and use shields to block your attacks. It takes someone like the Hulk to deal with the vast amounts of Frost Giants in this mission and break down the large Frost Giants' defenses and take them out.

Head down the street from the earlier bridge mission and you'll find Wasp's apartment building on the left. Smash through the ice blocks encasing the walls, then shift your attention to the Frost Giants as they spawn. Shatter ice and frost until the corner of the building is free and Wasp flies out to greet you. The whole Avengers team shows up to talk with Wasp, and she agrees to do some surveillance for you as you begin to unravel Loki's plans.

SIDE MISSION

A HEAVY DILEMMA

RECOMMENDED HERO: BLACK WIDOW

Mission Giver: Nick Fury
Type: Escort
Rewards: 250 Blue Sparks, Small Frost Giant

Speak with Nick Fury and he'll give you the rundown on your next side mission: transport a piece of S.H.I.E.L.D. equipment through enemy territory. Hop on the S.H.I.E.L.D. Motorcycle and follow the yellow objective marker to locate the equipment in the city.

Frost Giants will attack the area as you near the overpass. Engage them quickly before they have a chance to damage the equipment. If the equipment takes too much damage and its green bar is reduced to zero, the mission fails. Pick up the equipment after you've punched a hole in the ice blockade and begin carrying your cargo to its final destination.

As you walk down the street, equipment overhead, ice missiles will drop from the sky and form ice barricades as they land. Avoid getting hit by these or you and the equipment will take damage.

Drop the equipment off in the flare zone next to the S.H.I.E.L.D. vehicle. Prepare for an assault from a big group of Frost Giants, and as you beat away on the Giants, keep the equipment in your sight. Defend the equipment rather than straying too far out to defeat enemies. Use the flares as your guide as you keep coming back to them to protect the equipment. Remember, if you need a break at any time, Black Widow can use her stealth ability to slip out of combat and grab a few Sparks or sneak up behind an enemy. If the equipment survives and you defeat all the Frost Giants in the area, Fury signals mission accomplished.

CHASING DOWN THE BAD GUYS

MAKE MINE MARVEL

RECOMMENDED HERO: THOR

Mission Giver: Nick Fury
Type: Escort
Rewards: 250 Blue Sparks, Captain Marvel

For the next main mission, one of S.H.I.E.L.D.'s vehicles is en route to a safe house carrying an ally with crucial intel. The roads are jammed with ice barricades and Frost Giants, and the task at hand is to keep the S.H.I.E.L.D. ally safe as they drive to the checkpoint. Fly over to the bridge and meet the vehicle as it cruises into the city.

Follow the vehicle to the first intersection and destroy the ice barricades blocking the street. An Air Attack will strike multiple barricades at once. Once the barricades are in pieces, Frost Giants spawn to besiege the vehicle. Take them out one by one, and if you drift away too far, remember to throw Mjolnir and scatter any Frost Giants that near the vehicle.

Repeat your defense at the second and third intersections. Each will have ice barricades that stop the vehicle and Frost Giants that try to rip the vehicle apart. Thor's Lightning Strike area-effect attack can help destroy groups that surround the vehicle, especially when you're standing on one side of the vehicle and enemies may be attacking from the other. It's also clutch in the final encounter next.

The vehicle will pull off the street and park at a street corner after the third intersection. Prepare for an all-out slugfest in this final encounter: lots of Frost Giants and lots of running around to defend every side of the vehicle. Use your special abilities if you've got them and keep repelling enemies away from the vehicle. It's better to knock Frost Giants away than to stay with the same one until it's defeated and leave the vehicle vulnerable, even for a few seconds.

When you defeat the Frost Giant horde, Nick Fury arrives and opens the vehicle to reveal your new ally: Captain Marvel. She has intel on Loki's plans that says the trail leads to the warehouse district. While she investigates further, you now have Nick Fury and Captain Marvel to contact for main missions.

CHASING A LEAD

RECOMMENDED HERO: IRON MAN

Mission Giver: Captain Marvel
Type: Combat
Rewards: 250 Blue Sparks

Captain Marvel sends you on a hunt after roaming Frost Giants, hoping that if you follow them they will lead you to clues about Loki's master plan. It's easier if you're a flyer for this mission as you must race around the city and follow the Frost Giants from a distance. When you finally near each group, you will fight some normal and large Frost Giants.

There are three Frost Giant groups to fight. Follow the yellow objective markers to locate them and do your best to defeat the smaller Giants first. With smaller groups, it's easier to track the large Frost Giants and avoid a big blow from their spears. Once you destroy the remaining Frost Giant group, the trail leads to a secret access point on the sidewalk and your next mission inside the abandoned warehouse.

LOKI'S SWELLED HEAD

A.I.M. WEAPON FACTORY

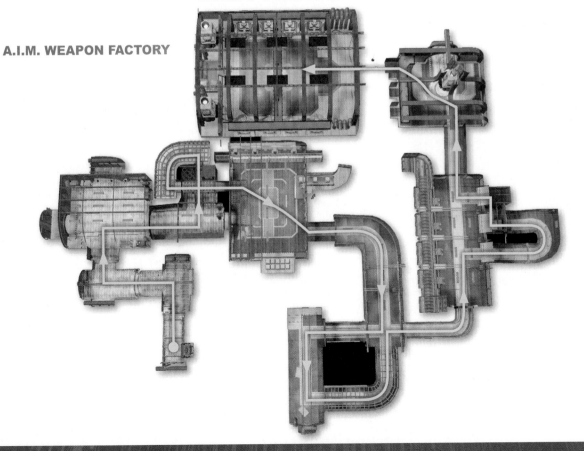

GAME BASICS

CHARACTERS

POWER DISCS

MARVEL'S THE AVENGERS

SPIDER-MAN

GUARDIANS OF THE GALAXY

TOY BOX

TOY BOX COLLECTION

ACHIEVEMENTS

RECOMMENDED HERO: **CAPTAIN AMERICA**

Mission Giver: Nick Fury
Type: Combat
Rewards: 250 Blue Sparks

The "Chasing a Lead" mission leaves you off at the doorstep to this mission. Use the control panel next to the nearby access point to open the doors into the abandoned warehouse serving as a secret A.I.M. Weapon Factory.

Follow the streaking Frost Giant until it leads you to the first room. Security lasers pop up, preventing you from leaving, and Security Drones fly into the area to neutralize the threat—you. Circle the room so the Drones can't lock on to you, and throw your shield at the closest Drone while avoiding the grounded Frost Giants. Take the Security Drones out first, then clean up the Frost Giants. When all is clear, smash the nearby security panel and shut off the lasers.

HERO TIP: HAWKEYE

Hawkeye's Open Fire ranged attack is also great against the flying Security Drones.

Head up the ramp and follow the yellow objective markers as they guide you through the warehouse. As you enter the next room, smash the nearby control panel to destroy the laser turret that defends the room. Jump down into the room and begin taking on targets. Throw your shield at the Security Drones and punch out Frost Giants. If they begin to swarm, back them off with Cap's Shield Assault.

Destroy the security panel and exit the room into the next corridor. More Security Drones and Frost Giants advance on your position. Before they reach you, smash the security panel on the left side and shut down the laser defenses. Engage the enemies, dodging left and right in the corridor as you strike the Drones out of the air with your shield. Mop up the Frost Giants last.

You'll reach a series of laser defenses next. Stand in front of the first laser and wait for the laser to move away from you, then sprint down the corridor. When the lasers return, perform a double-jump to clear the top laser and enter the next room. Jump through the second laser defense when it splits apart and the bottom laser is at its lowest point. The third laser setup is trickier. Wait for the top and bottom laser to move away from you and then run after it. After the middle laser passes overhead, time your jump so that you clear the bottom laser on its return trip. Smash the security panel on the right wall to drop the final laser defense and step into the intersection.

Turn to the right and follow the corridor to the next room. Dash toward the left wall and smash the security panel to shut down the laser cannon before it demolishes you. Next, avoid the Frost Giants and concentrate your shield throws on the two Security Drones. Alternatively, you can use Vibranium Defense (if you picked it up) to ricochet the Drones' laser pulses at the Frost Giants. Use your shield to continuously knock down the large Frost Giant while you cut apart the rest, then turn your attention on him.

At the end of the encounter, a door will open on the right wall. Grab the purple Sparks and jump through the next laser defense when it parts. Turn the corner and run through the last laser defense when the vertical lasers are at their farthest point from each other and the horizontal laser is high.

Climb the blue pole and trash the security panel on the upper ledge to drop the laser wall to your left. Turn right in the intersection and head toward the security room. It's a perfect opportunity in this next room to use Cap's Shield Assault and clear most of the room. Whatever enemies survive your assault, concentrate on any Security Drones first and then eliminate regular Frost Giants before wiping out their larger brethren.

Next, Loki will split into three. Continue dodging and striking if you can, or launch one of your specialty Cap's Shield Assault. As the shield circles around it should take out the fake Loki and deliver damage to the spawning Frost Giant. While the Frost Giant is stunned, combo melee attacks on it to eliminate it quickly. Do the same with the second and third Loki targets.

Climb the pole and head up into the security room where you can tap into the security monitors in the facility. You finally have found Loki, but he's not alone—he's working with M.O.D.O.K. to further his plans. When the villains realize they're being spied on, Loki confronts you while M.O.D.O.K. escapes.

Loki splits in two at the start of the fight: one real Loki and one mirror image. He likes to deflect your shield throws, so dodge frequently until you can get in close and land a series of blows on either of the Lokis. If Loki shimmers blue, avoid him; he can't be damaged in that state. Once you actually connect with a Loki, he transforms into a Frost Giant. Beat the Frost Giant and you end the first phase.

CO-OP COMBO: CAPTAIN AMERICA AND THOR

Loki is a tough boss fight, and who better to join forces with Cap than Loki's half-brother, Thor. Together the heroes have a much better chance at defeating Loki. As one distracts, the other can land blows on the unsuspecting villain, and when a Frost Giant spawns, tag-teaming on it will burst it apart in no time.

Finally, Loki will split into four. Repeat your pattern if you have enough purple Sparks to fire off Cap's Shield Assault. If not, you will have to go after each Loki in turn until only the real one is left. When a Loki transforms into a large Frost Giant, knock him down and keep up the melee attacks until you defeat him. Eventually, one Loki will be standing—that is, until you knock him down and complete the mission.

NOTE

If your hero gets defeated during the final Loki battle, don't opt to respawn at the previous checkpoint. Choose a different hero and continue where you left off to have a better chance at completing this difficult boss fight. There's no shame in using all of the Avengers to take down Loki!

 Feat Complete: Steady A.I.M.

A CHANGE IN THE AIR

RECOMMENDED HERO: THOR

Mission Giver: Wasp
Type: Combat
Rewards: 200 Blue Sparks

Fly over to the roof with the weather machine and clear out the enemies. You definitely want Thor or Iron Man on this mission; one wrong step or successful knock back from an opponent and you'll fall off the roof. With a flyer, you can zip back up no problem. With Thor, you can rocket a hammer at enemies while circling around the roof or drop to the roof and punch out the Frost Giants.

Stay on the roof until you defeat all your foes. Soon you will have repelled the defenders and then the weather machine is all yours. Smash away at it until you deplete its bar and the whole thing explodes. Mission accomplished, though the weather is still looking cold with a chance of blizzards.

Wasp will give you this mission immediately after completing "Loki's Swelled Head." Fly a hero like Thor across town to a door into an apartment complex. Take the elevator up to the roof and look across to the rooftop on the building below. Frost Giants and Security Drones are completing the final work on one of Loki and M.O.D.O.K.'s weather machines.

GAME BASICS CHARACTERS POWER DISCS MARVEL'S THE AVENGERS SPIDER-MAN GUARDIANS OF THE GALAXY TOY BOX TOY BOX COLLECTION ACHIEVEMENTS

SIDE MISSIONS

BAD PRESS

RECOMMENDED HERO: IRON MAN

Mission Giver: Wasp
Type: Combat
Rewards: 250 Blue Sparks, Medium Frost Giant A

Return to Wasp for a string of side missions involving the mayor and the city media. Loki has cast a spell on the mayor and they're using the media towers about the city to preach Loki's "good name." Fly toward Liberty Island and stop on the rooftop marked by the objective marker. Fire a Missile Barrage at them from range or fly straight into the rooftop for an Air Attack. Defeat the Frost Giants and then trash the tower to end the first of three transmission stations.

Repeat the process for the second and third transmission towers by following the objective markers. You'll be thankful you don't have to hear, "All Hail, Loki!" by the time you finish, though Wasp will be happy that you prevented the brainwashed mayor from spreading Loki's lies.

KEEPING IT LOKI

RECOMMENDED HERO: BLACK WIDOW

Mission Giver: Wasp
Type: Escort
Rewards: 1250 Blue Sparks

Wasp asks you to rescue the mayor and bring him to a designated S.H.I.E.L.D. safe zone for deprogramming. As Black Widow, you can slip in through the Frost Giant defenses with stealth and get off surprise attacks or unload from range with your twin pistols or stingers. Take out the Frost Giants guarding the mayor on the street.

HERO TIP: IRON MAN

Iron Man's Pulse Bolts can keep away bad guys from the mayor while you escort him to safety.

Pick up the mayor after you've cleared the area of Frost Giants and run toward the safe zone. Once you drop him off inside the safe zone, more Frost Giants attack.

If the attacks start coming in quickly, dodge out of the safe zone temporarily and then roll back in when it's cleared out or you have a target of opportunity on the side or back of one of your enemies. Defend the mayor from the Frost Giants to complete the mission.

A WORLDWIDE WEB

RECOMMENDED HERO: HAWKEYE

Mission Giver: Wasp
Type: Escort
Rewards: 250 Blue Sparks, A.I.M. Drone

This mission is similar to the previous one, only now Loki has put a spell on U.N. members and you're tasked with rescuing them and delivering them to S.H.I.E.L.D. safe zones. Zip over to the first safe zone and you'll find the first U.N. member encased in ice a few yards away. Shatter the ice layer, pick the U.N. member up, and drop her in the safe zone for your first success.

The second U.N. member is across the street. This time, though, Frost Giants spawn around the area, and you'll have to deal with them before picking up the U.N. member. Drop him off at the safe zone for another success.

Do the same for the third and fourth U.N. members. The third member is surrounded by ice; break through that and it's an easy jog back to the safe zone with her. The fourth member has Frost Giant bodyguards. So long as you take your time and spray the Frost Giants at range with Hawkeye's powerful arrow arsenal, you should handle this mission like a pro.

GAME BASICS

CHARACTERS

POWER DISCS

MARVEL'S THE AVENGERS

SPIDER-MAN

GUARDIANS OF THE GALAXY

TOY BOX

TOY BOX COLLECTION

ACHIEVEMENTS

CIVIL WARFARE

RECOMMENDED HERO: HULK

Mission Giver: Wasp
Type: Escort
Rewards: 100 Blue Sparks, Small Shielded Frost Giant

Just like the other Wasp escort missions, you have to save civilians this time and carry them back to the local S.H.I.E.L.D. safe zone. You must rescue six civilians in three minutes or the mission fails.

After you arrive at the safe zone, ignore the spawning Frost Giants and find the closest civilian encased in ice. Shatter the ice, pick up the civilian, and bring her back to the safe zone. You don't have a lot of time to fight off the Frost Giants, but you can use Hulk's Rampaging Rush to charge through Frost Giants on your way to a civilian.

If the enemy crowd gets thick, use Raging Roar to blast them away and then run for a new civilian. Once you get the sixth civilian into the safe zone, the danger immediately ends and you complete the mission.

AIR MAIL

RECOMMENDED HERO: BLACK WIDOW

Mission Giver: Nick Fury
Type: Collect
Rewards: 150 Blue Sparks, S.H.I.E.L.D. Sky-Cycle

After all your hard work, Fury wants to reward you with a new vehicle. Only problem? You have to go get it across town. Ride your old ground vehicle out to the docks and fetch your new S.H.I.E.L.D. Sky-Cycle.

The Sky-Cycle will ride like a regular bike, but if you transform it, the Sky-Cycle takes to

the air. Zip around on it for a while, then fly the Sky-Cycle up to the top of Avengers Tower to complete the mission.

 Feat Complete: Eyes to the Sky

WEATHERING THE STORM

SNOW END IN SIGHT

RECOMMENDED HERO: THOR

Mission Giver: Wasp
Type: Combat
Rewards: 200 Blue Sparks

The first weather machine is located on the small building to the right of Avengers Tower. Brush aside the Frost Giants and then bash the machine until it explodes. You can find the second weather machine a few building tops over with Frost Giants and Security Drones guarding it. Aim at the Drones first with Mjolnir, then sweep through the grounded Frost Giants before wiping out the machine.

HERO TIP: IRON MAN

Similar to Thor, Iron Man is a flyer, tough in hand-to-hand combat, and has a good ranged attack. He's also great for these rooftop battles.

Return to Wasp and she warns you of more weather machines threatening Manhattan. Seek out these five weather machines on the rooftops across the city and shut them down before it's too late.

The third, fourth, and fifth weather machines are easy flights away. As before, clear the Frost Giants and Security Drones before disabling the machines. After you beat the defenders around the fifth weather machine, Wasp thanks you for your assistance and pledges to work with S.H.I.E.L.D. to figure out how to stop these weather machines permanently.

 New Challenge Available: Super Jump Race

ICE BREAKER

RECOMMENDED HERO: CAPTAIN AMERICA

Mission Giver: Nick Fury
Type: Combat
Rewards: 250 Blue Sparks

S.H.I.E.L.D. tech has been devised to counteract the effects of the weather machines, and Nick Fury needs you to protect the heat generator until it comes online. Look for the generator in the park on the other side of Avengers Tower.

You must defend the generator for two minutes. It's best to have Cap powered up with purple Sparks so that you can use at least one Cap's Shield Assault during the skirmish. Throw your shield at the Security Drones to knock them out of the sky, and pay close attention to the large Frost Giants, since they do more damage to the heat generator if they strike it.

Be sure to dodge often to avoid damage, and it's even better if you can drag some of the enemies away from the generator to chase after you. Frost Giants will keep coming; this mission is not about destroying all enemies, it's about staying alive and destroying select enemies that are going after the generator. After two minutes, the generator sends out a pulse of fire that destroys any remaining enemies and signals victory.

SIDE MISSIONS

HASTY RETREAT

RECOMMENDED HERO: BLACK WIDOW

Mission Giver: Wasp
Type: Escort
Rewards: 250 Blue Sparks

Wasp needs you to escort civilians to the safe zone now protected by S.H.I.E.L.D.'s new heat generators. Use your new Sky-Cycle to zip over to the area. You have three minutes to save eight civilians.

Ignore the Frost Giants as best you can; you don't have time to fend them off and save all the people. Instead, dodge through them and run for the nearest ice-encrusted civilian. Shatter the ice on the civilian and carry her back to safety while avoiding Frost Giants. Continue the process until all eight are safe. If the Frost Giants become too thick, alternate between going left and right while gathering civilians to spread out the Frost Giants' defense.

CHILLING CHASE

RECOMMENDED HERO: IRON MAN

Mission Giver: Captain Marvel
Type: Combat
Rewards: 250 Blue Sparks

Captain Marvel wants you to seek out roaming Frost Giant and Security Drone forces and thin them out to help S.H.I.E.L.D. troops contain them. Fly across town to the first group near the A.I.M. Weapon Factory. Stay at range and pick off as many as you can; you can even hover up in the air and bombard them with Pulse Bolts from the sky.

After you defeat the first group, target the second group just up the block. Repeat the same process on this next group. You can bring out the big guns, Iron Man's Missile Barrage, if  you have enough purple Sparks as this is the last group. Blast away these Frost Giants and you complete the mission.

I'LL LET YOU OFF WITH A WARMING

RECOMMENDED HERO: THOR

Mission Giver: Captain Marvel
Type: Combat
Rewards: 350 Blue Sparks

Follow Captain Marvel's instruction to a heat generator out near the river. As with your last heat generator mission, "Ice Breaker," you must defend the generator from incoming Frost Giants, only this time you must hold them off for two-and-a-half minutes.

Use Mjolnir to knock out the flying Security Drones, and slam any Frost Giants attacking the machine directly with your hand-to-hand combos. When the enemies pile in close to the generator, launch a Lightning Strike to incinerate as many as possible. If you can hold out for the full two-and-a-half minutes, the heat generator unleashes a massive heat pulse and destroys all the remaining enemies for another win.

SUBWAY SERIES

TRAINING GROUND

RECOMMENDED HERO: CAPTAIN AMERICA

Mission Giver: Nick Fury
Type: Combat
Rewards: 250 Blue Sparks

A series of Frost Giant attacks have stopped one of the subway lines and trapped civilians in the tunnels under the city. Zip over to the intersection on the far side of Avengers

Plaza and look for the Frost Giant horde defending an icy pile in the street. Stay out wide and cut down Frost Giants with your shield as they converge outward. Work your way toward the icy pile until you've beaten all Giants.

Perform an Air Attack on the icy pile. This collapses the pile and opens access to the subway tunnel.

Destroy the Frost Giants in the tunnel and then take out the support beams to create a ramp for the oncoming train. Instead of colliding with the debris, the subway train now arcs up the ramp and out onto the street above.

Dispatch the Frost Giants that spawn on the train. It's easier to knock them off the train one by one with your shield and take them out solo. When the last one falls,

you save the civilians on the subway and complete the mission.

PIER PRESSURE

RECOMMENDED HERO: THOR

Mission Giver: Captain Marvel
Type: Combat
Rewards: 250 Blue Sparks

Captain Marvel automatically gives you this mission to save Sif from a band of Frost Giants at the completion of "Training

Ground." Head down to the harbor and you'll spot the first band of Frost Giants out on the pier.

Be careful of falling in the water or getting knocked out into the waves. Stick to the middle of the pier as you battle and try to use Mjolnir to destroy the floating Security Drones and any enemies at range. In close, Thor can combo hand-to-hand moves or blast a small radius of foes with Lightning Strike.

CO-OP COMBO: THOR AND HULK

It's a tough fight out on the pier, especially with the dangerous water so close. If you bring in another hero, try someone like Hulk who has amazing melee abilities. Hulk can jump into the thick of battle and use his Raging Roar to destroy enemy groups or pound away effectively with just his massive fists.

DISNEY
INFINITY
2.0
EDITION

MARVEL
SUPER HEROES

SIF'S SHIP-SHAPE

THE WHARF WAREHOUSE

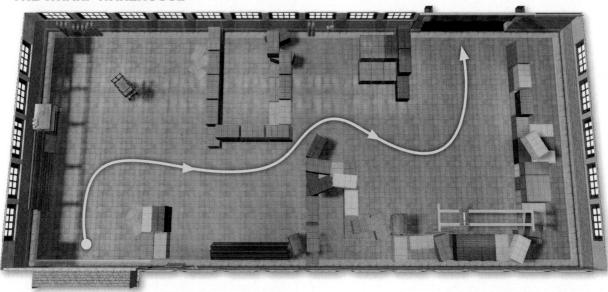

RECOMMENDED HERO: THOR

Mission Giver: Nick Fury
Type: Combat
Rewards: 250 Blue Sparks, Sif, S.H.I.E.L.D. Snowmobile

Nick Fury gives you this mission immediately following your battle on the pier, so you might as well stick with Thor as he continues to rescue Sif. Head inside the wharf area and throw Mjolnir at range to destroy enemies in the large interior. It's especially helpful if you've built up your skills around Mjolnir, such as Mjolnir Lightning Charge and Ranged Attack Upgrade.

Move to the second half of the wharf interior and battle through the Frost Giants there. Repeat your attack pattern. Don't let the Frost Giants swarm you, and use Mjolnir at range to pick them off. Only engage one-on-one if there is no one ready to smash you from behind.

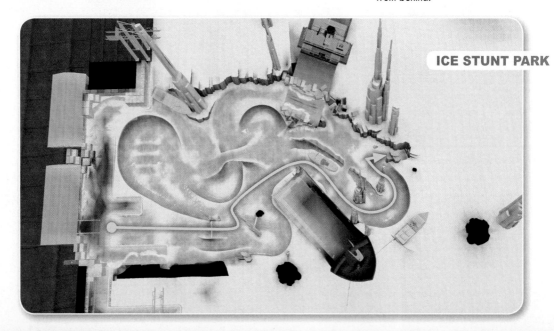

ICE STUNT PARK

Beating the second group opens the doors to the wharf's icy exterior. Hop on a snowmobile and drive through the icy stunt park, where you can do tricks with the snowmobile while driving up and down ice walls, and collect Sparks in the red-and-white balls scattered about the course. Once you've had your fun, cruise to the far end of the stunt park and climb up the cliff wall in the corner.

Enter the ice tunnel and smash any ice barriers in your way. Follow the path until it opens up into a large cavern filled with Frost Giants. Fight through these Frost Giants until you reach a second set on the cavern's far side.

Continue your smashfest on the next set of Frost Giants. When you defeat all of them, a Large Frost Giant appears. Besides being more durable than other Frost Giants, this Frost Giant can hurl ice boulders and clap his hands together to send out an icy shock wave that will paralyze you for several seconds if you get caught in the wave.

Charge up Mjolnir and start smacking the Large Frost Giant with ranged attacks. Avoid boulder throws and fly to the air when you see an icy shock wave, or back out of the way so as not to get caught in its path. Don't take the Large Frost Giant on face to face. If you want to throw down with him in hand-to-hand, dodge to one side and hit him with a combo from the side or from behind. Eventually you'll deal enough damage to shatter him apart.

You'll reach Sif up the ledge and through the tunnel beyond the Large Frost Giant. She fills you in on what Loki has been up to. He has been putting together items to build the Casket of Ancient Winters, which, if completed, will coat the world in eternal ice. Sif also joins you as a mission giver for a series of side missions. To acknowledge your hard work, Fury rewards you with the Snowmobile, which you can call upon at any S.H.I.E.L.D. transportation request station.

SIDE MISSIONS

JOINING THE FROZEN LEGION

RECOMMENDED HERO: BLACK WIDOW

Mission Giver: Sif
Type: Combat
Rewards: 250 Blue Sparks

Sif has reports that Loki is recruiting a Frost Giant general. She asks you to intercept some Frost Giants that have connections to the general. Hop on a Sky-Cycle and fly over to the first checkpoint via the yellow objective marker.

Land in the intersection and begin to dismantle the Frost Giants. Use both of Black Widow's pistols to blow apart the Frost Giants at range. When they close, dodge away from them and continue fire. Once you clear the street of foes, Sif alerts you that your mission is complete.

 New Challenge Available: Tread Dead Challenge

CHILL OUT

RECOMMENDED HERO: HAWKEYE

Mission Giver: Captain Marvel
Type: Combat
Rewards: 250 Blue Sparks, Ranged Attack Frost Giant

Speak with Captain Marvel and she'll alert you to a Frost Giant gathering that is causing havoc in the streets. Follow the yellow objective marker to the back side of the building and keep the peace. Use Hawkeye's charged-up arrows to deliver heavy damage to the Frost Giants as you clean the streets.

Continue following the objective markers and roaming the streets for bad guys. When Captain Marvel signals that all is clear, your mission is complete.

 New Challenge Available: Vs. Mode: Docks

GAME BASICS

CHARACTERS

POWER DISCS

MARVEL'S THE AVENGERS

SPIDER-MAN

GUARDIANS OF THE GALAXY

TOY BOX

TOY BOX COLLECTION

ACHIEVEMENTS

HOT SPOT

RECOMMENDED HERO: IRON MAN

Mission Giver: Captain Marvel
Type: Defend
Rewards: 250 Blue Sparks, Medium Frost Giant B

S.H.I.E.L.D. has placed another heat generator and needs time for it to warm up. Go defend the generator at the river. You have to hold on for three minutes as the Frost Giants pound away. Be careful not to get knocked into the water; dodge frequently to stay near the generator and concentrate your damage on the Giants actively focusing on the machine.

If a few Frost Giants begin to surround the generator, back up and launch a Missile Barrage to blow them off it. After three minutes of intense action, if you've kept the generator intact, a heat pulse blasts out and annihilates the rest of the foes for another victory.

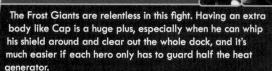

CO-OP COMBO: IRON MAN AND CAPTAIN AMERICA

The Frost Giants are relentless in this fight. Having an extra body like Cap is a huge plus, especially when he can whip his shield around and clear out the whole dock, and it's much easier if each hero only has to guard half the heat generator.

THINGS BEGIN TO HEAT UP

TAKING SOME HEAT

RECOMMENDED HERO: CAPTAIN AMERICA

Mission Giver: Wasp
Type: Combat
Rewards: 250 Blue Sparks

The second weather machine is easy to spot: just look down from your current rooftop to one below. This time the weather machine's energy pods are all on one rooftop. Exit your Sky-Cycle in the middle of the roof and start attacking Frost Giants. Cap's Shield Assault will single-handedly destroy most, if not all, of your enemies in one shot. If any are still standing, you can always go hand-to-hand with the tougher Frost Giants and combo them off the roof to get rid of them.

The third weather machine is a short jaunt over to a nearby rooftop. It's a similar setup, though there's also a Large Frost Giant included. Deal with his minions first, then concentrate on the Large Frost Giant. Jump or hover over his icy shock wave and return attacks with Shield Strike. You'll have more success if you've advanced to Shield Strike Upgrade 1 and 2. With the destruction of the final weather machine, you end Loki's grip on the skies and earn another victory against the God of Mischief.

New weather machines are working together to create a super-blizzard, and it's finally time to knock these weather machines out of commission for good. Fly up to the top of the rooftop high above Wasp and take on the Frost Giants guarding the first machine. Two energy pods on two different rooftops generate energy for the weather machine, so it's best to defeat enemies on one roof and destroy the two pods there before tackling the second roof. If you need to help getting up, there's a convenient lift on the outside of the building too.

JUST SAY NANO

RECOMMENDED HERO: IRON MAN

Mission Giver: JARVIS
Type: Defend
Rewards: 250 Blue Sparks

Upon completion of "Taking Some Heat," JARVIS calls out for help to defend two entrances to Avengers Tower that are under attack from the Frost Giants. If you're doing this mission solo, you will need someone like Iron Man with a potent ranged attack to cover both entrances. While defending one entrance, use your ranged attack to drive off enemies from the second entrance. If one entrance takes more damage, prioritize defending the weaker entrance.

**Marvel's The Avengers**

GAME BASICS CHARACTERS POWER DISCS **MARVEL'S THE AVENGERS** SPIDER-MAN GUARDIANS OF THE GALAXY TOY BOX TOY BOX COLLECTION ACHIEVEMENTS

The Frost Giants will come fast and furious. Don't follow Giants away from the entrances; even if they aren't dead, knock them away from the entrance and then return to enemies that are directly dealing damage to the doors. If you can get enemies to lock on you, dodge around and let them try to harm you while leaving the entrances alone.

JARVIS gives updates on the nano virus completion and the door strength. It's good news if the nano virus percentage to completion is lower than the doors' defenses; when you hear an entrance is down to 25 percent, look for the door that is more damaged and defend it until the end.

A Large Frost Giant will join during the fight. Avoid its icy shock wave, but don't put too much time and energy into defeating him. You don't have enough time to fight the Large Frost Giant and all the other minions. It's better to knock out multiple Frost Giants on a door rather than lower a Large Frost Giant's defenses.

If you can fend off the Frost Giants long enough for the nano virus creation process to complete, you finish the mission. This is a very difficult fight, so don't be discouraged if you have to retry several times to succeed. It's a big help if you can get another player to join with you and defend the doors together.

CO-OP COMBO: IRON MAN AND THOR

With two entrances to defend, it's a natural fit to have two Avengers battling to protect the nano virus. Iron Man and Thor work well together; each can hold out in melee, while armed with a powerful ranged attack that they can use to help with the other Avenger's Frost Giants if they have a breather. If each Avenger concentrates on protecting his door, S.H.I.E.L.D. gets its nano virus.

SIF'S SIDE MISSIONS

COLD RUSH

RECOMMENDED HERO: HULK
Mission Giver: Sif
Type: Combat
Rewards: 350 Blue Sparks

Sif is still on the trail of the Frost Giant general, and she sends you out into the field to trail Frost Giant groups in the hopes they lead to their commander. Follow the yellow objective markers to reach the street with the Frost Giant aggressors. As with many of your missions before, clear the Frost Giants from the area to continue with the mission. With Hulk, you can Charge in and finish off creatures left and right with your combo attacks.

The second checkpoint is just up the street. Stay with the same strategy: Charge in and upend enemies, then smash victims one by one until they explode. If you need a moment to think, jump up in the air and then down with an Air Attack to deal damage to those around you and momentarily clear the immediate area. When the final Frost Giant falls, you complete Sif's second Frost Giant general mission.

TAKE SNOW PRISONER

RECOMMENDED HERO: THOR
Mission Giver: Sif
Type: Combat
Rewards: 350 Blue Sparks, Large Frost Giant

Sif's final side mission sends you to the Frost Giant general's fortress. Follow the objective marker to the location and land at the ice blockade out front.

The first group of Frost Giants patrols the ring of ice beyond the entrance. Smash them around with a two-handed hammer swing, or let go of Mjolnir and rip through them from afar. Either way, they won't stand long against Thor.

More Frost Giants appear inside the second ice ring. Repeat your attack pattern from the first area. If you need some extra defense, retreat to the first ring for more space or take to the skies.

You meet the Frost Giant general in the third ring. Take out the smaller Frost Giants around him first, then turn your full attention to the general. Whenever he claps his hands and releases the icy shock wave, double-jump or hover to avoid the blast. Immediately after the shock wave passes, power up a Mjolnir Lightning Charge and throw your hammer at the general. It will take half a dozen blows or so, but eventually you'll shatter the general and complete Sif's final mission.

TO BEAT LOKI

SAFETY FIRST

RECOMMENDED HERO: HAWKEYE

Mission Giver: Captain Marvel
Type: Escort
Rewards: 250 Blue Sparks

Before you can deploy the nano virus on the Casket of Ancient Winters that Loki is building in the park by Avengers Tower, you must help all the civilians in the park to safety. S.H.I.E.L.D. has set up a heat generator on one side of the park. You have three-and-a-half minutes to free eight civilians and carry them to the heat generator.

Each civilian is encrusted in ice, and they are spread out in the park. As soon as you grab the closest one, the Frost Giants in the park will swarm on your location. Save your first civilian and then run to the next civilian. You want to reach the civilian in time to break them out of the ice and pick them up before any enemy lands an attack. If you need a little extra time, alternate going from one side of the park to the next to scatter the Frost Giants a bit.

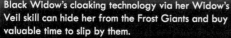
HERO TIP: BLACK WIDOW

Black Widow's cloaking technology via her Widow's Veil skill can hide her from the Frost Giants and buy valuable time to slip by them.

It will be close to get all the civilians back to safety. The farthest one is at the end of the park and a challenge to reach and return. Don't bother fighting the Frost Giants; you won't have time to fight them and save the civilians. When you bring the eighth civilian back to the heat generator, the area is secure and you're finally ready to take it to Loki.

VIRAL INFECTION

RECOMMENDED HERO: BLACK WIDOW

Mission Giver: Nick Fury
Type: Escort
Rewards: 250 Blue Sparks

The nano virus is ready, but it needs to reach the Casket of Ancient Winters. That's where you come in. Pick up the nano virus container and deliver it across the park to the Casket. Don't let the swarm of Frost Giants stop you.

Grab the nano virus container immediately and head toward the Casket. As Frost Giants converge, swing out wide and try to keep them from landing blows against you or the container. If they do close in, drop the container and roll out of harm's way with a dodge. Turn and unload your pistols on the Frost Giants until all that's left around the container are icy pieces. Pick up the container and continue on.

Little by little you should advance the container toward the Casket. Use Widow's Veil if you need to go invisible for a few seconds and escape for a better position. When you get near enough, dump the nano virus container on the Casket of Ancient Winters and stand back. Blowing up the Casket really, really upsets Loki, and he summons a gigantic Frost Beast to finish you off.

A CHILLING CONCLUSION

RECOMMENDED HERO: IRON MAN

Mission Giver: Nick Fury
Type: Combat
Rewards: 750 Blue Sparks

Loki is not happy at all with your meddling and sics his super-massive Frost Beast pet on you. The thing not only looks deadly, it actually is very deadly.

The Beast can destroy you a number of ways. When it rears back, watch out for its frost breath that will freeze you solid. Dodge to the right through the breath to avoid getting frozen by it.

The Frost Beast can also throw out a line of ice barricades that detonate when they hit you and cause serious damage. They detonate from right to left, so as the explosions approach you, roll away from them to the left to avoid as much damage as possible.

If the Frost Beast catches you with its claw, you'll be dead in one or two swipes. Dodge left or right to avoid this crushing blow.

However, the Beast's claws get caught in the ledge when it strikes. While it's stuck, hurry over and pound away at the claw.

When you deal enough damage to injure one of the claws, the Beast temporarily falls unconscious. Now's your chance to deal full damage to it directly. Slug it over and over again in the jaw, or use your most potent skill, to bring its life total down by a third.

HERO TIP: CAPTAIN AMERICA

Cap can land a blow on the Frost Beast's jaw just like any other Avenger. You will need as many Avengers as you have on hand to beat Loki's pet.

Frost Giants stream out of pit while the Frost Beast recovers. Try to clear as many of these Frost Giants as you can before the Beast attacks again. When the Beast starts spewing its icy breath, ignore the Frost Giants and return to battling the Beast. The Frost Giants will be frozen by the breath and eventually destroyed by the detonating ice barricades.

CO-OP COMBO: IRON MAN AND HULK

The end fight against the Frost Beast certainly goes better with two Avengers, and who better to smash with than Hulk. His Raging Roar can deal damage, but his big green fists do just fine.

Repeat the process of destroying the Beast's claws two more times to finally destroy it. If Iron Man gets knocked out of the fight, bring in the next Avenger to carry the torch against the big ice creature. It takes a team effort to finally conquer the Beast.

After its defeat, the Frost Beast slips back into its hole and disappears. Sif apprehends Loki and brings him back to Asgard to atone for his crimes. A few Frost Giants are still loose in the zoo, but what's that compared to day you've had. The Avengers assemble one last time with Nick Fury and Manhattan is safe—at least until Green Goblin starts menacing the place in the next Play Set with Spider-Man!

 Feat Complete: **Beastly Barrage**

 New Challenge Available: **Vs. Mode: Park**

GAME BASICS

CHARACTERS

POWER DISCS

MARVEL'S THE AVENGERS

SPIDER-MAN

GUARDIANS OF THE GALAXY

TOY BOX

TOY BOX COLLECTION

ACHIEVEMENTS

55

CROSSOVER COIN MISSIONS: NOVA

A.I.M. TO DESTROY

RECOMMENDED HERO: NOVA

Mission Giver: Captain Marvel
Type: Combat
Rewards: 250 Blue Sparks

See Captain Marvel for your first Crossover Coin mission as Nova. She needs you to take out M.O.D.O.K.'s Security Drones about the city, which are spying on S.H.I.E.L.D. and causing general mayhem. Fly to the first objective marker and engage the floating Drones in the street.

Stay in the air and weave back and forth as you send blue energy bolts back at the Security Drones. You have eight to blast out of the sky. Keep them all in front of you, so none get a surprise attack off on you. Hovering higher than them can give you the advantage of being able to fire on them while they readjust to get the right angle on you. After a little back and forth you'll shortly have your first victory as Nova in the Marvel's The Avengers Play Set.

M.O.D.O.K. STALK

RECOMMENDED HERO: NOVA

Mission Giver: Captain Marvel
Type: Combat
Rewards: 150 Blue Sparks

Your first successful mission drove M.O.D.O.K.'s Security Drones on the run. Chase the remaining group around the city and destroy them. Follow the yellow objective marker to the first group hovering above the street. As with your first mission, weave back and forth, avoiding Drone fire, as you return fire to destroy them. If you can get them close together, try using your Nova Core unique ability to destroy multiple Drones at once.

Chase after the second and third Drone groups as you did the first. If you're careful and accurate with your bolts, the hunks of metal will be molten slag before you break a sweat.

GETTING A HEAD

RECOMMENDED HERO: NOVA

Mission Giver: Captain Marvel
Type: Combat
Rewards: 250 Blue Sparks, S.H.I.E.L.D. Emergency Vehicle

Security Drones ambush you before Captain Marvel can even congratulate you on your last mission. You'll be swarmed by loads of M.O.D.O.K.'s Security Drones, but don't panic. Fly up and out of the ambush and then get all the Drones in front of you. By now you've had plenty of practice with Nova's Energy Blasts, and if you've had a chance to upgrade to Dual Energy Blasts, you'll be twice as effective.

Weave back and forth, dart up and down, as you pick the Drones off one by one. When the final one plummets, Captain Marvel and the rest of the Avengers swoop in and grab M.O.D.O.K. You may have only arrived with the Avengers and carried out three missions, but know that you were responsible for capturing Loki's partner in crime, M.O.D.O.K.

CROSSOVER COIN MISSIONS: ROCKET RACCOON

PORTAL CALL

RECOMMENDED HERO: ROCKET RACCOON

Mission Giver: Nick Fury
Type: Collect
Rewards: 150 Blue Sparks

See Nick Fury for your first Crossover Coin mission as Rocket Raccoon. According to Fury, Star-Lord air-dropped some tech packages, but his aim was a little shaky.

In order to assemble these into the teleporters S.H.I.E.L.D. wants to build around the city, Rocket has been tasked with retrieving the first tech package.

Follow the yellow objective marker until you reach the tech package. Pick it up and walk it over to the safe zone. Unfortunately, Rocket has short legs and it takes a while. Meanwhile, two separate groups of Frost Giants will spawn and try to stop you on the way. Dodge as many as you can, and if you're about to get hit, drop the package and fight back temporarily to clear the area, then pick up the package and continue on.

When you reach the safe zone, plunk the tech package down on the platform and you finish the mission. However, don't relax too long—your next mission begins right away.

━━━ **TECH TOCK** ━━━

RECOMMENDED HERO: ROCKET RACCOON

Mission Giver: Nick Fury
Type: Defend
Rewards: 250 Blue Sparks

The tech package needs time to power up: two minutes to be exact. As it powers up, you must defend it from the incoming Frost Giants. Stay close to the device and punch away any Giants that near. If they begin to swarm the package, retreat and use your Quantum Cannon to blast away at them.

Unless you have Rocket Raccoon leveled up a bit before joining the Avengers, this will be a difficult fight. Make sure to only attack the enemies directly around the tech package and don't go chasing foes at the expense of the device. After two minutes, the machine powers up and any remaining Frost Giants are repelled. Press the IN button to complete the mission.

━━━ **WE'RE GONNA ROCKET!** ━━━

RECOMMENDED HERO: ROCKET RACCOON

Mission Giver: Nick Fury
Type: Combat
Rewards: 250 Blue Sparks, S.H.I.E.L.D. Helicarrier

Travel back to Nick Fury. He gives your final mission: to get the teleporters all online. All you have to do is press the button on each teleporter. Alas, Frost Giants mill about each one preventing you from simply turning it on. Head over to the first teleporter and defeat all the Frost Giants in the area to be able to activate the device.

Once the teleporter is functioning, you can press the button to use it. You will be teleported into S.H.I.E.L.D. headquarters! Activate the teleport in there to zip out to any of the online teleporters via the city map: red dots are your teleport locations. For now, teleport back to where you came from and seek out the second teleporter the old-fashioned way.

Wipe out Frost Giants around the areas of the second and third teleporters and press the buttons when you're finished. If you accidentally teleport into S.H.I.E.L.D. headquarters, use the map to teleport back out to any of the locations and seek out the final teleporter.

Travel over to the final teleporter and attack all the Frost Giants in the area. Once the streets are clear, walk over to the teleport and press the final button. The teleporters are all online now, and S.H.I.E.L.D. has a major transportation system set up to fight back against Loki and his Frost Giants—all thanks to Rocket Raccoon and the Guardians of the Galaxy!

GAME BASICS

CHARACTERS

POWER DISCS

MARVEL'S THE AVENGERS

SPIDER-MAN

GUARDIANS OF THE GALAXY

TOY BOX

TOY BOX COLLECTION

ACHIEVEMENTS

DISNEY
INF🅝ITY
2.0
EDITION

MARVEL
SUPER HEROES

CROSSOVER COINS

MANHATTAN

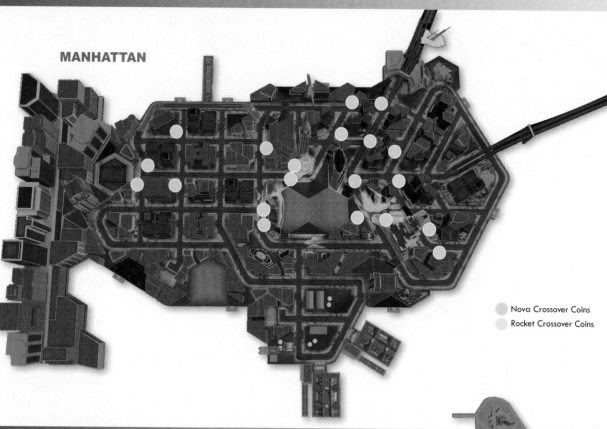

Nova Crossover Coins
Rocket Crossover Coins

TECH BONUS BOXES

MANHATTAN

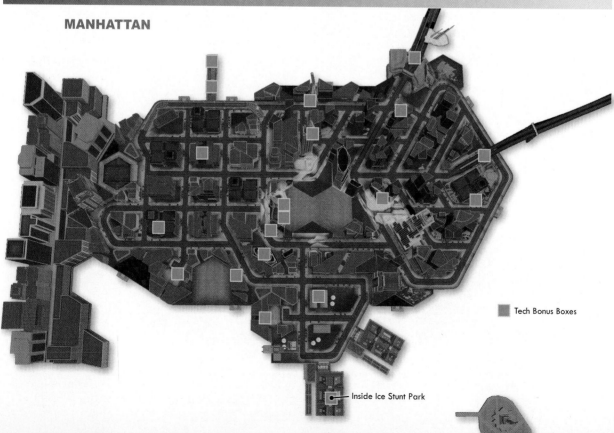

Tech Bonus Boxes

Inside Ice Stunt Park

WALL CRAWL BONUS BOXES

MANHATTAN

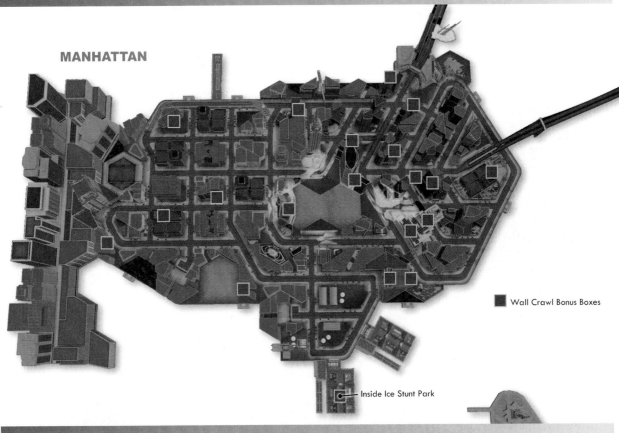

■ Wall Crawl Bonus Boxes

Inside Ice Stunt Park

FLIGHT BONUS BOXES

MANHATTAN

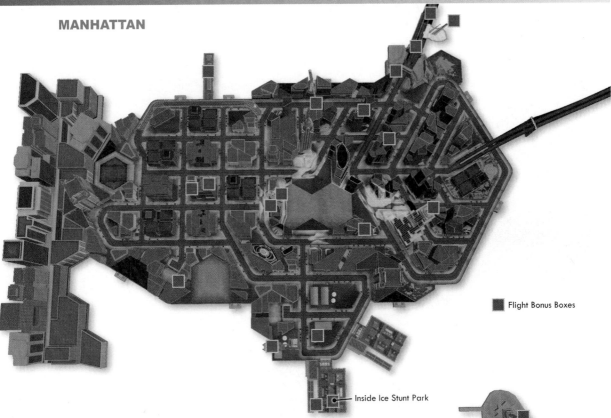

■ Flight Bonus Boxes

Inside Ice Stunt Park

GAME BASICS

CHARACTERS

POWER DISCS

MARVEL'S THE AVENGERS

SPIDER-MAN

GUARDIANS OF THE GALAXY

TOY BOX

TOY BOX COLLECTION

ACHIEVEMENTS

SUPER JUMP BONUS BOXES

MANHATTAN

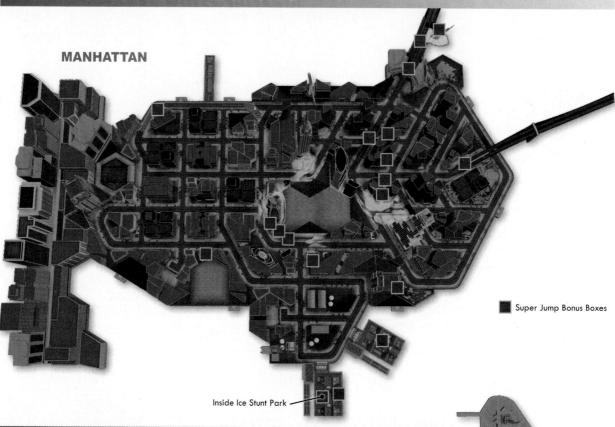

■ Super Jump Bonus Boxes

Inside Ice Stunt Park

MAXIMUM STRENGTH BONUS BOXES

MANHATTAN

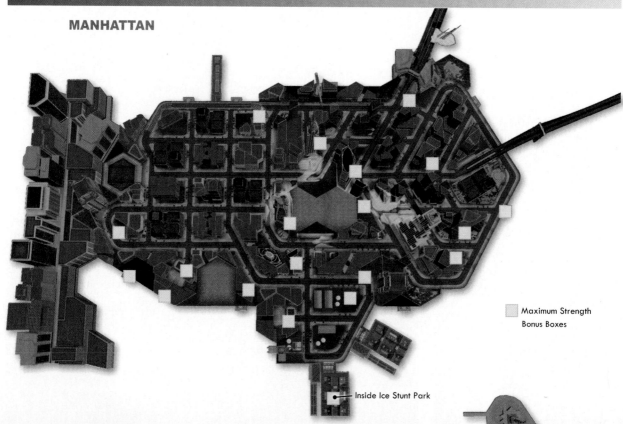

□ Maximum Strength Bonus Boxes

Inside Ice Stunt Park

AVENGERS FEATS

FEAT NAME	FEAT DESCRIPTION
Air Raid	Defeat 30 enemies while flying.
Avengers Away Team	Find all the hidden Crossover Coins in the Marvel's The Avengers Play Set.
Beastly Barrage	Destroy Loki's secret weapon.
Beginning Bonus	Collect your first bonus box in the Marvel's The Avengers Play Set.
Bird's Eye View	Arrive at the top of Avengers Tower.
Bonus Box Champion	Find and collect all Bonus Boxes in the Marvel's The Avengers Play Set.
Break the Ice	Break 25 chunks of ice around the city.
Bronze Hero	Collect 5 bronze medals from Marvel's The Avengers challenges.
Call for a Ride	Summon a vehicle from the S.H.I.E.L.D. transportation request station.
Cross Country Flight	Fly as Iron Man for a distance of 15 kilometers.
Damage Control	Deliver 16 civilians to the Heat Generators.
Damage Master	Deal 5,000 points of damage in Marvel's The Avengers destruction challenges.
Dancing Feat	Complete 150 feats.
Diving in with Both Feat	Complete 10 feats.
Enemy Eliminator	Defeat 200 enemies in Marvel's The Avengers combat challenges.
Eyes to the Sky	Unlock the Sky-Cycle.
Fast on Your Feat	Complete 100 feats.
Five by Five	Defeat 5 enemies as Hawkeye in 5 seconds.
Flight Master	Find and collect all Flight Bonus Boxes in the Marvel's The Avengers Play Set.
Getting Your Feat Wet	Complete 1 feat.
God of Thunder	Defeat 25 Small Frost Giants as Thor.
Gold Medalist	Collect 5 gold medals from Marvel's The Avengers challenges.
Grand Gold Medalist	Collect all gold medals from Marvel's The Avengers challenges.
Green Thunder	Attack Hulk as Thor.
Heavy Metal	Defeat 10 Medium Frost Giants as Iron Man.

FEAT NAME	FEAT DESCRIPTION
Job Well Done	Complete every mission in the Marvel's The Avengers Play Set.
Landing on Both Feat	Complete 50 feats.
Life Line	Revive another player 3 times.
Master of Verticality	Find and collect all Wall Crawl Bonus Boxes in the Marvel's The Avengers Play Set.
On Target	Defeat 15 M.O.D.O.K. Drones as Hawkeye.
Orb Smasher	Destroy 1,000 capsules in the Marvel's The Avengers Play Set.
Point Collector	Score 5,000 total points in Marvel's The Avengers challenges.
Points Champ	Score 10,000 total points in Marvel's The Avengers challenges.
Power Up	Restore power to every power generator.
Puny Tank	Defeat 3 Large Frost Giants as Hulk.
Road Trip	Ride the motorcycle as Captain America for 5 kilometers.
Romanoff's Revenge	Defeat 25 Small Frost Giants as Black Widow.
Running Rampage	Use Hulk's Rampaging Rush against 20 enemies.
Silver Medalist	Collect 5 silver medals from Marvel's The Avengers challenges.
Special Move Master	Defeat 50 enemies using Special Moves.
Springing to Your Feat	Complete 25 feats.
Steady A.I.M.	Defeat the opponent in the abandoned warehouse.
Super Jumper	Find and collect all Super Jump Bonus Boxes in the Marvel's The Avengers Play Set.
Super Soldier Sweep	Defeat 10 Shielded Medium Frost Giants as Captain America.
Supreme Strength	Find and collect all Maximum Strength Bonus Boxes in the Marvel's The Avengers Play Set.
Swept Off Your Feat	Complete 200 feats.
Tank Buster	Defeat 5 Large Frost Giants.
Team Player	Compete in 2 multiplayer challenges.
Technological Wonder	Find and collect all Tech Bonus Boxes in the Marvel's The Avengers Play Set.
Tower Power	Stabilize Avengers Tower.
Un-De-Feat-Able	Complete all feats.

AVENGERS CHALLENGES

MAP #	CHALLENGE NAME	DESCRIPTION	HOW UNLOCKED?
1	Hulk Smash!	As Hulk, destroy objects in the city for points.	Hulk challenge. Unlocked from beginning.
2	Fight or Flight	As Iron Man, defeat enemies to earn points.	Iron Man challenge. Unlocked from beginning.
3	Vs. Mode: Docks	Player vs. player combat on the docks.	Two-player challenge. Complete mission "Chill Out."
4	Vs. Mode: Park	Player vs. player combat in the park.	Two-player challenge. Complete mission "A Chilling Conclusion."
5	Vs. Mode: Avengers Tower	Player vs. player combat up on top of Avengers Tower.	Two-player challenge. Unlocked from the beginning.
6	A Shot at Glory	Earn points by breaking targets.	Unlocked from the beginning.
7	Quick Pace Race	Race the motorcycle to the finish line. Pass through all the gates in order.	Complete mission "Sheer Wheel Power."
8	Route to Victory	Complete a race on the motorcycle by passing through each of the gates.	Earn bronze on "Quick Pace Race" challenge.
9	Tread Dead	Defeat enemies while riding the snowmobile to earn points.	Earn bronze on "Route to Victory" challenge.
10	High Flier	Fly to the finish line as fast as you can. Pass through all the gates in order.	Flight challenge. Complete mission "Street Sweeper."
11	Skyward Score	Fly through the rings to earn points.	Flight challenge. Earn bronze on "High Flier" challenge.
12	Flight Targets	Fly through the rings to earn points.	Flight challenge. Earn bronze on "Skyward Score" challenge.
13	Super Jump Race	Compete in a race using the Super Jump to complete the event with the best time.	Super Jump challenge. Complete mission "Snow End in Sight."
14	Splash Landing	Collect points using the Super Jump.	Super Jump challenge. Earn bronze on "Super Jump Race" challenge.
15	Thrills and Chills	Earn a high score doing stunts on the snowmobile.	Located in the Wharf's Ice Stunt Park. Complete mission "Sif's Ship-Shape."
16	So Much Ice, So Little Time	Complete a race using the snowmobile before time runs out.	Located in the Wharf's Ice Stunt Park. Earn bronze on above challenge.

SPIDER-MAN

SPIDER-MAN PLAY SET

TOO MANY SYMBIOTES

──── DARK DAYS AHEAD ────

GREEN GOBLIN'S LAB

MAP LEGEND

MISSION GIVER

1 White Tiger

RECOMMENDED HERO: SPIDER-MAN

Mission Giver: White Tiger
Type: Combat
Rewards: 75 Blue Sparks

When Green Goblin starts recruiting heavyweights like Mysterio, you know it's going to be a bad day for the good guys. As our tale begins, White Tiger is spying on Green Goblin and Mysterio as they use Oscorp's resources to clone Venom. Green Goblin's ultimate goal is to bring down S.H.I.E.L.D., but Venom manages to escape, leaving Goblin with Symbiote clones to wreak chaos on the city. Spider-Man pops in, and White Tiger sends Spidey into the lab to confront the two villains.

Before you can do a thing, Mysterio lets loose his green gas and you're lost in a haze. Your new mission is to hunt down Mysterio—if you can figure out what's real and what's not.

Advance on Mysterio and watch as glass shards shoot out from the broken windows and stab at you, only to retract and disappear.

You get the feeling that illusion rules this place, and you can't trust your senses completely. Jump at the first platform, and double-jump at the second to keep pace with Mysterio.

Drop down the shaft and land on a series of ascending hexagon-shaped platforms. Continue jumping up them toward Mysterio. As he retreats, follow him to the next set of hexagon platforms and continue jumping toward him. Don't stand too long on the square platforms; they disappear from under your feet. When you land on the last platform, it vanishes and drops you way down to the floor below.

Race toward Mysterio and hop quickly over the green-bordered squares before they vanish. Avoid gaps in the squares and only rest on hexagon platforms. Double-jump over larger gaps until you reach Mysterio and a stable corridor at the far end.

Run through the corridor to another open space with floating corridor chunks. Double-jump across them until you land on the ledge with the yellow rail along its top edge. Jump up and grab the yellow rail, then jump again to end safely on the upper level.

Follow the corridor and then jump up the wall, holding on to the yellow rails. Slide to the left to position yourself better to grab higher rails. Climb over the Oscorp sign and flip yourself up to the next level. Traverse the next set of yellow hand-holds until you gain another level.

Use the yellow rails to reach the top level. At some points you will have to jump to the left while holding the rail to hold on. Run along the top level and into the green mist.

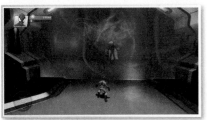

The final room has a large mirror on the wall in front of you. Mysterio appears, and though you can't see him directly, you can see him in the mirror. Watch your reflection in the mirror and fight Mysterio through your reflection's moves. A couple of reflection jabs will take care of him.

When the mirror shatters, Mysterio's illusion evaporates. Green Goblin swoops in to retrieve his ally and they jet off on the Goblin's glider. White Tiger thanks you for completing the first mission, but asks you to stay in the lab to rescue some trapped workers.

NOTE

You can choose any Marvel Character from this Play Set and be successful on these missions. Each hero is special and much of the fun is replaying through the missions with different heroes, leveling up and unlocking their special abilities as you go. However, there are some spots in each mission where a particular hero may be better suited to overcome an obstacle or a particular hero's skills may allow you to proceed through a mission easier. And sometimes we just thought it was cool to have that hero on a mission, like Iron Fist working with Luke Cage on a mission. With that in mind, we've chosen a Recommended Hero for each mission to maximize your superhero potential.

TRAPPED LIKE SARDINES

RECOMMENDED HERO: NICK FURY

Mission Giver: White Tiger
Type: Combat
Reward: 100 Blue Sparks, Swarming Symbiote

Your second mission requires a little stealth and a big gun: enter Nick Fury. White Tiger sends you back into the lab to rescue trapped scientists. You'll have to deal with security and Symbiotes to survive.

As you enter the first room, note that on the right there is a map of the lab complex hanging on the wall. It actually does show you the layout, including where the security defenses are up. On the left you'll find your first objective: a power cell. Knock the cell off its power conduit to drop the first security screen.

GREEN GOBLIN'S LAB (SECOND TRIP)

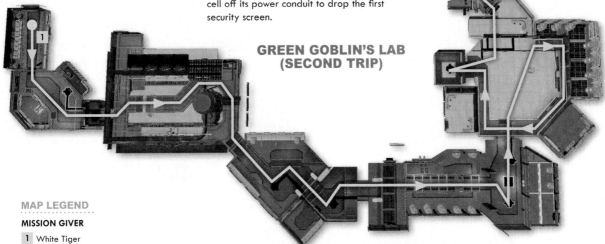

MAP LEGEND

MISSION GIVER

1 White Tiger

Side tabs: GAME BASICS · CHARACTERS · POWER DISCS · MARVEL'S THE AVENGERS · **SPIDER-MAN** · GUARDIANS OF THE GALAXY · TOY BOX · TOY BOX COLLECTION · ACHIEVEMENTS

Jump up the shaft ahead by grabbing each yellow rail. At the top, flip up into the next room and prepare to battle your first Symbiote. The Venom clone breaks out of its canister and attacks you as you traverse the upper walkway. Break out Fury's pistol to blast it to pieces, or practice some hand-to-hand combos on its gooey flesh.

Swarming Symbiotes attack you in the next room. They slither across the floor at you and nip at your legs. Take a couple of shots at them before they cover the distance, then whip through some spin kicks to turn them into puddles. Engage the other two Symbiotes in the second half of the room, and once they've been dealt with, knock the power cell off its conduit spot to lower the second security screen.

Pick up the power cell and carry it into the next room. Set the power cell on the empty conduit spot to power it up and open the blast door ahead.

A laser cannon defends the next area, and it will open fire as soon as you advance toward it. Here's a perfect opportunity to use Fury's Life Model Decoy if you've played Fury from the beginning and have enough skill points. As the cannon locks on the decoy, you can run invisibly across the room and knock the laser cannon's power cell off its conduit to disable the weapon. Otherwise, weave right and left as you dodge missiles and reach the far side.

Pick up the laser cannon power cell and carry it over to the empty conduit by the door. Power the door up and it opens. Enter the next large room and prepare for more combat. Use your pistol to wound Symbiotes from across the room; when they get close, combo a single Symbiote before dodging to a new position. You don't want to get surrounded, since Fury has very little health at this point to take much damage.

You also have to deal with homing missiles fired through the security screen. To take out the missile launchers, race up the stairs and follow the upper balcony around to the side room with the shattered glass floor. Perform an Air Attack on the glass floor to shatter it. You drop into the room with the power cell controlling the security screen and missile launchers. Remove the power cell from its conduit and you deactivate all the security defenses.

Navigate across the gap in the next room via the yellow rails on the left wall. If you fall to the pipes below, use the yellow pipe to climb back out and start again.

Let the missile launcher's projectile knock the first power cell off its conduit spot in the next room. This powers down the defenses and lets you walk over to the second power cell in the wall and smash it free. Carry one of the power cells to the elevator conduit and activate it. Carry the second power cell up to the next level and drop it on the door conduit to open the next room.

You can see the trapped scientists now through a security screen. Battle the Symbiotes in the room, then enter the side room and break free the power cell there. Carry it to the open conduit to activate the missile launcher, then run behind the second power cell's protective force field and let the homing missiles blow the second power cell off its conduit. Shut down the missile launcher and carry the second power cell to the empty conduit that unlocks the door to the scientists.

Enter the scientists' room to save them and claim your rewards. Nick Fury has helped S.H.I.E.L.D. take over Goblin's lab, and now it's up to the streets of Manhattan for more adventures.

SPIDER-MAN ENEMIES

SWARMING SYMBIOTE

These football-sized, chomping Symbiotes will gang up and gnaw you to pieces if you let them surround you. Usually one hit does them in.

TENDRILED SYMBIOTE

Tougher, buffer versions of a normal Symbiote. It has the annoying tendency to turn into a puddle and then reform somewhere else on the battlefield.

SYMBIOTE

Pieces of Venom that Green Goblin has transformed into minions to do his bidding. Most Symbiotes are all teeth and claws, but some throw ranged attacks and dodge around a lot.

LARGE SYMBIOTE

Bigger, stronger, and much uglier than all other Symbiotes. It can erupt into a repulsive gurgle that spews forth dozens of Swarming Symbiotes, and it can leap at you with a "belly flop" that devastates anything that it lands on—including you.

SYMBIOTE GRUNT

Your normal, shape-changing alien with a mean streak. You'll face more of these than any other enemy in the Spider-Man Play Set.

GOBLIN DRONE

Armed and dangerous, these mechanized, flying robots are the Green Goblin's chief weapon of the skies.

FROM TIGER TO CAGE

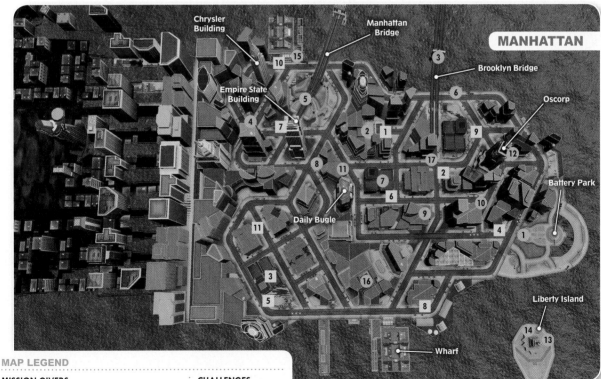

MANHATTAN

Chrysler Building
Manhattan Bridge
Brooklyn Bridge
Empire State Building
Oscorp
Daily Bugle
Battery Park
Liberty Island
Wharf

MAP LEGEND

MISSION GIVERS

1	White Tiger	7	S.H.I.E.L.D. Agent 4
2	Luke Cage	8	S.H.I.E.L.D. Agent 5
3	Black Cat	9	S.H.I.E.L.D. Agent 6
4	S.H.I.E.L.D. Agent 1	10	S.H.I.E.L.D. Agent 7
5	S.H.I.E.L.D. Agent 2	11	S.H.I.E.L.D. Agent 8
6	S.H.I.E.L.D. Agent 3		

CHALLENGES

1	City Web Race	6	Right on Target	11	Ring Run	16	Rat Trap
2	Ring the City	7	Crawl and Collect	12	Sonic Weaponry	17	Furious Frenzy
3	Race Gate Challenge	8	Combo Crawl	13	Nova Saves the Day		
4	Rooftop Rings	9	Wallopin' Wall Crawlers	14	Vs. Mode: Statue of Liberty		
5	Bridge Rings	10	Hover Car Race	15	Vs. Mode: Waterfront		

RECOMMENDED HERO: NOVA

Mission Giver: White Tiger
Type: Combat
Reward: 75 Blue Sparks

White Tiger informs you that Luke Cage needs help; your third mission is to track him down. Now's your chance to explore the city for the first time, and you can start with picking up the Hulk Crossover Coin floating near the building to your right. With Nova, you can fly around Manhattan and access anything from alleys to high rooftops easily.

Follow the yellow objective marker to Cage. A Symbiote will intercept at the intersection, but after you make it safe for pedestrians again, travel on to find Luke Cage a short distance away.

The alley near Luke Cage holds your first Iron Man Crossover Coin. Use the jump platform to leap up to the roof, where you'll find another Iron Man Crossover Coin. Continue up the side of the building for more, and you can retrieve two more on the adjacent rooftop for the complete Iron Man set.

HERO TIP: VENOM

Though not strictly a hero, you may want to face Venom off against his Symbiote clones. Just don't get confused with who's who in the fight.

Cage is on the other side of the building with all the Iron Man Crossover Coins. Defeat a pair of Swarming Symbiotes in the intersection next to Cage, then watch him beat up a Symbiote as you approach and finish your third mission.

UNFRIENDLY NEIGHBORHOOD

RECOMMENDED HERO: IRON FIST

Mission Giver: Luke Cage
Type: Combat
Reward: 150 Blue Sparks the "Symbiote Grunt", and the "S.H.I.E.L.D. Hovercar"

Luke Cage needs you to bust up the Symbiote party in the streets. The first Symbiote group he sends you after is right behind him in front of the Oscorp building. Run over and show them some of your lightning-fast moves.

When you're finished with the first group, cross the street and hunt down the second group. After you throw some martial arts mojo the Symbiotes' way, you will probably level up and can pick up your first skill. Think about holding that point to buy Shou-Lao the Undying, which conjures a fiery attack to damage nearby enemies in a small circle around you, when you level up again.

Head toward the bridge for the final group. Swarming Symbiotes threaten the S.H.I.E.L.D. agents desperately trying to hold them at bay. Give the enemies some grief, but even as you eliminate the first wave, a second wave spawns some regular Symbiotes for extra measure. If you've reached third level, use Shou-Lao the Undying as they converge on you, then one-two the closest targets as you dazzle them with your speed.

At mission's end, Luke Cage rewards you with your very own S.H.I.E.L.D. Hovercar. Now you can ride in style—and, even better, reach those rooftops without a spiderweb.

 New Challenge Available: Hovercar Race

INTERRUPTED UPLOAD

GREEN GOBLIN'S LAB (THIRD TRIP)

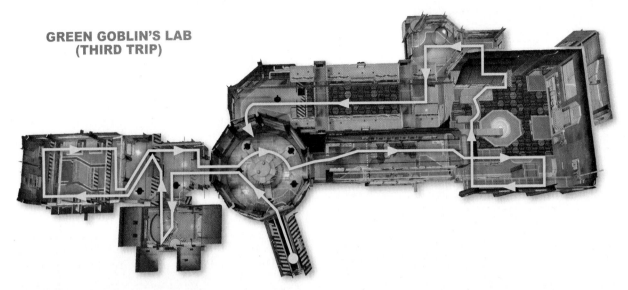

GAME BASICS

CHARACTERS

POWER DISCS

MARVEL'S THE AVENGERS

SPIDER-MAN

GUARDIANS OF THE GALAXY

TOY BOX

TOY BOX COLLECTION

ACHIEVEMENTS

RECOMMENDED HERO: NICK FURY

Mission Giver: White Tiger
Type: Defend
Reward: 200 Blue Sparks, "Black Cat", and "Symbiote"

White Tiger is sending you back into the lab. An important Oscorp scientist has gone missing, so the only option for getting his data is to get to his computer in the lab and upload the data to S.H.I.E.L.D. Straighten your trench coat, readjust your eye patch, and jump in the Hovercar for a cruise across town to the rooftop with the lab entrance.

Prepare for a mega-battle up on the rooftop. A variety of more than a dozen Symbiotes will assault you when you touch down on the roof. Dodge out of harm's way and start returning fire at range with your pistols as you circle the roof. Be careful not to fall off the roof during your circling, and if you see an opportunity to kick one of your enemies over the edge, go for it.

Take the door into the lab after making goo of the last of the Symbiotes. Inside the facility, walk to your right and break the power cell out of the wall. Pick it up and carry the cell into the central chamber. Drop down with the cell and drop it on the first empty conduit on the left. Destroy the three Symbiotes guarding the room and then enter the new wing opened by the power cell.

Jump down into the next area and smash the shuttered wall to your left. Beat back the Symbiotes in this side room and smash the power cell out of its wall socket. Carry your new power cell back into the other room and take the elevator up to the higher platform. Drop the power cell on the door conduit and enter the next area.

This side area contains a large battle area where you can hone your skills (and pump up your experience) on a Symbiote horde. Feel free to scoop up capsules here if you like, then exit and reclaim your power cell. Drop it on the far side of the platform on the elevator conduit to activate the elevator back to the central chamber.

Carry the power cell back into the central chamber and drop it on the next empty conduit going clockwise. You've just powered up the first part of the machine. Retrieve the other door power cell and carry it over to the second door conduit. Drop it in place to open the second wing.

This next room has a large gap that you must cross. Pay heed to the hexagons that look red hot—they are! One step on a red hexagon and you begin to burn up. Use the security console on the floor to shut off the red-hot hexagons and then cross the room to the other side. If you miss, fight a few Symbiotes and use the yellow pole to climb up.

Symbiotes swarm the next room. Stay to the right and climb the yellow pole to the walkway overhead. While the Symbiotes throw goo at you, jump across the upper platform and then across the air ducts.

Make one last leap to the yellow railing alongside the control room. Slide along the yellow rail and then drop down or hop up into the control room depending on which yellow railing you grabbed.

Battle through more Symbiotes in the largest portion of the control room and then head into the next room guarded by a floor of red-hot hexagons and two missile launchers. Use the security console to the right to deactivate the red hexagons. Trigger your Life Model Decoy to attract the homing missiles and run across to the missile launchers.

When the Life Model fades, let the missiles target you but stand on the other side of the force field protecting the power cell. The missiles will try to strike you, but blast the power cell off its conduit instead, deactivating the force field and shutting down the missile launchers. Pick up the power cell and drop down to the central chamber through the nearby open window.

Drop the power cell onto the second machine conduit. Walk over and dislodge the door power cell and carry it over to the third machine conduit.

Once you place your last power cell, the machine comes to life. You have two minutes to defend the computer and stay alive.

More and more Symbiotes will come at you. Be careful not to get surrounded while keeping an eye out for Symbiotes actively attacking the computer. Swat away enough Symbiotes from the machine and the timer runs down for a successful upload and S.H.I.E.L.D. victory. If you're having trouble, circle around the machine and blast away with Fury's twin pistols.

The more upgrades you have pumped into the pistol, the easier your task will be. For extra assistance in solo mode, pick up Armed Life Model Decoy and bring a second Fury into the battle.

CO-OP COMBO: NICK FURY AND VENOM

This fight to save the computer is vicious. You may want to recruit someone more vicious than the Symbiote clones—the original Symbiote, Venom. With the two of you guarding either side of the computer, the battle will go much smoother.

New Challenge Available: Crawl and Collect

SIDE MISSION

TRACK-A-MOLE

RECOMMENDED HERO: IRON FIST

Mission Giver: S.H.I.E.L.D. Agent 1
Type: Collect
Reward: 250 Blue Sparks

Someone is stealing S.H.I.E.L.D. tech, but a radar system has them tracked. Hop in the Hovercar and find the thief that pocketed the stolen goods.

Zip over to the yellow objective marker and tail the thief's gray car from a distance. You want to be close enough not to lose him, but not too close that you lose the car if

it makes a sharp turn. Stay high enough not to hit any street lamps or the overpass section near the end of the tail. Eventually, you will weave in and out of streets until you get to the warehouse section on the river.

Pieces of the stolen tech are spread around the warehouse. Destroy the S.H.I.E.L.D. crates one by one around the warehouse perimeter until you recover all ten

pieces. Symbiotes will spawn periodically to protect the crates. Chop them to pieces first before worrying about what's in the crates.

HERO TIP: SPIDER-MAN

Spidey's Wall Crawl ability comes in handy climbing all over the warehouse. He's also quick enough to dispatch Symbiotes simultaneously while searching crates.

Crates are scattered around the base and on the roof, along with a few nearly hidden groups on

the mezzanine level. The mission completes when you collect the tenth piece and recover all the tech for S.H.I.E.L.D.

DOUBLE POWER DISCS

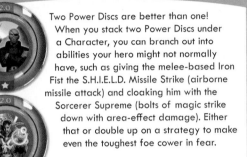

Two Power Discs are better than one! When you stack two Power Discs under a Character, you can branch out into abilities your hero might not normally have, such as giving the melee-based Iron Fist the S.H.I.E.L.D. Missile Strike (airborne missile attack) and cloaking him with the Sorcerer Supreme (bolts of magic strike down with area-effect damage). Either that or double up on a strategy to make even the toughest foe cower in fear.

SOMETHING STINKS

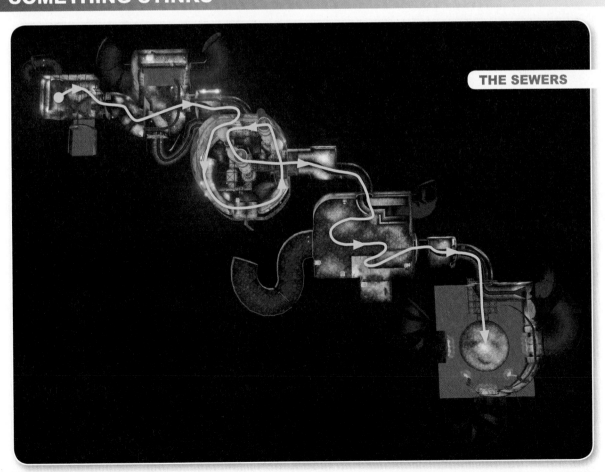

THE SEWERS

GAME BASICS · CHARACTERS · POWER DISCS · MARVEL'S THE AVENGERS · SPIDER-MAN · GUARDIANS OF THE GALAXY · TOY BOX · TOY BOX COLLECTION · ACHIEVEMENTS

SWEET AND SEWER

RECOMMENDED HERO: SPIDER-MAN

Mission Giver: Black Cat
Type: Combat
Reward: 200 Blue Sparks and "Tendriled Symbiote"

Seek out Black Cat for your next main mission. S.H.I.E.L.D. scientists are bringing heavy firepower into the sewers, and Black Cat thinks you're the guy to help them out. Web up your nostrils 'cause it's about to get stinky.

Feat Complete: Mission Master

Jump down off Black Cat's rooftop and walk around the corner to the sewer grate across the street. Symbiotes will intercept you. Puddle them before they jam up all the traffic and turn Manhattan into massive gridlock.

After you work out the cobwebs on your combat moves and smash all the Symbiotes, drop down into the sewer. Ignore the rats and veer around the big hole with nasty water pooling into it. On the far side of the chamber, jump up on the ledge and follow the tunnel as it curves to the right to defend the first two S.H.I.E.L.D. agents from a rush of Symbiotes.

A wall of goo blocks the tunnel. To get through, pick up the sonic weapon and carry it over to the goo. Fire the sonic weapon to blow through the goo and then walk over to the glowing green recharge station to power your weapon back up. Each sonic weapon gets five shots before it's drained dry.

Symbiotes rush after you as you enter the next chamber. Feel free to blast away with the sonic weapon; however, it's bulky and can be awkward to use in close combat, so it's usually a better idea to drop the weapon and use Spidey's acrobatic attacks to trash the bad guys. When the chamber isn't frantic with freaks, you can safely pick the sonic weapon back up again.

Avoid the bubbling pools of goo; these shoot Symbiote tendrils up to the ceiling when you come near. Cross the chamber to the goo mass in the center; its tendrils connect to the wall of goo blocking the exit tunnel. Blast the goo mass with your sonic weapon, then blast through the goo covering the exit tunnel. The two S.H.I.E.L.D. agents escape up the red ladder in the tunnel.

Approach the far ledge and double-jump up to engage the Symbiotes that guard the new tunnel. Kick, punch, and web them into the tunnel walls as you zip back and forth among them all.

Stay to the right, avoiding the goo pools, and follow the ramp to the recharge stations. Since you have unlimited power here, blast the spawning Symbiotes with your big weapon and recharge after you've cleared a path.

Drop the sonic weapon and double-jump on the first green hydraulic platform. Time your jumps to leap onto the second platform and then the steel catwalk. Cross the catwalk and double-jump over two more rising-and-falling platforms until you finally make it to the last green hydraulic platform. Follow it up to the final catwalk and exit the chamber.

HERO TIP: NOVA

If you're feeling daring, Spidey can web-swing across the chamber to the upper catwalks. If you have Nova, it's a simple flying trip up to the top.

Throw some more punches at the Symbiotes that appear in the upper tunnel. When there's nothing left but Sparks, continue up the tunnel until you reach the next chamber.

Circle around the goo tendrils and take out the Symbiotes that get in your way. Two more S.H.I.E.L.D. scientists need help here, so pick up the new sonic weapon and continue on toward the goo mass blocking the exit tunnel. Dispatch more Symbiotes with either the sonic weapon or a good, solid kick.

Obliterate the goo mass with the sonic weapon, then walk over and blast free the exit tunnel. Recharge the sonic weapon and continue on. The two S.H.I.E.L.D. agents will escape at the next red ladder.

Hop up onto the next tunnel section and splatter some Symbiotes that have decided that this particular part of the stench can be called home. After you get through the Symbiotes, you enter the final chamber.

Swing out onto the stone disk in the middle of the sewer water. Symbiotes, and their larger Symbiote Grunt cousins, will emerge from all angles and attack. Furiously fend them off, and tap in to your Web Barrage to pin down multiple enemies at once. Web Line also works wonders as you can pull Symbiotes from across the disk right to you for the take out shot.

Keep battling until the last Symbiote spawns. The Symbiote Grunts are much tougher than the normal Symbiote, and they can not only disappear and then reappear on you, but they can strike you with a heavy tendril attack from long range. Remember to dodge frequently and use the green and purple capsules around to your benefit. Beat the last Symbiote and you finish the mission and exit the sewers.

 New Challenge Available: Sonic Weaponry

SIDE MISSION

— AGENTS OF GOBLIN —

RECOMMENDED HERO: VENOM

Mission Giver: S.H.I.E.L.D. Agent 2
Type: Combat
Reward: 250 Blue Sparks

Meet up with the S.H.I.E.L.D. agent to learn about other agents being transformed into Symbiotes. Since, as Venom, you don't want a million Symbiotes running around town, your mission is to free the Symbiote-stricken agents and bring them back to the mission-giving S.H.I.E.L.D. agent.

Hitch a ride on a Hovercar or swing over to the building on the same street as the Daily Bugle. Look for a blinking red light; the trail of lights will lead you to the first agent.

HERO TIP: NOVA

If you don't feel like riding in style, ditch the Hovercar for Nova. As the Play Set's resident flyer, Nova can sub in for any long-distance missions.

Continue to follow the yellow objective markers until you find the seventh light up on the roof overlooking the harbor by Liberty Island.

Jump down and defend the first S.H.I.E.L.D. agent from the attacking Swarming Symbiotes. If the agent is covered in Symbiote goo, give him a whack to dislodge the coating and then pick him up.

Return to the S.H.I.E.L.D. agent who gave you the mission and drop off the first fellow agent. You have two more to fetch.

GAME BASICS

CHARACTERS

POWER DISCS

MARVEL'S THE AVENGERS

SPIDER-MAN

GUARDIANS OF THE GALAXY

TOY BOX

TOY BOX COLLECTION

ACHIEVEMENTS

Follow the trail of red lights to the second agent in the streets near the mission giver. Battle the Symbiotes trying to transform the agent, then pick him up and return to the mission giver.

The final agent is stuck in a parking lot. Follow the red lights to the agent, beat back the Symbiotes, and stomp across town to deliver the last agent to safety.

BACK TO THE SEWERS

TARGET THE TRAITOR

RECOMMENDED HERO: NOVA

Mission Giver: Luke Cage
Type: Escort
Reward: 150 Blue Sparks, Large Symbiote

Luke Cage asks you to turn on three radar stations, which will triangulate the position of the scientist who may be helping the Green Goblin. Your partner in the first half of this mission is a tech expert standing out in front of Oscorp; keep him safe and deliver him to each radar station to power them up as you defend against Symbiotes.

Your first destination is a rooftop below the big digital image of J. Jonah Jameson on the Daily Bugle building facade. Land on the roof and drop the tech expert on the platform. He turns on the radar station without a problem.

Follow the yellow objective marker to the second radar station. Land on the platform and let

the tech expert do his thing. The radar station takes a minute to power up, and during that time it's vulnerable to attack.

Symbiotes flood the rooftop and storm toward the radar station. Intercept them with Nova's blue energy bolts and try to repel some of them over the edge. Handle any that remain with a melee smackdown or circle the roof with continuous ranged fire until the Symbiotes are silent.

Fly the tech expert to the third and final radar station on the rooftop out in front of the Oscorp building. The generator powering the radar station actually is located on the next rooftop below, so get the tech expert to work and then drop down to combat the Symbiotes besieging the area.

Blow away any Symbiotes near the generator. If you can disintegrate your enemies from range, stay put. If they begin to swarm the generator, throw some punches and kicks in melee near the generator, then dodge out of danger when it gets too intense and return fire from range again.

Once the third radar station is operational, fly down to Luke Cage. He's spying on the scientist down by the bridge.

Now Luke Cage needs you to trail the scientist. Jump in the provided Hovercar and follow the scientist's gray car at a distance. Don't let the car get too far ahead of you where you can't see where it turns, but don't get close enough that you can't adjust to any sharp turns. Follow the scientist's car as it twists and turns through the city streets.

The scientist parks his car near the warehouse district and ducks into the sewers. You follow, only to run into a Large Symbiote blocking the sewer entrance. The Large Symbiote will hurl itself at you, causing major damage if it lands on you, but if it misses, you have an opportunity to land some blows while it's temporarily stunned.

Stay in motion during this fight. Between the ample amounts of spawning Symbiotes and the two Large Symbiotes you must defeat, combat is busy. Strike from range when you can, and dodge as soon as foes get close. If you have to fight hand-to-hand, hit for only two or three blows before jetting to a new area with a dodge. Continue punishing the bad guys until you defeat them all and can finally enter the sewer.

SEWER SEARCH

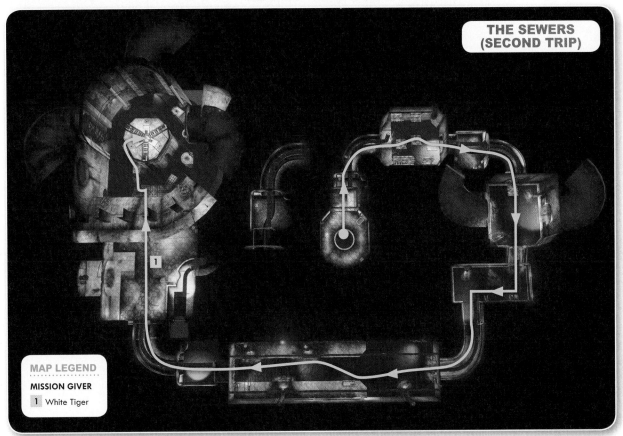

THE SEWERS (SECOND TRIP)

MAP LEGEND

MISSION GIVER

1 White Tiger

RECOMMENDED HERO: SPIDER-MAN

Mission Giver: Black Cat
Type: Combat
Reward: 150 Blue Sparks

Once you enter the first sewer chamber, pick up the sonic weapon and carry it over to the goo wall. Rip the wall apart with one blast and then press the IN button on the pipe. This flushes the water out of the central hole and you can now jump down to the lower level.

Continue ahead until Symbiotes drop from the ceiling and engage. Bounce around the tunnel from wall to wall as you dodge and assault the Symbiotes. Within seconds, you should have Sparks instead of goo.

GAME BASICS

CHARACTERS

POWER DISCS

MARVEL'S THE AVENGERS

SPIDER-MAN

GUARDIANS OF THE GALAXY

TOY BOX

TOY BOX COLLECTION

ACHIEVEMENTS

Press the IN button in the next chamber to lower the water level. Drop down into the basin and battle through all the Symbiotes that appear. When you have a minute to breathe, pick up the sonic weapon and place it on the wood planks nearest the goo wall.

Swing back up to the IN button and press it again. The water level rises again. Double-jump across the wooden platforms to reach the sonic weapon. Pick it up and blast a hole through the goo wall.

Fight more Symbiotes in the next tunnel. Eventually, you come out at the beginning of a waterway. A raft with a sonic weapon sitting on it bobs up and down in front of you. Jump on the raft and pick up the sonic weapon. You begin to float down the waterway.

Giant goo tendrils will shoot up from the water and damage the raft if you aren't careful. Position yourself so that the weapon always points directly ahead, which means you will have to rotate as the raft turns. Don't worry about the first two tendrils, but you will have to blast the goo wall blocking the tunnel ahead.

The water gushes you down into another chamber where you can charge against the wall as you drift by two charging stations. Quickly turn to face to your right and blast two more tendrils as they rise out of the water.

Blast the next goo wall. If you're low on energy for the sonic weapon, let the raft hit the goo wall and gently walk over to the edge and recharge at the charging station to your left. Then blow away the goo wall.

Now comes the hardest part. As the current sweeps you down into the final chamber, rotate to point the sonic weapon forward and blast the rising tendrils. One will rise to your right as you enter, a second to your left as you drift by the recharge stations, and a third and fourth to your right as you pass the final recharge stations.

Nuke the final goo wall to enter the tunnel leading out of the waterway. Jump off the raft to the solid stone tunnel and follow it until you see the Green Goblin talking with the scientist. As you listen in, you realize the scientist was forced to do the Goblin's bidding. Now you must rush in to save him before Goblin's Symbiotes eat him for lunch.

You have a lot of Symbiotes to dispatch here. Luckily, it's a vast chamber with plenty of room to dodge and counterattack. Use Spidey's speed to your advantage; don't sit still for more than a split second, and move back and forth from target to target quickly. Land a couple of blows on each enemy at a time, and they will add up to knockouts the longer the battle goes.

CO-OP COMBO: SPIDER-MAN AND IRON FIST

If you combine the two fastest heroes, the Symbiotes won't know what hit them. Flash around the chamber, dazzling them with your acrobatics, or combo on single foes for almost instant obliteration.

If you need help against the bigger targets, grab the sonic weapon and shoot them at close range. Just don't walk around with the sonic weapon too long; you can't move well with it, and you need to move well to overcome the Symbiotes here. Take out all the enemies and White Tiger arrives to escort the scientist out and send you after Green Goblin.

GOBLIN'S LAIR

RECOMMENDED HERO: SPIDER-MAN

Mission Giver: White Tiger
Type: Combat
Reward: 250 Blue Sparks

Continuing playing with Spidey as you hunt down the Green Goblin and the defense technology the scientist handed over to him. Enter the chamber past White Tiger and double-jump around the exterior of the circular platform in the middle. Clear each gap until you reach the yellow hand rails.

Carefully jump up the yellow rails and arc up onto the platform. If you're quick on your feet you'll beat the rising waters that now surround the whole platform.

There are three pressure plates—color-coded red, orange, and blue—with corresponding steam vents on opposite sides spaced out around the platform. Jump on any one of the pressure plates and Green Goblin flies in on his glider. Periodically, he will release an armed Goblin Drone to buzz around and attack you.

The Drone will circle around the platform. Time an Air Attack on the correct pressure plate to send a plume of steam up in the air to knock the Drone down. It will sputter on the platform for a few seconds before exploding.

Before it explodes, pick up the Goblin Drone and heave it at the circling Green Goblin. You know you have him in your sights when you see the target indicator lock on to him. Strike Green Goblin three times with the Drones to knock him out of the sky.

However, Green Goblin will not go down easily. After you hit him with the first Drone, he drops a slew of Goblin Grenades that detonate across the platform. Roll away from any grenade clumps and dodge as best you can to avoid major damage.

After your second successful Drone hit on Goblin, he summons Symbiotes onto the platform. Now you must wade through enemy attacks and exploding grenades as you set up for the final Drone strike.

Peg Green Goblin with a third Drone and he falls to the platform. S.H.I.E.L.D. arrives to scoop him up into custody, and you can finally get out of the sludge and back into the sunlight.

Feat Complete: **Subterranean Schemes**
Feat Complete: **Gross Misconduct**

SIDE MISSION

THE SOUND OF SAFETY

RECOMMENDED HERO: NICK FURY

Mission Giver: S.H.I.E.L.D. Agent 3
Type: Combat
Reward: 150 Blue Sparks after completion, Sky-Cycle upon accepting the mission

Symbiotes are crashing a checkpoint at the bridge. It may be too much for one hero to defend, except S.H.I.E.L.D. has graciously left three fully charged sonic weapons as support. Pick up a sonic weapon and stand between the two vehicles serving as a roadblock.

Wait until the Symbiotes are very close so you don't miss a single shot with the sonic weapon. You have fifteen charges and that's it. Defend the vehicles from taking damage, and if you run out of energy on a sonic weapon, drop it and go hand-to-hand for the finishing blows.

Save at least two or three shots on the sonic weapon for the Large Symbiote at the end of the fight. If you need more damage, switch to Fury's pistols and barrage the creature before it gets too close to the vehicles. Defeat the final Large Symbiote and you secure the checkpoint and show everyone who's the boss at S.H.I.E.L.D.

 New Challenge Available: Rat Trap

LEARNING TO FLY

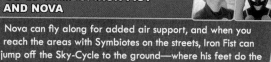
EARN YOUR WINGS

RECOMMENDED HERO: IRON FIST

Mission Giver: Luke Cage
Type: Combat
Reward: 100 Blue Sparks, Sky-Cycle

Luke Cage rewards you with a Sky-Cycle when you begin this mission. For those without flight or webs, the Sky-Cycle is a must-have for getting around the city. Take a ride on the Sky-Cycle and run through the training exercise by flying toward each floating IN symbol and shooting it with the Sky-Cycle's missiles.

CO-OP COMBO: IRON FIST AND NOVA

Nova can fly along for added air support, and when you reach the areas with Symbiotes on the streets, Iron Fist can jump off the Sky-Cycle to the ground—where his feet do the most damage.

Once you're trained on the Sky-Cycle, Luke Cage sends you to fend off some Goblin Drones. The first wave terrorizes the streets in front of the Daily Bugle. Zip in and start firing as soon as you can target them. The Goblin Drones will return fire—sometimes heavy at times—so weave left and right, and don't forget to bob up and down to dodge the deadly bolts.

The second enemy wave patrols the area in front of Oscorp. As before, stay on the move in the air as you blow the Goblin Drones apart. Unlike the first wave, the second wave includes ground enemies. After you defeat the Goblin Drones, lower the Sky-Cycle and use your martial arts to dismantle the Symbiotes wading through the streets.

The final wave mills about the bridge, and this group includes a Large Symbiote. Dive bomb the Goblin Drones and break them apart before you engage the Symbiotes. With your lightning-quick reflexes, pick off Symbiotes away from the Large Symbiote. When it's just you and the big guy, let loose with Shou-Lao the Undying or Chi State to deal enough damage to finish it off and set up S.H.I.E.L.D. to control the skies.

 New Challenge Available: Furious Frenzy

SIDE MISSIONS

SKY-CYCLE SALVO

RECOMMENDED HERO: VENOM

Mission Giver: S.H.I.E.L.D. Agent 4
Type: Defend
Reward: 350 Blue Sparks

For this mission you must defend three radar stations from Symbiote infestations. Granted, Venom hopping into a Hovercar or Sky-Cycle to reach the rooftops isn't necessarily his style, but you're going to love having him once he's tentacle-to-tentacle with the Symbiote horde.

Smash all the smaller Symbiotes away from the first station and keep defending it until the Large Symbiote arrives. Get in a couple of blows, but when it raises its arms to attack, dodge out of the way and counterattack from the side or rear. Use whatever special attacks you have available to puddle the Large Symbiote and save the first station.

Cruise up to the second station by the Daily Bugle. Goblin Drones rain green energy bolts down at you from the sky while the Symbiote horde pounds away at the station. You can either stay on the Sky-Cycle to blast the Drones, or you can land on the roof and use Venom's Web Line to destroy the annoying Drones. While the sky above you is clear, melee the Symbiotes and wipe them off the rooftop.

Continue besting normal Symbiotes until two Large Symbiotes appear. You must beat both of them before the radar station gets destroyed.

CO-OP COMBO: VENOM AND SPIDER-MAN

Normally, you don't see these two working together. In this case, though, two web shooters are better than one and can remove the Drones quickly enough to leave you extra time to defeat the Large Symbiotes.

The third radar station is atop a building overlooking the harbor in front of Liberty Island. The station lies on a lower roof, but you want to climb to the higher rooftop and shoot at the Goblin Drones from up here with your webs. There are too many Drones to survive long down below. Better to remove them all first before engaging the Symbiotes.

Keeping fighting till the last Symbiote falls and the radar station still has a few nuts and bolts left. You might have had to recruit a questionable ally to the S.H.I.E.L.D. cause, but the mission ends in success and you foil another part of Green Goblin's master plan.

WE INTERRUPT THIS BROADCAST

RECOMMENDED HERO: SPIDER-MAN

Mission Giver: S.H.I.E.L.D. Agent 5
Type: Combat
Reward: 250 Blue Sparks

It seems appropriate that Spider-Man should be the one to take out the big-screen TVs of J. Jonah Jameson shouting insults at S.H.I.E.L.D. and its allies. S.H.I.E.L.D. knows the real Jameson is out of town and wants to eliminate Mysterio's propaganda bombarding the city from the huge media screens. You're just the acrobatic superhero to make it happen!

Follow the yellow objective marker to the first TV. Target J. Jonah's big, fat heat, shoot your web line, and pull the whole thing down. You can also bring down a TV by crawling on it and performing an Air Attack to break the frame.

Continue to the first of the TV antennas. Smash the antenna until it's nothing but scrap metal and dust. Make sure you don't leave any of it left.

Destroy all ten of Mysterio's propaganda parts. There are no bad guys to stop you, so swing through town at your leisure and be happy that you can finally shut up J. Jonah Jameson—at least until the real one returns from out of town.

 Feat Complete: **Marvel's Agents of S.H.I.E.L.D.**

SLUDGE IN THE STREETS

ESCAPEE ESCORT

RECOMMENDED HERO: NOVA

Mission Giver: White Tiger
Type: Defend
Reward: 250 Blue Sparks

S.H.I.E.L.D. needs you to escort high-profile scientists to safety and Green Goblin's Symbiote forces don't want that to happen. After receiving your orders from White Tiger, fly over to the first S.H.I.E.L.D. vehicle and help the police officers in the streets control the Symbiotes. Eliminate any enemies attacking the vehicle first, then deal damage to the pipes spewing out Symbiote goo. You probably won't be able to turn away from the vehicle long enough to destroy a pipe in a single series of attacks. Be patient and guard the vehicle first; after a few successful rounds of attacks, you'll destroy the pipes and cut off enemies from attacking the first vehicle.

You'll see a formation of Goblin Drones shoot after the second vehicle. Turbo after them and intercept them before they can start attacking the vehicle. One by one nail them with your blue energy bolts before dropping to the ground.

Repeat your attack pattern against the Symbiotes and goo pipes around the second vehicle. If you get into a bad situation, let loose your Nova Core area-effect attack to rip apart anything immediately around you.

Follow more Goblin Drones to the next checkpoint. As before, destroy the flying enemies first, then descend to the asphalt. Smash the Symbiotes next to the vehicle, then destroy the pipes, and finally track down any enemies off the streets that may be looking to close in on the vehicle.

Next, the vehicle drives into an ambush with a Large Symbiote. Destroy the pipes while the Large Symbiote is away from the vehicles and keep more Symbiotes from showing up. When you can concentrate your energy on the one over-sized foe, use Nova Core to obliterate any collection of Swarming Symbiotes and keep blasting at range with your bolts until the creature bursts into dozen of Sparks.

The final fight to defend the S.H.I.E.L.D. vehicle occurs at a busy intersection in front of the Daily Bugle. Two goo pipes spit out enemies in the center; a vehicle is parked at three of the four corners. You must be able to defend each vehicle and also deal enough damage to the pipes to stop the continuous Symbiote threat. For good measure, a Large Symbiote is also trying to squash you.

HERO TIP: SPIDER-MAN

Spidey's speed can help in the final fight to defend the S.H.I.E.L.D. vehicles, and his Web Barrage can trap multiple foes when they converge in the intersection.

First things first, destroy one of the pipes with rapid-fire energy blasts. Then quickly scan the three vehicles and jet over to the one that has the most enemies. Ignore the Large Symbiote, who will be chasing you by this point, and quickly dispatch the enemies around the vehicle before moving to the next vehicle. You don't want to stand next to any vehicle for too long or else the Large Symbiote will leap on you and catch the vehicle with massive damage too.

Keep bouncing around to the vehicles, eliminating threats. As you pass by the center of the intersection, throw some damage at the last pipe. Once you destroy the second pipe, no new Symbiotes will spawn.

So long as you can keep all three vehicles whole, you have a chance. Defeat the Large Symbiote last, after all other Symbiotes have been destroyed, and you advance to the next stage of the mission.

Hop on the Sky-Cycle and tail the helicopter as it tries to escape. Goblin Drones will sweep in along the route and fire upon the weaponless copter. You must pick off each Goblin Drone before the helicopter takes too many hits.

CO-OP COMBO: NOVA AND IRON FIST

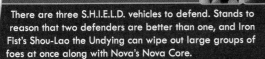

There are three S.H.I.E.L.D. vehicles to defend. Stands to reason that two defenders are better than one, and Iron Fist's Shou-Lao the Undying can wipe out large groups of foes at once along with Nova's Nova Core.

Fly up to the nearby rooftop where a S.H.I.E.L.D. helicopter with the scientists begins to take off. Symbiotes arrive to stop it. Show them a little cosmic mojo and remove them from the rooftop so the helicopter can lift off.

Fly in and out of the Manhattan buildings, firing your missiles at the Goblin Drones. If you can escort the helicopter all the way to Liberty Island, the scientists escape and you can return to the mainland, knowing you saved the lives of some very important people.

THE CAT'S OUT OF THE BAG

THE SEWERS (THIRD TRIP)

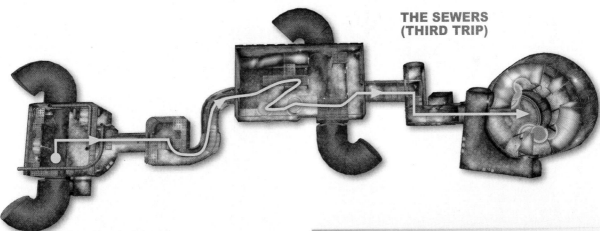

RECOMMENDED HERO: IRON FIST

Mission Giver: Black Cat
Type: Combat
Reward: 100 Blue Sparks

In this next mission, Black Cat has been captured and brought down into the sewers. Track down the sewer entrance out by the water and battle through the Symbiotes scattered about the plaza. When you've finally destroyed the Large Symbiote, plus any stragglers, the sewer entrance opens.

The first sewer chamber holds a big group of Symbiotes roaming about on the floor. The key, though, is to reach the platform high up above the goo wall. Fight the Symbiotes if you want, but when you're ready to continue, use the yellow hand rails and catwalks to navigate to the high tunnel. If you choose to play Nova instead of Iron Fist, simply fly up.

GAME BASICS

CHARACTERS

POWER DISCS

MARVEL'S THE AVENGERS

SPIDER-MAN

GUARDIANS OF THE GALAXY

TOY BOX

TOY BOX COLLECTION

ACHIEVEMENTS

Drop down through the hole in the floor of the high tunnel into the second chamber. Use Iron Fist's lightning-quick reflexes to wipe out all the Symbiotes in the chamber.

Because of his speed, Iron Fist is a great choice for all the melee battles throughout the sewers.

Climb up the yellow pole and double-jump over to the second catwalk. Pick up one of the two sonic weapons and drop back down. If you like, blow apart the goo wall leading back to the first chamber and collect a blue and an orange capsule along the way.

Charge up at the recharging station and destroy the goo wall blocking access to the next tunnel. Leave behind the sonic weapon and jump over the pipes and trenches between you and the next chamber. Symbiotes will spawn too, and you'll have to deal with them to make it through.

You need another sonic weapon to get through the next goo wall. To obtain it, cross to the first hydraulic lift to the right and ride it up to the platform. Jump off and get on the second hydraulic lift to the top. Double-jump off the top platform and land on the catwalk that holds the sonic weapon. Pick up the sonic weapon and drop down to the ground.

Symbiotes spawn as soon as you touch the weapon. Hurry toward the hydraulic lifts and repeat your route to reach the top platform again. Drop down off the far side of the platform to land on the catwalk with the recharging station. Symbiotes will attack in front of the goo wall; however, standing next to a recharging station, you have unlimited ammo with the sonic weapon, so enemies should not be a problem.

Rip through the goo wall with the sonic weapon, then jump over the pipes and climb the yellow poles to discover the final chamber. Along the way you can smash through a barricaded side chamber for a purple capsule and an orange capsule.

Black Cat is held in a specially designed prison cell that hangs from the ceiling. Three goo tendrils hang down, attached from prison cell to goo masses on the various platform levels. You must locate the sonic weapon and destroy all the goo masses to free Black Cat.

Use the hydraulic lifts to gain access to the middle level where you'll find the sonic weapon. Destroy the nearby goo wall for easier access to the lifts and destroy another link in the goo connections holding Black Cat prisoner.

Work your way around the chamber using the hydraulic lifts to locate the goo masses. Pull the trigger on the sonic weapon when you're close to obliterate a goo mass.

The hardest goo mass to reach is the one up top. Take the hydraulic lifts up to the top level and smash through the barricade to discover a side tunnel that links to the far catwalk in the main chamber. Put your melee skills to work in the side tunnel, which is filled with Symbiotes. When cleared, pick up the sonic weapon, blow through the second barricade, and destroy the final goo mass.

You free Black Cat—but wait a second! It's not Black Cat! Mysterio has cast an illusion over the whole area. You really just knocked out a whole facility of S.H.I.E.L.D. agents and broke Green Goblin out of prison. You've just put Green Goblin back into play, and he's going to be an even greater menace than before.

SIDE MISSIONS

SYMBIOTE AMBUSH

RECOMMENDED HERO: NICK FURY

Mission Giver: S.H.I.E.L.D. Agent 6
Type: Combat
Reward: 250 Blue Sparks, Police Horse

S.H.I.E.L.D. needs help cleaning Symbiotes off the streets, and who better than the big boss, Nick Fury, to pick up the broom. Fury's "broom" can either be his boot heels or his twin pistols—your choice. Follow the yellow objective marker to the first street location and unleash your Fury on the Symbiote congregation.

A Large Symbiote forms at the end of the first skirmish. Use Fury's pistols to take on the Large Symbiote, and if you have extra skill points to spend, Ranged Attack Upgrade and Explosive Shells are a big improvement.

HERO TIP: SPIDER-MAN

Web Line attacks work just as well as Fury's ranged pistols against the Symbiotes in the streets. Spidey's acrobatic attacks will also make quick work of any enemy except the Large Symbiotes.

With the first Symbiote threat gone, S.H.I.E.L.D. sends you out to a second spot. Repeat your attack pattern here, and when you finish off the second Large Symbiote, you finish off the mission.

ROOFTOP RENDEZVOUS

RECOMMENDED HERO: NOVA

Mission Giver: S.H.I.E.L.D. Agent 7
Type: Escort
Reward: 250 Blue Sparks, Symbiote Spawn

Fly Nova out to a rooftop on the shoreline next to Liberty Island. A scientist needs saving from the Symbiotes, and there is a rooftop full of the creatures when you arrive. Slam into the roof and knock a couple over the edge before firing off an arc of energy blasts to cut through the horde.

After defeating the rooftop-bound Symbiotes, Goblin Drones zoom into the air. Now you have to deal with a combination of flying and ground enemies. Eliminate all the airborne enemies first, then you can drop down onto a more deserted section of the rooftop and start leveling the rest of the Symbiotes.

When the scientist comes out of hiding, fly up to him and pick him up quickly. Swarming Symbiotes converge on the scientist, but if you're quick enough, you can lift off with him before they have a chance to bite. Escort the scientist down to his safehouse on the other side of the city. Another satisfied scientist thanks you for a mission well done.

OSCORP ESCORT

RECOMMENDED HERO: VENOM

Mission Giver: S.H.I.E.L.D. Agent 8
Type: Escort
Reward: 350 Blue Sparks

How about some fun irony and invite Venom to a mission saving Oscorp VIPs? Hop on a Sky-Cycle and jet across town to the S.H.I.E.L.D. helicopter taking off from the rooftop near Liberty Island. It's going to circle around town and escape by the bridge, and, without webs, it's your job to keep the passengers safe with Sky-Cycle missiles.

As you go up and down over elevated train platforms and back and forth over the Manhattan streets, Goblin Drones will fly in and assault the chopper. Keep your target on the helicopter when the skies are clear, so when a Goblin Drone appears, it's a quick move to target it and release a deadly missile.

Keep the helicopter from taking too much damage and it will make it to the bridge. Blast away the last group of Goblin Drones and the chopper flies off into the distance safely. Venom may not like scientists and their experiments, but you can show them what he can do with a Sky-Cycle and unlimited destruction at his fingertips.

GOING AFTER THE GOBLIN

─── MYSTERIO'S HIDEAWAY ───

RECOMMENDED HERO: NOVA

Mission Giver: Luke Cage
Type: Defend
Reward: 350 Blue Sparks

Well, good news—the scientists you helped escort to safety out of Manhattan have given S.H.I.E.L.D. the location of Mysterio's lair. All you need to do is help some S.H.I.E.L.D. techs set up three radar stations. Pick up the first tech in the street and fly him up to the first control center.

The tech will begin configuring the radar station. While it boots up, you must defend both the tech and the radar station from Symbiotes. Your top priority, however, is the radar station. If that goes boom, the mission fails. If the tech gets harassed by Symbiotes, the boot-up sequence will pause, but the Symbiotes can't hurt the tech.

When a goo pipe appears to spawn more Symbiotes, destroy that as quickly as possible. Don't leave the radar station to take damage, but if the station is safe, the goo pipes should be wrecked next. After the boot-up sequence is complete, the goo pipes are all eliminated, and you vanquish the last Symbiote enemy, the radar station activates.

For the second radar station, you need two techs. Fly your first tech to the first of two control centers, and a second tech will join him to operate a separate set of controls. As they start working on the boot-up sequence, the Symbiotes arrive. As before, destroy goo pipes early to avoid too many enemy reinforcements. Defend the radar station at all costs, and if a tech gets knocked off his control center, scoop him back up and put him back at the controls. After a long battle, you will secure the second radar station.

If you're having trouble at any point, take to the air. You can nuke goo pipes from above and blast enemies without worrying about getting swarmed. Just watch out for the ranged goo attacks that can knock you to the ground.

Carry both techs over to the adjacent rooftop and get them started on the third radar station's boot-up sequence. This setup has one control center and the radar station up on a higher rooftop; the second control center rests on a lower rooftop. Hover up in the air to watch both control centers and the radar station and fly to whichever area needs your assistance.

Continue to destroy goo pipes, clear Symbiotes off the rooftops, and return techs to their control centers if they are forced to leave. This is a long fight, so unless you have a teammate helping you out, be patient.

CO-OP COMBO: NOVA AND NICK FURY

Nick Fury's fearsome pistols can help with support at the radar station. If Nova has the air covered, Fury can sit at the radar station and blow apart any Symbiotes foolish enough to approach.

Swat the Symbiotes away from the radar station as it completes its final programming. As soon as the third radar station comes online, it reveals Mysterio's secret location and your next mission begins.

ILLUSIONS OF GRANDEUR

MYSTERIO'S HIDEAWAY

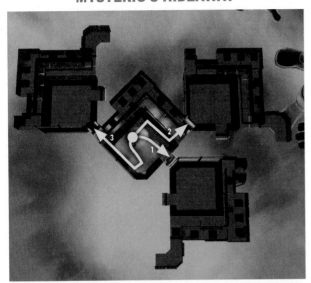

RECOMMENDED HERO: NICK FURY

Mission Giver: White Tiger
Type: Combat
Reward: 350 Blue Sparks, White Tiger

Send Fury on the Sky-Cycle to Mysterio's Hideaway in the tall building on the edge of the city. Goblin Drones circle the building like angry hornets around a disturbed hive. Stay at a distance and pick them off one by one until you can land on the roof and enter the Hideaway rooftop door one level down.

You run across the cube in the first room. Mysterio has locked himself in a fortress of puzzles. The key to unlocking the puzzles is manipulating the cube to expose its sides to matching colors and shapes. For example, in the first room, the door is locked by a blue square. Let the cube roll toward you to expose the blue side and punch it. The door unlocks and opens for you.

The doorway transports you to Mysterio's puzzle platform. Its simplest version has two wings: one with a blue door and a missing red square, and one with a red door and a missing blue square. Punch the blue cube side to close the blue door, but fill in the missing blue square. You can now pass through the open red door, hop up on the blue square, and retrieve the power cell on the end square.

Carry the power cell back to the central power conduit and drop it in. The wings temporarily disappear as you fight to stay alive on the central platform. Fight off the wave of Symbiotes until the wings appear again. Punch the red cube side to fill in the missing red square and retrieve the second power cell. As soon as you drop in the power conduit, you're transported back to the first room.

A new door has appeared in the first room on the upper level. Punch the blue side to fill in a missing square of the staircase, then punch the circle shape on the cube side and enter the door to proceed to the next level of the puzzle platform.

HERO TIP: NOVA

Flight can make the puzzles easier. If you have Nova, for example, you can skip punching the cube for blue and simply fly up to the top level and the open circle-shape door.

The second puzzle platform gets harder. Punch the triangle cube side to open one of the closed doors.

Punch the red cube side to fill in a missing square to reach the first power cell. Pick up the cell and deposit it in the central power conduit. Battle the Symbiotes until you've destroyed enough to reset the platform and call back the second wing.

Open the second wing by punching the circle-inside-square symbol on the cube and then punching the blue side to unlock the double-locked door. Now punch the circle symbol on the cube to fill in the missing squares on the lower level.

Punch the green cube side to fill in the green square next. Now, run up, grab the power cell, and drop it in the conduit to finish the puzzle.

Back in the first room, punch the circle cube side and the green cube side to open the double-locked door on the upper level. Punch

the red cube side to fill in the missing step in the stairs. Enter the new doorway to transport back to the puzzle platform.

Back on the puzzle platform, punch the red cube side and go to the now-closed red door. Double-jump to the floating white square to the left of the red door, then double-jump

to the next floating square, and finally back to the main platform behind the red door. With the red door closed, the red square on the floor is filled in and you can cross. Pick up the power cell and drop it off back at the closed red door. Return to the central platform via the floating side squares, punch the red side on the cube, cross through the open door, pick up the power cell, and drop it on the power conduit.

Mysterio sends the largest Symbiote horde yet at you. Constantly stay on the move, circling the central platform (without falling off) and strafing the enemies with Fury's

high-octane pistols. If you try to go toe-to-toe with these foes, you're likely to get crushed by multiple attacks.

After fighting through the Symbiotes and seeing the second wing return, leave the blue door closed and punch the green cube side to fill in one of the green squares in that wing. As you did with the other side, use the floating white squares off to the side to bypass the blue door and climb up the main path to reach the power cell.

Pick up the power cell and bring it back to the green square. Leave it for now and return to the cube to punch the blue side, then punch the square symbol on the cube to fill

in that missing square in the wing, and then punch the blue cube side again to fill in the final square. Return to the power cell and get it back to the square in front of the now-closed blue door. Skirt around the blue door using the floating white squares and punch blue on the cube for the last time.

Drop the power cell into the power conduit and it is light's out Mysterio. The energy backfires on Mysterio and the illusions fade. S.H.I.E.L.D. swoops in to capture the villain

and leave you with only the Green Goblin to apprehend.

 Feat Complete: Dispelled Illusions

GREEN GOBLIN'S GRIM GAUNTLET

RECOMMENDED HERO: SPIDER-MAN

Mission Giver: Luke Cage
Type: Combat
Reward: 750 Blue Sparks, Luke Cage

The final battle against the Green Goblin is a flying chase through Manhattan. To bring him to justice, you must continually pick off his four Goblin Drones to

drop his shield and then deal damage directly to the glider before the shields come back up and four more Drones appear. It's going to take multiple loops around Manhattan and dozens of Drone detonations to punch through Green Goblin's defenses.

Run into any green capsules floating above the streets. The green Sparks will trail after you and eventually give you health back. You will stay alive much longer if you capture as many green Sparks as you can along the race.

Green Goblin is not without his tricks. His first big defense comes in the form of giant, blue energy Goblin Bombs. Hit one and you'll spin out of control. Three knocks you out of the chase for sure.

Once you drop the Goblin's shields, pelt him with as many missiles as you can from your Sky-Cycle. You only have a few seconds before the shields return, so make those shots count.

Out by the bridge, Goblin launches his second big defense— Goblin Drones in the form

of an energy "X." This "X" rolls through the sky, and if any part strikes the Sky-Cycle, it electrocutes you and spins you out of control. Speed through the gaps and stay on the same path through the multiple "X"s if you make it through the first one.

After the bridge, Green Goblin's Drones develop laser fire. Dodge the green beams as they cut through the air. It's important now more than ever to eliminate Goblin's Drones quickly.

As you wear Goblin down, he will blow a hole through a skyscraper. Follow him and his Drones through the skyscraper and pursue them down into the streets below.

Take your time and steady your shot when you want to pick off the Goblin Drones or smack the glider.

When Goblin throws out his Goblin Bombs or lets loose his electrifying "X"s, hang back to give yourself more room to maneuver.

Eventually, you will drop Goblin's shields for the final time. Pepper him with the last few missiles and bring him down.

Green Goblin's glider plummets out of control and ends up in the Hudson River. S.H.I.E.L.D. fishes him out and takes him away. The

whole crew meets up to pal around after nabbing another nefarious villain, but there are plenty of Symbiotes running around town for those still itching for a fight.

Feat Complete: High and Mighty

CROSSOVER COIN MISSIONS: HULK

CAPTURED CAPTAIN

RECOMMENDED HERO: HULK

Mission Giver: Luke Cage
Type: Combat
Rewards: 100 Blue Sparks

Luke Cage gives Hulk a side mission close to home. Captain Marvel has been captured a block away down by the bridge. Run over to the tunnels under the bridge and fetch the sonic weapon first.

Use the sonic weapon, if you like, to blast the surrounding Symbiotes to smithereens. If you do, be sure to charge the sonic weapon up at the recharge station on the nearby wall.

Of course, Hulk's fists are fearsome too, and he's perfectly capable of bashing Symbiotes with his bare knuckles. Clear the Symbiotes away from the tunnel in front of Captain Marvel's cell long enough to destroy the goo wall with the sonic weapon.

S.H.I.E.L.D. is happy to have their agent back when you finally free Captain Marvel. Return to Luke Cage because he's got two more side missions that require muscle—lots and lots of green muscle.

━━ TRAFFIC TROUBLE ━━

RECOMMENDED HERO: HULK

Mission Giver: Luke Cage
Type: Escort
Rewards: 100 Blue Sparks

A S.H.I.E.L.D. convoy is headed out and needs a big, green bodyguard to see it safely through. Follow the yellow objective marker to the convoy vehicle and smash through the Symbiotes on the scene.

Destroy the goo pipe the first chance you get to prevent Symbiote reinforcements from spawning. You don't want to abandon the vehicle to do so; however, Hulk's Roar can demolish the pipe and the surrounding Symbiotes in a single, mighty attack.

Follow the vehicle to the second roadblock. As with the first, clear the goo pipe from the road, but only remove it when Symbiotes aren't attacking the vehicle directly.

Continue on to a third roadblock. The vehicle will reach there before you, so Charge in and wipe out the Symbiotes on either side of the vehicle first. Once the vehicle is safe, lumber up the street and pound the goo pipe until it's pulverized into useless scrap.

The last battle takes place at the base of the bridge. When you finally flatten the goo pipe and annihilate all the Symbiotes in the area, the convoy motors over the bridge and out of town safe and sound.

━━ TOWER ASSAULT ━━

RECOMMENDED HERO: HULK

Mission Giver: Luke Cage
Type: Defend
Rewards: 100 Blue Sparks

Your final Hulk crossover mission sends the muscle-bound Avenger up to the rooftops to defend an important S.H.I.E.L.D. radar station. The first Symbiote wave will already be assaulting the station when you arrive. Jump into the fray immediately and start swinging. Clear the enemies away from the station as quickly as possible. Don't stay on one enemy too long; knock them away and stay near the station until all is quiet.

That quiet does not last. More waves of Symbiotes will jump down off the upper roof, and after more fisticuffs, a Large Symbiote spawns to take Hulk on. Unlike other heroes that want to stay back and use ranged attacks against the Large Symbiote, Hulk is made to go head first at the beast. Out-slug the creature and the victory is yours.

Hulk has helped S.H.I.E.L.D. stay in the tech race with the Green Goblin. Since he's already in Spider-Man's neighborhood, feel free to use Hulk's destructive talents against other Symbiote threats that may take a little more muscle than brains.

CROSSOVER COIN MISSIONS: IRON MAN

VILE AND INVISIBLE

RECOMMENDED HERO: IRON MAN

Mission Giver: White Tiger
Type: Combat
Rewards: 100 Blue Sparks

Unlock this series of missions by collecting all ten Iron Man Crossover Coins in Manhattan. White Tiger recruits Iron Man's help to track down tech that's been stolen by the Symbiotes to turn them invisible.

Fly over to the warehouse buildings out on the tip of Manhattan near Liberty Island. Symbiotes pour out of pipe and will continue to pour out endlessly until you destroy the pipe. In between attacking targets of opportunity, focus your firepower on the pipe to pulverize it quickly. If you don't destroy the pipe, you will have to battle wave after wave of Symbiote foes.

NOTE

These are not your normal Symbiote foes; they can become invisible. If you look closely, you can trace the shimmer of an outline around the invisible foes.

The second pipe pollutes Liberty Island. As Symbiotes spew out of it, use the same tactics as the first battle. Destroy foes close to the pipe, deal as much damage as you can to the pipe, then dodge out of the way if any counterattacks are incoming. Repeat until there is no pipe and there are no Symbiotes left.

The final pipe lies on the rooftop overlooking the harbor. A Large Symbiote joins the mass of Symbiotes around this pipe. Rely on similar tactics, only keep

an eye on the Large Symbiote at all times so it doesn't sneak attack you while you damage the pipe. When you destroy the pipe and the last of the Symbiote horde, you end the threat of unseen enemies and complete your first Crossover Coins mission as Iron Man.

BOMB'S AWAY

RECOMMENDED HERO: IRON MAN

Mission Giver: White Tiger
Type: Defend
Rewards: 100 Blue Sparks

White Tiger sends you on a second mission to defend a S.H.I.E.L.D. vehicle from Goblin Drones and guided bombs. Follow the yellow objective market to the vehicle and hover over it.

Bombs, some with Goblin Drones, fly toward it from each street.

Pinpoint the bombs with a Pulse Bolt and they blow up with a single hit. You can detonate multiple bombs if they are close together. Prioritize bombs near the vehicle so they don't explode and damage the vehicle's armor.

Follow the vehicle to its second location. Hover above it and prepare for bombs and Goblin Drones. If you survive, you earn another victory.

GLIDER GETAWAY

RECOMMENDED HERO: IRON MAN

Mission Giver: White Tiger
Type: Combat
Rewards: 100 Blue Sparks

In the third Iron Man mission, another piece of Stark tech has been stolen. Follow the giant glider as it weaves through the Manhattan skyline. Riding the Sky-Cycle, you can blast away at the glider, but your goal is to dodge the Goblin Drones as they stream by and survive till Liberty Island.

The glider crashes on Liberty Island. Fly in and destroy all the Goblin Drones hovering over the tech. Dodge left, right, up, and down as you return fire and sputter each one to the ground. After destroying the Drones, capture the tech to complete this mission and Iron Man's Crossover Coin missions.

GAME BASICS

CHARACTERS

POWER DISCS

MARVEL'S THE AVENGERS

SPIDER-MAN

GUARDIANS OF THE GALAXY

TOY BOX

TOY BOX COLLECTION

ACHIEVEMENTS

CROSSOVER COINS

MANHATTAN

Hulk Crossover Coins
Iron Man Crossover Coins

WEB SWING BONUS BOXES

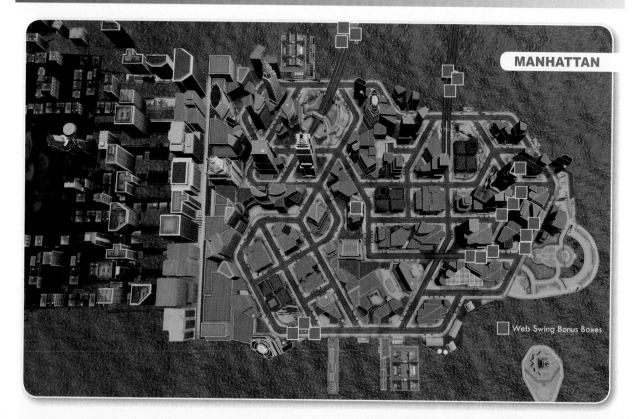

MANHATTAN

Web Swing Bonus Boxes

WALL CRAWL BONUS BOXES

MANHATTAN

☐ Wall Crawl Bonus Boxes

FLIGHT BONUS BOXES

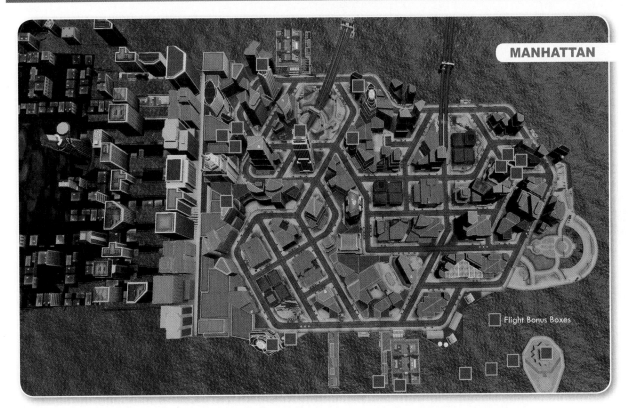

MANHATTAN

☐ Flight Bonus Boxes

SUPER JUMP BONUS BOXES

MANHATTAN

☐ Super Jump Bonus Boxes

MAXIMUM STRENGTH BONUS BOXES

MANHATTAN

☐ Maximum Strength Bonus Boxes

SPIDER-MAN FEATS

FEATS	
FEAT NAME	**FEAT DESCRIPTION**
Marvel's Agents of S.H.I.E.L.D.	Complete 5 S.H.I.E.L.D. Agent missions in the Spider-Man Play Set.
Back Off!	As Iron Fist, repel enemies during combat.
Bonus Box Master	Find and collect all Bonus Boxes in the Spider-Man Play Set.
Bridge Spotter	Fly under each bridge as Nova.
Bronze Champ	Collect 5 bronze medals in the Spider-Man Play Set.
Clear a Path	Destroy 5 cars in 10 seconds in the Spider-Man Play Set.
Clear the Skies	Destroy 10 Goblin Drones.
Climbing the Walls	Wall Crawl for 5 minutes as Spider-Man or Venom.
Contest of Champions	Compete in 2 multiplayer challenges in the Spider-Man Play Set.
Damage Champion	Deal 5,000 points of damage in Spider-Man destruction challenges.
Dancing Feat	Complete 150 feats.
Disinfectant	Remove the symbiote infection from 5 citizens.
Dispelled Illusions	Defeat Mysterio in his secret Lair.
Diving in with Both Feat	Complete 10 feats.
Double Trouble	Use Nova's Dual Energy Blasts upgrade to defeat an enemy.
Enemy Eradicator	Defeat 200 enemies in Spider-Man combat challenges.
Fast on Your Feat	Complete 100 feats.
Getting Your Feat Wet	Complete 1 feat.
Go for the Gold	Collect 5 gold medals in the Spider-Man Play Set.
Great Gobs of Gold	Collect all gold medals in the Spider-Man Play Set.
Gross Misconduct	Defeat Green Goblin in the Sewers.
High and Mighty	Defeat Green Goblin above the streets of New York.
How the Mighty Have Fallen	Destroy 10 Large Symbiotes.
Landing on Both Feat	Complete 50 feats.
Liberty's Landing	Fly to the top of the Statue of Liberty as Nova.

FEATS	
FEAT NAME	**FEAT DESCRIPTION**
Master Crawler	Find and collect all Wall Crawl Bonus Boxes in the Spider-Man Play Set.
Mission Master	Get a mission from Luke Cage, White Tiger, and Black Cat.
Orb Demolisher	Destroy 1,000 Orbs in the Spider-Man Play Set.
Points Pro	Score 5,000 total points in Spider-Man challenges.
Points-a-Plenty	Score 10,000 total points in Spider-Man challenges.
Rise and Shine	Help revive another character 5 times in the Spider-Man Play Set.
Scrape the Sky	Reach the top of the 4 tallest buildings in the Spider-Man Play Set.
Silver Star	Collect 5 silver medals in the Spider-Man Play Set.
Sky Master	Find and collect all Flight Bonus Boxes in the Spider-Man Play Set.
Spider Speed	Upgrade Spider-Man to his maximum running speed.
Springing to Your Feat	Complete 25 feats.
Strong Arm of the Law	Find and collect all Maximum Strength Bonus Boxes in the Spider-Man Play Set.
Subterranean Schemes	Complete 3 missions in the sewers.
Super Jump Extraordinaire	Find and collect all Super Jump Bonus Boxes in the Spider-Man Play Set.
Swarmer Sweep	Defeat 8 Swarming Symbiotes in 1 second.
Swing Savvy	Find and collect all Web Swing Bonus Boxes in the Spider-Man Play Set.
The Immortal Weapon	Perform Iron Fist's special move 4 times in 30 seconds.
Two to Tango	Complete any 2 missions in the Spider-Man Play Set with 2 players.
Un-De-Feat-Able	Complete all feats.
Venomous Combo	As Venom, use a full combo move against an enormous symbiote enemy.
Webs Away!	Carry a townsperson while web swinging as Spider-Man or Venom.
Welcome Wagon	Find all the hidden Crossover Coins in the Spider-Man Play Set.

SPIDER-MAN CHALLENGES

CHALLENGES			
MAP #	**CHALLENGE NAME**	**DESCRIPTION**	**HOW UNLOCKED?**
1	City Web Race	Web swing to the finish line as quickly as possible! Pass through all the gates in order.	Unlocked from beginning.
2	Ring the City	Earn points by swinging through the rings.	Earn bronze on "City Web Race" challenge.
3	Race Gate Challenge	Web swing to the finish line as quickly as possible! Pass through all the gates in order.	Earn bronze on "Ring the City" challenge.
4	Rooftop Rings	Earn points by swinging through the rings.	Earn bronze on "Race Gate Challenge" challenge
5	Bridge Rings	Earn points by swinging through the rings.	Earn bronze on "Rooftop Rings" challenge.
6	Right on Target	Earn points by breaking targets. Utilize your character's special moves!	Unlocked from beginning.
7	Crawl and Collect	Jump onto the wall and collect Orbs for points.	Complete "Interrupted Upload" mission.
8	Combo Crawl	Jump onto the wall and collect Orbs for points.	Earn bronze in "Crawl and Collect" challenge.
9	Wallopin' Wall Crawlers	Prepare for the onslaught! Collect Orbs and avoid attacks!	Earn bronze in "Combo Crawl" challenge.
10	Hovercar Race	It's a race against time in the S.H.I.E.L.D. Hovercar.	Complete "Unfriendly Neighborhood" mission.
11	Ring Run	Collect Orbs and pass through rings in the S.H.I.E.L.D. Hovercar.	Earn bronze on "Hovercar Race" challenge.
12	Sonic Weaponry	Earn points by destroying Symbiotes with the sonic weapon.	Complete "Sweet and Sewer" mission.
13	Nova Saves the Day	Save the citizens as quickly as possible! Deliver them to the safe zone near the vehicles.	Earn bronze in "Sonic Weaponry" challenge.
14	Vs. Mode: Statue of Liberty	Player vs. player combat on Liberty Island.	Unlocked from beginning.
15	Vs. Mode: Waterfront	Player vs. player combat on the waterfront.	Complete "Agents of GOBLIN" mission.
16	Rat Trap	Complete the challenge before time runs out.	Complete "The Sound of Safety" mission.
17	Furious Frenzy	Complete the challenge before time runs out.	Complete "Escapee Escort" mission.

GUARDIANS OF
THE GALAXY

GUARDIANS OF THE GALAXY PLAY SET

KNOWHERE BUT HERE

SPATIAL DELIVERY

CRASH SITE

Jump up and grab the lowest blue rail and continue climbing up the right side of the space station. Follow the blue rails until you cross over the spinning blades to the left side. Jump across the gaps, then make your way up the blue rails to the top of the platform. Double-jump across one more gap and take the final blue rails to the top level. Smash open the door to enter.

RECOMMENDED HERO: STAR-LORD

Mission Giver: Cosmo
Type: Explore
Rewards: 50 Blue Sparks, The Collector, Mining Transport

Double-jump up to the next level and break open the door. Double-jump up again to a higher level and then jump on the horizontal blue rail to slide across to the other side of the chamber.

Follow the corridor and bash through the next door. Jump over the pipe and climb the blue rails to the higher platform. Once you reach the vertical rail, you'll

capture your first Iron Man Crossover Coin. Collect nine more to allow Iron Man to join this Play Set.

The crew of the *Milano*— Star-Lord, Gamora, Rocket Raccoon, Drax, and Groot— hold one of the most destructive artifacts in the universe, an infinity gem. Unfortunately for them, that doesn't make them deadly or feared— it makes them wanted fugitives! The world conqueror, Ronan, wants the infinity gem for himself and has chased Star-Lord and crew to Knowhere. After a crash landing, it's up to Star-Lord to navigate Knowhere and find The Collector.

NOTE

You can choose any Marvel Character from this Play Set and be successful on these missions. Each hero is special and much of the fun is replaying through the missions with different heroes, leveling up and unlocking their special abilities as you go. However, there are some spots in each mission where a particular hero may be better suited to overcome an obstacle or a particular hero's skills may allow you to proceed through a mission easier. And sometimes we just thought it was cool to have that hero on a mission, like Gamora squaring off against the first Sakaarans, sword against sword. With that in mind, we've chosen a Recommended Hero for each mission to maximize your superhero potential.

Enter the green square with a pile of metal plates inside. Perform an Air Strike to shatter the plates and drop down to the lower level below. Cross the chamber and greet The Collector to fulfill your contract—handing over the infinity gem and completing your first mission.

KNOWHERE TO RUN

DOCKING BAY

MAP LEGEND

MISSION GIVERS

1 Cosmo ("Knowhere to Run")
2 The Collector ("Power Full")
3 Yondu ("Out of the Frying Pan...")
4 Yondu ("...Into the Fire")

CHALLENGES

4 Vs. Mode: Docking Bay
10 Knowhere Fast
11 Intruder Alert
12 Galactic Games

RECOMMENDED HERO: GAMORA

Mission Giver: Cosmo
Type: Combat
Rewards: 75 Blue Sparks, Sakaaran Foot Soldier

Under Ronan's order to retrieve the infinity gem, the Sakaarans attack Knowhere. The Sakaarans are your main enemies in the Guardians of the Galaxy Play Set, and in this mission you get to practice combat moves on the Sakaaran Foot Soldiers and their drop pods. Don't waste a prime opportunity to let Gamora go sword-to-sword with the first foes to invade Knowhere.

Pick up the Nova Crossover Coin to your left and open the door to the Docking Bay. Speak with Cosmo and he asks you to intercept the incoming Sakaarans before they deactivate Knowhere's shields and bring in a whole invasion fleet.

Sakaaran Foot Soldiers will come at you with big blades and big muscles. Dodge any swings in your direction, and wield your own blade with precision. Cut apart each Sakaaran as soon as you have an opportunity to strike from the side or rear. If you don't have time to dodge, block and counterattack.

DOCKING BAY (LOWER LEVEL)

Once you defeat the Foot Soldiers on the lower deck, omni-blaster turrets spring up to guard the ramp to the upper level. The laser turret sensors sweep the area, and if you're caught in the green scan field, the turrets open fire. Wait for the scan field to sweep past, then charge in and destroy the turrets with one or two power thrusts.

Continue up the ramp and demolish the remaining omni-blaster turrets. More drop pods descend on the upper level. When a drop pod first touches down, you have a second to destroy the pod and prevent the Sakaaran inside from exiting. Try to destroy as many drop pods as you can to lessen the number of foes you have to fight.

Tear through the last of the Sakaarans to complete your second mission. You've saved the station for the time being, but there are more challenges ahead, and many more battles that will require all the Guardians' talents to triumph.

GUARDIANS OF THE GALAXY ENEMIES

SAKAARAN FOOT SOLDIER (BLASTER)

The base version of a Sakaaran, equipped with a laser gun that delivers minor damage. Once you gain a level or two, pushing around these guys won't be a problem.

SAKAARAN FOOT SOLDIER (SWORD)

Like the blaster-equipped version of the Foot Soldier, these Sakaarans aren't that strong but wield a sword that can sting in combat if you let them get close enough.

FLYING SAKAARAN

These Sakaarans take to the air and prove a nuisance for ground-based heroes. Air Attacks and ranged fire are the way to go to knock them down.

SAKAARAN GUNNER

Tougher than the Foot Soldier and armed with a laser cannon that hurts if you get scorched by one. You will have to land several blows to vaporize these enemies.

LARGE SAKAARAN

The most powerful Sakaaran resembles a tank on legs. Keep your distance from this brute and deal as much ranged damage as possible. Of course they shoot a devastating laser beam from their visor, so stay on the move.

SCARAB

Small and skittery, these robots will attempt to swarm you. Certain Scarabs spawned by Large Sakaarans can explode and deal unexpected damage to you.

LET'S BE CLEAR

RECOMMENDED HERO: GROOT

Mission Giver: Cosmo
Type: Combat
Rewards: 100 Blue Sparks

It's time to bring in Groot to clean up the debris blocking the Docking Bay bridges. As powerful as Groot may be, he can't bash his way through the debris. You need to pick up a fuel cell from the illuminated conduits on the floor and hurl the fuel cell at the debris. Upon contact, the fuel cell explodes and removes the first barrier.

Cross the bridge and engage the Sakaarans guarding the next platform. With Groot's long reach, you shouldn't have too much trouble sweeping the Sakaarans aside and pulverizing anyone that tries to get back up.

Grab a fuel cell from next to the crates and throw it at the ship. Three fuel cell hits will send the ship spinning out of control, only to detonate on the deck below. After the ship burns up in a fiery poof, let Groot give one of his huge grins and enjoy another mission accomplished.

Before you can reach safety, however, one of the Sakaaran fighters hovers in front of the exit and opens fire on you. Run away from the ship and duck behind the stack of crates to the right. Hide there until the ship pauses and reloads.

New Challenge Available: Vs. Mode: Docking Bay

SIDE MISSIONS

SENTINEL SKIRMISH

CENTRAL OPERATION TOWER

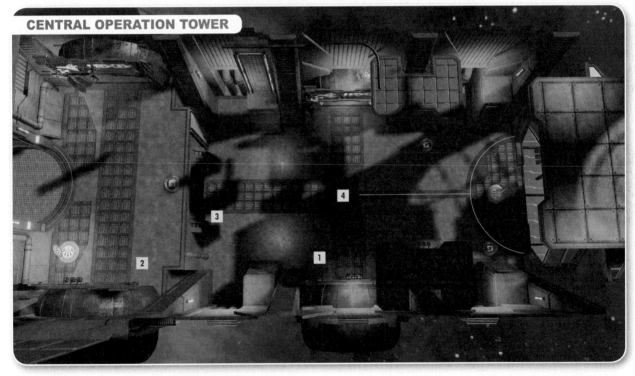

MAP LEGEND

MISSION GIVERS

1 The Collector ("Sentinel Skirmish")
2 Cosmo ("Pest Control")
3 The Collector ("Metal Detection")
4 Yondu ("Launch Time")

RECOMMENDED HERO: DRAX

Mission Giver: The Collector
Type: Combat
Rewards: 250 Blue Sparks, Sakaaran Omni-Blaster Turret

Drax can take a hit or two, so when The Collector needs someone to knock out surveillance sentinels—heavily armed sentinels, that is—volunteer the guy who is big, brave, and bald. With a little timing, Drax can easily knife each one of the surveillance sentinels without any return fire.

Exit to the Docking Bay, look for the first surveillance sentinel, and avoid its sweeping green scan. As the scan circles around, wait for it to pass your position and then sprint for the sentinel. Rip through the sentinel with your blades before the scan completes its full rotation and you won't even take a minor burn.

HERO TIP: ROCKET RACCOON

Drax may be smooth with his moves and whirling blades, but Rocket makes up for his small strides by blasting sentinels from afar.

Your second objective marker points below the main deck to a secret area. Creep to the edge and peer over until you see a section of landing that you can drop down onto and not plummet out into space. Quickly move toward the second sentinel and tear it apart before it can fire.

 Feat Complete: **Eureka!**

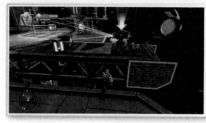

Another sentinel guards the far end of the secret area. Take a running start and double-jump over the large gap to the sentinel's platform before its scan registers a threat. Destroy the turret and take the elevator back up to the main deck.

Follow the ramp up to the top level. Halfway up the ramp stands the fourth sentinel. As with the others, charge up as the scan sweeps away from you and turn it to scrap metal before its laser can fire.

The final sentinel defends the far end of the top platform. Rush around and skewer it before the scan locks on to you. With the *Dark Aster* looming in the background, it's a grim reminder that you may have dismantled these Sakaaran devices, but there are many more to go.

POWER FULL

RECOMMENDED HERO: ROCKET RACCOON

Mission Giver: The Collector
Type: Delivery
Rewards: 150 Blue Sparks

The Collector needs you to power up his delivery alert systems, which requires two fuel cells to be inserted in the nearby power station. Run over to the glowing blue dispenser farthest from the station and pick up the fuel cell there. Carry it over to the station and insert it. You'll hear the gears winding down. You only have a few seconds to insert the second fuel cell.

Run over to the dispenser closest to the station and retrieve the second fuel cell. Hurry back to the station and plug it into the machine before time runs out. Just like that you've completed another mission!

LIVING DANGEROUSLY

PEST CONTROL

LIVING QUARTERS

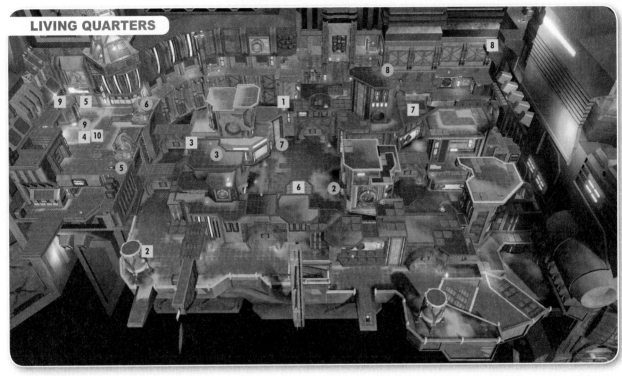

MAP LEGEND

MISSION GIVERS

1	The Collector ("Power Outage")		**6**	The Collector ("Cosmic Creatures")
2	The Collector ("Spy Sweep")		**7**	The Collector ("Rockin' Ronan")
3	Cosmo ("Miner Catastrophe")		**8**	The Collector ("What's Yours is Mine's")
4	Cosmo ("Drop Everything!")		**9**	The Collector ("Free Your Mine")
5	Cosmo ("Time for Paws")		**10**	Yondu ("To Peace in a Pod")

CHALLENGES

2	Space Station Sprint		**8**	You're the Collector!
3	Vs. Mode: Living Quarters		**9**	Space Pace
5	Munitions Expert			
6	Shooting Gallery			
7	Path of Destruction			

RECOMMENDED HERO: STAR-LORD

Mission Giver: Cosmo
Type: Combat
Rewards: 150 Blue Sparks

Cosmo opens the access gate to the Living Quarters zone at the beginning of this mission. Enter and look to the upper platforms for Sakaarans who are causing havoc to the locals. The first drop pod zone lies on the platform to your right. Climb up the rails, dismantle the omni-blaster turret on the midpoint landing, then climb the pole to the upper platform. Run for the initial drop pod and release a flurry of attacks as a new drop pod lands. Remember, if you destroy a drop pod quickly, you will prevent the Sakaaran from exiting and attacking you in combat.

After dealing with the first Sakaaran group, look for the second group on the next platform over. Jump off the side and glide with Star-Lord's Boot Jets until you sail over to the glowing blue poles. Climb up either of the poles to the top platform and engage the Sakaarans. Drift over to the third group once there are no more moving targets up on your current platform. You can sail across a large section of the Living Quarters and climb up the rails to destroy the third group as you did to the first two.

CO-OP COMBO: STAR-LORD AND GAMORA

These two make a great team in combat and will dispatch large Sakaaran groups more efficiently than a single hero can. Both can shoot at range, or work together side by side to knock out adversaries.

Follow the yellow objective marker and make your way to the fourth Sakaaran group. Climb up to the top of the platform and charge for the drop pod. As soon as you destroy the lone drop pod, the mission completes and any remaining Sakaarans are instantly destroyed.

New Challenge Available: You're The Collector!

THEMED POWER DISCS

Each of the Play Sets has its own hexagonal Power Discs that can give your play experience a whole new level of entertainment. Want a breathtaking view of the entire galaxy? Pick up The Rip, a Guardians of the Galaxy-themed Power Disc. Playing around in the Toy Box and want to create your own worlds? Boost your textures with surfaces and objects inspired by Groot when you pick up the Power Disc Groot's Roots. Look for the special themes tied to each Play Set, or mix them up for customizable heaven.

SIDE QUESTS

POWER OUTAGE

RECOMMENDED HERO: GAMORA

Mission Giver: The Collector
Type: Delivery
Rewards: 250 Blue Sparks

The security monitor feed in the Living Quarters is down and The Collector needs it activated again. Speak to him in the Living Quarters area, and he assigns you the task of plugging two fuel cells into nearby sockets.

Pick up a new fuel cell and double-jump out onto the first movable platform. Quickly double-jump to the second movable platform and dunk the fuel cell into the socket on the wall as you pass by.

HERO TIP: STAR-LORD

Having trouble with jumps? Recruit Star-Lord and let his Boot Jets glide you farther on a jump. Getting to those sockets won't be an issue any longer.

Use the jump disk on the same platform as The Collector to reach the nearby, higher platform. Look for the yellow objective marker and jump down towards it. Pick up a fuel cell from the dispenser near the platform's edge and carry it over to the right to plug into another socket. This activates the movable platforms.

Return to pick up another fuel cell and activate the movable platforms again. Grab a new fuel cell, double-jump out to the far platform, and turn to face the wall at the end. As you move towards that far wall, position yourself into the middle of the platform and jump up at the last second before the movable platform disappears into the wall slot. If you time it just right, you can slam the fuel cell into the second socket, crank up the security monitor feed, and finish off the mission.

New Challenge Available: Path of Destruction

SPY SWEEP

RECOMMENDED HERO: ROCKET RACCOON

Mission Giver: The Collector
Type: Combat
Rewards: 250 Blue Sparks

More surveillance sentinels have been placed around the Living Quarters, and The Collector wants them removed—pronto! Rocket's up for the task with his smaller (and harder to hit) frame and twin (easier to hit with) Quantum Cannons. There are six sentinels scattered about the Living Quarters, with the first one a short climb up the nearby rails. Sneak up on the first sentinel from above and either drop down and punch it out of existence or shoot it up from above.

You can spot the next surveillance sentinel easily from the first location. Follow the yellow objective marker up to the platforms on your left and destroy that sentinel before moving on to the third. Descend the platforms and, much like you did with the first, attack the third sentinel from above.

Wipe out the fourth with your Quantum Cannons as you cross its platform, and climb a series platforms to get in range to blow the fifth sentinel apart.

Finally, look for the sixth sentinel across the Living Quarters. It's partially hidden under an overhang, so drop down and quickly fire on it as it swings its sensor around to you. When it explodes, you complete the mission and secure some peace and quiet for The Collector's citizens.

 New Challenge Available: Space Station Sprint

MAJOR PROBLEMS IN THE MINER ZONE

MINER CATASTROPHE

RECOMMENDED HERO: GROOT
Mission Giver: Cosmo
Type: Combat
Rewards: 150 Blue Sparks

Seek out Cosmo for your next main mission to stop the Sakaarans from overrunning the new Anti-Air Gun he just installed. His mission giver hologram is on the platform above the Mining Zone access gate. After you receive the mission, drop down and pick up a fuel cell from the nearby dispenser. Toss the fuel cell into the socket on the other side of the gate to activate the elevator.

Ride the elevator up to the platform above. Step out in the middle of the platform and you complete the mission. However, this is only the prelude to the harder mission ahead.

DROP EVERYTHING!

RECOMMENDED HERO: STAR-LORD
Mission Giver: Cosmo
Type: Defend
Rewards: 150 Blue Sparks, The Mini Milano

Now it's time to defend Knowhere with Cosmo's giant Anti-Air Gun. If you can power it up, that is. Glancing around quickly, there appear to be no fuel cells in the area.

Use the blue poles behind Cosmo to climb up to the series of platforms that lead to the roof of a sealed room. Jump through the hole in the roof to enter the sealed room, only to discover a fuel cell dispenser. Assuming you've been running around all the areas, exploring this hidden area might also complete the "All Access Pass" feat for you.

 Feat Complete: All Access Pass

Carry two fuel cells back to the Anti-Air Gun and shove them in the sockets to get the big weapon started. As soon as you do, the first wave of Sakaaran ships begins the attack. Hold the trigger to bombard the skies with laser fire and target Sakaaran ships as they fly by. Once you get one in your sights, don't pull away until you've brought the ship down.

GAME BASICS · CHARACTERS · POWER DISCS · MARVEL'S THE AVENGERS · SPIDER-MAN · GUARDIANS OF THE GALAXY · TOY BOX · TOY BOX COLLECTION · ACHIEVEMENTS

103

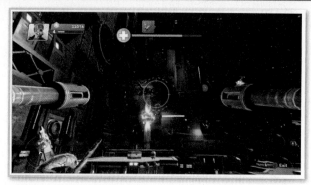

The Sakaarans will damage you by releasing energy balls that float down to the base. If the energy ball strikes a platform, the resulting explosion deals heavy damage to your Anti-Air Gun. Four such explosions will do you in. You can, however, shoot the energy ball as it's descending to eliminate the threat.

After you vanquish the first wave, a second wave of Sakaaran ships attacks. Midway through this wave you should complete the "Enemy Down!" feat on your way toward victory. Blast the last Sakaaran ship out of your restricted air space and you save the Mining Zone. Plus, you show off Star-Lord's expertise with weapons of any size!

Feat Complete: Enemy Down!

New Challenge Available: Munitions Expert

— TIME FOR PAWS —

MINING ZONE

RECOMMENDED HERO: GAMORA

Mission Giver: Cosmo
Type: Combat
Rewards: 150 Blue Sparks, Scarab, Starblaster, Knowhere Omni-Blaster Turret

Bring in the agile Gamora to explore the new Mining Zone that Cosmo unlocks at the start of this mission. Look to the right of Cosmo for a floating Guardians token that gives you the Scarab Toy Box item and a floating Nova Crossover Coin near the wall. Use the blue rails on the wall to cross the gap and enter the main section of the Mining Zone.

As you land on the first platform in the main Mining Zone, a new enemy type—Scarabs—drops in and surrounds you. Keep the Scarabs away with a sweep of your sword and cut them down one by one as you dodge back and forth.

Perform a double-jump over the gap ahead and charge toward the omni-blaster turret in the center of the next platform. Take that out first, then engage the Flying Sakaarans. Use an Air Attack to knock them to the ground and then penetrate their defenses with melee strikes, or whip out your blaster and hit them at range. Just be careful because they can do the same to you. Once you defeat the Flying Sakaarans, collect the Iron Man Crossover Coin in the corner.

Return to the platform that held the Scarabs and look for a set of side platforms that stretch under active incinerators. Time your double-jumps across the platforms to avoid both incinerators and an omni-blaster turret on the third platform. Wait for the turret's scan to move away from the platforms, then watch as the first incinerator's exhaust flames die down. Quickly double-jump to the platform in front of the first incinerator and wait for the second incinerator's flames to die down. Move quickly again before the first incinerator's flames start back up. Then double-jump again and smash the omni-blaster turret.

Pick up the Iron Man Crossover Coin in the back of the far alcove and grab the fuel cell from its dispenser. Return to the main platform and shove the fuel cell in the lone socket there. This activates more machinery in the Mining Zone, and you can use the rising and falling platforms to reach deeper regions inside the zone.

Hop across the three circular platforms to the far ledge and pick up another Iron Man Crossover Coin. Turn to your left and jump onto a smaller circular platform that descends to a lower catwalk.

Creep to the edge and watch below. Two omni-blaster's scans trace the area. If you drop off and land right next to the closest turret, you can destroy it quickly and remain just out of reach from the second turret's scan. Once that scan passes, charge over to the second omni-blaster turret and blow it apart before it returns fire.

Spring over to the last platform to destroy one final omni-blaster turret. Once you do this, you can freely climb around the area without getting pelted by enemy laser fire. Return to the blue rails next to the incinerator and collect a Nova Crossover Coin as you climb the rails to the upper levels. Navigate the rail system until you reach a glowing blue pole that takes you up to the top of a square platform.

Cut through the two omni-blaster turrets that appear atop the platform, then go after the Flying Sakaarans. Rely on your blaster as you circle around the platform, avoiding the Sakaaran laser fire while providing accurate laser fire of your own. When you have no more targets, leap off the platform to the two small, circular platforms that rise and fall slowly.

Ride the second of the circular platforms up to a new level with an omni-blaster turret. Wait for the turret's scan to pass overhead, then jump up to the platform and quickly dispatch the turret. A second turret guards the next area. Jump on the horizontal blue rail and slide down to the turret before it can lock on to you. Rip the turret apart, then turn the corner and jump past two more incinerators. Climb up the final ledge and cut up the last omni-blaster turret that guards the entrance to Cosmo's control room corridor.

Grab the Guardians token that unlocks the Starblaster and earns you the "Ticket to Ride" feat. Now that you have access to the flying Starblaster, it's much easier to reach the higher platforms and balconies around Knowhere. Punch the access panel to the gate that opens into Cosmos' control room corridor.

 Feat Complete: **Ticket to Ride**

> **NOTE**
>
> Once you gain the Starblaster, the Guardians, who usually do all their travel on the ground, can now fly. Seek out a Starblaster at any of the Guardians' transportation request stations for a superior travel mode.

GAME BASICS

CHARACTERS

POWER DISCS

MARVEL'S THE AVENGERS

SPIDER-MAN

GUARDIANS OF THE GALAXY

TOY BOX

TOY BOX COLLECTION

ACHIEVEMENTS

Sakaarans line up at the control room gate trying to get in. They won't see you coming, so avoid the Scarabs that skitter down the corridor at you and pick up a fuel cell from the dispenser on the left side. Carry the fuel cell ahead to the socket on the left wall and jam it in. Knowhere omni-blaster turrets spring out of the corridor and unload on the backs of the Sakaarans. Before they can figure out what is happening, the defenses take out all the Sakaarans.

You finally get to meet Cosmo and discover he's a telepathic astronaut dog! Since you have a genetically engineered talking raccoon in your group, maybe that's not so weird after all. Cosmo is appreciative of your efforts to help him against the Sakaarans and introduces you to Yondu, who will be your main mission giver from here on out.

 Feat Complete: Canine Encounter

 New Challenge Available: Intruder Alert

WILD BLUE YONDU

RECOMMENDED HERO: DRAX

Mission Giver: Yondu
Type: Explore
Rewards: 150 Blue Sparks, Starfoil

LIVING QUARTERS (RAIL SLIDE VIEW)

Yondu immediately gives you this mission after you complete Cosmo's "Time For Paws." Enter the upper balcony of the Living Quarters and jump up on the green rail system that runs high above the main platforms below. Ride the green rail as it curves out to the right and then back to the left.

MAP LEGEND

CHALLENGES

1 Riding the Rails

Back on the main rail, wait until you reach the end of the first rail. Jump off to a short rail on the right, ride that to the end, then jump back to the left onto the main rail system again as it corkscrews down around a support post.

On the next stretch, look to jump on a short rail to the right if you need the Guardians token that unlocks the Starfoil. Jump over to that rail, grab the coin, and immediately jump back to the main rail before you crash into the end post.

HERO TIP: GAMORA

Athletic Gamora is a fine pick to ride the rails. Her acrobatic flips can keep her on rails and avoid the energy spikes.

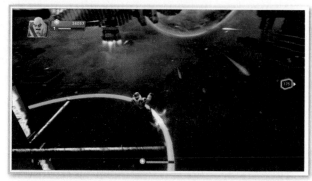

As you descend, jump over the red energy spikes in the rail. These will derail you if you run into them. Leap over three energy spikes as you wind down to the next straightaway.

Now comes the hardest part. Jump over a final energy spike and then jump to the left off the current rail before it ends and land on the new rail. Execute a series of rapid jumps to clear the rest of the energy spikes, including one more rail-to-rail jump, and reach the deck near the Mining Zone entrance.

Yondu makes an explosive entrance near the Mining Zone gate. He tells you that Ronan's weakness is his ship, the *Dark Aster*, and Yondu has a plan to take out Ronan once and for all.

New Challenge Available: Riding the Rails

SIDE MISSIONS

COSMIC CREATURES

RECOMMENDED HERO: ROCKET RACCOON

Mission Giver: The Collector
Type: Escort
Rewards: 250 Blue Sparks

The shock wave from a Sakaaran blast has jostled open one of The Collector's vaults and three rare creatures have escaped. Why not send another rare creature, Rocket Raccoon, out looking for them? The first one is easy to track down. Look over the edge from The Collector's platform and you'll see it on the bottom level of the Living Quarters. Jump down and grab it before the creature can scurry away.

Carry the creature into the Central Operation Tower. Follow the yellow objective marker and deposit it on the walkway where it will be safe.

HERO TIP: GROOT

Groot's long reach can scoop up the creatures that try to scurry away from you, and his gentle nature will keep the creatures safe.

Head back into the Living Quarters and pick up the second creature. The drop-off point is the same spot in the Central Operation Tower as the first. The third creature wanders the Docking Bay. Collect it from the upper level and bring it back to the Central Operation Tower for another successful mission completion.

ROCKIN' RONAN

RECOMMENDED HERO: STAR-LORD

Mission Giver: The Collector
Type: Combat
Rewards: 250 Blue Sparks

Ronan has planted more surveillance sentinels around the area, and it's in The Collector's best interest (and yours) if you remove them before they can spy on your every move.

Drop off The Collector's platform and head for the nearby blue access gate. Be careful, though—the first sentinel's scan will reach out past the gate and can lock on to you before the gate even opens. Burst through the gate as it automatically opens and destroy the first sentinel on the left with your ranged blaster fire.

Two more sentinels guard the next access gate. Wait until their scans sweep away from you and charge for the nearest one. Open fire with your pistols and destroy one sentinel after the other.

Don't go through the access gate; the final two sentinels are on the ledge above you. Look for the blue poles to your left. Climb up one of the poles and immediately blast away at the closest sentinel after you pull yourself up on the ledge. Once the fourth sentinel is down, turn toward the fifth sentinel, wait for its scan to rotate away from you, and cross the ledge to destroy it. Ronan's "eyes" on you go dead and The Collector rewards you with some blue Sparks at mission's end.

WHAT'S YOURS IS MINE'S

RECOMMENDED HERO: GAMORA

Mission Giver: The Collector
Type: Delivery
Rewards: 250 Blue Sparks

Jump in a Starblaster and fly up to the ledge in the corner where The Collector offers you this mission. Make sure your Starblaster lands on the ledge with you, and after you accept the mission, jump back in the Starblaster and hover up to the ledge above. Now you have an easier route to recovering a rare item for The Collector.

Go through the nearby doors and turn left. Follow the corridor to a sealed gate. Open the gate to enter the Mining Zone and drop down to a series of platforms stretching under two big incinerators. Time your jumps to pass by the incinerators when the exhaust flames aren't blasting out.

Pick up the fuel cell in the dispenser after the second incinerator. Ride the horizontal rail by the third incinerator and then use the two rising-and-falling circular platforms to reach the larger square platform. Cross that platform and double-jump to a second platform where a pile of debris in the corner hides The Collector's item. Toss the fuel cell at the debris to destroy it and The Collector gets his rare item and you complete another side mission!

FREE YOUR MINE

RECOMMENDED HERO: DRAX

Mission Giver: The Collector
Type: Delivery
Rewards: 250 Blue Sparks, Flying Sakaaran

The power grid is offline in the mines, and since The Collector uses the mine for a smuggling route, he wants the grid back online. Sign up Drax to go hunt down a fuel cell and shove it in the mine's main socket. First, drop down off The Collector's platform and enter the Mining Zone access gate. As you did earlier, climb across the blue rails on the right wall and open the gate to the main section of the Mining Zone.

Use the platforms that lead under the incinerators and cross them without getting burned to reach the alcove with the fuel cell dispenser. Pick up the fuel cell and retrace your steps back to the main platforms.

Follow the yellow objective marker down to the socket. Use the three large circular rising-and-falling platforms to eventually get down to the lower catwalk with the socket. It's also possible to jump off the second circular platform and land directly on the socket catwalk if you're careful. Plug in the fuel cell to the socket, and, just like that, The Collector's smuggling operation is back on and you're a little bit wealthier.

PEST BEHAVIOR

COSMO'S CONTROL ROOM

MAP LEGEND

MISSION GIVERS

1 Cosmo ("Pest Behavior")
2 Cosmo ("Tough Cell")
3 Cosmo ("Disruptive Behavior")

RECOMMENDED HERO: GROOT

Mission Giver: Cosmo
Type: Combat
Rewards: 250 Blue Sparks, Sakaaran Gunner

Cosmo warns you that Sakaarans have invaded the Living Quarters again in force. You can spot the first group through the window next to Cosmo. Enter the Living Quarters and climb to this first platform. When you reach the top, sprint for the omni-blaster turret in the middle and remove that first. Go after the Sakaarans next, either pulverizing them with your huge wooden fists or sweeping them over the edge.

Continue around the Living Quarters following the objective markers to each Sakaaran group. With each encounter, attack the omni-blaster turret so it doesn't gun you down and then out-flank the other Sakaarans as you bash them with your bruising melee attacks.

The final group is a big one. Fight them off as they swarm around you, and if you get knocked over the edge, climb back up via the blue poles to try again. With Groot's strength, you will bash through them all and claim the Living Quarters back for the citizens of Knowhere.

HERO TIP: STAR-LORD

Star-Lord's Boot Jets come in handy moving around the Living Quarters, and his pistols can pick off targets before they reach him.

CO-OP COMBO: GROOT AND ROCKET RACCOON

Always partners, these two complement each other with Groot's formidable melee attacks and Rocket's fearsome ranged attacks. Any of the larger fights in the Living Quarters can use any extra pair of hands in combat.

TO THE DARK ASTER

— COOL MINERS FODDER —

RECOMMENDED HERO: ROCKET RACCOON

Mission Giver: Yondu
Type: Delivery
Rewards: 150 Blue Sparks

POD GARAGE

Yondu explains his plan to you: Ronan's ship is vulnerable, and the only way to defeat your foe is to fly a mining pod to the *Dark Aster*. Yondu needs a mining pod powered up, and you can do this with fuel cells, sockets, and nimble hairy feet.

MAP LEGEND

MISSION GIVERS

1 Yondu ("Cool Miners Fodder")

Jump back to the fuel cell dispenser and pick up your second fuel cell. Jump back over the track and stick the fuel cell in the second socket; the track extends further. Return to the dispenser and get your third fuel cell. Jump back to the third socket and stick in the fuel cell to drop the final blockade.

The mining pod moves along the glowing blue track in the Pod Garage. However, you want to corral it to the far platform where Yondu can access it. Open the first gate by picking up the fuel cell and stuffing it in the socket next to the first "X" blockade. When you do, the blockade drops and a new track opens.

Wait for the mining pod to follow the blue track to the end. Once it moves over to the far platform, Yondu gets in and sets up a series of missions to protect the pod.

GAME BASICS · CHARACTERS · POWER DISCS · MARVEL'S THE AVENGERS · SPIDER-MAN · GUARDIANS OF THE GALAXY · TOY BOX · TOY BOX COLLECTION · ACHIEVEMENTS

TO PEACE IN A POD

RECOMMENDED HERO: GAMORA

Mission Giver: Yondu
Type: Defend
Rewards: 200 Blue Sparks, Large Sakaaran

Yondu has the mining pod, and the Sakaarans know it. They send an assault team to destroy the pod, and it's up to you to stop the massacre. After you speak with Yondu in the pod, you immediately man the Anti-Air Gun and the enemies starting dropping in.

Try to blow up the drop pods as soon as they appear to prevent Sakaarans from exiting and attacking Yondu's mining pods. Sweep over the platform and rain down heavy laser fire on any enemies that escape drop pods.

Large Sakaarans will appear on the ledges above the mining pod. Continue hammering each one with laser fire until it explodes. Don't let the Large Sakaarans concentrate their laser beams on the mining pod or it will take heavy damage. After defeating the Large Sakaarans, return to the main platform and eliminate the Sakaarans and omni-blaster turrets that spawn.

 Feat Complete: Tanked

A Sakaaran ship shows up last. It will drop energy balls down on the mining pod to try and finish it off. Protect the mining pod by shooting the energy balls before they land. Once you've destroyed an energy ball, rotate up to the ship and get off some laser strikes on it. Continue repeating this process until the ship explodes and you complete the mission.

UP AND RUNNING

RECOMMENDED HERO: DRAX

Mission Giver: Yondu
Type: Escort
Rewards: 200 Blue Sparks, Short Ranged Drone

Yondu needs to drive the mining pods across the facility. The Sakaarans want to prevent that at all costs. Escort Yondu's mining pod as it drives slowly through the various access gates. Open each gate and then defend the mining pod in the following area from Sakaaran troops arriving in drop pods.

HERO TIP: ROCKET RACCOON

Use Rocket's Quantum Cannons to destroy foes at range, or at least stun them long enough to get into better position and keep the mining pod functioning that much longer.

The fights will be intense. The Sakaaran groups will contain a mix of troops, from Foot Soldiers up to Large Sakaarans. Rely on Drax's blades to rip apart most foes, and when you need a boost, tap into his Drax the Destroyer special ability to soup up his strength and attack speed.

CO-OP COMBO: DRAX AND GAMORA

Defending the mining pod is hard work, and it's much easier with two. Drax stays close to the pod, while Gamora can stray and strafe any ranged foes with her pistol shots.

Obstructions will stop the mining pod. Clear them, but only after you've defeated the enemies in the area first. It matters little if Yondu gets ahead of you if the Sakaarans continue to assault him.

Continue defending the mining pod as you near the Central Observation Tower. When you finally beat the final group and the last Large Sakaaran explodes in a burst of Sparks, guide the mining pod through the blue gate and into safety.

LAUNCH TIME

RECOMMENDED HERO: GROOT

Mission Giver: Yondu
Type: Escort
Rewards: 250 Blue Sparks, Sakaaran Omni-Missile Turret

Much like the last mission you must escort Yondu, but this time it's through the Docking Bay toward the launch pad. Groot's long reach will be a big plus as you sweep aside any foes that try to storm the mining pod. Race ahead of the mining pod and engage the first set of Sakaarans outside the access gate.

Follow the mining pod as it hovers along the path toward the far end of the Docking Bay. Use Groot's melee attacks to guard against the near foes, and send out his Burrowing Arm to strike targets at range.

When enemies surround the pod, use Groot's I Am Groot! special ability to grow and let loose a series of close-range attacks that will destroy all weaker foes and severely damage tougher foes. Wade into the remaining foes with your melee combo attacks to finish enemies still standing.

Once the gate opens, follow the mining pod up the ramp to the upper level. Scatter the Scarabs on the ramp, then stomp up to the top and crush the laser turrets one by one. Groot will take some hits here, but it's best to let the turrets focus on him rather than the mining pod. Clear the laser turrets quickly before turning your attention to the last group of Sakaarans.

Keep the Large Sakaarans off the mining pods. If you strike a Large Sakaaran enough, it will concentrate on you. Dodge often and use your I Am Groot! ability if you have enough purple Sparks to trigger it. You don't have to beat all the Sakaarans to complete the mission; as soon as Yondu pilots the mining pod to the launch pad area, the mission ends and all remaining enemies are destroyed.

OUT OF THE FRYING PAN...

RECOMMENDED HERO: STAR-LORD

Mission Giver: Yondu
Type: Defend
Rewards: 250 Blue Sparks

You get to play with the biggest gun on Knowhere in this mission to defend Yondu's mining pod. Like the previous Anti-Air Gun missions, you must shoot down waves of Sakaaran ships as they drop bombs and drain energy from the mining pod. However, your gun this time causes larger explosions and you can catch multiple enemy ships in the blasts much easier. Hit one enemy ship in a group and they all go up in flames!

As the first wave appears, watch the flight patterns and hold the trigger of your gun to warm it up. When the entire targeting circle is green, it's ready to fire a charged blast

that destroys most ships in a single hit and causes big explosions. Track an enemy ship and zap it when you're at full energy.

A second wave appears after you defeat the first wave. Be careful not to let any ships drop energy bombs on the deck. The bombs explode and deplete the mining pod's shields. Continue blasting away at the circling Sakaaran ships until the second wave ends.

The final wave begins much like the first two. Track ships and destroy them, hopefully chaining multiple explosions and eliminating multiple ships at once. The final enemy ship will be a large Sakaaran vessel, and it drains energy from the mining pod's shields very quickly. Charge up your weapon, aim at the ship, and when the targeting circle is green, let loose. Two hits will down the enemy ship and keep Yondu alive to finally take off for the *Dark Aster*.

Feat Complete: Man the Guns!

New Challenge Available: Knowhere Fast

GAME BASICS

CHARACTERS

POWER DISCS

MARVEL'S THE AVENGERS

SPIDER-MAN

GUARDIANS OF THE GALAXY

TOY BOX

TOY BOX COLLECTION

ACHIEVEMENTS

...INTO THE FIRE

RECOMMENDED HERO: STAR-LORD

Mission Giver: Yondu
Type: Explore
Rewards: 250 Blue Sparks

Yondu and the mining pod are a short trip up on the top of the launch pad. Climb the stairs and walk up the long launch pad to speak with Yondu. He asks you if you're ready to take the fight to Ronan and head off to the *Dark Aster*.

Jump in the mining pod and you fly straight through the space combat between Sakaaran ships and Knowhere defenses. Yondu pilots you through the battle, finds a hole in the *Dark Aster*'s hull, and crash-lands you on one of the *Dark Aster*'s abandoned decks. With your mining pod smoking, you might want to explore the *Dark Aster* and give the pod time to cool down before returning to Knowhere.

DEFEATING RONAN THE ACCUSER

UNWELCOME WAGON

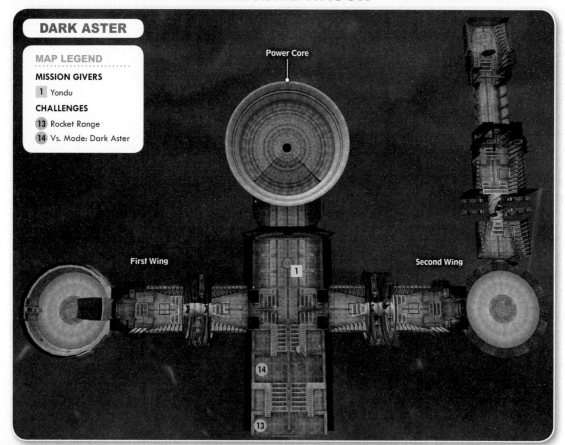

DARK ASTER

MAP LEGEND

MISSION GIVERS
1 Yondu

CHALLENGES
13 Rocket Range
14 Vs. Mode: Dark Aster

Power Core

First Wing

Second Wing

RECOMMENDED HERO: GROOT

Mission Giver: Yondu
Type: Combat
Rewards: 350 Blue Sparks, Kamikaze Drone

Step out of the crashed mining pod and look around the *Dark Aster*'s gloomy interior. Yondu stands on the other side of the deserted deck, and he tells you that the plan is to get through the huge bulkhead door nearby, but first you have to discover a power source for the bulkhead door.

DARK ASTER (FIRST WING)

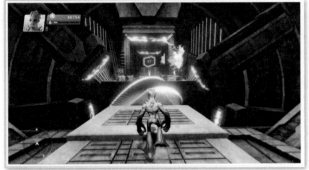

Turn around and head to the door on your right. It opens as you near and you can proceed through the next chamber. At the end of the platform you'll see a spinning drill with rods that generate electricity between the sides and the drill. Jump on the drill as one of the grooves comes up from the right side and run down the groove. If you get too close to falling off the left side, jump over the lighted edge to the next groove (avoiding getting electrocuted by random bolts of electricity) and finish off your run down that groove.

HERO TIP: ROCKET RACCOON

Rocket can hop across the spinning drill almost effortlessly, and his Quantum Cannons drive foes away in the power gun chamber.

Enter the large chamber at the end and prepare for a long battle. As the drop pods land, attack them immediately to minimize the number of enemies you will have fight. Use Groot's Burrowing Arm attack to strike at foes across the chamber and dodge close enemies with Groot's shuffle. Continue moving around the chamber, crushing Sakaarans with your sweeping melee attacks, until you deal with all of the enemy waves.

CO-OP COMBO: GROOT AND DRAX

If you want to maul your opponents, these are the two Guardians to do it. Team up to melee through the waves of Sakaaran troops that try to stop you in the power weapon chamber.

The lights shut off when you beat the final Sakaaran, and the power gun glows in the middle of the chamber. Pick up the power gun and shoot a blast at the glowing circle in the wall. The blast powers up a panel that rises and reveals a symbol (three arrows pointing to the right). Turn around and shoot the circle on the opposite side. The panel rises and a strip on the wall begins to circle around the chamber.

The strip contains many symbols. Look for the same symbol as the door panel (three arrows pointing to the right) and zap that symbol with your power gun. The symbol glows and when it rotates into the door panel, the symbol unlocks a hidden panel that reveals the corridor back to the main deck.

Retrace your steps over the spinning drill and back to Yondu. Destroy two new laser turrets on the way and show off your new power weapon to the Guardians' crew.

 New Challenge Available: Rocket Range

GAME BASICS   CHARACTERS   POWER DISCS   MARVEL'S THE AVENGERS   SPIDER-MAN   **GUARDIANS OF THE GALAXY**   TOY BOX   TOY BOX COLLECTION   ACHIEVEMENTS

113

DOOR AND PIECE

DARK ASTER (SECOND WING)

RECOMMENDED HERO: ROCKET RACCOON

Mission Giver: Yondu
Type: Combat
Rewards: 400 Blue Sparks

After speaking with Yondu, pick up the power gun and aim it at the circle in front of you. One blast powers up the circle, which opens the door to the next wing. Your mission: To retrieve the key that opens the bulkhead door.

Enter the new wing and continue straight ahead. Cross the spinning drill and take out the two laser turrets guarding the chamber beyond.

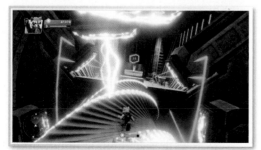

As you approach the center of the chamber, the door slides closed and Sakaarans ambush you. Stay on the move and keep firing. Circle the room, choose a target, unload on that target till it explodes, then choose another target. It's a long battle, but one that you can win with Rocket if you stay out of all-out melee combat.

HERO TIP: GAMORA

If you want melee mixed with ranged combat, you can take Gamora into this battle. Her guns aren't as good as Rocket's, but her fists are better.

Like last mission's door puzzle, this chamber has rotating symbols that unlock the way out: only this time there are three. Shoot each panel circle with the power gun to activate it, then shoot that row's symbol that matches the symbol to unlock the door. Once all three activated symbols rotate into place, the panel slides up and reveals the exit.

Carry the power gun with you, jump over another spinning drill, and engage the enemies on the next corridor. Aim at the Large Sakaaran and rip it apart quickly with the power gun. Unfortunately, the battery supply doesn't last long on the power gun; destroy as many enemies as you can with it, then switch to your Quantum Cannons.

Dodge back and forth in the corridor as you fire away with your Quantum Cannons. Avoid melee with the Large Sakaarans; when they near, dodge and head to the opposite end of the corridor. Continue blasting away, eliminating the other Sakaarans, until only the Large Sakaarans are left. It will take you several back-and-forth trips across the corridor to vaporize them all.

When the last Sakaaran slumps, the seal at the end of the corridor rises and reveals the bulkhead door key. You've just unlocked the key to entering Ronan's inner chamber.

DOOR BUSTERS

RECOMMENDED HERO: GAMORA

Mission Giver: Yondu
Type: Combat
Rewards: 500 Blue Sparks

Pick up the key to the bulkhead door and carry it back toward the main deck. You will have to drop it any time enemies attack; after each fight, pick it back up and continue your journey.

Square off against any foes that block your path. Use Gamora's formidable melee moves to deal damage, then flip out of harm's way with her dodge. Most enemies, even the Large Sakaaran, won't stand up long to her punishment.

An explosion rips through the complex in the next area and the spinning drill speeds up. Carefully carry the key across, jumping from groove to groove as you avoid hitting the ceiling with the key and getting caught by a stray electricity bolt. Continue ahead and enter the large circular chamber.

Head immediately to the center of the chamber and collect the power gun. Charge up and begin zapping everything in sight. If you stick to the power gun, you can clear the chamber in seconds instead of the minutes it would take you with old flesh and bone.

Make your way through the final section back to the main deck. Laser turrets will lock on to you as you pass through the corridor; drop the key, cut through the laser turrets, then pick the key back up. After you jump across the final spinning drill and knock out the laser turret, the door opens back to the main deck and you plug in the key to unlock the door to the *Dark Aster*'s power core.

 New Challenge Available: Vs. Mode: Dark Aster

DARK ASTER DISASTER
DARK ASTER (POWER CORE)

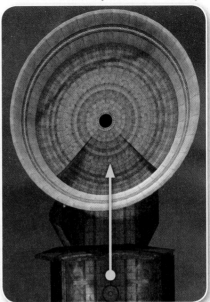

RECOMMENDED HERO: STAR-LORD

Mission Giver: Yondu
Type: Combat
Rewards: 0 Blue Sparks

It's time to go up against Ronan in the final battle! Enter the power core, grab a power gun from one of the dispensers on the floor, and shoot the power gun at the main energy stream. The power core overloads and seems to shut down the whole ship—until Ronan himself shows up to start the ship back up.

 Feat Complete: To the Depths

Ronan makes for a very difficult foe. First, he has a shield that protects him from all damage; you can't approach him, and you can't hit him directly with a ranged attack. Second, he summons forth scores of Sakaarans to defend the power core. It will be a challenge to move around the chamber without getting struck by enemy attacks. Third, Ronan can throw an earthquake attack at you; the floor ripples in a long strip and deals major damage if you get caught in the upheaval.

GAME BASICS

CHARACTERS

POWER DISCS

MARVEL'S THE AVENGERS

SPIDER-MAN

GUARDIANS OF THE GALAXY

TOY BOX

TOY BOX COLLECTION

ACHIEVEMENTS

The trick to beating Ronan is outsmarting him. You don't have to beat Ronan with damage; you need to beat him with your mind. There is another way to shut down the ship: overload it by powering up each of the sockets that rotate high overhead in the power core chamber. How do you do it? Shoot the power gun at Ronan's shield. It won't deal damage to him, but it will create an energy ball.

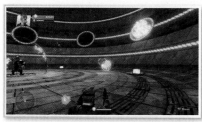

Now you have to get the energy ball into a socket. Shoot the energy ball with the power gun or your pistols—the energy ball will roll off across the chamber in the opposite direction. Put enough force behind it and the energy ball reaches the upper section of the power core. Start up multiple energy balls and get them rolling to increase your odds of them rolling into a socket.

HERO TIP: ROCKET RACCOON

Sub any of the other Guardians into the fight against Ronan if Star-Lord goes down. Rocket's Quantum Cannons can catapult the energy balls into the sockets as well.

Of course, you have the other Sakaarans to worry about too. In between creating energy balls, use the power gun to mow down Sakaarans. There is an endless supply of power guns around the chamber. If one runs out, run over to any dispenser and pick up a new one.

More and more Sakaarans arrive the madder Ronan gets. Continue circling around the chamber, alternating between energy balls and blasting Ronan's Sakaaran troops.

It gets crazy near the end, with energy balls, laser fire, and Sakaaran bodies all over the place. Don't stop until the final energy ball rolls into place. Standing still is a recipe for disaster.

When the last energy ball clicks into place, the power core overloads again and it takes all of Ronan's strength to keep the resulting explosion from destroying him. The weakened Ronan is no longer a threat, and you leave the *Dark Aster* content in knowing that Knowhere is safe for the time being.

Back on Knowhere, you discover that Yondu betrayed you. While you were busy saving the galaxy, he stole the infinity gem and sailed off to sell it for himself. What he doesn't know is that The Collector switched it with a decoy, and it wouldn't have mattered anyway since Ronan is hot on his trail. You get a good laugh at your old "friend," but now that you have new friends to explore the galaxy with—who needs him anyway.

Feat Complete: Accuser Diffuser

CROSSOVER COIN MISSIONS: IRON MAN

METAL DETECTION

RECOMMENDED HERO: IRON MAN

Mission Giver: The Collector
Type: Explore
Rewards: 250 Blue Sparks

SERVE AND DEFLECT

RECOMMENDED HERO: IRON MAN

Mission Giver: The Collector
Type: Combat
Rewards: 250 Blue Sparks

Once you collect all ten Iron Man Crossover Coins, Cosmo and The Collector need Iron Man's help in retrieving bio-scanners from the Mining Zone. After you speak with The Collector, follow the yellow objective markers and fly over to the Mining Zone. The first bio-scanner sits right next to the incinerators beside the entrance.

> **NOTE**
>
> Once you add either of the Crossover Coin heroes, Iron Man or Nova, you now have characters with flight. It's much easier to reach Knowhere's ledges and many different zones when you can fly. Use Iron Man or Nova to do your scouting, especially if you're looking for Bonus Boxes or mission givers.

The second bio-scanner rests on a platform way below the first bio-scanner. Look for the yellow objective marker and fly down to the new platform. Walk over and collect your second scanner after you're done sightseeing.

Rise straight up from the second bio-scanner and you'll spy the third scanner. Look for it inside the circular tower with the open roof. You have to drop inside the tower to retrieve it. Then blast out of there to the opposite side of the Mining Zone and land on the marked catwalk to gain the fourth bio-scanner.

The last bio-scanner is stationed on the opposite side of the tower from the fourth bio-scanner. Fly around to the other side of the tower and you'll see the bio-scanner on the back side of the catwalk. Fly down, scoop the bio-scanner up, and you complete the first Crossover Coin mission for The Collector.

Return to The Collector for the second mission. This time his hologram appears at the door to the Mining Zone that you used for the "What's Yours is Mine's" side mission. The Collector wants you to defend two bio-scanners under attack in the Mining Zone.

There are two platforms to defend divided by a large expanse of open air. Luckily, as Iron Man, you can fly back and forth between these two platforms as the Sakaarans appear to attack the bio-scanners. Shoot over to the platform where the Sakaaran drop pods land first. Wipe out the first wave, which is just a warm-up act for the larger waves to follow.

Now zip over to the second platform and defend it with everything you've got—which is quite a lot with the Iron Man suit. Use Pulse Bolts to knock around Sakaarans, especially Flying Sakaarans, Air Attacks can trip up foes, and your melee combos can pound enemies too. Missile Barrage should only be triggered when you think you can hit more than a single opponent or really need to destroy an enemy in a hurry. You can even pick up Sakaarans and heave them over the edge to their doom.

Keep going back and forth until you finish off the last of the drop pods. When there are no more Sakaarans to assault the bio-scanners, the area is secure and you're ready for your final Iron Man Crossover Coin mission.

AGGRESSOR ASSESSOR

RECOMMENDED HERO: IRON MAN

Mission Giver: The Collector
Type: Combat
Rewards: 250 Blue Sparks

Head back to the Central Operation Tower for the final side mission. The Collector needs bio-scans of each type of Sakaaran troop to better prepare Knowhere's defenses. Take off into the Living Quarters Zone and battle each Sakaaran group until you've catalogued them all.

Engage the first group of Sakaaran Foot Soldiers. Armed with blasters, these enemies can strike at you from range, but they aren't that durable in melee and your ranged attacks are much more destructive. Wipe them out quickly and move on to your second target.

The next foe is a bit more challenging: a Large Sakaaran. Don't try to trade punches with this brute. Instead, stay at range and unload with your Pulse Bolts or Missile Barrage. If you have to get in close, strike from the side, dodge, then get behind him and back up while firing more ranged damage. After a lot of damage, the Large Sakaaran will crumple and collapse into Sparks.

Follow the yellow objective marker to a side balcony that holds the Scarabs. Pick them off one by one from range, then zoom out to the Docking Bay for your fourth battle against Sakaaran Gunners. Move quickly as you mix Pulse Bolts with punches and dismantle your foes before they can mount much of a counterattack.

Fly up to the upper levels of the Docking Bay for your last two battles. First, power through the sword-armed Foot Soldiers on their platform. Next, zip over to the last platform and land amidst the falling drop pods that release Flying Sakaarans. Hit as many as you can while they're on the ground, then take to the air and trade ranged fire with them until the last of them plummets. With your final enemy bio-scan you complete The Collector's objectives and wrap up Iron Man's missions on Knowhere.

CROSSOVER COIN MISSIONS: NOVA

DISRUPTIVE BEHAVIOR

RECOMMENDED HERO: NOVA

Mission Giver: Cosmo
Type: Explore
Rewards: 250 Blue Sparks

Once you collect all ten Nova Crossover Coins, Cosmo has a set of three missions for Nova. Look for Cosmo atop the Central Operation Tower where he gives you the first mission to request your help disabling disruptors in the Mining Zone.

Fly to the Mining Zone and follow the yellow objective markers to each disruptor. The first resides on a lower platform, and you can spot a reddish energy glow emanating from the disruptor. Float down to it and detonate it with an Energy Blast.

Fly up to the second disruptor, burn it to the ground, then fly across to another platform a short distance away for the third disruptor. After exploding the third disruptor, look for the fourth disruptor on a high corner platform to your left.

The final disruptor lies down on a protruding catwalk below you. Fly down, trigger a couple of well-aimed Energy Blasts, and you complete your first Nova Crossover Coin mission.

TOUGH CELL

RECOMMENDED HERO: NOVA

Mission Giver: Cosmo
Type: Defend
Rewards: 250 Blue Sparks

Return to Cosmo atop the Central Operation Tower and pick up your second side mission. Fly out to the Docking Bay to prevent the Sakaarans from destroying the fuel cell dispensers out there that are critical to maintaining power to the defensive weapons. As soon as you accept the mission, the Sakaarans begin to attack and you have one minute to reach the scene or you fail the mission.

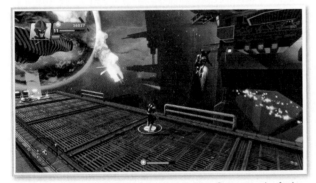

The Sakaarans will keep spawning in the area. Stay near the fuel cell dispenser and repel the Sakaarans with melee combos and ranged Energy Blasts. If the enemies begin to swarm around you, take to the sky and start knocking them over the edge with ranged fire.

When the final Sakaaran falls, you save the fuel cell dispenser. Wipe off the metal shards from your fallen foes and jet back to Cosmo for the third mission.

DROPPING IN

RECOMMENDED HERO: NOVA

Mission Giver: Cosmo
Type: Combat
Rewards: 250 Blue Sparks

Drop pods are now invading the Living Quarters. Cosmo sends you there to defend against the Sakaaran threat. Fly into the Living Quarters and zip from encounter to encounter as quickly as you can: You have five minutes to defeat every enemy. It's not going to be easy.

The first Sakaaran group guards a large platform to your left. Come in full speed in

their midst and knock some of them off their feet when you collide with the rooftop. Use your melee moves and ranged fire to clear the roof, then fly on to the next group.

Continue assaulting each group. Repeat your attack pattern at each site: land with an Air Attack, throw melee combos on the nearby foes, then flank out to avoid enemy damage and blast away at range. If you get in trouble at any point, trigger your Nova Core special ability to eliminate multiple foes at once.

Your final two foes will be Large Sakaarans. Avoid their devastating laser beams and circle around them to continually deal ranged damage. If you have to get in close, strike from the side or rear, then dodge back out of the way and return to your ranged fire. You are on the clock and don't have much time, so make sure you are getting in as much damage as possible on the Large Sakaaran as you dodge around. If you can burst apart both Large Sakaarans before the time runs out, you silence the Sakaarans in the Living Quarters and complete your Nova Crossover Coin missions for Cosmo.

GAME BASICS

CHARACTERS

POWER DISCS

MARVEL'S THE AVENGERS

SPIDER-MAN

GUARDIANS OF THE GALAXY

TOY BOX

TOY BOX COLLECTION

ACHIEVEMENTS

119

CROSSOVER COINS

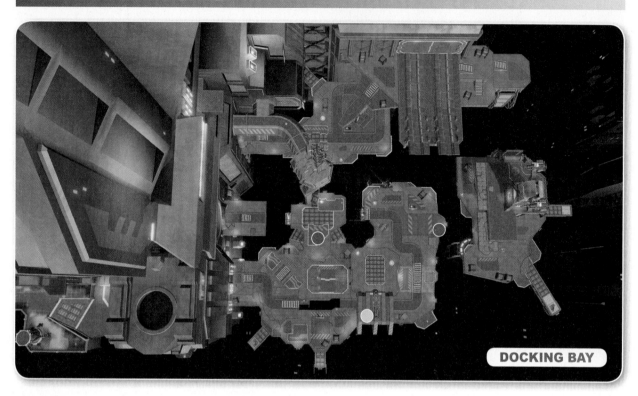

DOCKING BAY

○ Nova Crossover Coins
● Iron Man Crossover Coins

CENTRAL OPERATION TOWER

GAME BASICS

CHARACTERS

POWER DISCS

MARVEL'S THE AVENGERS

SPIDER-MAN

GUARDIANS OF THE GALAXY

TOY BOX

TOY BOX COLLECTION

ACHIEVEMENTS

LIVING QUARTERS

COSMO'S CONTROL ROOM

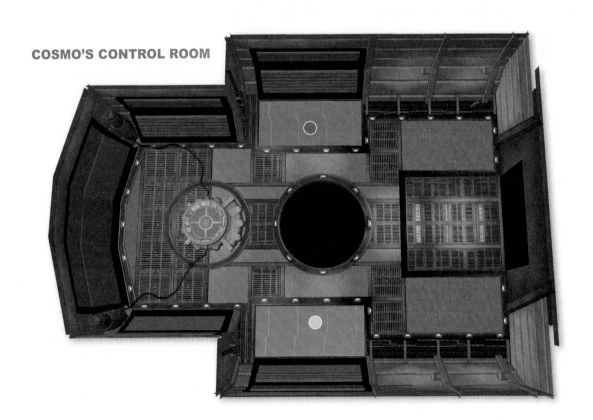

MINING ZONE

- Nova Crossover Coins
- Iron Man Crossover Coins

TECH BONUS BOXES

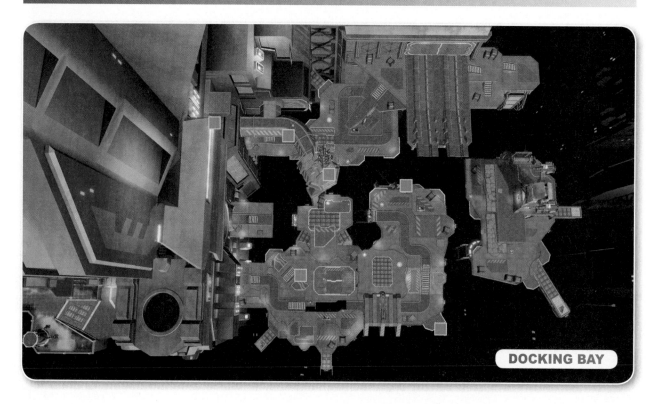

DOCKING BAY

GAME BASICS

CHARACTERS

POWER DISCS

MARVEL'S THE AVENGERS

SPIDER-MAN

GUARDIANS OF THE GALAXY

TOY BOX

TOY BOX COLLECTION

ACHIEVEMENTS

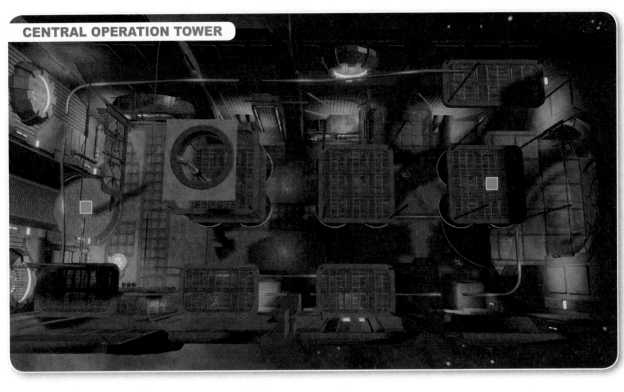

CENTRAL OPERATION TOWER

■ Tech Bonus Boxes

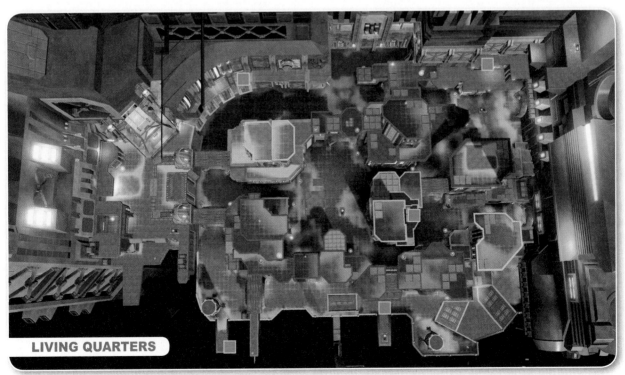

LIVING QUARTERS

MINING ZONE

■ Tech Bonus Boxes

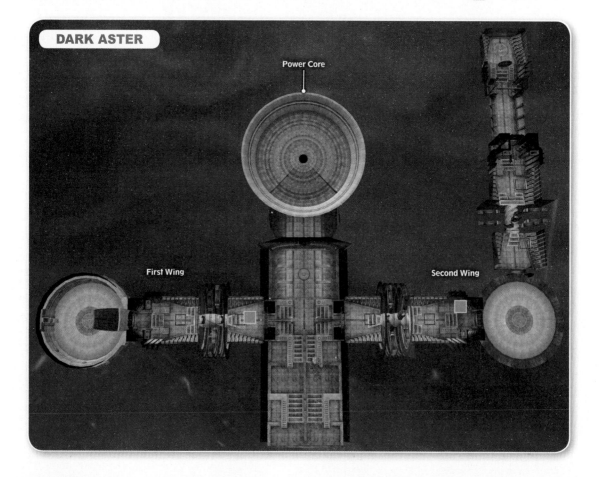

DARK ASTER

Power Core

First Wing

Second Wing

WALL CRAWL BONUS BOXES

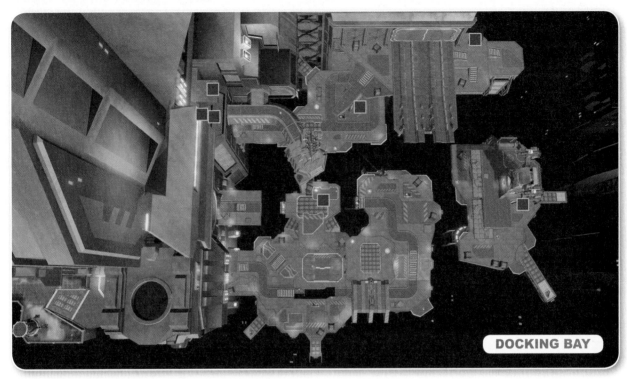

DOCKING BAY

■ Wall Crawl Bonus Boxes

CENTRAL OPERATION TOWER

GAME BASICS

CHARACTERS

POWER DISCS

MARVEL'S THE AVENGERS

SPIDER-MAN

GUARDIANS OF THE GALAXY

TOY BOX

TOY BOX COLLECTION

ACHIEVEMENTS

LIVING QUARTERS

Wall Crawl Bonus Boxes

MINING ZONE

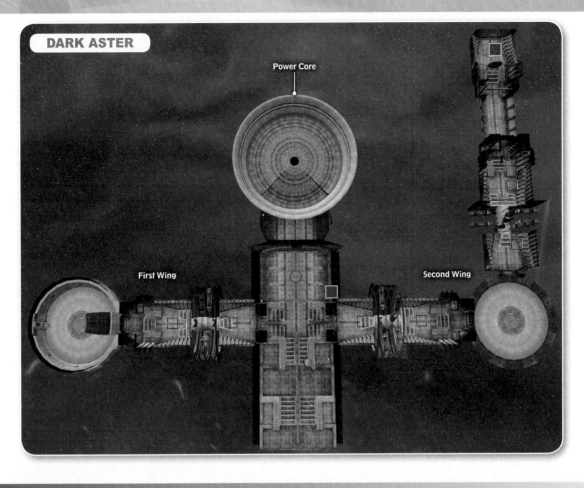

DARK ASTER

Power Core

First Wing

Second Wing

FLIGHT BONUS BOXES

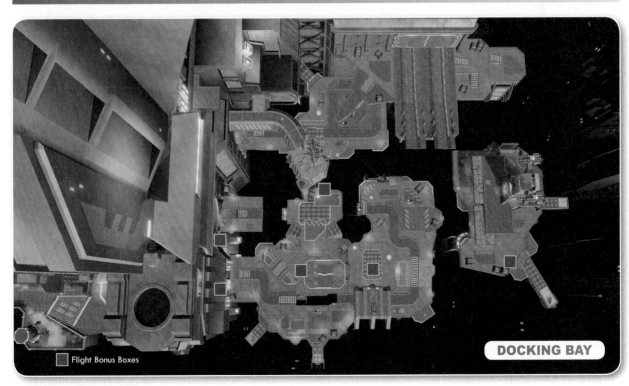

☐ Flight Bonus Boxes

DOCKING BAY

GAME BASICS

CHARACTERS

POWER DISCS

MARVEL'S THE AVENGERS

SPIDER-MAN

GUARDIANS OF THE GALAXY

TOY BOX

TOY BOX COLLECTION

ACHIEVEMENTS

CENTRAL OPERATION TOWER

■ Flight Bonus Boxes

LIVING QUARTERS

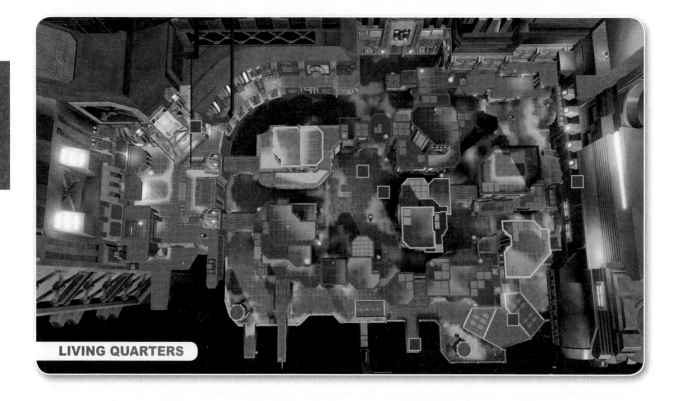

MINING ZONE

DARK ASTER

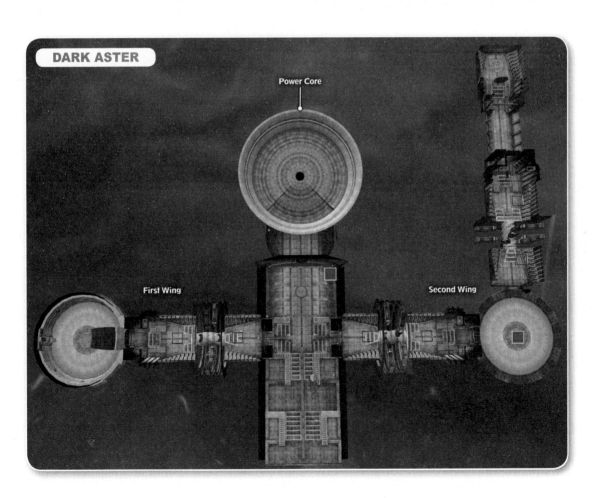

Power Core

First Wing

Second Wing

SUPER JUMP BONUS BOXES

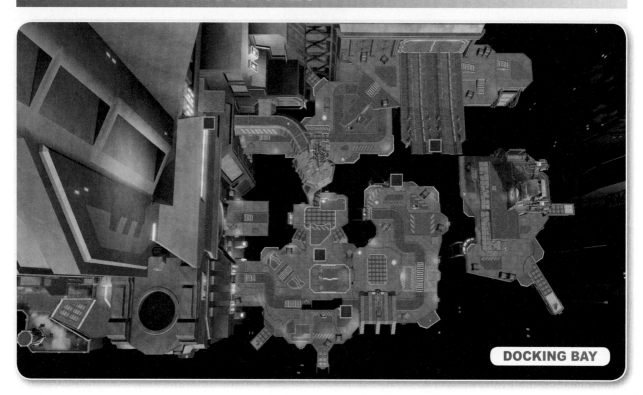

DOCKING BAY

■ Super Jump Bonus Boxes

CENTRAL OPERATION TOWER

LIVING QUARTERS

MINING ZONE

GAME BASICS

CHARACTERS

POWER DISCS

MARVEL'S THE AVENGERS

SPIDER-MAN

GUARDIANS OF THE GALAXY

TOY BOX

TOY BOX COLLECTION

ACHIEVEMENTS

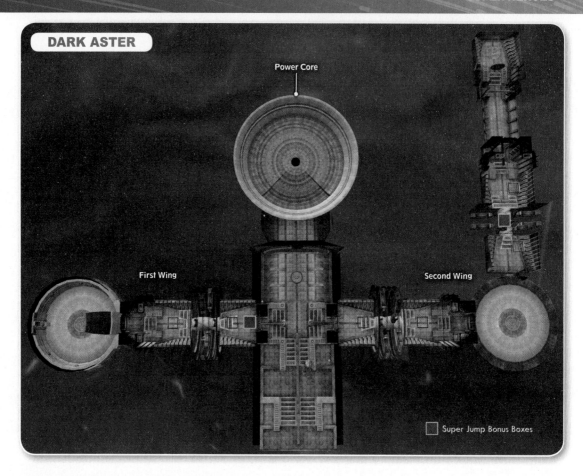

DARK ASTER

Power Core

First Wing

Second Wing

☐ Super Jump Bonus Boxes

MAXIMUM STRENGTH BONUS BOXES

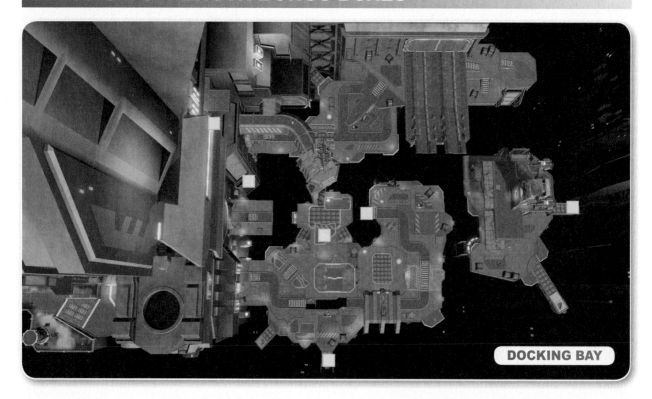

DOCKING BAY

GAME BASICS

CHARACTERS

POWER DISCS

MARVEL'S THE AVENGERS

SPIDER-MAN

GUARDIANS OF THE GALAXY

TOY BOX

TOY BOX COLLECTION

ACHIEVEMENTS

CENTRAL OPERATION TOWER

 Maximum Strength Bonus Boxes

LIVING QUARTERS

MINING ZONE

Maximum Strength Bonus Boxes

DARK ASTER

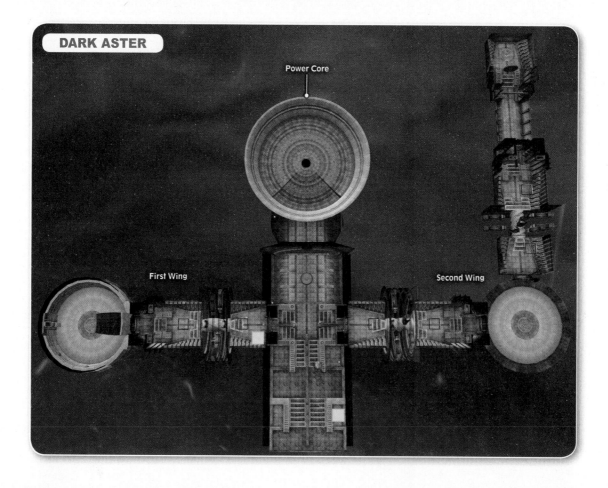

Power Core

First Wing

Second Wing

GUARDIANS OF THE GALAXY FEATS

FEATS	
FEAT NAME	**FEAT DESCRIPTION**
Accuser Diffuser	Defeat Ronan.
Ace of Points	Score 5,000 total points in Guardians of the Galaxy challenges.
All Access Pass	Explore every area of Knowhere.
All Together Now	Complete 2 challenges in a 2-player game.
Batteries Not Included	Use the charger gun to power a socket on Knowhere.
Big Boomer	Blow up 10 fuel cells.
Bonus Box Buster	Find and collect all Bonus Boxes in the Guardians of the Galaxy Play Set.
Bough Break	Defeat 3 or more enemies with Groot's Special Move.
Bronze Medalist	Collect 5 bronze medals from Guardians of the Galaxy challenges.
Canine Encounter	Enter Cosmo's control room.
Carpool	Unlock all of the vehicles.
Catching Air	Unlock Star-Lord's Leaps and Bounds ability.
C'mon Over!	Find all of the hidden Crossover Coins in the Guardians of the Galaxy Play Set.
Damage Dealer	Deal 5,000 points of damage in Guardians of the Galaxy destruction challenges.
Dancing Feat	Complete 150 feats.
Deadliest Woman in the Universe	As Gamora, defeat 5 enemies in 10 seconds.
Deeply Grooted	Defeat 20 enemies with Groot's Root for Groot ability.
Diving in with Both Feat	Complete 10 feats.
Double Team	Defeat a Large Sakaaran in a 2-player game.
Enemy Demolisher	Defeat 200 enemies in Guardians of the Galaxy combat challenges.
Enemy Down!	Destroy 25 Sakaaran ships.
Eureka!	Discover the secret area below the docks.
Fast On Your Feat	Complete 100 feats.
Flash of Green	Upgrade Gamora to her maximum running speed.
Galactic Gold Medalist	Collect all gold medals from Guardians of the Galaxy challenges.

FEATS	
FEAT NAME	**FEAT DESCRIPTION**
Galactic Strength	Find and collect all Maximum Strength Bonus Boxes in the Guardians of the Galaxy Play Set.
Galactic Super Jumper	Find and collect all Super Jump Bonus Boxes in the Guardians of the Galaxy Play Set.
Getting Your Feat Wet	Complete 1 feat.
Gold Medal Guardian	Collect 5 gold medals from Guardians of the Galaxy challenges.
Knowhere Safe	Defeat 10 elite Sakaaran soldiers.
Landing on Both Feat	Complete 50 feats.
Man the Guns!	Fend off the second Necrocraft attack.
Master Pilot	Find and collect all Flight Bonus Boxes in the Guardians of the Galaxy Play Set.
Onward and Upward	Wall Crawl as Drax for 5 minutes.
Orb Obliterator	Destroy 1,000 Orbs in the Guardians of the Galaxy Play Set.
Points Master	Score 10,000 total points in Guardians of the Galaxy challenges.
Quill is Mightier Than the Sword	Defeat 10 enemies with Star-Lord's turret.
Rabid Rodent!	Defeat 5 enemies as Rocket without firing a weapon.
Rocket Power	Defeat 5 enemies as Rocket using the Hadron Enforcer.
Silver Champion	Collect 5 silver medals from Guardians of the Galaxy challenges.
Springing to Your Feat	Complete 25 feats.
Swept Off Your Feat	Complete 200 feats.
Tanked	Defeat a Large Sakaaran.
Tech Collector	Find and collect all Tech Bonus Boxes in the Guardians of the Galaxy Play Set.
The Destroyer	As Drax, defeat 10 enemies in Destroyer Mode.
Ticket to Ride	Unlock a flying vehicle.
To the Depths	Reach the Power Core Room in the Dark Aster.
Un-De-Feat-Able	Complete all feats.
Wall Conqueror	Find and collect all Wall Crawl Bonus Boxes in the Guardians of the Galaxy Play Set.

GUARDIANS OF THE GALAXY CHALLENGES

	CHALLENGES		
MAP #	**CHALLENGE NAME**	**DESCRIPTION**	**HOW UNLOCKED?**
1	Riding the Rails	Collect Orbs for points while riding the rail!	Complete mission "Wild Blue Yondu".
2	Space Station Sprint	Earn points by breaking targets. Utilize your character's special moves!	Complete mission "Spy Sweep".
3	Vs. Mode: Living Quarters	Challenge a friend at the Living Quarters. The player with the most knockouts wins!	Earn bronze on "Space Station Sprint" challenge.
4	Vs. Mode: Docking Bay	Challenge a friend at the Docking Bay. The player with the most knockouts wins!	Complete mission "Let's Be Clear".
5	Munitions Expert	Destroy Sakaaran ships for points using the Anti-Air Gun.	Complete mission "Drop Everything!".
6	Shooting Gallery	Shoot targets with the Anti-Air Gun for points.	Earn bronze on "Munitions Expert" challenge.
7	Path of Destruction	Gain points by destroying all you can before time runs out.	Complete side mission "Power Outage".
8	You're The Collector!	Earn points by jumping to collect Orbs.	Complete mission "Pest Control".
9	Space Pace	Race around the moving platforms using the Super Jump.	Earn bronze on "You're The Collector" challenge.
10	Knowhere Fast	Race a flying vehicle for points.	Complete mission "Out of the Frying Pan...".
11	Intruder Alert	Use a vehicle to destroy targets for points.	Complete mission "Time For Paws".
12	Galactic Games	Hop aboard a vehicle and race through Knowhere.	Earn bronze on "Intruder Alert" challenge.
13	Rocket Range	Defeat enemies aboard the *Dark Aster* for points.	Complete mission "Unwelcome Wagon." Only Rocket Raccoon can start it.
14	Vs. Mode: Dark Aster	Challenge a friend aboard the *Dark Aster*. The player with the most knockouts wins!	Complete mission "Door and Piece".

GAME BASICS
CHARACTERS
POWER DISCS
MARVEL'S THE AVENGERS
SPIDER-MAN
GUARDIANS OF THE GALAXY
TOY BOX
TOY BOX COLLECTION
ACHIEVEMENTS

TOY BOX

INTRODUCTION TO THE TOY BOX

Disney Infinity: Marvel Super Heroes is a huge game with infinite possibilities. The Toy Box is a key feature of the game, and it can be somewhat daunting at first as there is so much to do. This part of the guide focuses on the Toy Box, which encompasses all parts of *Disney Infinity: Marvel Super Heroes* that are outside of the various Play Sets.

LEARNING ABOUT THE TOY BOX

After completing the start of the game where you get a brief taste of what is in store for you in *Disney Infinity: Marvel Super Heroes*, you enter the Toy Box Introduction world. This is the place where you can learn everything you need to know about playing, creating, and just having fun in the Toy Box. There are several hosts that provide missions, which are lessons on the various aspects of the Toy Box. It is a very good idea to take some time and go through these instructional missions, even if you are a veteran of *Disney Infinity*, because some of the controls and features have changed.

Move the Disney Infinity Toy Stand onto the platform to enter the Toy Box Intro World.

REWARDS IN THE TOY BOX

Not only do you learn about the Toy Box by completing the host missions, you also earn some cool rewards. In addition to blue Sparks (the money in the Toy Box) and orange Sparks (experience for your character), you also unlock some very cool toys. While you could purchase them in the Toy Store, some are quite expensive and you can unlock them for free just by completing all of the missions.

Toy Box Host Missions Rewards	
MISSIONS COMPLETED	**REWARD**
5 missions	King Louie Townsperson
10 missions	Collector Challenge Kit template
20 missions	Toy Box Door
30 missions	King Louie's Throne
36 missions	Enchanted Bed

There are five main hosts for the Toy Box. There is no specific order in which you need to visit them. However, it is usually best to save the combat host for last so you can build up some experience for your character and then upgrade your character's skills prior to going into combat. So let's get started.

CREATION HOST

Merlin is the Creation Host.

The Merlin townsperson is the host who teaches you the basics of creating in the Toy Box. As such, he offers a good place to start. He is the host with the icon of the world above his head. Walk over and talk to Merlin. As soon as you do, you gain blue and orange Sparks and complete the first mission. Also, the Toy Box World expands as a city is built right before your eyes.

Talk to Merlin again and you can choose from two topics—Toy Box Creation Help or Travel Help. Start off with creation help and then go through the four options one at a time. The first teaches you how to place an item in the Toy Box. Next you learn how to customize the look of the Toy Box. Third is about changing the Toy Box sky and the last choice is about getting more toys.

Press the editor button to open the Toy Box editor. Here you can select from all of the toys that are unlocked for you. Learn to use the editor and the filter to find the correct toy. Pick one and then move it around and rotate it to get it just how you want it. Then place it into the Toy Box following the in-game directions to complete the mission.

Learning how to place items in the Toy Box is an important lesson to learn right at the start.

The next lesson teaches you how to change the look of your Toy Box. Follow the directions to access your wand from the Packs and Tools menu and then use the wand to select an item. You can then change the look of the object. When you select the palette, you can change the style of just that object or even apply that theme to the entire Toy Box. That will change all of the items whose style can be changed to that new style. Play around with this to see the different themes that are available initially. You can purchase more themes in the Toy Store later.

Use the magic wand to select an item to customize.

After changing the look of an item, you can now learn about Spark Mode. This lets you move around the Toy Box quickly and edit or build lots of things. Open the editor and then follow the instruction to enter Spark Mode and complete the assigned tasks.

Then ask Merlin about changing the look of the sky. He tells you how to use either Power Discs or the sky changer toy to do this. Finally, ask Merlin about getting more toys.

The next options in the Creation Host menu are about travel. The first is how to go to a Play Set and then how to download a Toy Box. Ask Merlin for a tip to complete another mission. He will help you get to those hard to reach Sparks. His advice is to build structures that will allow your characters to reach those.

> **NOTE**
>
> As you complete these missions, once you collect enough orange Sparks, you will level up your hero to level 1 and unlock the Hall of Heroes Door and the Marvel's Hall of Super Heroes Door.

> **TIP**
>
> While you can explore the city that the Creation Host made for you and look for Sparks, it is better to complete all of the Host Missions first because some of the things you learn will help you get some of those hard-to-reach Sparks.

Creation Host Missions		
MISSION	**SPARK REWARDS**	**UNLOCKS**
Talk to Creation Host for the first time	100 orange, 300 blue	
Place an item in the Toy Box	20 orange	
Change the look of the Toy Box	35 orange, 300 blue	Toy Box Terrain
Use Spark Mode	25 orange, 25 blue	
Change the sky	25 orange, 200 blue	
Getting more toys	15 orange, 100 blue	
How to go to a Play Set	15 orange, 100 blue	
How to download a Toy Box	15 orange, 100 blue	
Ask the Creation Host for a tip	5 orange, 10 blue	
Ask how to collect hard-to-reach Sparks	10 orange, 25 blue	
Unlock the Hall of Heroes and Marvel's Hall of Super Heroes Doors	35 orange, 300 blue	

VEHICLE HOST

Luigi from *Cars* is the Vehicle Host who teaches you all about vehicles and mounts, which you can use to travel quickly and get to places some characters could not otherwise reach. When you walk over and talk to him, a race track is automatically created, plus the Autopia Car appears on the track. Go and hop in it to unlock the car and complete the first mission.

Luigi is ready to help you learn about vehicles.

Talk to Luigi again and ask him to teach you to drive a car. Then hop back in the car and start driving. When you drive over the race button in the middle of the road, you are asked to start the race—don't start it yet. Follow the on-screen directions to learn how to accelerate and how to drift. Drifting is a great way to take turns at high speed and also build up turbo. Luigi even lets you know how to use turbo to get a boost of speed from your car. Try to stay on the track. However, if you drive off the edge, you will respawn back on the track. Finally, learn how to do a quick 180-degree turn to complete this mission. Continue along the track back to Luigi.

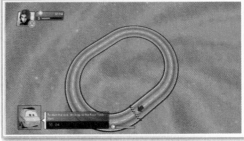

Drift around the turns so you can build up turbo.

Luigi's next mission is to teach you how to fly. He provides a helicopter for you for this mission, so get in and get started. Follow the on-screen prompts to learn how to take off, fly forward, and strafe to the left and right, as well as how to attack. Once you have tried all of these, the mission is complete, so fly back to Luigi.

A helicopter is a great way to get some of those Sparks that are on top of the buildings and other locations that are up high.

> **TIP**
>
> When flying the helicopter, press the Item select button and select from four different types of weapons. Try them out. They are great for defeating enemies.

Next, learn how to ride animals. Luigi provides Merida's horse, Angus, for you to ride. Mount up and then follow the directions to learn how to run, jump, and even sprint. Following that mission, talk to Luigi about how to build your own tracks. This is quite easy and all of the pieces you need are already unlocked in the Toy Box. However, you don't actually need to build a track to complete this mission—just listen to Luigi and learn. The basics of building a track are to make sure all of the pieces are connected, create a complete circuit, and be sure to include a race track start piece. Then just drive up to the Race Track Start piece to begin a race. The Toy Box will automatically provide some competition for you.

Learn how to make your own race tracks.

Now that you know how to drive, it is time to learn about doing tricks. Luigi will create a stunt park and a stunt buggy for you to drive. Drive up the sides of the stunt park to get airborne, then follow the directions to perform some tricks. The mission is completed once you have performed a total of five tricks. Exit the stunt buggy to return to Luigi.

GAME BASICS · CHARACTERS · POWER DISCS · MARVEL'S THE AVENGERS · SPIDER-MAN · GUARDIANS OF THE GALAXY · TOY BOX · TOY BOX COLLECTION · ACHIEVEMENTS

Practice getting air and doing tricks. Notice that as you do tricks, you build up turbo just like when you drift.

Finally, ask Luigi how to reach hard-to-reach Sparks. Since he is the Vehicle Host, he will tell you to try using a helicopter. This tip counts as another mission complete, and by now you should be getting close to your third reward.

Vehicle Host Missions		
MISSION	**SPARK REWARDS**	**UNLOCKS**
Talk to Vehicle Host for the first time and drive the car	35 orange, 100 blue	Autopia Car
Learn how to drive a car	35 orange, 300 blue	
Learn how to fly	35 orange, 200 blue	
Learn how to ride animals	35 orange, 200 blue	
Learn how to build your own track	25 orange, 50 blue	
Learn how to do tricks in a car	35 orange, 300 blue	
Ask how to collect hard-to-reach Sparks	10 orange, 25 blue	

EXPLORATION HOST

When you first talk to Mulan, an Agrabah market structure appears and challenges you to get to a Spark capsule. An indicator shows the location of an orange Spark capsule. As you go after it, you learn about jumping as well as rope/pipe climbing and grinding to get to get to the capsule to complete another mission. Next you have to collect ten blue Spark capsules that are scattered about the market area

Once you have completed the Agrabah missions, talk to Mulan again and ask her how to jump. She will provide some platforms with blue Spark capsules. Jump across the platforms to get to the blue Sparks. Next ask her how to jump farther. She will teach you how to double jump. Then double jump across some more platforms to collect even more blue Spark capsules. The final lesson is how to grab a ledge. Now you have to double jump towards platforms and grab on to the ledge. Then press the jump button again to pull yourself up to collect a blue Spark capsule. Move across all of these platforms to complete this mission. Finally ask her about collecting hard-to-reach Sparks. She will suggest using a flying character. Complete all of these missions and you are on your way to your next reward.

Mulan is ready to teach you how to get around obstacles in the Toy Box.

Make your way through Agrabah to collect capsules and complete a couple missions along the way.

Jump onto platforms and grab ledges to complete Mulan's three instructional missions.

Once you have completed the instructional missions, it is time to try out the Agrabah challenge. An indicator shows the location of an orange Spark capsule. Use what you have learned about jumping as well as rope/pipe climbing and grinding to get to get to the capsule to complete another mission. Next you have to collect ten blue Spark capsules that are scattered about the market area. Get them all and you have completed yet another mission and are on your way to your next reward.

Exploration Host Missions		
MISSION	**SPARK REWARDS**	**UNLOCKS**
Learn how to jump	20 orange, 50 blue	
Learn how to jump farther	20 orange, 50 blue	
Learn how to grab a ledge	20 orange, 50 blue	
Collect orange capsule in Agrabah challenge	100 orange, 300 blue	
Collect 10 blue Spark capsules in Agrabah challenge	70 orange, 100 blue	
Ask what to do if you get stuck	10 orange, 25 blue	
Ask how to collect hard-to-reach Sparks	10 orange, 25 blue	

TOY STORE HOST

Remember Oaken from *Frozen*? He is the Toy Store Host and is here to teach you all about the Toy Store and how to get more toys for your Toy Box. As soon as you walk over to him, he gives you some blue Sparks. These are the currency in the Toy Box.

Start off by asking Oaken what he has for sale. This opens up the Toy Store. Look through the menus and pages of toys. You don't have to buy anything at this time. When you exit the Toy Store, you complete the mission. The next mission is to learn how to get more toys. You can purchase them from the Toy Store Host or from the pause menu. Ask the remaining two questions about Blue Sparks and Disney Infinity 1.0 Toys to complete two more missions.

Talk to Oaken to learn about the Toy Store.

The Toy Store consists of several different pages of toys that you can unlock by spending blue Sparks, by playing through the Play Sets and Toy Box Games, or by completing Toy Box Host missions.

Toy Store Host Missions		
MISSION	SPARK REWARDS	UNLOCKS
Talk to the Toy Store Host	10 blue	
What does Oaken have for sale?	10 blue	
How do you get more toys?	50 blue	
What do blue Sparks do?	10 blue	
How do you get your Disney Infinity 1.0 toys?	10 blue	

COMBAT HOST

The last of the main Toy Box hosts is Phil, the same person—or satyr—that trained Hercules as well as several other heroes. He can make you a hero too!

Phil, the Combat Host, will teach you all you need to know about fighting enemies.

When you first talk to Phil, he sends two enemies to attack you. Follow the directions and press the attack button to defeat them. Be sure to gather the Sparks they leave behind once defeated.

Use melee combat moves to defeat the two enemies by tapping the attack button rapidly.

Many characters have projectile weapons while others do not. However, you can equip items to all characters no matter whether they have a projectile weapon or not. Ask Phil bout this. He will show you how to press the Item select button to open up the Packs and Tools menu. Here you can assign a weapon such as the Toy Box Blaster to your character so they can use it to attack enemies. Next ask Phil about Toy Box games. He explains how to place a Toy Box game piece onto the hexagonal slot on the Disney Infinity base to play these games. Finally talk to Phil about placing enemies in your Toy Box. He shows you how to use the enemy generator to cause enemies to spawn in the Toy Box. Push the button on this toy if you want some more enemies to fight.

The Fairy Godmother gives you the combat challenge. Use ranged attacks to hit the Omnidroids from a distance.

Now all that is left is the combat challenge. Walk across the race track to talk to the Fairy Godmother. Cinderella is being help captive. You must rescue her.

Move into the courtyard area and defeat several Omnidroids so you can get to a button. Push it to lower a bridge so you can reach the tower where Cinderella is located. As you take damage, be sure to

collect the green Spark capsules as well as green Sparks left behind by defeated enemies.

TIP

By this time, you should have leveled up your character a few levels. Be sure to go to the skill tree from the pause menu and purchase some skills for your character that will help them be more effective in combat.

The Tank Omnidroid is defending the tower.

Once you get across the bridge, you must face the boss—a Tank Omnidroid. This is one strong enemy and it can take a lot of damage. Stay back and use the Toy Box Blaster or your character's ranged attack to hit this boss. When it begins firing its lasers at you, move behind the tower for cover. Then resume your attack when the laser stops firing. Keep at it until the Tank Omnidroid is defeated.

Pick up Cinderella and get her to Phil to complete the challenge.

The tower opens and you can pick up Cinderella. Carry her across the bridge. However, there are more Omnidroids waiting. If you try to fight, you will drop Cinderella. So just run as fast as you can through the courtyard and out into the Toy Box main area. Get her to Phil to complete this challenge. If you have already completed all of the other missions and challenges, you will have unlocked the final reward at the same time.

Combat Host Missions		
MISSION	SPARK REWARDS	UNLOCKS
Talk to the Combat Host for the first time	35 orange, 100 blue	
Learn how to hold a weapon	25 orange, 50 blue	
Learn how to go to a Toy Box game	25 orange, 100 blue	
Learn how to fill your Toy Box with enemies	25 orange, 100 blue	
Complete the combat challenge	150 orange, 300 blue	

INTERIORS

Disney Infinity: Marvel Super Heroes offers several new features to the Disney Infinity universe. One of those is the ability to create INteriors. When you begin playing *Disney Infinity: Marvel Super Heroes*, you can create your very own INterior. This is like your own house or location where you can display items and objects that you have collected while progressing through the Play Sets or that you have purchased with your blue Sparks. The INterior is a reflection of you. Customize it and make it your very own.

LEARNING ABOUT INTERIORS

Cogsworth, the butler from the castle in Beauty and the Beast, is your INteriors Host.

It may not look like much to begin with. However, talk to Cogsworth and complete the INterior missions to get your INterior looking nice. Plus you can unlock some cool toys.

There is a Toy Box host that is in charge of teaching you all about INteriors. Cogsworth appears near Luigi after you complete a few of the Toy Box host missions. Go talk to him to learn about INteriors. As soon as you do, he disappears and a giant treehouse is created. Climb up to the treehouse by jumping up the ledges of the ladder to get to a platform where Cogsworth is once again waiting for you. Once you arrive, you unlock the INterior Door and it appears on the side of the small house on the platform. Move to the door and enter your INterior to continue.

This door will take you to your very own INterior.

Upon entering your INterior, you find a single, large room—the lobby—which is in dire need of some decorating. However, it is a blank slate ready for you to shape as you wish. Cogsworth has some missions to help you get your INterior all decorated while teaching you how you can customize it yourself. Therefore, talk to Cogsworth to find out what to do next.

TIP

Later on as more townspeople come to visit your INterior, several of them will provide missions for you to complete. Many of these INterior missions unlock toys that you can immediately use either in your INterior or outside in the Toy Box.

TUTORIAL MISSIONS

In addition to the normal INterior missions, there are also five tutorial missions that cover the basics of INterior design. You can access these by talking to Cogsworth and asking him questions. The Tutorial missions are as follows:

The Floor is Yours—Learn how to place furniture and other items in your INterior.

Picturesque—Learn how to place pictures, art, and other wall decorations in your INterior.

More Room—Learn how to add rooms to your INterior.

Interior Design—Learn how to customize the walls, floor, and trim of a room.

Finishing Touches—Learn how to customize lights and other parts of your rooms. The lobby is a great place to do this because it has many features to customize that are not available in other rooms.

THE INTERIOR MISSIONS

There are several different INterior missions. While they do not always come in the same order, there are several that require you to complete previous missions in order to be offered them.

PERSONAL SPACE

■ **Townsperson Mission Giver:** Cogsworth

■ **Requirement:** Select the magic wand from the Packs and Tools menu, then use it to customize your INterior walls.

■ **Unlock:** Vintage Theme, Lamp, Space Station X-1 Lighting

While in the lobby of your INterior, select the wand from the Packs and Tools menu, aim at a wall, and press the button with the palette on the screen in the lower-right corner. This allows you to customize the look of a room. Walls is the initial category. You have a choice of three different themes. Select one and then press the apply button to change the theme of the walls. Then exit the customizer. You have decorated your first walls.

HOME FURNISHING

■ **Townsperson Mission Giver:** Cogsworth

■ **Requirement:** Select a piece of furniture from the Toy Box Editor and place it in your INterior.

■ **Unlock:** Chair, Green Couch, Toon Window, Potted Vine, Disney Infinity Painting

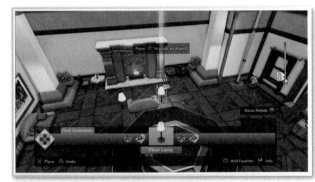

Now you need to start adding some furniture to your INterior. Press the editor button to enter the Toy Box Editor. You are already in the Floor Decoration category, which is where all furniture you have unlocked is available. Select from a chair, a lamp, or a plant, rotate it as needed, and then place it into your INterior. Continue to place as many pieces of furniture as you want into the room. Once you unlock a toy, you do not have to pay each time you place one. Exit the Toy Box Editor when you are done.

ROOM TO GROW

■ **Townsperson Mission Giver:** Cogsworth

■ **Requirement:** Select a room from the Toy Box Editor, and place the room in the highlighted area.

■ **Unlock:** 2-Door Room B, Long Hall, Short Hall, 1-Door Room

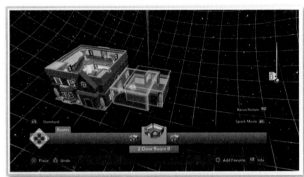

While the lobby of your INterior is nice, you can make your INterior much larger. Let's start off by adding a room. Open the Toy Box Editor and you will already be in the Rooms category. There is only one room from which to choose—2-Door Room B. This room has two doors on adjacent walls. Select this room and then drag if over to your lobby. You can rotate the room to get it so that one of the doors of your new room is facing your lobby. Next, move it so that the two doors connect and then press the connect button to add a room to your INterior. Exit the Toy Box Editor to complete the mission. Once you return to the INterior, you can walk into your new room and even customize it if you want.

YOU'RE WELCOME

■ **Townsperson Mission Giver:** Cogsworth

■ **Requirement:** Select the Guest Gatherer from the Toy Box Editor and place it in your INterior.

■ **Unlock:** Guest Gatherer, Carl Fredricksen Costume, Kuzco Costume, Mr. Toad Costume, Cogsworth Costume, Sleeping Beauty Costume

Now that you have expanded your INterior, why not invite some guests over to visit. Open the Toy Box Editor and select the Guest Gatherer from the Floor Decorations category. Place it anywhere in your INterior and then exit the Toy Box Editor. Placing this Toy in your INterior causes townspeople guests to arrive and begin visiting your INterior. This is important since some of these guests will have INterior missions for you to complete. You unlock five townspeople in costumes of various Disney characters. You can go into the Toy Box Editor and place these townspeople into your INterior as well as your Toy Box on the outside.

NOTE As you complete the above missions and accomplish some Feats, you receive a reward. The Basin Trophy is your first award and appears near the front door of your INterior. Go pick it up and then you can begin using this Toy to decorate your INterior.

SPECIAL ADDITION

■ **Townsperson Mission Giver:** Scrooge McDuck

■ **Requirement:** Select two rooms and two hallways from the Toy Box Editor, and add them to your INterior.

■ **Unlock:** Hallway Turn, 3-Door Room B, 2-Door Room A

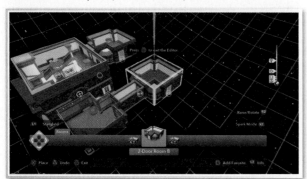

Scrooge McDuck wants to eventually keep his money hidden from the Beagle Boys in your INterior. However, you need to expand some more. Open the Toy Box Editor and start adding some rooms. You need to add at least two hallways and two new rooms to complete this task. Hallways are a great way to separate rooms so you are not walking right from one room into the next—providing a transition from one room to another. They also allow you to connect rooms with shapes that might make it difficult to connect together. Attach two hallways and two rooms to your existing rooms and then exit the Toy Box Editor to complete this mission.

GOLD PLATE REAL ESTATE

■ **Townsperson Mission Giver:** Scrooge McDuck

■ **Requirement:** Select Scrooge McDuck's Money Bin from the Toy Box Editor, and place it in the Toy Box.

■ **Unlock:** 4-Door Room A, Scrooge McDuck's Money Bin (in Toy Box)

This mission requires you to leave the INterior and return to the Toy Box. There are several missions that must be completed outside of your INterior. Therefore, head to the front door of the lobby and exit the INterior. When you get out into the Toy Box, you will probably need to add some flat terrain to the Toy Box so you have a location on which to build. Use the Toy Box Editor to do this. Then go to the Set Pieces category and select Uncle Scrooge's Money Bin and place it to complete this mission.

HOME BASE

■ **Townsperson Mission Giver:** Agent Coulson

■ **Requirement:** Select the Helicarrier Consoles from the Toy Box Editor and place it in your INterior.

■ **Unlock:** Agent Coulson Costume, Helicarrier Consoles

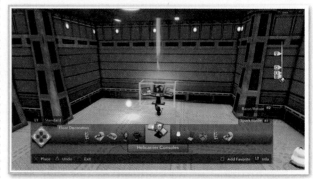

This is a quick and easy mission. Go into the Toy Box Editor, and under the Floor Decoration category, select Helicarrier Consoles. Then just place it in one of the rooms of your INterior. That is it.

CHANGE OF VIEW

■ **Townsperson Mission Giver:** Belle

■ **Requirement:** Use the magic wand to customize the walls, floors, and trim to create a Beast's Castle-themed room.

■ **Unlock:** The Beast's Castle Theme

This mission is quick to complete. Find a room in need of decorating and then use the magic wand. Change the wall to The Beast's Castle Walls, the floor to The Beast's Castle Floors, and the trim to The Beast's Castle Accents. Then exit the customizer to earn your reward.

CHIMNEY SNEAK

- **Townsperson Mission Giver:** Darkwing Duck

- **Requirement:** Aim the magic wand at the door in the fireplace, and set it to open.

- **Unlock:** Darkwing Duck Costume

This is another quick mission and gives you some experience with using Logic Connections on toys. Aim at the fireplace in the lobby and use the magic wand to select it. Then press the button that corresponds to the connections icon of two gears. This opens the Logic Connections menu. Select Properties, then change the Door Open option to Open. You can also use the slider to adjust how long the door stays open as well as choose if you want the door to always stay open. Once you have set the Door Open option, exit this menu to complete the mission.

AIR OF RECOGNITION

- **Townsperson Mission Giver:** Agent Coulson

- **Requirement:** Use the magic wand to customize the walls, floors, and trim to create a Helicarrier-themed room.

- **Unlock:** Helicarrier Theme, Helicarrier Light

Agent Coulson has another mission for you. He wants a command center to look like the Helicarrier. Pick a room, possibly the one where you placed the Helicarrier Consoles, and then get out your magic wand and start customizing. Change the walls to Helicarrier Walls, the floor to Helicarrier Floor, and the trim to Helicarrier Accents. You might also want to change the light to the Helicarrier Light after you unlock it by completing this mission so it fits in better with the Helicarrier look.

SUCCESS STORIES

- **Townsperson Mission Giver:** Scrooge McDuck

- **Requirement:** Select an elevation room from the Toy Box Editor, and add it to your INterior.

- **Unlock:** Pipe Climb Room, Elevator Room, 4-Door Room B

Scrooge McDuck wants you to add another room to your INterior. This time he wants a room that will connect two levels of floors. Open the Toy Box Editor, and go to the Rooms category. You now have the Pipe Climb Room. Attach it to one of your first floor rooms. Then characters can climb the pipe to get up to the higher floor.

WARM RECEPTION

- **Townsperson Mission Giver:** Belle

- **Requirement:** Select Beast's Fireplace from the Toy Box Editor, and place it in your INterior.

- **Unlock:** Beast's Fireplace

While you can do this in any room, why don't you go back to the room you themed after The Beast's Castle. Then open the Toy Box Editor and select Beast's Fireplace from the Wall Decorations category. Put it along any wall in the room to complete the mission and then exit the editor. Once placed, you can use the magic wand on the fireplace and, using the Logic Connections menu, either turn the fire on or off. This fireplace does not have a secret door built into it.

GAME BASICS

CHARACTERS

POWER DISCS

MARVEL'S THE AVENGERS

SPIDER-MAN

GUARDIANS OF THE GALAXY

TOY BOX

TOY BOX COLLECTION

ACHIEVEMENTS

PETER'S PLAN

■ **Townsperson Mission Giver:** Peter Pan

■ **Requirement:** Return to the Toy Box or a Toy Box Game and defeat 10 enemies.

■ **Unlock:** None

This is another mission where you need to return to the Toy Box. It is also a mission you can complete while playing in any Toy Box or by playing one of the Toy Box Games. Another option is to go into the Toy Box, open the Toy Box Editor, and place 10 enemies for you to defeat. The enemy generator can also spawn enemies in the Toy Box for you. Whatever you choose, defeat a total of 10 enemies to complete this mission.

CINDERELLA SWITCH

■ **Townsperson Mission Giver:** Cinderella

■ **Requirement:** Use the magic wand to customize the walls, floor, and trim to create a Cinderella-themed room.

■ **Unlock:** Cinderella Castle Theme, Cinderella's Pink Dress

Pick a room in your INterior, or add a new one, and then use the magic wand to customize it. Change the walls to Cinderella Castle Walls, the floor to Cinderella Castle Floor, and the trim to Cinderella Castle Accents.

GARDENER'S GRIP

■ **Townsperson Mission Giver:** Cinderella

■ **Requirement:** Return to the Toy Box and collect 10 flowers.

■ **Unlock:** Cinderella Castle Shrub, Cinderella Castle Fern

Head back out to the Toy Box and begin collecting flowers. They can be found all over. Therefore, this is a good mission to combine with another you have to do out in the Toy Box, like one of Peter Pan's missions. Once you have collected 10 flowers, the mission is complete.

ELEVATED THREAT

■ **Townsperson Mission Giver:** Agent Coulson

■ **Requirement:** Select the Communications Array from the Toy Box Editor and place it in the Toy Box.

■ **Unlock:** Communications Array

This is one of those missions that requires you to leave the INterior and venture out into the Toy Box. When you do, open up the Toy Box Editor and find the Communications Array under the Set Pieces category. Place it anywhere in the Toy Box to complete this mission.

CONTRIVED CONTRAPTIONS

■ **Townsperson Mission Giver:** Darkwing Duck

■ **Requirement:** Use the magic wand to assign two Logic Connections to toys in your INterior.

■ **Unlock:** None

There are a lot of ways you can complete this mission. However an easy way is to go into a room and set up a counter to keep track of how many characters are in the room. To do this, open the Toy Box Editor and go to the Creativi-Toys category. Select the Counter and place it in the corner of the room. Now exit the editor, and use the magic wand in the room. Select the button related to the connection icon and open the Logic Connection menu. Select New Logic Connection and then choose to send a message when Entered. Pick Any from the next menu so that when any character or townsperson enters, it triggers this action. Now use the magic wand and aim at the Counter toy. Press the designated button to Connect the logic instructions for the room to the Counter. Finally, in the next menu for what you want the Counter to do when it receives a message that someone has entered the room, select Increment and then By 1. Do this same thing or experiment with other connections in the same room or another area to complete this mission.

FLORAL ARRANGEMENT

■ **Townsperson Mission Giver:** Cinderella

■ **Requirement:** Select the Garden Ballroom from the Toy Box Editor and place it in the designated, highlighted area.

■ **Unlock:** Garden Ballroom

You now get to add a specialty room to your INterior. Open the Toy Box Editor and select Garden Ballroom from the Rooms category. A good place for this is next to your Cinderella Castle-themed room; however, you can put it anywhere you want. Connect it to an existing room and you are ready to go.

TIP

When you add the Garden Ballroom to your INterior, there are several planters with an icon on them. When the princess townsperson that matches that icon comes and stops in front of that planter, the planter will customize to that princess's theme. For example, if Snow White comes to the planter with the apple, an apple tree will replace the tree there. Unlock or purchase all of the princess townspeople and place them in this room to help move this along.

BUILD AWAY

■ **Townsperson Mission Giver:** Scrooge McDuck

■ **Requirement:** Return to the Toy Box and have a Builder create a new home for you.

■ **Unlock:** Toy Box City Builder, Toy Box Treehouse Builder, New Concept

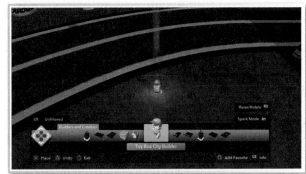

This is another easy mission; however, you will have to leave the INterior and go back out into the Toy Box. Once there, open the Toy Box Editor and go to the Builders and Creators category. Choose either the Treehouse or City Builder and place him down in the Toy Box. Builders will go around your Toy Box and begin building structures within their theme. Once the Builder is placed, the mission is complete. After a while, you will find that the Builder has built something for you.

NEVERLAND STAND

■ **Townsperson Mission Giver:** Peter Pan

■ **Requirement:** Return to the Toy Box or a Toy Box Game and defeat 25 more enemies.

■ **Unlock:** None

As with the previous Peter Pan mission, you just have to defeat enemies out in the Toy Box. Next time you are out there, find someone to fight—actually 25 of them.

GAME BASICS CHARACTERS POWER DISCS MARVEL'S THE AVENGERS SPIDER-MAN GUARDIANS OF THE GALAXY TOY BOX TOY BOX COLLECTION ACHIEVEMENTS

147

THE HIGH NOTE

■ **Townsperson Mission Giver:** Cinderella

■ **Requirement:** Select a music-playing toy from the Toy Box Editor and place it in your INterior.

■ **Unlock:** Cinderella's Slipper (reward for completing all of the Princess missions—delivered to your lobby)

For this mission, you will need to go to the Toy Store from the pause menu. Then select Toys and then INterior Decorations. One of the music-playing toys you can choose is the Grand Piano from the Basic Decorations–Page 1 menu. However, to purchase this toy, you must first buy the Table, the Nightstand, the Round Ornate Rug, the Tall Dresser, and the Bed in order to get to the Grand Piano on the toy tree. Then return to the game and open the Toy Box Editor. Select the Grand Piano from the Floor Decoration category and place it in one of your rooms. It will automatically start playing music on its own.

IT'S OFFICIAL

■ **Townsperson Mission Giver:** Agent Coulson

■ **Requirement:** Select the Command Center Room from the Toy Box Editor, and place it in your INterior.

■ **Unlock:** Command Center, The Tesseract (reward for completing all of Agent Coulson's missions—delivered to your lobby)

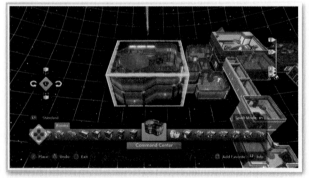

Time to add another specialty room. Open up the Toy Box Editor and select the Command Center from the Rooms category. Connect it to one of the doors of your INterior to complete this mission. The Command Center is a room where you can train, fighting against enemies. Enter the room and press the button along one wall. Then go down into the training area and let the combat begin.

HOME SAFE HOME

■ **Townsperson Mission Giver:** Scrooge McDuck

■ **Requirement:** Select the INterior Money Bin from the Toy Box Editor and place it in your INterior.

■ **Unlock:** Money Bin, Scrooge McDuck's Money Pile (reward for completing all of Scrooge's missions—delivered to your lobby)

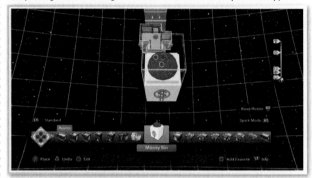

Open up the Toy Box Editor and select the Money Bin from the Rooms category. Then attach it to your interior. When you enter this room, you will see some money down at the bottom. As you collect blue Sparks, the level of the money rises. It reflects the blue Sparks you collect—not what you currently have in your account. So the Money Bin will fill as you continue to play and collect blue Sparks. When you invite friends to visit your Toy Box, they can see just how successful you are.

PAN'S DEFENSE

■ **Townsperson Mission Giver:** Peter Pan

■ **Requirement:** Return to the Toy Box or a Toy Box Game and defeat 100 more enemies.

■ **Unlock:** Neverland Map (reward for completing all of the Peter Pan missions—delivered to your lobby)

This is the last of the Peter Pan missions and the toughest. The best way to do this is to just go out and play in the Toy Box and Toy Box Games. However, you can also place 100 Soldier of Hearts or Soldier of Clubs enemies in the Toy Box. Then hop into the Autopia car, select a weapon, and defeat all of them.

SIDE MISSIONS

There are also six INterior side missions which you can complete. They focus on decorating your INterior. Be sure to get one of these missions before you spend a lot of time decorating because what you have done in the past will not go towards the current side mission. Then use these missions as opportunities to work on your INterior. While these missions do not unlock toys, they reward you with blue Sparks for your efforts.

TIDYING UP

■ **Townsperson Mission Giver:** Fairy Godmother

■ **Requirement:** Select the magic wand from the Packs and Tools menu, then use it to customize INterior rooms 20 times.

As you add new rooms to your INterior, take some time to customize their walls, floors, and trim. If you want to complete this mission quickly, just change one item and then exit the customizer. Then use the magic wand again to change another item. By doing this, you can get three or four changes in each room and get to that 20 requirement much quicker.

CHANGE OF SCENERY

■ **Townsperson Mission Giver:** Fairy Godmother

■ **Requirement:** Select the magic wand from the Packs and Tools menu, then use it to customize 20 additional INterior rooms.

This is essentially similar to the previous mission. Just customize rooms 20 more times.

REVAMPING THE ROOM

■ **Townsperson Mission Giver:** Fairy Godmother

■ **Requirement:** Select the magic wand from the Packs and Tools menu, then use it to customize 20 additional INterior rooms.

Customize rooms an additional 20 times.

SOFA, SO GOOD

■ **Townsperson Mission Giver:** The Genie

■ **Requirement:** Select 25 individual furniture pieces from the Toy Box Editor, and place them in your INterior.

You have unlocked some floor decorations, so start putting them into your rooms. While 25 may seem like a lot, they can be spread out through your entire INterior. Put a few in each room and you will easily get this mission completed.

FURNITURE FULFILLMENT

■ **Townsperson Mission Giver:** The Genie

■ **Requirement:** Select 50 additional individual furniture pieces from the Toy Box Editor, and place them in your INterior.

Continue decorating your INterior with 50 more floor and wall decorations.

FULLY FURNISHED

■ **Townsperson Mission Giver:** The Genie

■ **Requirement:** Select 100 additional individual furniture pieces from the Toy Box Editor, and place them in your INterior.

Place 100 more floor and wall decorations into your INterior.

GAME BASICS

CHARACTERS

POWER DISCS

MARVEL'S THE AVENGERS

SPIDER-MAN

GUARDIANS OF THE GALAXY

TOY BOX

TOY BOX COLLECTION

ACHIEVEMENTS

GAME CREATION

There is still one more Toy Box host in *Disney Infinity: Marvel Super Heroes*. Quorra, from *Tron: Legacy* is the Gameplay Host. If you drop down the side of the cliff near Merlin to a lower area in the Toy Box, you can find Quorra near a door.

> Quorra will teach you all about game creation.

The Toy Box Door is your first lesson with Quorra. This one has already been placed in the Toy Box for you. However, you can go into the Toy Box Editor and place these doors anywhere you want. Toy Box Doors are very powerful. They allow you to essentially connect different Toy Box worlds. For this lesson, you are going to set up this Toy Box Door. First, you will need to take out the magic wand. Then use it to select the Toy Box Door and choose the connections icon.

Once in the connections menu, select Properties. Now you can select the destination where the door will take you. You can choose to have the door lead to a new Toy Box, import a Toy Box, or link to an existing Toy Box. You can also select a destination locator tag and even decide whether the door will automatically take players who open it to the next destination or require a confirmation before travel. While you can link the door to any destination, test it out by selecting an existing Toy Box and choosing Toy Box Launch. Then when you go through the door, it will take you to the main level of your current Toy Box where you entered at the very start.

After connecting the Toy Box Door to another Toy Box—even the one you are currently in—Quorra disappears. However, don't worry, she still has some missions for you. Follow the brick walkway leading from the Toy Box Door you just connected to another Toy Box Door that will take you to the Game Creation Toy Box.

> Edit the properties of the Toy Box Door so you can use it to get to other Toy Boxes.

> This second Toy Box Door takes you to Quorra and some lessons on creating your own games.

TIP

When designing your own Toy Box Worlds and games, use pathways to help direct players to where you want them to go.

LEARNING ABOUT GAME CREATION

Upon arriving in the Game Creation Toy Box, you find Quorra waiting. Walk up to and talk to her. She is here to teach you how to make toys communicate with one another and work together. You can search for hidden treasure, which is a tutorial to the basics of connecting and programming toys. You can also choose to learn about five different types of kits or templates, which are mini-games that have already been set up for you. Exploring these kits is a great way to learn about creating games. However, start off with the search for hidden treasure to get your feet wet in game creation.

NOTE

The Toy Box Door near Quorra will take you back to the Toy Box Introduction whenever you want.

> Quorra is waiting for you in the Game Creation Toy Box.

TREASURE MOUNTAIN

Once you select to search for hidden treasure, a mountain appears with a treasure at the top. To get to the treasure, you will need to learn how to make toys communicate with one another. To start off, Quorra reveals a switch that serves as a trigger for the replayer toy. When you step on the switch, it sends a signal to the replayer toy to build a bridge so you can get across the gap to the other side where your mission continues. The replayer toy has recorded a bridge being built across the gap. When you step on the switch, the replayer "plays" the building process and the bridge appears in the Toy Box.

Step on the switch to make a bridge appear.

NOTE

Creativi-Toys is the name of toys that can be programmed by assigning them logic functions. While you can connect other toys such as doors or even rooms in the INterior, they need to connect to a Creativi-Toy for a behavior or action. In fact, there are two main factors in connecting toys. One toy acts as a trigger while the other toy receives a signal from the trigger and then performs an action. So while learning about game creation and connecting toys, think of which is the trigger and which is the action or behavior.

TIP

If you want to learn more about using Creativi-Toys as you play this mission, use your magic wand to study and analyze how each of the toys in this mission were programmed.

Follow Quorra across the bridge to the other side and then continue up a path to a locked door. In order to get the door to open, you need to connect it to the switch. To connect toys, you need to use your magic wand, so select it from the Packs and Tools menu. Select the switch by aiming at it with the magic wand and then pressing the connection button.

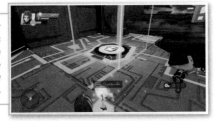

The switch is your trigger for this connection. When you step on it, the switch will send a signal to the door.

In the connection menu, select New Logic Connection and then Stepped On and finally Any. When you, or any character or AI step on the switch, it will send a signal or trigger to another toy.

Now you need to select the behavior or action caused by the trigger. Select the door by using your magic wand. Now you decide what happens when the door receives the message or trigger. Select Open. The two toys are now connected. Walk over to the switch and step on it. The door will then open. Walk into a cave and collect some orange Sparks in a capsule and then continue to the next door, which opens as you approach it.

Once you have connected the switch to the door, you can continue to the next task—after opening the door by stepping on the switch.

On the other side of the door, you find a checkpoint toy. This toy can save your progress. If your character dies, then he or she will return to the last checkpoint toy stepped on. You don't know what dangers await you, so be sure to save your progress by stepping on the checkpoint.

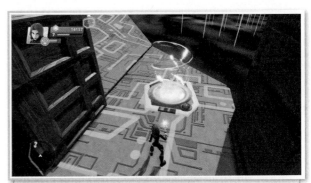

Checkpoint toys save your progress within a game. If you are making a large game, be sure to put a few in your Toy Box.

As you continue following Quorra up the side of the mountain, you come across a pool of lava that you must get across. To help you do this, you have a super cannon and an Action Button. You need to connect them. Whip out your magic wand and select the Action Button. Select New Logic Connection and then Pressed. When you press the Action Button, this sends a message. Now connect it to the Super Cannon and decide what you want the action to be. Select Tilt to 45 degrees to complete the connection. Finally, press the Action Button to tilt the Super Cannon and then walk into it and soar up and across the pool of lava.

GAME BASICS

CHARACTERS

POWER DISCS

MARVEL'S THE AVENGERS

SPIDER-MAN

GUARDIANS OF THE GALAXY

TOY BOX

TOY BOX COLLECTION

ACHIEVEMENTS

The Action Button serves as a trigger. Then connect it to the super cannon to tilt it up 45 degrees so you can launch yourself over the lava.

Quorra leads you farther up the mountain. You finally come to a large yellow cube. This is a trigger area. It acts like the trigger you stepped on to open the door. However, all you have to do to activate the trigger area is enter it. Plus, it is normally invisible unless you are editing. Try putting away your magic wand and the trigger area becomes invisible. There is also a checkpoint, so be sure to step on it.

Trigger areas are a great way to activate an action during a game without the players knowing it or having them step on a trigger.

This time you are breaking a connection between toys.

The pathway leading farther up the mountain is blocked. A falling object generator is spawning mine toys that roll down the path until they hit a Kill Switch and blow up. If you try to go up the path, you will be destroyed by the mine toys. Therefore, you need to break the logic connections between some toys.

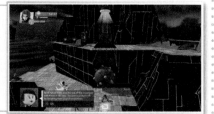

Falling mine toys are preventing you from advancing. You need to stop that falling object generator from dropping mine toys.

Something is sending a message to the falling object generator to tell it to drop mine toys. Look around and find the Repeater toy. Aim at it and then use the magic wand to select it. In the menu, scroll down to the connection with the falling object generator and delete the link. The mine toys stop dropping and now you can get up the ramp. Just be careful not to touch the Kill Switch or your character will be destroyed instead of the mine toy.

Move up the ramp to the ledge. Step onto the manhole cover and it will launch you up to the top of the ledge. Then climb up the ladder to the top of another ledge to find Quorra waiting for you. She is next to an elevator. However it is not working. It needs a trigger to activate it. Open up the Toy Box Editor and from the Creativi-Toys category, select the trigger. Place it on the ground.

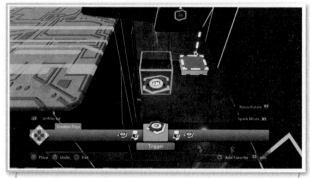

This time you need to select a toy to use as a trigger and place it in the Toy Box.

Now select the trigger using the magic wand and create a new logic connection so that it sends a message when it is stepped on by anyone. Next, connect it to the elevator platform and select the On choice so that when the message is received, the elevator will start going up and down. Once it is all connected, step on the trigger and ride the elevator to a higher ledge.

TIP

The falling mine toy obstacle is a simple connection of two toys with a third to help out. The Pulse toy sends a signal to the falling object generator to drop a mine toy as soon as the previous mine toy is destroyed. The Kill Switch at the bottom destroys the mine toy and causes another to be dropped. Thus this creates an endless loop of action until the connection is broken.

Game Creation

GAME BASICS | CHARACTERS | POWER DISCS | MARVEL'S THE AVENGERS | SPIDER-MAN | GUARDIANS OF THE GALAXY | TOY BOX | TOY BOX COLLECTION | ACHIEVEMENTS

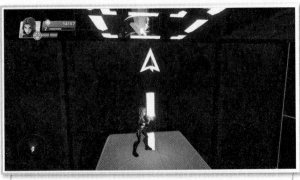

Notice that when you have your magic wand out, some toys (such as the elevator platform) have dashed lines showing the extent of their movement. However, if you put the wand away, those lines disappear. They are there to help you in editing the Toy Box.

It is nice to have big friends to help you defeat your enemies.

At the top of the ledge, walk onto the checkpoint to save your progress. Now you have to deal with some enemies. Notice that they have an orange color around them. They have been created by the enemy generator and set to the orange team. They will attack anyone who is not on the orange team—since you have not been assigned to the orange team, they will attack you.

Those enemies are on the orange team. You need to get some help for your team.

Use the magic wand to select the enemy generator on the far left side, which is not activated. Select Properties, and from the Team menu, select Blue Team and then exit. When you do, a couple small bridges and a team assigner appear. Move across the bridges and touch the team assigner. This causes a Tank Omnidroid to appear and be assigned to the blue team. Since you touched the team assigner, you are on the blue team. Watch as your new teammate goes after the orange enemies.

Climb up the ladder and follow Quorra the rest of the way to the top of the mountain. Here is your final challenge you must complete in order to get the treasure. The treasure is locked in a chamber behind a gate. The only way to open the gate is to drop something from the falling object generator into the basketball hoop. You will need to use Creativi-Toys to do this. There is no one way to complete this. You can make a simple way to get the ball into the hoop, or create a complex method—the choice is yours.

You have to get a ball into the hoop to score the treasure.

The first thing you need to do is put a trigger or other toy that you can connect to the falling object generator to get it to start dropping balls. Open the Toy Box Editor, go to the Creativi-Toys category, and select the trigger or the Action Button. Place it on the ground. Now select it with the magic wand, create a trigger event, and then connect it to the falling object generator. Select an ESPN basketball or other ball to drop when the trigger is activated.

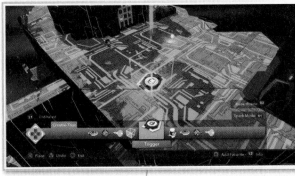

Start off with a trigger to activate the falling object generator. Make the connection between the two.

Now you have to figure out a way to get the ball from the generator to the hoop. A simple way is to use conveyor belts from the Platforming Toys category. Place one under the generator and then a couple more in a line all the way to the hoop. Now when a ball drops, it should be carried by the conveyor belts all the way to the hoop.

Conveyor belts can carry the ball to the hoop. Make sure they are all going in the same direction—towards the hoop.

Once you get your connections made, step on the trigger to drop a ball. Then watch to see if it goes in. You may need to use the magic wand to move toys around to get it just right. There are several different types of toys you can use to complete this. Once a ball goes into the hoop, the gate opens and you can enter to collect several capsules of orange and blue Sparks.

Watch the ball go into the hoop.

Then go collect the treasure!

TREASURE DEFENSE KIT

Games consist of several toys that are connected together. One of the games Quorra can show you is the treasure defense. In this, you have money to spend on some defenses and then must protect an object from waves of enemies. While the game kit that Quorra provides is fairly simple compared to the Toy Box Games you can play, this kit shows the basics and the vital connections. In addition to placing the kit in the Toy Box World, Quorra also explains several of the key toys and how they are connected to each other.

This is the treasure defense kit. All of the toys are grouped together. However, in a real game, you could move many of them out of sight, such as behind terrain or objects.

The inventory manager and storefront toys allow you to set up the ability for players to purchase toys during a game. You can customize when and what items are available as well as how much they will cost.

The first toy that Quorra introduces is the inventory manager. It is used in this game to limit the choices of toys that players can select in the editor. By setting the properties of this toy, you can choose exactly what toys are available. Next she discusses the storefront. This toy has two menus. One is used to organize a shop of items for sale. The other menu is for players to actually purchase those items during the game.

Because this game involves money, the money manager toy is a must. It lets you choose the type of currency you want to use as well as how it appears in the game, such as when you defeat enemies or break items. This money can then be spent in the storefront. The amount of money dropped by these things can be set using the loot drop manager toy. As you can see, if you want to use money and be able to buy things in the game, you need several different toys connected together.

While Quorra explains how some of the toys create an economy to introduce you to the importance of connecting toys to complete a function, where a game really starts is with the challenge maker. In order to begin a game, a player must first step on the challenge maker. For this game, the challenge maker is connected to the text displayer. This provides instructions to the player that have been written within these toys. After the text is displayed and the player presses a button to remove the instructions to start the game, the text displayer sends a signal to other toys to get the game going.

Each game needs a challenge maker as the interface players use to access and start a game. This is a feature new to the game.

TIP

The challenge maker is like the brain of the game. It starts the game and connects to several different toys to help progress a game along and then determine the victory conditions. When making your own games, always start with the challenge maker.

For example, in this game, the text displayer gives instructions to pick items to use in the game. Then it sends a message to the storefront to open and let the players start picking. It also activates the money manager, which provides money for the players to spend. When the players close the storefront after picking items, the storefront sends a message to the text displayer to give the next set of instructions—in this case, to place items to help defend the treasure. This opens another storefront toy and another money manager toy are activated so that players can access the storefront—by pressing the Toy Box Editor button—to purchase more items with the money they collect by defeating enemies. The editor manager then opens and lets the players place as many objects as desired until the money runs out.

Because this game has two different purposes for the storefront—setting up and during the game—you need two sets of storefronts and money managers. This allows you to also have different prices for the two storefronts.

Use the enemy wave generator to configure the types and numbers of enemies. If you connect this toy to locator toys, you can specify where you want the enemies to appear.

When the player is finished placing items and closes the storefront, the enemy wave generator begins creating groups of enemies to charge and attack Odin's treasure. In the enemy wave generator, you can choose the types of enemies and how many appear in each wave. For this game, there is only one wave. If the enemies destroy the treasure, then the game is over. However, if the player defeats all the enemies with the treasure intact, then the result is a victory.

Try playing the game to see how everything works within the game. Then take some time to select each toy with the magic wand and look at all the properties and connections with other toys. The designers have left a note for you with descriptions about the game. Just walk over the toys with a "?" over them.

Try out the game to see how it works. These toys with the "?" on them contain information about how the game was made. Walk over them to access their text.

TIP

The treasure defense type of game is quite complicated with lots of different toys and multiple connections. However, by using the kit, you can quickly place this game into a Toy Box World and then make modifications so it suits your purposes.

COLLECTOR CHALLENGE KIT

The collector challenge kit is another template that is a complete game. This type of game requires players to collect objects within a certain amount of time. Quorra walks you through the basics of this type of game.

The collector challenge kit has everything you need to create a collection game. Of course, when making your own game, you will want to move those colored orbs around to make it more difficult to collect them. However, they are already connected to the other toys when you use a kit or template.

As with all games, you start with a challenge maker. It usually has more connections than any other toy. For a collection game, you need a collectible tracker. It can keep track of orbs, rings, and other collectible items. As you can see, there are three of these toys—one for each color of orb. The collectible trackers have a couple different functions. For this game, when all of the assigned color of orb are collected, the collectible tracker sends a message to the counter. Also, whenever a player collects one of the orbs, it sends a message to the scoreboard. You can set each collectible tracker to a different score value so that each color of orb is worth different amounts of points.

The collectible trackers keep track of the various collectibles in the game and send a message when all of a certain type is collected.

The counter is busy in this game. It receives messages from each of the collectible trackers. When it receives one from each, it send a message back to the collectible trackers to reset and place the orbs back into the game area. It also resets itself so that it is ready to begin receiving messages again. The other main controlling toy is the timer. It begins counting down when the challenge maker sends a message to it and the game starts and, when time runs out, it sends a message to the challenge maker that the game has ended. When using a timer, you need to set the amount of time you want the game to last in its properties.

The counter and timer help keep this game running by providing points and limiting the time players have to get as many collectibles as they can.

The scoreboard keeps track of how many points the players have earned and displays it on the screen. This also provides the scores for the challenge maker at the end of the game for the final tally. Then when the game is over, the level starter toy sends a message to the collectible trackers to hide the orbs and to the scoreboard to reset so that the game is all ready for the next time it is played. Think of this as cleaning up.

Try out the game to see how it works now that you know how all the toys work together. Try making changes such as the points for each orb or the amount of time you have. Use the magic wand to move the orbs around as well.

TIP

If you want to try making a game from scratch, a collectible game is one of the easier games to create. To begin with, you may only want to use one type of collectible, and once you have that working, add more later.

── SOCCER KIT ──

There are a number of different types of sports games you can create in the Toy Box. However, most are similar in the way they function. Quorra provides a soccer kit for you to try out and explore. However, you can easily use the same concept to make a hockey game or, with a few more modifications, create a basketball game. The Toy Box offers several different sports toys to help you create these types of games. However, let's start with soccer.

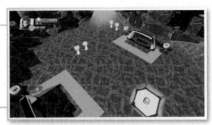

> The soccer kit is another simple template. However, it can teach you a lot about scoring.

The central toy for the soccer kit is the challenge maker. Players step on it to start a game. When the game begins, the challenge maker sends messages to the timer and the scoreboard telling them to reset back to their initial values.

At the start of the game, the timer and scoreboard reset. Then, during the game, the timer counts down and the scoreboard counts up as goals are scored.

When a ball goes into a goal, it triggers several actions that are caused by messages sent from the goal to other toys such as the party cannons and the scoreboard.

A soccer game needs a soccer ball. So when the game begins, the challenge maker sends a message to the falling object generator to drop a soccer ball onto the field. Then, when the game is over, it sends another message to remove the ball from the Toy Box World.

The soccer game ends when the timer reaches zero. The timer sends a message to the challenge maker to end the game. The challenge maker then sends messages to the falling object generator to remove the soccer ball and to the party cannons to do a grand finale.

The falling object generator drops a soccer ball onto the field at the start of the game.

The soccer game ends with a bang of fireworks and the final score. You can add some more toys to this kit so you can have sound effects and other actions.

The goals in this game are also connected to other toys. When the soccer ball goes into the game, it causes several things. The ball resets to a position in the middle of the field. If you look while you have your magic wand out, you can see a locator there. The goal also sends a message to the scoreboard to advance the score by one. Finally, messages are sent to the two party cannons on either side of the goal so they launch confetti into the air.

> **TIP**
>
> Templates are a great place to start. It is very easy to use the soccer kit and convert it to a hockey game. Edit the falling object generator to drop a hockey puck and change the grassy terrain to ice.

GAME BASICS

CHARACTERS

POWER DISCS

MARVEL'S THE AVENGERS

SPIDER-MAN

GUARDIANS OF THE GALAXY

TOY BOX

TOY BOX COLLECTION

ACHIEVEMENTS

EASY PINBALL KIT

Pinball games are a lot of fun to play in the Toy Box, but can be tough to make. Therefore, Quorra has a kit all ready for you to explore. She also explains some of the tricks you can use to help create some physics such as gravity.

The pinball kit is a complete game that is ready to play. However, you can still modify it once you learn how it works.

As with all games, the challenge maker is where you start the game. It also connects several of the key components and ties them together to make the game work. Quorra also introduces a new toy that is very important to this game—the remote controller. This actually lets you assign controller inputs for game play. The remote controller only works when a character steps onto it. Then the character is temporarily removed from play and the player gains control of specific Creativi-Toys in the game rather than controlling the character.

The remote controller is a powerful tool that gives the player control over different elements in a game.

The remote controller in the pinball game lets you control the left and right pinball flippers.

The previous kits and templates have all used the default camera view, which is focused on the character. However, in this game, a target camera is used. This lets you set the view of the game the player will see when playing. Once the target camera is placed, then a locator is used to show where you want the camera to look.

The target camera lets you set the perfect angle of view for the game.

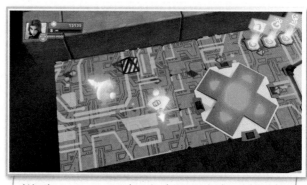

Weather vanes are used to simulate gravity by pushing the ball in specific directions. In this case, towards the flippers.

TIP

There are several other types of cameras available for purchase in the Toy Box Store. These allow you to view top down, side scrolling, and much more. Selecting the correct camera for a game can make a lot of difference.

There are several other toys that help make the game work. When a player steps on the challenge maker to begin the game, the character is automatically dropped right onto the remote controller. When the player presses the button to use the remote controller, this sends a message to activate the target camera. The remote controller also tells the falling object generator to drop a ball via the logic gate toy.

One of the challenges of a pinball game is gravity. The Toy Box Worlds are flat while pinball games are set on an angle. Therefore, the game needs a way to simulate gravity so that the balls will move towards the flippers just like they would in real life. To accomplish this, the game uses weather vanes. These weather vanes are then connected to locators to choose the direction of the force they use to move the ball. You can even adjust how hard the forces push the ball by adjusting the properties of the weather vanes.

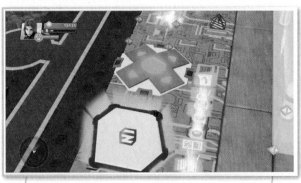

All of these toys work together to create the game.

When the ball is released, super cannons propel it up the chute. At the corner, the ball enters a trigger area. When this happens, a second weather vane is activated and blows the ball into the pinball table area. It deactivates as soon as the ball exits this small trigger area. The table area is another trigger area that activates the first weather vane that blows the ball towards the flippers. Every time the ball hits a pinball bumper or pinball bouncer, it sends a message to the scoreboard to increase the score. A racing gate is positioned behind the flippers. The racing gate is connected to a kill switch. If the ball hits this gate, the ball is destroyed and disappears. This then sends a message to the counter toy to reduce the number by one. The counter toy keeps track of how many balls the player has. When the counter reaches zero, a message is sent to the challenge maker to end the game. If the counter is not yet zero, it sends a message to the logic gate which then sends another message to the falling object generator to drop another ball.

There are two trigger areas that activate and deactivate the weather vanes. This is important since you only want them moving the ball in specific directions at certain places in the game.

TIP

If you want to add the ability to earn extra balls, you could create a link between the scoreboard and the counter. For example, you could state that when the score reaches 100, the counter is increased by one—thus giving an extra ball.

You may have noticed a large, bluish, transparent object over the top of the pinball table area. This is a scalable barrier block. This is a new feature to the Toy Box. For the pinball game, it prevents the ball from leaving the table area. In other games, it can help keep characters in the game area without being a visible barrier. When you put your magic wand away, the barrier becomes invisible. If you are doing a side-scroller game, you can use a vertical barrier to keep characters from falling off edges. Remove the barrier from the pinball game and see what happens. The ball may hit a bumper or bouncer and get flipped out of the table area. Then the game does not work anymore.

The scalable barrier block is used to keep the balls in play for the pinball game.

TIP

The scalable barrier block can be set in properties to have a collision effect. If something hits it, the block gives off an animation like hitting a forcefield. However, for most games, you want it to be completely invisible. Therefore, for the pinball game, that collision effect is turned off.

RACING GATE KIT

The last kit that Quorra shows you is the racing gate kit. When you ask her about it, not only does the kit appear in the Toy Box World, but also a large area where you can set up a race.

> The racing gate kit lets you create a race game without the limitations of the race track creator or using race track pieces. In fact, you can make a race anywhere.

The challenge maker is the starting place for this game. When a player steps on it, this begins the game. The ready up checker toy waits for all the players in the Toy Box World to join the game before the race starts. Because up to four players can play this game, there are four counters—one for each player. These keep track of the number of laps the players complete. In this case, when a player has completed three laps and moves through the last racing gate, the counter sends a message to the challenge maker to record the player's time and finish the race for that player. It also sends a message to the ready up checker to hold the player at the end of the race until all of the other players finish.

Because up to four players can participate in this game, the kit includes four counter toys to keep track of laps in the race.

When the game begins, just the first racing gate is activated. After you run through it, the next racing gate activates and this one deactivates.

When the race begins, the challenge maker deactivates all of the racing gates except for the first racing gate. The challenge maker also sends a message to the timer to start timing. As each player moves through the first racing gate, it deactivates—just for that player—and then sends a message to the next racing gate to activate—once again just for that player. This ensures that each player has to go through all of the racing gates in order so no one can cheat.

Try out this game with just your one character to see how it works. The racing gates are all positioned close by. When designing such a game, keep all the toys close by while you make connections. Test it out to make sure it works. Then you can move the racing gates around the course. Otherwise it is difficult to connect all the gates if they are scattered about the Toy Box World.

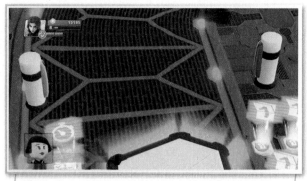

The racing gates are connected to each other so as one deactivates, the next activates. Each player has only one active racing gate at a time.

At the end of the race, the challenge maker displays your time.

The counters keep track of the laps. Once all players have completed the race, and the counters have all sent a finished message to the challenge maker, this toy then ends the race and displays the results. It also sends messages to the other toys to reset so they are ready for the next game.

NOTE

While Quorra shows you five kits, there are more than seventy additional kits available in the Toy Store. Kits are unlocked when you purchase all of the toys included in the kit or when you complete some of Quorra's tasks. Some kits can be connected together to create a large game with several small games. Each kit can be customized and modified. For beginning Toy Box users, as well as those with experience, kits are a quick way to make a game and also learn how to connect toys together for different functions.

ASSAULT ON ASGARD

Disney Infinity: Marvel Super Heroes includes two Toy Box Games. These are unlocked by placing the corresponding hexagonal Power Disc onto the Disney Infinity base. Assault on Asgard is one of these games. It is similar to a tower defense game where you must defend an object from the enemies. The best way to learn how to play this game is to play it. The introduction serves as a tutorial.

The game consists of the introduction and ten levels. You can play the game with any character you choose. If your character is defeated (health bar runs out) during a level, you can swap in another character. However, you can't swap your original character in for the remainder of the level, so have some extra characters ready to go since the enemies don't stop while you are swapping characters. Defeated heroes can be used again if you restart the level or complete the level.

Loki is planning on taking over Asgard with the help of the Frost Giants. He has opened a portal and will begin his attacks as soon as Odin goes into the Odinsleep.

> **TIP**
>
> Depending on the enemies you face, you may want to use a couple heroes during a level anyway. For example, you may want a fast hero to deal with normal, weaker enemies and then bring in a more powerful, but slower, hero to deal with the really big and tough enemies.

THE SAGA'S START

When you first begin Assault on Asgard, you are taken to the introductory level where you learn the basics. The object of the game is to protect Odin's treasures, which are in golden, cylinder-shaped objects. There is only one in the introduction, but some later levels have as many as four that you must protect. Each level also has three Asgardian townspeople. If you pick them up and then throw them into the townsperson door, you can earn more loot as you defeat enemies. For this introduction, there is only one Asgardian.

You must protect Odin's treasure and prevent the enemies from destroying it.

At the start of each level, you begin by picking the traps you will use. These are defensive toys that help you defeat the enemies. The menu that appears not only lists the traps available, but also the types of enemies you will be facing. For this level, you only have to worry about Small Frost Giants. There is also only one trap available to begin with. As you advance through each level in turn, you unlock an additional trap so that by level 10, you have lots of traps from which to choose. For now, select the Asgardian spread turret.

At the start of the level, you select which traps you will be using. Choose carefully because you are stuck with those traps for the entire level.

Once you select the traps you will be using, you then have the opportunity to place those traps. Each trap costs a certain amount of money. You begin the level with some initial money. Use that money to place traps. For the introduction, you have only enough money to place a single turret. Put it somewhere between Odin's treasure and the enemy door from which the enemies appear. This level only has one wave. However, in all of the other ten levels, you must fight off six waves of enemies. As you defeat enemies, they drop coins. Be sure to collect those so you can spend the money in between each wave to place more traps.

Place the turret in the path the enemies follow. Look for the purple arrows on the ground. They show likely pathways the enemies will take to get to Odin's treasure.

As the countdown to the enemy wave begins, move to the left side of the area and pick up the Asgardian. Then take aim at the townsperson door on the right side and throw him into it. You score some extra gold as a reward. By now, the Frost Giants are approaching.

While waiting for enemies to appear, pick up the Asgardian and throw him into the door to save him. You get some extra loot for your efforts.

There are only a few Frost Giants in this level, so it is not too difficult. The turret will open fire when they get into range. However, the turret by itself is not enough to defeat them—though it will do some damage and make it easier for you to finish them off. Use your character's melee and ranged attacks to defeat the enemies. While some will stop to fight you if you are in their path, others will rush towards Odin's treasure and begin attacking it. The treasure has a health bar. If the bar is completely depleted, the treasure is destroyed and the level ends in defeat. To win, you must defeat all of the enemies without the treasure being destroyed. So fight off these Small Frost Giants to complete this level—and your training.

Engage the enemies before they get to Odin's treasure.

Keep an eye on the treasure. It is easy to be distracted in a fight and have other enemies sneak past you to attack the treasure.

TIP

When playing with more than one player, divide up the responsibilities. Have one stay back to protect Odin's treasure while the rest attack the enemies before they can get to the treasure.

THE ASGARD HUB

After completing the introduction, The Saga's Start, you are taken to the hub. There are ten levels in Assault on Asgard. Since you finished the intro level, an enemy door has been removed from the first level, Spawn of Niflheim. In addition, the intro level is also available in the middle of the hub if you want to play it again. There is a skill tree spot where you can purchase new skills as your characters level up. Finally, there is the Survival Mode, which unlocks after you complete the first level. Move your character to the open door on the left to get started on the first level.

The hub is where you come between levels.

SPAWN OF NIFLHEIM

Traps Available

- Asgardian Spread Turret
- Asgardian Freeze Mine

Enemies

- Small Frost Giants
- Medium Frost Giants
- A.I.M. Drones

NOTE

While you used the spread turret in the intro level, you also get the freeze mine for this level. The freeze mine is triggered when an enemy gets close to it. The mine detonates and freezes all enemies on the ground within its blast radius. This not only slows down the waves, but also provides some easy targets that your character can attack without them fighting back. The spread turret is not very powerful, but can fire in an arc and hit several enemies near each other at the same time. Traps all have a recharge time after they attack. The turret fires several bursts, then has to reload. The mines recharge after a while and then can detonate again.

When this level begins, you can pick two traps. Since you only have two from which to choose, select both. The spread turret and the freeze mine can be used through all ten levels and work well together. After selecting the traps, you can place them. This first level requires you to defend a single Odin's Treasure. Look for the purple arrows to see where the enemies will travel. There are two enemy doors from which enemies enter. However, for the first wave, they will only come out of the enemy door on the left side. You have 600 points to spend on traps. This lets you either place a couple turrets or two freeze mines and a single turret. The latter is a better idea. While turrets cause damage, an enemy wave can quickly walk by them without taking a lot of damage. Therefore, place a freeze mine across the path in a narrow area and then place a turret right behind it. Then when the enemies are frozen by the mine, the turret can fire on them while they are immobile. Put another freeze mine in another narrow area—a chokepoint—to slow down more enemies that get past your turret. Once you have your traps set, it is time to begin the first wave.

GAME BASICS · CHARACTERS · POWER DISCS · MARVEL'S THE AVENGERS · SPIDER-MAN · GUARDIANS OF THE GALAXY · TOY BOX · TOY BOX COLLECTION · ACHIEVEMENTS

Since enemies are only coming from one enemy door this time, place your traps along the path they must follow. If they don't work well, you can always sell them and put new traps out after the first wave is defeated.

Defend near the treasure. While you can engage away from the treasure at the beginning, you don't want enemies to get to the treasure to attack it with no defences around.

When the first wave begins, you have a bit of time. Quickly grab an Asgardian and throw him into the door. You get enough money to buy an extra turret when you get to place more traps after the first wave is defeated. After taking care of one of these little guys, check out the treasure. The Frost Giants have most likely been slowed down by the freeze mines and some may be destroyed by the turret while frozen. However, the A.I.M. Drones can bypass the mines and are not affected by them (however turrets can fire at flying enemies). You will need to use a ranged attack to hit these drones.

After each wave, you can spend the money you have collected by defeating enemies and throwing Asgardians into the door on more traps. If your first traps were not in a good position, sell them back and then start over. This time the enemies will still come from the same enemy door. There are two paths that lead directly to the treasure. By now you should have enough to purchase a couple turrets to place near the treasure and freeze mines along the paths. The turrets near the treasure can also fire on the flying A.I.M. Drones and help eliminate those threats. When you are ready, start the second wave.

> **TIP**
>
> As the early waves are the weakest, it is usually a good time to get those Asgardians. Plus the money you earn can be used on traps before the next wave. The earlier you get the bonus money, the more you get to use those traps.

Saving Asgardians is a great way to score some extra money for traps. Just don't neglect the enemies for too long.

Position some traps near the treasure because enemies are all moving towards this location. This ensures that all enemies will hit at least some of your traps.

> **TIP**
>
> As a general rule, it is best to position traps close to the treasure during the early waves. You know that all enemies will be headed to that location and then when they get there, they stop to attack, giving the turrets targets that won't move away. Then as you earn more money, begin expanding your traps out from the treasure along paths that most of the enemies will follow. That will help slow down the waves and whittle down their numbers. The second wave follows the same path at the first. Keep them away from the treasure and be sure to collect as many coins as you can so you can buy more traps.

The A.I.M. Drones will get to Odin's treasure first because they are not affected by the freeze mines.

Try to stay near the treasure because you know that is where all enemies will eventually end up. Plus you need to make sure the treasure is protected. If your character has some area attacks (such as a special move) that can affect several enemies at once, wait until there is a large group of enemies and then release it. Remember that you have to collect purple Sparks to charge up special moves. There are some purple capsules in the level to help you do this. Once the first wave is defeated, you have a few seconds to gather up any remaining coins before preparing for the next wave.

A group of frozen enemies makes for an easy target. Jump up in the middle of them, and then press the attack button to come down with a ground slam to damage all of them.

The third wave comes from both enemy doors. Keep your traps in the narrow parts of the path where you know enemies have to travel. This wave also includes Medium Frost Giants, so you will have to spend a little extra time defeating these larger enemies. There is a total of six waves. Each subsequent wave is a bit more difficult. However, if you have been diligent about collecting coins, by the final wave, you should have traps all over the pathways to the treasure. Stay near the treasure because there are so many Frost Giants in the later waves that many will still get through your traps. That is why it is good to have several turrets surrounding your treasure.

Medium Frost Giants are more powerful and can take more damage. However, they are easier to defeat if you wait until a freeze mine turns them into ice.

STORM OF JOTNAR

Traps Available

- Asgardian Spread Turret
- Asgardian Freeze Mine
- Asgardian Barrier

Enemies

- Small Frost Giants
- Medium Frost Giants

NOTE

The barrier is the new trap for this level. It is the least expensive trap and is basically a low wall that you can use to block passageways. However, it is destructible and enemies will break them down and then advance. They are best used to slow down enemies along one path so you can deal with those on another path first.

The Asgardian Barrier is unlocked for this level. Use it to slow down enemies.

The second wave has attacks from two enemy doors—on opposite sides of the area. Position your defenses accordingly. Wave 3 also has attacks from two enemy doors. However, this time it is the other two enemy doors. You may want to sell back all your traps and then put down new ones to cover those two directions. Start bringing your turrets in close to the treasure so those Frost Giants that do get through will come under fire while they are attacking the treasure.

This level has only one treasure—but it is surrounded by enemy doors.

This level is tougher than the previous level. You must defend one treasure located in the middle of the area. However, there are four enemy doors that surround you. Luckily, for the first wave, the Frost Giants only come from one enemy door. Try using some barriers to see how they work. Then back them up with turrets.

Because you are attacked from all directions, stay near the treasure to deal with enemies that get through your traps.

In wave 4, you get attacked from all four directions. Stay near the center for this one. If you try to engage enemies from one direction, others get to the treasure behind you. Surround the treasure with turrets to help you defeat the Frost Giants that try to destroy the treasure. By staying in one spot, you can more quickly gather the coins from the defeated enemies. Wave 5 is a bit tougher. Medium Frost Giants attack towards the end. Try to clear out all of the Small Frost Giants before the larger enemies arrive. The final wave hits you with lots of Small Frost Giants. Then eight Medium Frost Giants attack all at once—two from each direction. Your turrets will help weaken them, so move in and finish them off to complete this level.

LOKI'S MACHINATIONS

Traps Available

- Asgardian Spread Turret
- Asgardian Freeze Mine
- Asgardian Barrier
- Asgardian Catapult Trap

Enemies

- Small Frost Giants
- Medium Frost Giants
- A.I.M. Drones

NOTE

The catapult trap is less expensive than a turret. When an enemy steps on it, it launches them in one direction. When placing this trap, you can see the flight path of the enemy when it springs. Rotate the trap so you can send the enemy in the direction you want—preferably into one of the pools of lava where they will be destroyed.

The conveyor belts near the enemy doors help the enemies move much faster towards the treasure.

This level has a single treasure in the middle of the area. There are only two enemy doors on opposite sides of the treasure. One is closer to the treasure than the other. There are conveyor belts in front of each enemy door. This prevents you from placing traps along those paths and helps the enemies move faster as they advance.

For the first wave, the enemies come from both enemy doors. For the one closest to the treasure, you don't have a lot of depth for traps due to the conveyor belts. Place a freeze mine near the conveyor belt and back it up with a turret. Then place another freeze mine and turret along the narrow pathway from the other enemy door, as close to the treasure as possible. Focus on defeating the enemies from the close enemy door first, then turn your attention to the enemies from the other enemy door since they take longer to get to the treasure.

TIP

Grab the Asgardian close to the treasure and throw him through the doorway to safety. However, the other two are tough to get to. You have to jump over lava and across moving conveyor belts to get to them and then back across to get to the doorway. If your character falls into the lava, they are out for the rest of this level. Plus it can take some time to get this—time that Odin's treasure can come under attack. So you may consider just leaving those two Asgardians alone for this level.

The enemies from the closest enemy door are the first threat you need to eliminate.

After the first wave, spend your money on more traps. However, begin concentrating them along the narrow pathway between the treasure and the far enemy door. You then focus on fighting off the enemies from the closest enemy door with a few defenses near the treasure. By the time you have finished them off, you can turn your attention to the attacks from the other enemy door, which have been delayed and weakened by your traps.

Position most of your defenses along the pathway from the farther enemy door to the treasure.

Waves 2 and 3 add some Medium Frost Giants as part of the attack. Again, focus on the attacks from the close enemy door and then deal with the other attacks. As you add more traps to that side, you will find that there are fewer enemies getting through and that they are taking longer to get to the treasure.

Freeze mines can stop an entire group of enemies. This is a great chance to move in and finish them off before they thaw and renew their attacks.

The A.I.M. Drones begin attacking in the last few waves. Plus you have more Medium Frost Giants and lots of Small Frost Giants. Use the same strategies as before and you will be fine. Load up on turrets around the treasure if you have already saturated the pathway with traps. In the final wave, the enemy sends lots of Medium Frost Giants to try to occupy you while Small Frost Giants rush in behind and try to get past you. Defend near the treasure to prevent the enemy from attacking it. Defeat all the enemies and victory is yours.

BURNING FROST

Traps Available

- Asgardian Spread Turret
- Asgardian Freeze Mine
- Asgardian Barrier
- Asgardian Catapult Trap
- Asgardian Energy Shield

Enemies

- Small Frost Giants
- Medium Frost Giants
- A.I.M. Drones

NOTE

The energy shield is the new trap you get for this level. This device provides protection from missiles and projectiles. It can be good to use to protect your treasure from enemies with ranged attacks.

This is a tough level. While previous levels have had only one treasure, this level has two that you must protect. If that were not tough enough, they are on opposite sides of the area. There are also four enemy doors that all lead into the center. Then from there, they can go to either treasure. Since you can't be at both treasures at the same time, you have to decide how you want to use your traps. You can split them up at each treasure, concentrate them in the center, or heavily defend one treasure with traps and spend your time at the other treasure. The catch is that if either treasure is destroyed, you are defeated.

There are two Odin's treasures in this level and they are located on opposite sides of the area.

The first wave comes out of one enemy door. However, they then split up and head for both treasures. Be sure to place a turret near each treasure with a freeze mine in front of it. Then place another freeze mine or other trap somewhere near the intersection by the enemy door where the Frost Giants have to split up. Try to defeat as many enemies as you can near the enemy door and then mop up any that get to the treasures. Be sure to collect all the coins because you need them to build more traps. This first wave is a good chance to get at least one of the Asgardians since each gives you enough loot to get a turret.

Try to defeat as many enemies as you can as they emerge from the enemy door and before they can split up and head to the two different treasures.

Wave 2 comes from two enemy doors across from each other. It starts out with several A.I.M. Drones that fly towards each of the treasures. Therefore, be sure you have at least two turrets near each treasure to help deal with them. Also position some freeze mines along the pathways leading directly towards each treasure. Wave 3, on the other hand, sends out Frost Giants first and then, while you are engaging them, sends in the Drones. The Medium Frost Giants arrive in wave 4. The dangerous aspect of them is that while you are busy fighting them, the Small Frost Giants are running to the two treasures. By this time, you should have at least three turrets around each treasure with a nearby freeze mine. Be sure to have turrets all around your treasures. The enemy likes to go to the other side and uses the treasure as cover if there is only one turret.

Make sure your characters have a block breaker attack. That makes defeating these Medium Frost Giants a bit easier. In fact, you might want to switch out to a character that has this type of attack if your first character does not.

By the time you get to wave 5 and the final wave, one of your treasures is probably in worse shape than the other. Make that treasure your priority. Try to stop the enemies headed towards the healthier treasure at the start, then rush over to the weaker treasure and defend it up close. Position more freeze mines and other traps near the healthier treasure to help keep it safe until you can get back to it and mop up the remaining enemies.

CHAMPION OF ASGARD

Traps Available

- Asgardian Spread Turret
- Asgardian Freeze Mine
- Asgardian Barrier
- Asgardian Catapult Trap
- Asgardian Energy Shield
- Asgardian Mine Deployer

Enemies

- Small Frost Giants
- Medium Frost Giants
- A.I.M. Drones

> **NOTE**
>
> The mine deployer is similar to the freeze mine. However, instead of freezing the enemies when it detonates, it causes damage. This is great for damaging several enemies at once. Its down side is the time it takes to recharge.

This level once again features two treasures. However, this time, both are in the center of the area and relatively close to one another. There are four enemy doors with paths that approach the treasures from two main directions. The best way to defend the treasures is to position turrets near the treasures and then freeze mines at the chokepoints where the paths approach the treasures. Then, as you can place more traps later in the level, expand your traps out along the pathways.

Because both treasures are in the center, that is where you should build your defenses at the start.

The first wave consists of only Small Frost Giants. However, it gives you a good feel of how they approach and if your traps are working. As usual, place a turret near each treasure along with some mine deployers. In fact, try placing a mine deployer as close as you can to a turret. It will blow up when enemies approach it, and then once it recharges, it will blow up again to damage any remaining enemies.

By concentrating traps near the center, the defenses can work together to cause as much damage to the enemies as possible.

As you advance through the waves, enemies begin coming out of more enemy doors. By wave 4, they are coming at you from all four and all about the same time; plan on enemies getting to your treasures. There are too many and they move quickly so traps along the pathways can't stop them all. Therefore, be sure to have at least two turrets around each treasure. They are good for shooting down the A.I.M. Drones as well as hitting Frost Giants who are attacking your treasures.

By the later waves, be sure to have turrets all around your treasures because lots of enemies are headed your way.

Use teleporters to quickly get to the doorway so you can throw Asgardians to safety. Scout out the area during trap placement and plan the routes you will take to get to these little people.

In wave 5, the Medium Frost Giants begin attacking. Because they are slower, go after the Small Frost Giants first and then you can deal with the Mediums. The final wave throws everything at you. It starts with drones, then Small Frost Giants, and then lots of Medium Frost Giants at the end. Be sure to have either freeze mines or mine deployers near your turrets to deal with them. Their attacks are slow and these mines can detonate once or twice while they are there to slow them down or cause damage until you can get there to finish them off.

Don't let those Medium Frost Giants attack your treasures. They can cause a lot of damage.

The first wave hits you from all four enemy doors. Therefore, a good tactic is to place freeze mines at the base of each flight of stairs, two turrets on either side of each treasure to attack the enemies as they are frozen as well as those near the treasures, and a mine deployer right next to each trap. That makes for a great initial deployment. In fact, since there are only Small Frost Giants in the first wave, these defenses can usually take care of them on their own, allowing you to go after those Asgardians. Get all three of them and that is a lot of money to spend on the second wave.

You start out with enough money to have some pretty good defenses for the first wave.

THUNDER STRIKE

Traps Available

- Asgardian Spread Turret
- Asgardian Freeze Mine
- Asgardian Barrier
- Asgardian Catapult Trap
- Asgardian Energy Shield
- Asgardian Mine Deployer
- Asgardian Healing Rune

Enemies

- Small Frost Giants
- Medium Frost Giants
- A.I.M. Drones

NOTE

The healing rune is not really a trap. Instead, it is a device that will heal nearby characters. If your characters have been taking a lot of damage and are even being defeated during the levels, consider placing one or two of these around so you can heal while in the middle of the battle.

This level is large. However, most of the fighting takes place in the central area. You have two treasures here like the previous level. However, they are a bit more spread apart. There are four different enemy doors and they all have paths leading down stairs to get to the treasures—two paths moving towards each treasure from opposite sides. Therefore, you need to place traps all around your treasures and plan on defending them up close.

This is a large area. However, most of the fighting takes place right in the center.

You need some bonus loot for traps. Therefore, consider going after some of the Asgardians. Even through they are spread out, there are teleports around that can help you get from one end of the area to the other side where the doorway is located. Try to do this in the early levels when the threats to your treasures are not quite as great.

The second wave has some Medium Frost Giants. However, between your traps and your own efforts, this is not a very tough wave either. Be sure to collect coins from the defeated enemies and use them to buy more mines and turrets. In fact, try putting two freeze mines on either side of each treasure and two mine deployers on the other two sides. Along with turrets, any enemies that get close to your treasures will take a lot of damage.

Even Medium Frost Giants will have a hard time getting to your treasures and causing them damage.

TIP

When you have to defend two different treasures, consider putting more traps around one to defend it while you have less around the second. Then spend most of your time defending the second while the traps take care of the first treasure. If you position a variety of traps around your treasures, the enemy will have a hard time getting to the treasure and then staying there very long to inflict much damage.

JOTUNHEIM INCURSION

Traps Available

- Asgardian Spread Turret
- Asgardian Freeze Mine
- Asgardian Barrier
- Asgardian Catapult Trap
- Asgardian Energy Shield
- Asgardian Mine Deployer
- Asgardian Healing Rune
- Asgardian Decoy

Enemies

- Small Frost Giants
- Medium Frost Giants
- Large Frost Giants
- A.I.M. Drones

NOTE

The decoy is inexpensive and can distract enemies. Place them along the paths away from treasures to slow down enemies who stop to attack the decoys.

This level takes place in a large hall. You only have one treasure to defend. However, that also means that all the enemies are going to go after that one. One enemy door is fairly close to the treasure while the other two are at a distance on the other side of the hall. Start off with your traps fairly close in to the treasure on both sides. Then as you progress through the waves, put more traps along the path to the two enemy doors farther away.

TIP

The pathways in this level are wider. Therefore, individual mines are not as effective, as some enemies run around them. You may want to deploy mines in pairs to be sure to cover the entire width of the pathways to the treasure.

One of the enemy doors is closer to the treasure. This is where you need to be at the start of each wave.

The first wave consists of Small Frost Giants. Put yourself between the treasure and the closest enemy door and fight off the enemies as they approach. Then move back to the treasure to protect it up close. Unless your defenses are very effective, you may not have a lot of time to get the Asgardians without risking some damage to the treasure. The second wave includes some A.I.M. Drones, so be sure you have several turrets to deal with them.

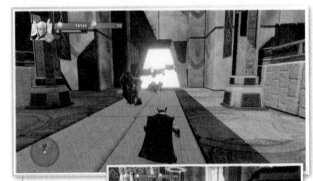

Because your treasure is attacked from two directions, keep turrets and other traps all around your treasure. The turrets can make short work of the A.I.M. Drones.

Later waves include some Medium Frost Giants. You need to worry about those who have a ranged attack. They can stand back and throw ice projectiles at you as well as at the treasure. Because they are a bigger threat when they come from the far side, place some mine deployers along their paths; that should help take care of them with a little help from you. In the final level you have to deal with Large Frost Giants. Not only do they throw ice at you, they also have a freezing attack that inflicts damage after it freezes you. Press the jump button to break out of it and hit these big guys with your most powerful attacks. Since they lob ice at the treasure, you need to go out and fight them or they will stand back and destroy Odin's treasure.

Go after the enemies as they emerge from the enemy door closest to the treasure. By the time you finish them off, head back towards the treasure. If you planned your defenses along the long pathway well, there will be few enemies that ever get to the treasure.

TRICKSTER'S GAMBIT

Traps Available

- Asgardian Spread Turret
- Asgardian Freeze Mine
- Asgardian Barrier
- Asgardian Catapult Trap
- Asgardian Energy Shield
- Asgardian Mine Deployer
- Asgardian Healing Rune
- Asgardian Decoy
- Asgardian Focus Turret

Enemies

- Small Frost Giants
- Medium Frost Giants
- Large Frost Giants
- A.I.M. Drones

NOTE

The focus turret uses lightning to attack enemies and is more focused than the spread turret. Combine the two with each other to bolster your defenses around your treasures.

This level gives you a single treasure to defend. However, there are three enemy doors around you and four different pathways to get to the treasure. Because you get enemies coming from all three enemy doors right at the start in the first wave, concentrate your traps near the treasure. The Asgardians are scattered around and take some time to retrieve and deliver to the doorway, so you may want to hold off on that.

Enemies can attack your single treasure from three different enemy doors along narrow pathways surrounded by lava.

Because you get attacked from several different directions, stay close to the treasure. Try to engage enemies at the closer enemy doors with ranged attacks, but don't stray too far away. You have to deal with Medium Frost Giants in the first wave—so be ready with a character that can break blocks and has some powerful melee attacks. Be sure to collect all the coins as you need all the money you can get for more traps.

This level sends Medium Frost Giants right in the first wave.

The second wave is not too tough. It consists of Medium Frost Giants and A.I.M. Drones. The third and fourth waves are very similar. Position freeze mines along the pathways and then attack them when they are frozen. Be sure to include a turret near the mines to hit them while they are chillin'. Wave 5 sends in a Large Frost Giant along with the Mediums. You need a character with a block breaking attack and some heavy melee damage to deal with these enemies. The final wave is more of the same with two Large Frost Giants at the end. You need to go out and fight them or they will throw projectiles at your treasure and destroy it before they get to your traps.

Medium and Large Frost Giants can take a lot of damage. Position mines and turrets along the way to weaken them before you have to fight them.

ASGARD UNDER SIEGE

Traps Available

- Asgardian Spread Turret
- Asgardian Freeze Mine
- Asgardian Barrier
- Asgardian Catapult Trap
- Asgardian Energy Shield
- Asgardian Mine Deployer
- Asgardian Healing Rune
- Asgardian Decoy
- Asgardian Focus Turret
- Asgardian Implosion Mine

Enemies

- Small Frost Giants
- Medium Frost Giants
- Large Frost Giants
- A.I.M. Drones

NOTE

You get one of the most powerful traps for this level. The implosion mine detonates like the other mines. However, instead of just causing damage, it opens a small black hole and sucks in nearby enemies. It gets rid of them completely! Be sure to try out this trap for this level.

This level contains four different treasures to defend. They are all close together and will split up the enemies to give you more time to defeat them before they can be destroyed. However, all it takes is one to be destroyed and it is a defeat for you. Keep your traps in close because there are enemy doors in four different directions—and all fairly close to the treasures.

This time you have to defend four treasures. Luckily they are close together in the center of the area.

The area where the treasures are located is surrounded by a low wall with only four openings. These chokepoints are great spots for freeze mines. Then spend your remaining money on turrets to cover the mines. While this is not the greatest defense, it will get you through the first wave so you can collect some coins and get more traps for later waves. The first wave only has Small Frost Giants, so collect lots of coins and then, if you can afford it, sell back some of those freeze mines and replace them with implosion mines. Add some more turrets too. Ideally you should try to get a couple turrets for each treasure—one focus turret and one spread turret. Then place implosion mines at all the entrances. This may take a few waves until you can afford it, but that is your goal.

Put mines in the entrances and turrets near the treasures.

Wave 2 adds A.I.M. Drones to the attack, so those turrets come in handy in to shoot the drones down. Medium Frost Giants make their appearance in waves 3 and 4. Then the Large Frost Giants come in wave 5. Watch out for their freeze attacks and their ice projectiles. The final wave has everything including four Large Frost Giants—attacking in pairs from opposite enemy doors. Get near a pair and then let loose with your character's special move if it causes a lot of damage.

Large Frost Giants are tough. Use block breaker attacks and keep hitting them hard with your full chain of melee attacks. If your character can charge up his or her attacks, those work even better.

THUNDER GOD'S CHALLENGE

Traps Available

- Asgardian Spread Turret
- Asgardian Freeze Mine
- Asgardian Barrier
- Asgardian Catapult Trap
- Asgardian Energy Shield
- Asgardian Mine Deployer
- Asgardian Healing Rune
- Asgardian Decoy
- Asgardian Focus Turret
- Asgardian Implosion Mine
- Asgardian Battle Wedge

Enemies

- Small Frost Giants
- Medium Frost Giants
- Large Frost Giants
- A.I.M. Drones

> **NOTE**
>
> The battle wedge is actually a vehicle that characters can drive around. It is so powerful, just running into an enemy destroys the enemy! While it can cause a lot of damage as it mows through groups of enemies, you have to maneuver it carefully to get around the terrain in this level.

This level has only one object to defend. However, it is not one of Odin's treasures. Instead, it is Odin himself, deep in Odinsleep in his bed. There are four enemy doors in two different directions. However, Odin is on a raised platform and there are only two flights of stairs that lead up to it. Therefore, you have two access points through which the enemies must move. Use a combination of mines and turrets to protect Odin.

You must protect Odin himself while he lies in Odinsleep.

You don't have a lot of money at the start. However, spend it on some powerful traps. Place an implosion mine at the base of each flight of stairs and spend the rest on a turret to put next to Odin. Then stay on the platform and defend Odin during the first wave. It consists of only Small Frost Giants, so you should have little trouble with them. As you can afford it, add a few more turrets to the platform around Odin to protect him from A.I.M. Drones and Frost Giants that get up the stairs.

Place an implosion mine at the base of each flight of stairs right from the beginning. When it detonates, it can destroy an entire group of enemies.

Medium Frost Giants join the attack during the second wave. As you can afford it, place a second implosion mine at each staircase. Sell the first and then position them next to each other so they block the stairways. If you do this, few if any enemies will get up onto the platform in wave 3. Large Frost Giants join in wave 4. You may have to go out and fight them if they don't get in close enough to the implosion mines. Meanwhile build several turrets on the platform around Odin, since wave 5 has some A.I.M. Drones as well. The final wave opens up with A.I.M. Drones and Medium Frost Giants. Stay on the platform and deal with anything that gets near Odin. The second part of this wave contains Small and Large Frost Giants. However, with your implosion mines, you may only have to deal with a few of these enemies. Your defenses will do most of the job for you. After you defeat this final wave, you have completed all of the levels in Assault on Asgard.

Stay up on the platform to protect Odin from those enemies that get in close to attack.

DEFENSE SURVIVAL MODE

After you complete the first level of Assault on Asgard, you unlock the Defense Survival Mode. This is a game that is not themed after Asgard. Instead, it uses various themes from the Toy Box and even changes themes as you advance through the levels. In addition, you have access to all types of traps right from the start. Everything is unlocked.

This door takes you to the survival mode for this Toy Box Game.

In survival mode, you have four different treasures to defend. There are six enemy doors, but they don't all open until later waves. You must fight off wave after wave of enemies until all of your treasures have been destroyed. As you lose one, sell back the traps around it and move it to your other treasures. You face all types of enemies. They come from different Play Sets and are the enemies available for unlock or purchase in the Toy Store, so you may be be fighting Frost Giants, outlaws, pirates, and even monsters. The objective is to see how many waves you can survive before

losing all of your treasures. Use the same strategies as you did in the Assault on Asgard levels and you should do well. Good luck!

The theme of the survival mode changes every few levels. However, the game stays the same.

ESCAPE FROM THE KYLN

Escape from the Kyln is another of the Toy Box Games included with *Disney Infinity: Marvel Super Heroes*. To play it, just place the hexagonal Power Disc onto the Disney Infinity base and you gain access to this game. Escape from Kyln is essentially a Toy Box dungeon crawler with a Guardians of the Galaxy theme.

> *Your character is stuck in the Kyln and is about to break out of a cell. Escape is the objective of this game.*

GETTING STARTED

When you play Escape from the Kyln for the first time, you are put right into the introduction level. This is a tutorial to help you learn how to play the game. You start off right in the middle of the escape. As the character you have selected and placed on the Disney Infinity base, you have to save a prisoner as your first mission. After learning the controls from the on-screen instructions, move forward and defeat three enemies.

TIP

One of the cool features of this game is the ability to zoom the view in and out. Since these levels are huge, and some enemies have ranged attacks, it is a good idea to zoom out as you move about, then zoom in during combat if needed.

> *Go after the enemies to save the prisoner who will become your sidekick.*

After defeating the enemies, the prisoner becomes your sidekick. A sidekick can be very useful in this game. They follow you around and will automatically attack enemies. In addition they can get into small spaces and find items or complete tasks. Shortly after gaining your sidekick, you need to use your new ally to help deactivate a shield. Pick up and throw your sidekick through an access panel. The sidekick then deactivates the shield protecting a security key that you need to continue.

Pick up and throw sidekicks into these access panels to do things you can't do on your own.

The Kyln uses energy fields to prevent prisoners from escaping. Therefore, in order to continue your escape, you need to find security keys. Most are protected by some sort of shield. You need to figure out how to deactivate the shield in order to get them. Your sidekick can come in handy, just like for the first key. Walk over to the key. The energy field blocking your path will shut down and you can continue.

> *Look for these security keys to shut down energy fields. Most are protected by shields, which you must find a way to deactivate.*

As you are advancing through the Kyln, you can find loot chests. Attack them to break them open and you receive some type of loot for your sidekick. Collect all of this that you can find and you are awarded it at the end of the level. There are different types of loot that you can use to outfit your sidekicks. These loot chests are scattered about the Kyln and are often not on the direct route to your objectives. Therefore, you need to do bit of exploring to find them all.

> *Look for these loot chests and break them open to find some sidekick loot.*

Your goal for each level is to get to the exit. Once you have deactivated any energy fields in your path and made your way clear across the level, you come across the circular-shaped gate that automatically opens when you approach it. This is the exit and represents the end of the level. Walk through the gate and all of the sidekick loot you have collected will be unlocked and awarded to you. Finally, walk through the portal to exit the level.

> *Pass through the exit gate at the end of the level and all of the sidekick loot you collected will be unlocked.*

GAME BASICS

CHARACTERS

POWER DISCS

MARVEL'S THE AVENGERS

SPIDER-MAN

GUARDIANS OF THE GALAXY

TOY BOX

TOY BOX COLLECTION

ACHIEVEMENTS

THE HUB

Once you complete the tutorial level, the portal brings you to the Hub. At this location, you can do several different things. First, you can recruit a sidekick. There are several of them wandering around the Hub area. Once you find a suitable sidekick, you can outfit them. Then you can enter one of the doors to explore one of the cell blocks.

The Hub is where you pick and outfit sidekicks to help you explore the cell blocks to make good your escape from the Kyln.

There are several different sidekicks in the Hub. As you approach one, their stats will appear over their heads. Each sidekick has three different stats that consist of an icon and a number. The sword icon and number show you how much damage or healing the sidekick can inflict. The shield icon and number indicate how much damage the sidekick can take before passing out. Finally, the eye icon and number represent the sidekick's ability to uncover hidden secrets and enter access panels.

Check out the values of the sidekicks. Recruit one with a good balance of statistics.

Once you have recruited a sidekick, it is time to outfit your new friend. Walk over to the sidekick outfitter and activate it. Here you can assign your sidekick a helmet, a weapon, and some armor. As you explore the cell blocks and open up loot chests, you will unlock more equipment for outfitting your sidekick. The equipment can boost one, two, or even three of your sidekick's statistics and make them more effective.

Outfit your sidekick with the look you have collected while exploring.

Now that you have a fully outfitted sidekick, you are ready to explore the cell blocks. After finishing the tutorial, the doorway to Cell Block 1 is unlocked. After you complete that cell block, you unlock the doorway to the next cell block. You must advance through all eight cell blocks to escape the Kyln.

> **TIP**
>
> There is a skill tree pad located in the Hub. After leveling up your characters while exploring the cell blocks, be sure to spend those skill points to make your characters more powerful and to unlock some new moves or attacks.

Enter the doors that you have unlocked to explore the eight cell blocks. The final cell block will get you out of the Kyln for good.

EXPLORING THE CELL BLOCKS

The main part of the game is exploring the cell blocks. Your objectives in the cell blocks are to get to the exit and to find as much loot as possible. In order to get to the exit, you need to find several keys or complete tasks to deactivate energy fields to progress through the level. Along the way, defeat a lot of enemies to earn all colors of Sparks. When you first enter a cell block, you are in an entrance area. There is a sidekick outfitter here in case you want to make any last minute equipment changes. Plus there are access panels for throwing your sidekick into and Spark capsules lying about. Look around this area and get some goodies while you wait for the level to be created.

> **TIP**
>
> If you have a new character and want to level them up quickly, use that character to play the first cell block of Escape from the Kyln. You fight a lot of enemies and can easily level up a couple times while also earning blue Sparks to purchase toys in the Toy Store.

The entrance area can be explored for some Sparks while you are waiting to begin.

While moving through the cell block after passing through the entrance gate, you will trigger Kyln braziers. The barrel-shaped lights can cause enemies to spawn in your area. When you see colored targets appear on the ground, get ready for a fight. That is where Sakaarans will appear and begin attacking you. In addition, as you walk near cells, the prisoners inside may break out and attack. So you not only have to fight the guards, but also the prisoners as well. The prisoners consist of Symbiotes and Frost Giants. Don't think of it as danger—think of it as an opportunity to collect some more Sparks!

When you see these targets appear, get ready for an attack.

Other prisoners can also break out of cells and attack you.

A yellow hexagonal icon appears, showing you the direction of your next objective. If you just want to get through the cell block as quickly as possible, follow this icon. However, if you wan to collect as much loot as possible, explore the areas off to the sides of the direct path. That is where a lot of the game can take place. The choice is up to you.

Your sidekick cannot enter some access panels because his or her search stat is not high enough. The sidekick will let you know which panels he or she can enter.

During your explorations, you will move past series of braziers and trigger a security area lockdown. As a result, an energy field will activate and block your path to the next part of the cell block. In order to deactivate the energy field, you need to collect a number of security keys—usually two or more of them.

When there is a security area lockdown, an energy field blocks your path.

These keys are not just lying around. They are protected by shields that must be shut down. Sometimes your sidekick can help you take care of the shields by letting you throw him or her through an access panel. Other security keys require you to defeat enemies or turrets to lower the shields. There are several different types of shields with different requirements to deactivate them so you can get the security keys.

Some keys are protected by a shield linked to pressure plates. You must step on and deactivate each pressure plate. However if you, your sidekick, or an enemy steps on the pressure plates again, they will reactivate. So pick up your sidekick while doing this and your life will be a lot easier.

As you fight off enemies, if your sidekick's health bar is depleted, your sidekick will pass out. Don't worry, your sidekick is not dead. You just need to revive your sidekick. Walk over to them and press the button that appears on the screen to bring your sidekick back into the fight. While reviving takes some time, it also has another cost—your character's health. After reviving a sidekick, your character's health bar will decrease. However, no matter how low your health, you can always revive a sidekick and still have some health remaining.

Revive your sidekicks when they are passed out from taking too much damage. You need them to continue through the cell blocks and they can help you defeat enemies along the way. Plus every hero needs a sidekick.

> **TIP**
>
> There are a few skills that come in handy when playing this game and working with a sidekick. The Helping Hand ability reduces the amount of health it costs your character to revive a sidekick or even another character. The Team Player skills decrease the amount of time it takes to revive a sidekick or another character. You may want to have one character with these abilities that you can swap in when your sidekicks need help and then swap out for another more powerful character when you need to fight.

Once you have retrieved all the security keys and deactivated the energy fields, you must advance to the exit gate. After passing through the gate and receiving your sidekick loot, move through the portal to get back to the Hub safe zone and unlock the doorway to the next cell block.

> **NOTE**
>
> After completing Cell Block 1, you not only unlock the doorway to Cell Block 2, but also the doorway to the Exploration Survival Mode.

Getting to the cell block exit is your main objective.

When you return to the Hub, you can recruit another sidekick in exchange for your current sidekick. Since you unlocked some sidekick loot in the cell block, be sure to visit the sidekick outfitter and give your sidekick some more powerful equipment. Then when you are ready, go explore the next cell block.

GAME BASICS

CHARACTERS

POWER DISCS

MARVEL'S THE AVENGERS

SPIDER-MAN

GUARDIANS OF THE GALAXY

TOY BOX

TOY BOX COLLECTION

ACHIEVEMENTS

Don't forget to outfit your sidekick with the latest equipment you found in the last cell block.

As you progress through the cell blocks, you will find that the Kyln has creative ways of protecting their security keys. Always follow the shield from the key to an object to determine what you have to do to deactivate the shield so you can get to the key.

This key is protected by enemies. Defeat them so you can collect the key.

Your character must stand on the pad for a number of seconds in order to deactivate this shield. Enemies will keep spawning until this is accomplished. The counter at the top of the screen lets you know how much time is remaining and only counts down while you are on the pad.

TIP

If your character is defeated within a cell block level, swap out for another character. Defeated characters cannot be used until the level is completed or you exit the level. A good tactic is to have several characters on hand. When one gets low on health, bring in another character with full health. Then when you find some green Sparks and the threat is over, bring back characters with low health and heal them. You may also want to use different characters for different types of enemies, depending on the skills you have unlocked for them.

EXPLORATION SURVIVAL MODE

This doorway appears at the Hub after you exit Cell Block 1. This game offers you a chance to explore new locations and defeat enemies that are randomly generated each time. As a result, you never get the same game twice.

The doorway to the Exploration Survival Mode is located next to the Tutorial doorway.

Search for enemies and then defeat them. Use the minimap in the lower left corner to see in which direction the remaining enemies are located.

When you begin this game, the levels are generated while you wait and watch.

Once you clear a level of all enemies, the game is not over. Another level is randomly generated and then populated with enemies. Go find them and defeat them.

In this mode, there is only one objective—search for and destroy all enemies. There is a timer at the top of the screen keeping track of how long it takes to accomplish this. Unlike in the cell block levels, there are no loot chests and your sidekick is only needed to help you defeat the enemies.

How many levels can you complete and how long will it take you? The game will keep creating new levels for you.

CREATING IN THE TOY BOX

There are so many things you can do in *Disney Infinity: Marvel Super Heroes*. While you can complete the Play Sets, play all of the Toy Box Games, finish all of the missions from the Toy Box hosts in the Toy Box Introduction world, and decorate your INterior, there is still much more to do. In fact, the only limit is your imagination as you create your own Toy Box Worlds.

UNLOCKING TOYS

When you want to create in the Toy Box, you want some toys to place in your world. Therefore, you need to unlock the toys you want. One way to unlock toys is to go to the Toy Store and purchase them. The blue Sparks you collect as you play in the Toy Box Games and Play Sets, as well as by completing the Toy Box host missions, are the currency you use to purchase toys. Some toys are inexpensive while others are quite costly. However, there are other ways to unlock toys—and some toys can't be purchased: they must be unlocked as a reward.

Many toys can only be unlocked by completing tasks in the Play Sets and Toy Box Games. When you go into the Toy Store, these toys are not connected in the toy trees for purchase. If you want them, you will have to earn them.

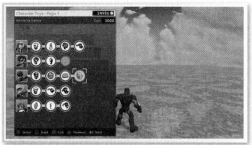

Many of the toys in the Toy Store are from *Disney Infinity 1.0*. These are all available for purchase. However, if you have the original *Disney Infinity*, you can unlock a lot of these toys. If *Disney Infinity: Marvel Super Heroes* detects that you have a Disney Infinity account on your game system, you automatically unlock all of the Toy Box toys from *Disney Infinity 1.0*. Place one of the Play Set pieces on the Disney Infinity base in order to unlock all of the Play Set toys from that Play Set. Finally, by placing characters from *Disney Infinity 1.0*, you unlock the character toys. Therefore, if you have the characters and Play Sets, you can unlock a lot of toys without spending a single blue Spark.

> **TIP**
>
> Be sure to complete all of the Toy Box host missions in the Toy Box Introduction world. You unlock some toys that would be very expensive if you had to purchase them.

BASIC TOY BOX WORLDS

When you want to create your very own Toy Box World, you can use one of these basic worlds to help you get started. Some of these worlds are complete, while others are just starters that you can then build up how you want.

EMPTY TOY BOX

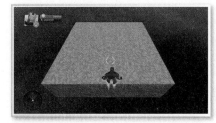

This Toy Box contains a few large pieces of flat terrain that create a small square of land. This is the best place to start if you want to create a world from scratch and don't want anything in your way. Add the terrain how you want it and then start placing toys.

NEW CITY TOY BOX

Select this Toy Box if you need a city. It lays out a grid of streets and then generates several tall buildings, complete with decorations. This takes a lot of the time and work out of making a city. Then you can go ahead and modify it and decorate it as much as you like. This world also comes complete with enemies.

NEW TREEHOUSE TOY BOX

Treehouses are automatically generated when you open this Toy Box. You can then use their giant trees for creating games or other activities. Or try connecting the trees with rails and make a fun roller-coaster-like experience. The Toy Box provides the treehouses—you provide the fun.

NEW RACE TRACK TOY BOX

This Toy Box automatically constructs a race track along with some simple terrain underneath the track pieces. The track is ready for racing. All you need to do is supply the vehicles and any decorations to customize this experience.

GAME BASICS

CHARACTERS

POWER DISCS

MARVEL'S THE AVENGERS

SPIDER-MAN

GUARDIANS OF THE GALAXY

TOY BOX

TOY BOX COLLECTION

ACHIEVEMENTS

NEW TERRAIN TOY BOX

NEW MOUNTAIN TOY BOX

NEW LEDGE LAND TOY BOX

By using simple terrain blocks, this Toy Box creates a world that provides a rough landscape that you can then add other types of terrain to smooth out or leave it as it is. There are different sizes of terrain blocks arranged to create various elevations.

Mountains, caves, ladders, and rails are used to create this Toy Box. You can easily customize it by changing the terrain theme or using terrain Power Discs. The rails that connect the several mountains in this world can be used for a number of different types of games, including foot races using racing gate toys as checkpoints along the race course.

This Toy Box is a ready-made challenge by itself. It contains several different pieces of terrain at various elevations. They are connected by rails, and super cannons are positioned so a character can be launched through the air from one platform to another. In addition, characters have to climb up series of ledges to get to the rails and super cannons. Set triggers at the bottom of this world and at the top, connect them to a timer toy, and you have a game that times how long it takes for players to get to the top.

BUILDERS AND CREATORS

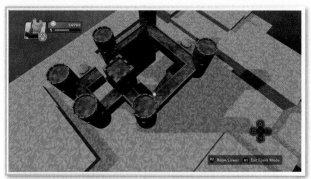

One of the new features that can help you build structures quickly are builders and creators. These are actually toys that you can purchase in the Toy Store. Builders are special townspeople that, when placed in a Toy Box, will begin building their assigned type of structures. For example, a city builder will move around your Toy Box and will begin building city buildings and structures wherever there is empty space. Builders assemble their structures a piece at a time, so it can take a while to build things. There are ten types of builders.

- Toy Box Cottage Builder
- Toy Box Pirate Town Builder
- Toy Box Treehouse Builder
- Toy Box Castle Builder
- Toy Box Forest Builder
- Toy Box Rail Builder
- Toy Box Platform Builder
- Toy Box City Builder
- Toy Box Logic Builder
- Toy Box Agrabah Builder

Creators, unlike builders, make a structure all at once. Using creators is a great way to quickly put together a world with lots of large structures. This toy also allows you to decide where you want something while builders build wherever they want. For most creators, you select a spot to begin and then drag the cursor across an area to create the dimensions of what you want. Then the creator will build the structure. There are seventeen types of creators you can purchase in the Toy Store and use for your Toy Box Worlds.

- Toy Box Race Track Creator
- Toy Box Wide Race Track Creator
- Toy Box Winding Race Track Creator
- Toy Box Wide Winding Race Track Creator
- Toy Box Stunt Track Creator
- Toy Box Wide Stunt Track Creator
- Toy Box Treehouse Creator
- Toy Box Cottage Creator
- Toy Box Forest Creator
- Toy Box City Creator
- Toy Box Platform Creator
- Toy Box Rail Creator
- Toy Box Wide Track Creator
- Toy Box Track Creator
- Toy Box Terrain Creator
- Toy Box Pirate Town Creator
- Toy Box Castle Creator

DOORS

Doors are another new feature and can add a lot to your Toy Box Worlds. Doors are not just decorative toys. They actually are used to connect different Toy Box Worlds. There are six different doors and they can be found in the Creativi-Toys category in the Toy Box Editor. Doors can be placed anywhere in a world. The Toy Box door is the only one you can edit to connect to other Toy Box Worlds of your choosing by using the magic wand. You can actually use this type of door to connect up to ten Toy Box Worlds. This allows you to create a game with up to ten different levels. The INterior door takes you into your INterior. So on any of your worlds, you can have a link to your INterior. The Hall of Heroes door and the Marvel's Hall of Super Heroes door take you to those respective halls. Finally, if you want to add a link to some games that are randomly generated, use the Defense Survival Mode door or the Exploration Survival Mode door.

ONLINE/MULTIPLAYER

While there is a lot to do solo in the *Disney Infinity: Marvel Super Heroes* Toy Box, it is even more fun to play with others and show off your hard work. There are two main ways you can interact with other players online. The first is to invite them into your worlds to explore, play games you have created, or challenge them to play the Toy Box Games with you. The second is to use the Toy Box Share to upload Toy Box Worlds that you have created or to download Toy Box Worlds created by others.

Join up with your friends by inviting them to play with you in one of your Toy Box Worlds, or join another player's game to visit his or her worlds. Use Xbox Live, the PlayStation Network, or whatever online network you have for your gaming system. You can have a total of four players in one world at a time. Take some time to show your friends around the world that you have created. If you are in one of the Toy Box Games, you can open the pause menu and select Online/Multiplayer to connect with friends and have them join you as you play these games.

While you can invite three friends over to one of your Toy Box Worlds to check it out, you can also submit your worlds for the entire planet to enjoy and explore. To do this, open the pause menu and then select Online/Multiplayer. Next select Toy Box Share. Follow the on-screen directions for uploading one of your saved Toy Box Worlds. Disney will review your submission and may feature it on their collection of user-created Toy Box Worlds for other people to try out.

Several lucky people will be selected to share their Toy Box creations with the entire world in Disney's Toy Boxes. It is a lot of fun to see what other people have designed and to explore how they were able to do it. This is especially true for worlds with lots of Creativi-Toys linked together. Who knows what you might find when you take millions of players' imaginations to the power of Infinity.

In addition to submitting your Toy Box Worlds, you can also download featured Toy Box Worlds from Disney's collection. These are usually released throughout the month, so be sure to check back frequently.

HALL OF SUPER HEROES

The Hall of Super Heroes is a part of the game where you can see how your Marvel characters have progressed and keep track of all the Marvel Power Discs you have collected. You can get to the Hall of Super Heroes from any Marvel's Hall of Super Heroes Door, which you can place in any Toy Box World. You can also access it from the Toy Box menu, which is off of the main menu when you start the game.

When you first begin playing, the Hall of Super Heroes is fairly plain. There are several holographic pedestals around the room. Once you take ownership of a character and it reaches level 1, some holographic sparks appear over the pedestal. Walk up to it and a hologram of the character appears. The pedestals for Marvel's The Avengers are located on the ground floor. The pedestals for the characters from the Spider-Man and Guardians of the Galaxy Play Sets appear along the upper walkways on the sides of the hall. Finally, the villain pedestals are along the back wall on the upper walkway.

When you get certain collections of characters all to level 1, you can unlock some cool features. There are three hologram buttons located along the upper walkway. You have to level up Marvel characters to unlock these. The buttons turn red when unlocked. Standing on these buttons causes holograms to appear in the middle of the hall. The buttons are unlocked when you level up three, then eight, and then finally fifteen Marvel characters.

There are also rewards for leveling up collections of characters. When you have all of Marvel's The Avengers characters, the Quinjet flies by the large window at the front of the hall. Get three of the five Spider-Man characters leveled up and a New York City skyline appears in the distance out the window. Level up all five and a Spider-Man background appears behind their pedestals. If you level up three of six Guardians of the Galaxy characters, a space scene appears out the window. Get them all leveled up and a background appears behind their pedestals. Finally, level up all three of the villains characters to unlock a background behind their pedestals.

As you collect and use Power Discs, they will appear in the hall. The sixteen round Power Discs are along the back wall.

The hexagonal Power Discs for vehicles and objects appear along one side of the hall...

...while the hexagonal Power Discs for textures and skies appear on the other side of the hall.

However, that is not all. If you level up all twenty-one of the Marvel characters, you unlock a door to a hidden room.

Finally, if you collect all thirty of the Disney Infinity 2.0 characters and level them up, you unlock Luke Skywalker's landspeeder, which appears on display in the middle of the Hall of Super Heroes to encourage you. Once unlocked, you can place this vehicle into a Toy Box and drive it around.

TOY BOX FEATS

Be sure to take a look at the feats you can complete. Some are easy to get and only require you to do a simple task. Others will take a lot of building or other actions to earn.

While you are in a Toy Box, you can earn feats. These are small awards that you get for a variety of actions, ranging from building things, to driving, or even defeating enemies. There are 116 feats in all that can be earned in the Toy Box (in addition to those that can be earned in the Play Sets). Some are specific to the INteriors and others can only be earned in the Toy Box Games. While some feats are easy to earn, others will take a while. Some feats also reward you with a toy or even an achievement or trophy. The following table has all the info you need on feats.

TOY BOX FEATS		
FEAT	**REQUIREMENT**	**REWARD**
A Deadly Blow	Hit 10 targets with Jasmine's Windstorm.	—
A Fighting Chance	Defeat 250 enemies.	—
A Friend in Need	Bring a sidekick into the Toy Box, and tell the sidekick to follow you.	—
A Matter of Life and Death	Activate a Defeat Manager 3 times.	—
A Night at the Symphony	Place 5 music objects in one INterior room.	—
Adding On	Add 10 rooms to your INterior.	—
Again and Again and Again	Use the Repeater to trigger 100 reactions from other toys.	—
All Over Creation	Have 3 Builders building at the same time.	—
All Trapped Up	Place 50 traps in Toy Box Games.	—
And They're Off!	Sprint on a rideable animal for 30 consecutive seconds.	—
Animal Shelter	Gather 10 animals in the same room.	—
Arabian Nights	Place 50 Agrabah buildings and objects in a Toy Box while using the Jasmine's Palace View sky.	—
Arcade Ace	Place 4 arcade game items in a single room.	—
Art Gallery	Decorate a single room with at least 8 wall hangings.	—
Auto-Pilot	Spend 60 minutes in flying vehicles.	—
Avengers Assemble	Customize a room with Helicarrier-themed walls, ceiling, and floors. Have 8 Avengers guests in the room.	—
Battling It Out	Defeat 50 enemies in one play session in any Toy Box Game.	—
Belle of the Ball	Place a guest in a Belle costume in a room that includes many Beauty and the Beast customizations and objects.	—
Bigger Trigger	Link 100 Creativi-Toys.	—
Building Friendships	Have 2 Builders building at the same time.	—
Building Up	Complete all the My INterior Builder missions.	Scrooge McDuck's Money Pile
Catching a Ride	As Hiro, ride on Baymax's back.	—
Collection Selection	Track 100 Collectibles with Collectible Trackers.	—
Coming Together	Place toys from 5 different Play Sets in a single Toy Box.	—
Control Freak	Link the Remote Controller to other toys 10 times.	—

TOY BOX FEATS		
FEAT	**REQUIREMENT**	**REWARD**
Count On It!	Track 100 points on Counters.	—
Creating a Scene	Use a Creator 50 times.	—
Creating a Stir	Use a Creator 10 times.	—
Creating an Uproar	Use a Creator 100 times.	The Magic Lamp
Creation Complete	Acquire all sets of toys for all Creators.	Mystery Shack Jackalope Exhibit
Dancing Feat	Complete 150 feats.	150 Feat Trophy
Delayed Reaction	Use the Time Delayer to delay 10 triggered toy reactions.	—
Diving in with Both Feat	Complete 10 Feats.	10 Feat Trophy
Drivin' You Crazy	Do 100 tricks in ground vehicles.	—
Fast On Your Feat	Complete 100 Feats.	100 Feat Trophy
Fiddling Around	Modify a Builder's creation before it has been completed.	—
Fighting a Winning Battle	Defeat 1,000 enemies.	Gaston's Portrait
Five Can Play That Game	Using the Challenge Maker, create 5 different endings.	—
Flight of Fancy	Fly for a total of 10 minutes as Tinker Bell.	—
Fly the Hoop	Fly through an arch.	—
From Rags to Riches	Spawn each variety of Toy Box currency from the Money Manager.	—
Fully Armed and Operational	Defeat 50 enemies with armed, flying vehicles.	—
Get the Ball Rolling	Make 10 townspeople dance at the same time.	Dwarfs' Pipe Organ
Getting Your Feat Wet	Complete 1 feat.	1 Feat Trophy
Going Door-to-Door	Place a Toy Box Door that links to another Toy Box.	Monster's Inc. Door Station
Good as Gold	Change the loot in a Loot Chest 3 times, and then plunder the Loot Chests!	—
Hi Ho Hiro	As Baymax, fly with Hiro on your back.	—
Hulk Decorate!	Decorate a room with Hulk walls, Hulk floors, and 3 Hulk furniture pieces.	—
I Can See My House From Here	Place a terrain piece or object 500 meters high.	—
In Too Deep	Reach the final level of Escape from the Kyln or Brave Forest Siege.	Hero's Duty Arcade Game
Instant Replay	Use the Replayer toy.	—
It Takes Two	As Aladdin, defeat 2 Agrabah Guards.	—
It's About Time	Link a Timer to a Challenge Maker.	—
Just a Fling	Launch 10 enemies with a launcher.	—

GAME BASICS · CHARACTERS · POWER DISCS · MARVEL'S THE AVENGERS · SPIDER-MAN · GUARDIANS OF THE GALAXY · TOY BOX · TOY BOX COLLECTION · ACHIEVEMENTS

TOY BOX FEATS		
FEAT	**REQUIREMENT**	**REWARD**
Keep Your Guard Up	Finish a level without allowing your base to receive any damage.	Lock, Shock, and Barrel's Tub
Landing on Both Feet	Complete 50 feats.	50 Feat Trophy
Leap Frog	Jump a vehicle over another character.	—
Legions of Legions	Use the Enemy Wave Manager to spawn 20 enemy waves.	—
Like Gaston	Have a guest in a Gaston costume sit in Gaston's Chair in the same room as Gaston's Portrait.	—
Location, Location, Location	Link 20 different Locators to other toys.	—
Long Road Ahead	Place connecting track or street pieces that stretch at least 1,000 meters.	—
Look Behind You!	Drive 1,000 meters in reverse.	—
Look Ma, No Road!	Get over 10 minutes of air time while driving a ground vehicle.	—
Lying Low	Place a terrain piece as low as the Toy Box allows.	—
Making Connections	Connect one toy to at least 8 other toys.	—
Maxed Out	Have your Builder's buildings hit the Toy Box's capacity limit.	—
Meet Your Maker	Use a builder.	—
More of the Same	Connect a Repeater to any Generator toy.	—
Now You Shall Deal With Me	Defeat 10 targets using Maleficent's Diaval's Drive.	—
Off to a Running Spark	Collect all Sparks in the Toy Box Intro.	—
Oh Boy, Oh Boy, Oh Boy!	Attack 5 targets with Donald Duck's Donald's Rage.	—
On Camera	Assign 10 Target Cameras to different targets.	—
Original Condition, New In Box	Create and save an original Toy Box.	—
Perfect Princess	Complete all the My INterior Princess missions.	Cinderella's Slipper
Photo Finish	Ride an animal through a race gate.	—
Pirate Haven	Place 50 pirate buildings and pieces in a single Toy Box.	—
Putting Up a Fight	Defeat 100 enemies.	—
Putting Up Barriers	Place 5 Barrier walls on a single level.	—
Quick on the Trigger	Set off a chain of at least 10 Logic Connections.	—
Raise Your Glass	Scale the size of a Scalable Barrier Block 5 times.	—
Remodel Citizen	Customize 200 times with the magic wand.	—
Roommate Round-Up	Gather 2 guests in Woody and Buzz costumes in the same room.	—
Saddle Sore	Ride an animal for over 50 kilometers.	—
Score!	Link a Scoreboard to a Challenge Maker.	—
Shooting for Your Own Hand	As Merida, freeze 10 targets.	—
Shop-Keeping	Create a Storefront Inventory, and activate that Storefront 5 times.	—

TOY BOX FEATS		
FEAT	**REQUIREMENT**	**REWARD**
Sixteenth Birthday Surprise	Have a guest in a Maleficent costume put a guest in a Sleeping Beauty costume to sleep in the same room as Maleficent's Spinning Wheel.	Aurora's Dress
Slumber Party	Make 10 townspeople sleep at the same time.	Andy's Bed
Smash Hit	Destroy 25 breakable objects as the Hulk.	—
Springing to Your Feat	Complete 25 feats.	25 Feat Trophy
Standing Tall	Appear on the top of the 1st Place Podium.	—
Starter Home	Begin building and save a Toy Box INterior.	—
Steamroller	As Stitch, roll into 10 enemies.	—
Steep Steep Steeplechase	Drop 50 meters in a single fall while riding an animal.	—
Swept Off Your Feat	Complete 200 feats.	200 Feat Trophy
Switching Gears	Change your Packs and Tools 5 times with Packs and Tools Managers.	—
Taking Inventory	Use the Inventory Manager to change your inventory, and activate the Manager 5 times.	—
Taking the Plunge	Complete the 4th level or higher of Escape from the Kyln or Brave Forest Siege without being knocked out.	—
Taking Up a Collection	Collect 10 pieces of equipment for your sidekicks.	—
Teaming Up	Link Team Activators to Enemy Generators or Enemy Wave Managers 10 times.	—
The Enchanted Tiki Room	Place 2 Enchanted Tiki Room objects in the same room.	—
The Sky's the Limit	Ascend to a height of 1,000 meters.	—
The Sum of All Creation	Acquire a complete set of toys for any Creator.	—
Three in One	Defeat 3 enemies using an Asgardian Implosion Mine or an Imploding Pineapple.	—
Throw Your Create Around	Pick up and throw a Builder.	—
Time's On Your Side	Have your Builders build for a total of 60 minutes.	—
To the Rescue	Complete all the My INterior Hero missions.	The Tesseract
Trap of All Trades	Place 6 different types of traps in a single play session.	—
Trigger Happy	Link 500 Creativi-Toys.	Tron Arcade Game
Trigger Twenty	Link 20 Creativi-Toys.	—
Try This Five for Size	Scale Trigger Areas 5 times.	—
Un-De-Feat-Able	Complete all feats.	Mega Feat Trophy
Well-Connected	Create Logic Connections between the Victory Tracker and 5 other toys.	—
Winds a Blowin'	Use 10 Weather Vane toys.	—
Wordsmith	Trigger text to appear 10 times from the Text Creator or Text Displayer.	—
You've Changed A Loot	Customize what the Loot Drop Manager makes enemies leave behind, and then try it out.	—

DISNEY INFINITY TOY BOX
THE COLLECTION

There are more than a thousand toys that you can collect and use in the Toy Box. Some are available right from the start. Others can be unlocked by spending blue Sparks. Finally, others are collected in the Play Sets and Toy Box Games. As new Play Sets and characters are released in the future, there will be even more toys for you to use.

The following tables include information on all the toys available at the release of *Disney Infinity: Marvel Super Heroes*. It contains the name, the type of toy, and how it is unlocked. Plus we have included a check box so you can keep track of the toys you have in your collection and what you still need to get.

The function of a toy refers to how it interacts with characters or other toys. Here is a key for these attributes:

Air Vehicle: These vehicles can fly through the air and move off the edges of the land in Toy Box Worlds.

Breakable: This toy can be destroyed by attacking it or hitting it with projectiles or vehicles.

Builder: These are special townspeople that, when you put them into a Toy Box World, will start building their specific type of structures a little bit at a time.

Capsule: You can place down capsules to provide health or special move power for players to collect in your Toy Box Worlds.

Collectible: These objects can be used in games you create where players have to collect specific items.

Creator: These will automatically build a large structure or track all at once.

Critter: These are animal townspeople that can't be destroyed, but you can still pick them up.

Custom: This toy can be connected with other toys for interaction.

Decoration: These are items that you can put inside your INterior rooms.

Enemy: Watch out for these toys. They can attack you.

Ledge Hang: These objects can be placed along the side of a wall or cliff and allow characters to climb up or hang on.

Mission Givers: These toys are non-player characters in the Toy Box and provide missions in the Play Sets.

Motorcycle: These are smaller ground vehicles that can be driven on land.

Mount: These animal toys can be ridden by characters.

Pack: This toy is carried on the back of a character and activated by pressing the attack button.

Physics Ball: This ball moves and bounces according to the laws of physics.

Physics Block: These blocks obey the laws of physics. They fall and some can break.

Rail Grind: Characters, even Cars characters, can grind on these toys. Connect them together for long periods of grinding.

Room: Expand your INterior by adding some rooms.

Sidekick: These small townspeople can follow you around and help attack your enemies.

Static: These toys just sit there. Come back later, they are still there. They can't be destroyed.

Template: These are several toys connected together to create a mini game, which you can use individually or to make a larger game in your world.

Tool: This is a toy that can be carried by a character and activated by pressing the alternate attack button.

Townspeople: These small townspeople can be picked up, thrown, and even drop-kicked. They do not attack, nor can they be destroyed.

Track: Connect these toys together to create a race track.

Vehicle: These toys can be driven by characters, but stay on land—unless you drive off a cliff or jump.

> **NOTE**
>
> Customization Cluster is a type of terrain that can be changed when you use a magic wand to customize it. The default is Fantasy Terrain in the editor. However, by selecting a themed terrain toy, you can change the theme to any that you have unlocked. This terrain also changes when you place a texture set Power Disc on the Disney Infinity base.

The following tables containing all of the toys are organized in the same way that they are in the Toy Store to help you find them quickly.

GAME BASICS · CHARACTERS · POWER DISCS · MARVEL'S THE AVENGERS · SPIDER-MAN · GUARDIANS OF THE GALAXY · TOY BOX · TOY BOX COLLECTION · ACHIEVEMENTS

183

PLAY SETS

——— AVENGERS ———

	**Marvel's The Avengers**
GOT IT?	**ICON**	**TOY NAME**	**DESCRIPTION**	**CATEGORY**	**FUNCTION**	**UNLOCK**	**TOY STORE PAGE**
✓		A.I.M. Drone	An A.I.M. hover drone from the Marvel's The Marvel's The Avengers Play Set.	Enemies	Enemy	Marvel's The Marvel's The Avengers Play Set Reward	Avengers - Page 1
✓		Blue Car	A decorative car from the Marvel Play Sets.	Decorations	Breakable	Toy Store Purchase (Avengers Landmark)	Avengers - Page 1
✓		Captain Marvel	Carol Danvers, the super-powered Avengers heroine.	Cast Members	Mission Giver	Marvel's The Marvel's The Avengers Play Set Reward	Avengers - Page 1
✓		Female Townsperson 1	A townsperson from the Marvel's The Marvel's The Avengers Play Set.	Marvel Townspeople	Townspeople	Toy Store Purchase (Avengers Landmark)	Avengers - Page 1
✓		Female Townsperson 2	A townsperson from the Marvel's The Marvel's The Avengers Play Set.	Marvel Townspeople	Townspeople	Toy Store Purchase (Avengers Landmark)	Avengers - Page 1
✓		Horizontal Laser Fence	A dangerous Avengers-themed gate.	Platforming Toys	Custom	Toy Store Purchase (Avengers Landmark)	Avengers - Page 1
✓		Large Frost Giant	A large Frost Giant from the Marvel's The Marvel's The Avengers Play Set.	Enemies	Enemy	Marvel's The Avengers Play Set Reward	Avengers - Page 1
✓		M.O.D.O.K.'s Weather Machine	Make it freeze and snow in your world with this weather machine.	Creativi-Toys	Custom	Toy Store Purchase (Avengers Landmark)	Avengers - Page 1
✓		Male Townsperson 1	A townsperson from the Marvel's The Avengers Play Set.	Marvel Townspeople	Townspeople	Toy Store Purchase (Avengers Landmark)	Avengers - Page 1
✓		Male Townsperson 2	A townsperson from the Marvel's The Avengers Play Set.	Marvel Townspeople	Townspeople	Toy Store Purchase (Avengers Landmark)	Avengers - Page 1
✓		Medium Frost Giant A	A medium-sized Frost Giant from the Marvel's The Avengers Play Set.	Enemies	Enemy	Marvel's The Avengers Play Set Reward	Avengers - Page 1
✓		Medium Frost Giant B	A medium-sized Frost Giant from the Marvel's The Avengers Play Set.	Enemies	Enemy	Marvel's The Avengers Play Set Reward	Avengers - Page 1
✓		Puffy Coat Townsperson 1	A townsperson from the Marvel's The Avengers Play Set.	Marvel Townspeople	Townspeople	Toy Store Purchase (Avengers Landmark)	Avengers - Page 1
✓		Puffy Coat Townsperson 2	A townsperson from the Marvel's The Avengers Play Set.	Marvel Townspeople	Townspeople	Toy Store Purchase (Avengers Landmark)	Avengers - Page 1
✓		Ranged Attack Frost Giant	A medium-size Frost Giant marksman from the Marvel's The Avengers Play Set.	Enemies	Enemy	Marvel's The Avengers Play Set Reward	Avengers - Page 1
✓		Red Car	A decorative car from the Marvel Play Sets.	Decorations	Breakable	Toy Store Purchase (Avengers Landmark)	Avengers - Page 1
✓		S.H.I.E.L.D. Emergency Vehicle	An Avengers-themed vehicle.	Vehicles and Mounts	Vehicle	Marvel's The Avengers Play Set Reward	Avengers - Page 1
✓		S.H.I.E.L.D. Helicarrier	An Avengers-themed vehicle.	Vehicles and Mounts	Air Vehicle	Marvel's The Avengers Play Set Reward	Avengers - Page 1
✓		S.H.I.E.L.D. Motorcycle	An Avengers-themed vehicle.	Vehicles and Mounts	Motorcycle	Marvel's The Avengers Play Set Reward	Avengers - Page 1
✓		S.H.I.E.L.D. Sky-Cycle	An Avengers-themed vehicle.	Vehicles and Mounts	Motorcycle	Marvel's The Avengers Play Set Reward	Avengers - Page 1
✓		Sensor Switch	Turn things on and off by going through this doorway.	Creativi-Toys	Custom	Toy Store Purchase (Avengers Landmark)	Avengers - Page 1
✓		Sif	The warrior goddess from Thor.	Cast Members	Mission Giver	Marvel's The Avengers Play Set Reward	Avengers - Page 1
✓		Silver Car	A decorative car from the Marvel Play Sets.	Decorations	Breakable	Toy Store Purchase (Avengers Landmark)	Avengers - Page 1
✓		Sliding Laser Fence	A dangerous Avengers-themed gate.	Platforming Toys	Custom	Toy Store Purchase (Avengers Landmark)	Avengers - Page 1
✓		Small Frost Giant	A small Frost Giant from the Marvel's The Avengers Play Set.	Enemies	Enemy	Marvel's The Avengers Play Set Reward	Avengers - Page 1
✓		Small Shielded Frost Giant	A small, shielded Frost Giant from the Marvel's The Avengers Play Set.	Enemies	Enemy	Marvel's The Avengers Play Set Reward	Avengers - Page 1
✓		Snowmobile	An Avengers-themed vehicle.	Vehicles and Mounts	Motorcycle	Marvel's The Avengers Play Set Reward	Avengers - Page 1
✓		Tony Stark's Sports Car	An Avengers-themed vehicle.	Vehicles and Mounts	Vehicle	Marvel's The Avengers Play Set Reward	Avengers - Page 1

Toy Box Marvel Decorations Continued

GOT IT?	ICON	TOY NAME	DESCRIPTION	CATEGORY	FUNCTION	UNLOCK	TOY STORE PAGE
✓		UN Female Delegate 1	A townsperson from the Marvel's The Avengers Play Set.	Marvel Townspeople	Townspeople	Toy Store Purchase (Avengers Landmark)	Avengers - Page 1
✓		UN Female Delegate 2	A townsperson from the Marvel's The Avengers Play Set.	Marvel Townspeople	Townspeople	Toy Store Purchase (Avengers Landmark)	Avengers - Page 1
✓		UN Guard	A townsperson from the Marvel's The Avengers Play Set.	Marvel Townspeople	Townspeople	Toy Store Purchase (Avengers Landmark)	Avengers - Page 1
✓		UN Male Delegate 1	A townsperson from the Marvel's The Avengers Play Set.	Marvel Townspeople	Townspeople	Toy Store Purchase (Avengers Landmark)	Avengers - Page 1
✓		UN Male Delegate 2	A townsperson from the Marvel's The Avengers Play Set.	Marvel Townspeople	Townspeople	Toy Store Purchase (Avengers Landmark)	Avengers - Page 1
✓		Vehicle Summoner	Place this toy to summon nearby vehicles.	Creativi-Toys	Custom	Toy Store Purchase (Avengers Landmark)	Avengers - Page 1
✓		Vertical Laser Fence	A dangerous Avengers-themed gate.	Platforming Toys	Custom	Toy Store Purchase (Avengers Landmark)	Avengers - Page 1
✓		Wasp	The fashionable heroine from the Avengers.	Cast Members	Mission Giver	Marvel's The Avengers Play Set Reward	Avengers - Page 1
✓		Air System Fan	A city-themed building piece.	City Building Set	Breakable	Toy Store Purchase (Avengers Landmark)	Avengers - Page 2
✓		Air Vent	A city-themed building piece.	City Building Set	Breakable	Toy Store Purchase (Avengers Landmark)	Avengers - Page 2
✓		Avengers Open Shipping Container	An Avengers-themed furniture piece.	Decorations	Static	Toy Store Purchase (Avengers Landmark)	Avengers - Page 2
✓		Avengers Shipping Container	An Avengers-themed furniture piece.	Decorations	Static	Toy Store Purchase (Avengers Landmark)	Avengers - Page 2
✓		Avengers Tower	An Avengers-themed building.	Set Pieces	Static	Toy Store Purchase (Avengers Landmark)	Avengers - Page 2
✓		Bike Stand	A city-themed building piece.	City Building Set	Breakable	Toy Store Purchase (Avengers Landmark)	Avengers - Page 2
✓		Building Fan	A city-themed building piece.	City Building Set	Breakable	Toy Store Purchase (Avengers Landmark)	Avengers - Page 2
✓		Bus Stop Sign	A city-themed building piece.	City Building Set	Breakable	Toy Store Purchase (Avengers Landmark)	Avengers - Page 2
✓		Cell Tower	A city-themed building piece.	City Building Set	Breakable	Toy Store Purchase (Avengers Landmark)	Avengers - Page 2
✓		Chess Table	A city-themed building piece.	City Building Set	Breakable	Toy Store Purchase (Avengers Landmark)	Avengers - Page 2
✓		City Water Tank	A city-themed building piece.	City Building Set	Breakable	Toy Store Purchase (Avengers Landmark)	Avengers - Page 2
✓		City Water Tower	A city-themed building piece.	City Building Set	Breakable	Toy Store Purchase (Avengers Landmark)	Avengers - Page 2
✓		Construction Barrel	A city-themed building piece.	City Building Set	Breakable	Toy Store Purchase (Avengers Landmark)	Avengers - Page 2
✓		Construction Barrier	A city-themed building piece.	City Building Set	Breakable	Toy Store Purchase (Avengers Landmark)	Avengers - Page 2
✓		Construction Crane	A climbable Avengers-themed building piece.	Decorations	Static	Toy Store Purchase (Avengers Landmark)	Avengers - Page 2
✓		Construction Post	A city-themed building piece.	City Building Set	Breakable	Toy Store Purchase (Avengers Landmark)	Avengers - Page 2
✓		Corner Air Duct	A city-themed building piece.	City Building Set	Breakable	Toy Store Purchase (Avengers Landmark)	Avengers - Page 2
✓		Corner Ice Stunt Ramp	A cold and slick stunt park piece.	Race Track Pieces	Static	Toy Store Purchase (Avengers Landmark)	Avengers - Page 2
✓		Garbage Can	A city-themed building piece.	City Building Set	Breakable	Toy Store Purchase (Avengers Landmark)	Avengers - Page 2
✓		Ice Shard	A breakable ice chunk.	Decorations	Breakable	Toy Store Purchase (Avengers Landmark)	Avengers - Page 2
✓		Ice Spike	A breakable ice chunk.	Decorations	Breakable	Toy Store Purchase (Avengers Landmark)	Avengers - Page 2
✓		Ice Stalagmite	A breakable ice chunk.	Decorations	Breakable	Toy Store Purchase (Avengers Landmark)	Avengers - Page 2
✓		Ice Stunt Block	A cold and slick stunt park piece.	Race Track Pieces	Static	Toy Store Purchase (Avengers Landmark)	Avengers - Page 2

GAME BASICS

CHARACTERS

POWER DISCS

MARVEL'S THE AVENGERS

SPIDER-MAN

GUARDIANS OF THE GALAXY

TOY BOX

TOY BOX COLLECTION

ACHIEVEMENTS

Toy Box Marvel Decorations Continued

GOT IT?	ICON	TOY NAME	DESCRIPTION	CATEGORY	FUNCTION	UNLOCK	TOY STORE PAGE
✓		Ice Stunt Hill	A cold and slick stunt park piece.	Race Track Pieces	Static	Toy Store Purchase (Avengers Landmark)	Avengers - Page 2
✓		Ice Stunt Mound	A cold and slick stunt park piece.	Race Track Pieces	Static	Toy Store Purchase (Avengers Landmark)	Avengers - Page 2
✓		Ice Stunt Pipe	A cold and slick stunt park piece.	Race Track Pieces	Static	Toy Store Purchase (Avengers Landmark)	Avengers - Page 2
✓		Ice Stunt Ramp	A cold and slick stunt park piece.	Race Track Pieces	Static	Toy Store Purchase (Avengers Landmark)	Avengers - Page 2
✓		Ice Stunt Rollover	A cold and slick stunt park piece.	Race Track Pieces	Static	Toy Store Purchase (Avengers Landmark)	Avengers - Page 2
✓		Large Electrical Box	A city-themed building piece.	City Building Set	Breakable	Toy Store Purchase (Avengers Landmark)	Avengers - Page 2
✓		Large Ice Stalagmite	A breakable ice chunk.	Decorations	Breakable	Toy Store Purchase (Avengers Landmark)	Avengers - Page 2
✓		Parking Meter	A city-themed building piece.	City Building Set	Breakable	Toy Store Purchase (Avengers Landmark)	Avengers - Page 2
✓		Sidewalk Bush	A city-themed building piece.	City Building Set	Breakable	Toy Store Purchase (Avengers Landmark)	Avengers - Page 2
✓		Sidewalk Shrub	A city-themed building piece.	City Building Set	Breakable	Toy Store Purchase (Avengers Landmark)	Avengers - Page 2
✓		Small Electrical Box	A city-themed building piece.	City Building Set	Breakable	Toy Store Purchase (Avengers Landmark)	Avengers - Page 2
✓		Subway Directory	A city-themed building piece.	City Building Set	Breakable	Toy Store Purchase (Avengers Landmark)	Avengers - Page 2

SPIDER-MAN

Spiderman

GOT IT?	ICON	TOY NAME	DESCRIPTION	CATEGORY	FUNCTION	UNLOCK	TOY STORE PAGE
✓		Black Car	A decorative car from the Marvel Play Sets.	Decorations	Breakable	Toy Store Purchase (Spider-Man Landmark)	Spider-Man - Page 1
✓		Black Cat	The feline mission giver from the Spider-Man Play Set.	Cast Members	Mission Giver	Spider-Man Play Set Reward	Spider-Man - Page 1
✓		Cab Driver	A townsperson from the world of Marvel.	Marvel Townspeople	Townspeople	Toy Store Purchase (Spider-Man Landmark)	Spider-Man - Page 1
✓		Construction Worker 1	A townsperson from the world of Marvel.	Marvel Townspeople	Townspeople	Toy Store Purchase (Spider-Man Landmark)	Spider-Man - Page 1
✓		Construction Worker 2	A townsperson from the world of Marvel.	Marvel Townspeople	Townspeople	Toy Store Purchase (Spider-Man Landmark)	Spider-Man - Page 1
✓		Female S.H.I.E.L.D. Agent 1	A townsperson from the world of Marvel.	Marvel Townspeople	Townspeople	Toy Store Purchase (Spider-Man Landmark)	Spider-Man - Page 1
✓		Female S.H.I.E.L.D. Agent 2	A townsperson from the world of Marvel.	Marvel Townspeople	Townspeople	Toy Store Purchase (Spider-Man Landmark)	Spider-Man - Page 1
✓		Green Car	A decorative car from the Marvel Play Sets.	Decorations	Breakable	Toy Store Purchase (Spider-Man Landmark)	Spider-Man - Page 1
✓		Hazard Plate	A dangerous Spider-Man-themed floor plate.	Platforming Toys	Custom	Toy Store Purchase (Spider-Man Landmark)	Spider-Man - Page 1
✓		Hipster 1	A townsperson from the world of Marvel.	Marvel Townspeople	Townspeople	Toy Store Purchase (Spider-Man Landmark)	Spider-Man - Page 1
✓		Hipster 2	A townsperson from the world of Marvel.	Marvel Townspeople	Townspeople	Toy Store Purchase (Spider-Man Landmark)	Spider-Man - Page 1
✓		Lab Elevator	An elevator from the laboratories in the Spider-Man Play Set.	Platforming Toys	Custom	Toy Store Purchase (Spider-Man Landmark)	Spider-Man - Page 1
✓		Large Symbiote	An enormous enemy symbiote from the Spider-Man Play Set.	Enemies	Enemy	Spider-Man Play Set Reward	Spider-Man - Page 1
✓		Luke Cage	S.H.I.E.L.D.'s one and only Power Man.	Cast Members	Mission Giver	Spider-Man Play Set Reward	Spider-Man - Page 1
✓		Male S.H.I.E.L.D. Agent 1	A townsperson from the world of Marvel.	Marvel Townspeople	Townspeople	Toy Store Purchase (Spider-Man Landmark)	Spider-Man - Page 1
✓		Male S.H.I.E.L.D. Agent 2	A townsperson from the world of Marvel.	Marvel Townspeople	Townspeople	Toy Store Purchase (Spider-Man Landmark)	Spider-Man - Page 1

	Spiderman Continued						
GOT IT?	ICON	TOY NAME	DESCRIPTION	CATEGORY	FUNCTION	UNLOCK	TOY STORE PAGE
✓		Police Car	A decorative car from the Marvel Play Sets.	Decorations	Breakable	Toy Store Purchase (Spider-Man Landmark)	Spider-Man - Page 1
✓		Police Horse	A Spider-Man-themed mount.	Vehicles and Mounts	Mount	Spider-Man Play Set Reward	Spider-Man - Page 1
✓		Radar Tower	A radar tower from the Spider-Man Play Set.	Set Pieces	Static	Toy Store Purchase (Spider-Man Landmark)	Spider-Man - Page 1
✓		S.H.I.E.L.D. Hovercar	A Spider-Man-themed vehicle.	Vehicles and Mounts	Vehicle	Spider-Man Play Set Reward	Spider-Man - Page 1
✓		Scientist 1	A townsperson from the world of Marvel.	Marvel Townspeople	Townspeople	Toy Store Purchase (Spider-Man Landmark)	Spider-Man - Page 1
✓		Sky-Cycle	A Spider-Man-themed vehicle.	Vehicles and Mounts	Motorcycle	Spider-Man Play Set Reward	Spider-Man - Page 1
✓		Spider-Man Taxi	A decorative car from the Marvel Play Sets.	Decorations	Breakable	Toy Store Purchase (Spider-Man Landmark)	Spider-Man - Page 1
✓		Swarming Symbiote	A small symbiote from the Spider-Man Play Set.	Enemies	Enemy	Spider-Man Play Set Reward	Spider-Man - Page 1
✓		Symbiote	A fast enemy symbiote from the Spider-Man Play Set.	Enemies	Enemy	Spider-Man Play Set Reward	Spider-Man - Page 1
✓		Symbiote Grunt	An enemy symbiote from the Spider-Man Play Set.	Enemies	Enemy	Spider-Man Play Set Reward	Spider-Man - Page 1
✓		Symbiote Spawn	A small symbiote from the Spider-Man Play Set.	Enemies	Enemy	Spider-Man Play Set Reward	Spider-Man - Page 1
✓		Tendriled Symbiote	A tendriled enemy symbiote from the Spider-Man Play Set.	Enemies	Enemy	Spider-Man Play Set Reward	Spider-Man - Page 1
✓		Thug 1	A townsperson from the world of Marvel.	Marvel Townspeople	Townspeople	Toy Store Purchase (Spider-Man Landmark)	Spider-Man - Page 1
✓		Thug 2	A townsperson from the world of Marvel.	Marvel Townspeople	Townspeople	Toy Store Purchase (Spider-Man Landmark)	Spider-Man - Page 1
✓		Thug 3	A townsperson from the world of Marvel.	Marvel Townspeople	Townspeople	Toy Store Purchase (Spider-Man Landmark)	Spider-Man - Page 1
✓		Tourist 1	A townsperson from the world of Marvel.	Marvel Townspeople	Townspeople	Toy Store Purchase (Spider-Man Landmark)	Spider-Man - Page 1
✓		Tourist 2	A townsperson from the world of Marvel.	Marvel Townspeople	Townspeople	Toy Store Purchase (Spider-Man Landmark)	Spider-Man - Page 1
✓		White Tiger	Ava Ayala, the spectacular White Tiger!	Cast Members	Mission Giver	Spider-Man Play Set Reward	Spider-Man - Page 1
✓		Barrier Fence	A city-themed building piece.	City Building Set	Breakable	Toy Store Purchase (Spider-Man Landmark)	Spider-Man - Page 2
✓		Building Scaffolding	A city-themed building piece.	City Building Set	Breakable	Toy Store Purchase (Spider-Man Landmark)	Spider-Man - Page 2
✓		Business Man 1	A townsperson from the world of Marvel.	Marvel Townspeople	Townspeople	Toy Store Purchase (Spider-Man Landmark)	Spider-Man - Page 2
✓		Business Man 2	A townsperson from the world of Marvel.	Marvel Townspeople	Townspeople	Toy Store Purchase (Spider-Man Landmark)	Spider-Man - Page 2
✓		Business Man 3	A townsperson from the world of Marvel.	Marvel Townspeople	Townspeople	Toy Store Purchase (Spider-Man Landmark)	Spider-Man - Page 2
✓		Business Woman 1	A townsperson from the world of Marvel.	Marvel Townspeople	Townspeople	Toy Store Purchase (Spider-Man Landmark)	Spider-Man - Page 2
✓		Business Woman 2	A townsperson from the world of Marvel.	Marvel Townspeople	Townspeople	Toy Store Purchase (Spider-Man Landmark)	Spider-Man - Page 2
✓		City Cistern	A city-themed building piece.	City Building Set	Breakable	Toy Store Purchase (Spider-Man Landmark)	Spider-Man - Page 2
✓		Construction Scaffolding	A city-themed building piece.	City Building Set	Breakable	Toy Store Purchase (Spider-Man Landmark)	Spider-Man - Page 2
✓		Construction Spool	A city-themed building piece.	City Building Set	Breakable	Toy Store Purchase (Spider-Man Landmark)	Spider-Man - Page 2
✓		Construction Wheelbarrow	A city-themed building piece.	City Building Set	Breakable	Toy Store Purchase (Spider-Man Landmark)	Spider-Man - Page 2
✓		Daily Bugle	A Spider-Man-themed building.	Set Pieces	Static	Toy Store Purchase (Spider-Man Landmark)	Spider-Man - Page 2
✓		Fire Hydrant	A city-themed building piece.	City Building Set	Breakable	Toy Store Purchase (Spider-Man Landmark)	Spider-Man - Page 2

GAME BASICS

CHARACTERS

POWER DISCS

MARVEL'S THE AVENGERS

SPIDER-MAN

GUARDIANS OF THE GALAXY

TOY BOX

TOY BOX COLLECTION

ACHIEVEMENTS

			Spiderman Continued				
GOT IT?	ICON	TOY NAME	DESCRIPTION	CATEGORY	FUNCTION	UNLOCK	TOY STORE PAGE
✓		Firefighter	A townsperson from the world of Marvel.	Marvel Townspeople	Townspeople	Toy Store Purchase (Spider-Man Landmark)	Spider-Man - Page 2
✓		Hazmat Specialist	A townsperson from the world of Marvel.	Marvel Townspeople	Townspeople	Toy Store Purchase (Spider-Man Landmark)	Spider-Man - Page 2
✓		Hot Dog Stand	A city-themed building piece.	City Building Set	Breakable	Toy Store Purchase (Spider-Man Landmark)	Spider-Man - Page 2
✓		Mailbox	A city-themed building piece.	City Building Set	Breakable	Toy Store Purchase (Spider-Man Landmark)	Spider-Man - Page 2
✓		Newspaper Stand	A city-themed building piece.	City Building Set	Breakable	Toy Store Purchase (Spider-Man Landmark)	Spider-Man - Page 2
✓		Newspaper Vending Machine	A city-themed building piece.	City Building Set	Breakable	Toy Store Purchase (Spider-Man Landmark)	Spider-Man - Page 2
✓		Nick Fury Billboard	A Spider-Man-themed piece of furniture.	City Building Set	Breakable	Toy Store Purchase (Spider-Man Landmark)	Spider-Man - Page 2
✓		Oil Drum	A city-themed building piece.	City Building Set	Breakable	Toy Store Purchase (Spider-Man Landmark)	Spider-Man - Page 2
✓		Oscorp Tower	A Spider-Man-themed building.	Set Pieces	Static	Toy Store Purchase (Spider-Man Landmark)	Spider-Man - Page 2
✓		Pile of Bricks	A city-themed building piece.	City Building Set	Breakable	Toy Store Purchase (Spider-Man Landmark)	Spider-Man - Page 2
✓		Pile of Pipes	A city-themed building piece.	City Building Set	Breakable	Toy Store Purchase (Spider-Man Landmark)	Spider-Man - Page 2
✓		Police Officer 1	A townsperson from the world of Marvel.	Marvel Townspeople	Townspeople	Toy Store Purchase (Spider-Man Landmark)	Spider-Man - Page 2
✓		Police Officer 2	A townsperson from the world of Marvel.	Marvel Townspeople	Townspeople	Toy Store Purchase (Spider-Man Landmark)	Spider-Man - Page 2
✓		Rooftop Fan	A city-themed building piece.	City Building Set	Breakable	Toy Store Purchase (Spider-Man Landmark)	Spider-Man - Page 2
✓		Sewer Rat	A rat from the Spider-Man Play Set.	Critters	Critter	Toy Store Purchase (Spider-Man Landmark)	Spider-Man - Page 2
✓		Small AC Unit	A city-themed building piece.	City Building Set	Breakable	Toy Store Purchase (Spider-Man Landmark)	Spider-Man - Page 2
✓		Small Cistern	A city-themed building piece.	City Building Set	Breakable	Toy Store Purchase (Spider-Man Landmark)	Spider-Man - Page 2
✓		Spider-Man Billboard	A Spider-Man-themed piece of furniture.	City Building Set	Breakable	Toy Store Purchase (Spider-Man Landmark)	Spider-Man - Page 2
✓		Stack of Bricks	A city-themed building piece.	City Building Set	Breakable	Toy Store Purchase (Spider-Man Landmark)	Spider-Man - Page 2
✓		Telephone Booth	A city-themed building piece.	City Building Set	Breakable	Toy Store Purchase (Spider-Man Landmark)	Spider-Man - Page 2
✓		Toxic Drum	A city-themed building piece.	City Building Set	Breakable	Toy Store Purchase (Spider-Man Landmark)	Spider-Man - Page 2
✓		Trash Receptacle	A city-themed building piece.	City Building Set	Breakable	Toy Store Purchase (Spider-Man Landmark)	Spider-Man - Page 2
✓		Wall Air Duct	A city-themed building piece.	City Building Set	Breakable	Toy Store Purchase (Spider-Man Landmark)	Spider-Man - Page 2
✓		Woman 1	A townsperson from the world of Marvel.	Marvel Townspeople	Townspeople	Toy Store Purchase (Spider-Man Landmark)	Spider-Man - Page 2
✓		Woman 2	A townsperson from the world of Marvel.	Marvel Townspeople	Townspeople	Toy Store Purchase (Spider-Man Landmark)	Spider-Man - Page 2
✓		Woman 3	A townsperson from the world of Marvel.	Marvel Townspeople	Townspeople	Toy Store Purchase (Spider-Man Landmark)	Spider-Man - Page 2
✓		Wooden Pallets	A city-themed building piece.	City Building Set	Breakable	Toy Store Purchase (Spider-Man Landmark)	Spider-Man - Page 2

GUARDIANS OF THE GALAXY

GOT IT?	ICON	TOY NAME	DESCRIPTION	CATEGORY	FUNCTION	UNLOCK	TOY STORE PAGE
			Guardians of the Galaxy				
✓		Crusader with Extension	A flying vehicle from Guardians of the Galaxy.	Vehicles and Mounts	Air Vehicle	Guardians Play Set Reward	Guardians of the Galaxy - Page 1
✓		Elite Sakaaran	A powerful and armed enemy Sakaaran from the Guardians of the Galaxy Play Set.	Enemies	Enemy	Guardians Play Set Reward	Guardians of the Galaxy - Page 1
✓		Flying Sakaaran	An armed flying enemy Sakaaran from the Guardians of the Galaxy Play Set.	Enemies	Enemy	Guardians Play Set Reward	Guardians of the Galaxy - Page 1
✓		Kamikaze Drone	Enemy drone from the Guardians of the Galaxy Play Set.	Enemies	Enemy	Guardians Play Set Reward	Guardians of the Galaxy - Page 1
✓		Knowhere Omni-Blaster Turret	A Guardians of the Galaxy-themed weapon.	Instant Fun	Custom	Guardians Play Set Reward	Guardians of the Galaxy - Page 1
✓		Large Sakaaran	An enormous and dangerous enemy Sakaaran from the Guardians of the Galaxy Play Set.	Enemies	Enemy	Guardians Play Set Reward	Guardians of the Galaxy - Page 1
✓		Mining Transport	A flying vehicle from Guardians of the Galaxy.	Vehicles and Mounts	Air Vehicle	Guardians Play Set Reward	Guardians of the Galaxy - Page 1
✓		Procyon	A flying vehicle from Guardians of the Galaxy.	Vehicles and Mounts	Air Vehicle	Guardians Play Set Reward	Guardians of the Galaxy - Page 1
✓		Sakaaran Foot Soldier	A sword-wielding enemy Sakaaran from the Guardians of the Galaxy Play Set.	Enemies	Enemy	Guardians Play Set Reward	Guardians of the Galaxy - Page 1
✓		Sakaaran Gunner	An armed enemy Sakaaran from the Guardians of the Galaxy Play Set.	Enemies	Enemy	Guardians Play Set Reward	Guardians of the Galaxy - Page 1
✓		Sakaaran Omni-Blaster Turret	A Guardians of the Galaxy-themed weapon.	Instant Fun	Custom	Guardians Play Set Reward	Guardians of the Galaxy - Page 1
✓		Sakaaran Omni-Missile Turret	A Guardians of the Galaxy-themed weapon.	Instant Fun	Custom	Guardians Play Set Reward	Guardians of the Galaxy - Page 1
✓		Scarab	A vehicle from Guardians of the Galaxy.	Vehicles and Mounts	Air Vehicle	Guardians Play Set Reward	Guardians of the Galaxy - Page 1
✓		Short Ranged Drone	Enemy drone from the Guardians of the Galaxy Play Set.	Enemies	Enemy	Guardians Play Set Reward	Guardians of the Galaxy - Page 1
✓		Starblaster	A flying vehicle from Guardians of the Galaxy.	Vehicles and Mounts	Air Vehicle	Guardians Play Set Reward	Guardians of the Galaxy - Page 1
✓		Starfoil	A flying vehicle from Guardians of the Galaxy.	Vehicles and Mounts	Air Vehicle	Guardians Play Set Reward	Guardians of the Galaxy - Page 1
✓		The Collector	Taneleer Tivan, from Guardians of the Galaxy.	Cast Members	Mission Giver	Guardians Play Set Reward	Guardians of the Galaxy - Page 1
✓		The Mini Milano	A flying vehicle from Guardians of the Galaxy.	Vehicles and Mounts	Air Vehicle	Guardians Play Set Reward	Guardians of the Galaxy - Page 1
✓		Alien 1	An alien from the Guardians of the Galaxy Play Set.	Marvel Townspeople	Townspeople	Toy Store Purchase (Guardians Landmark)	Guardians of the Galaxy - Page 2
✓		Alien 2	An alien from the Guardians of the Galaxy Play Set.	Marvel Townspeople	Townspeople	Toy Store Purchase (Guardians Landmark)	Guardians of the Galaxy - Page 2
✓		Female Scientist	A miner from the Guardians of the Galaxy Play Set.	Marvel Townspeople	Townspeople	Toy Store Purchase (Guardians Landmark)	Guardians of the Galaxy - Page 2
✓		Intergalactic Traveler	A traveler from the Guardians of the Galaxy Play Set.	Marvel Townspeople	Townspeople	Toy Store Purchase (Guardians Landmark)	Guardians of the Galaxy - Page 2
✓		Knowhere Blue-Spotted Critter	An alien critter from the Guardians of the Galaxy Play Set.	Critters	Critter	Toy Store Purchase (Guardians Landmark)	Guardians of the Galaxy - Page 2
✓		Knowhere Bristle Critter	An alien critter from the Guardians of the Galaxy Play Set.	Critters	Critter	Toy Store Purchase (Guardians Landmark)	Guardians of the Galaxy - Page 2
✓		Knowhere Brown Critter	An alien critter from the Guardians of the Galaxy Play Set.	Critters	Critter	Toy Store Purchase (Guardians Landmark)	Guardians of the Galaxy - Page 2
✓		Knowhere Container	A Guardians of the Galaxy-themed decoration piece.	Decorations	Static	Toy Store Purchase (Guardians Landmark)	Guardians of the Galaxy - Page 2
✓		Knowhere Dock Worker	A dock worker from the Guardians of the Galaxy Play Set.	Marvel Townspeople	Townspeople	Toy Store Purchase (Guardians Landmark)	Guardians of the Galaxy - Page 2
✓		Knowhere Fin Critter	An alien critter from the Guardians of the Galaxy Play Set.	Critters	Critter	Toy Store Purchase (Guardians Landmark)	Guardians of the Galaxy - Page 2
✓		Knowhere Floor Fan	A Guardians of the Galaxy-themed decoration piece.	Platforming Toys	Custom	Toy Store Purchase (Guardians Landmark)	Guardians of the Galaxy - Page 2
✓		Knowhere Fuel Tank	A Guardians of the Galaxy-themed decoration piece.	Decorations	Static	Toy Store Purchase (Guardians Landmark)	Guardians of the Galaxy - Page 2

Guardians of the Galaxy Continued

GOT IT?	ICON	TOY NAME	DESCRIPTION	CATEGORY	FUNCTION	UNLOCK	TOY STORE PAGE
✔		Knowhere Maroon Critter	An alien critter from the Guardians of the Galaxy Play Set.	Critters	Critter	Toy Store Purchase (Guardians Landmark)	Guardians of the Galaxy - Page 2
✔		Knowhere Mechanic	Mechanic from the Guardians of the Galaxy Play Set.	Marvel Townspeople	Townspeople	Toy Store Purchase (Guardians Landmark)	Guardians of the Galaxy - Page 2
✔		Knowhere Mining Boss	A mining boss from the Guardians of the Galaxy Play Set.	Marvel Townspeople	Townspeople	Toy Store Purchase (Guardians Landmark)	Guardians of the Galaxy - Page 2
✔		Knowhere Purple Critter	An alien critter from the Guardians of the Galaxy Play Set.	Critters	Critter	Toy Store Purchase (Guardians Landmark)	Guardians of the Galaxy - Page 2
✔		Knowhere Red-Legged Critter	An alien critter from the Guardians of the Galaxy Play Set.	Critters	Critter	Toy Store Purchase (Guardians Landmark)	Guardians of the Galaxy - Page 2
✔		Knowhere Restaurateur	A restaurateur from the Guardians of the Galaxy Play Set.	Marvel Townspeople	Townspeople	Toy Store Purchase (Guardians Landmark)	Guardians of the Galaxy - Page 2
✔		Knowhere Robot 1	A robot from the Guardians of the Galaxy Play Set.	Marvel Townspeople	Townspeople	Toy Store Purchase (Guardians Landmark)	Guardians of the Galaxy - Page 2
✔		Knowhere Robot 2	A robot from the Guardians of the Galaxy Play Set.	Marvel Townspeople	Townspeople	Toy Store Purchase (Guardians Landmark)	Guardians of the Galaxy - Page 2
✔		Knowhere Shop Owner	A shop owner from the Guardians of the Galaxy Play Set.	Marvel Townspeople	Townspeople	Toy Store Purchase (Guardians Landmark)	Guardians of the Galaxy - Page 2
✔		Knowhere Spotted Stripe Critter	An alien critter from the Guardians of the Galaxy Play Set.	Critters	Critter	Toy Store Purchase (Guardians Landmark)	Guardians of the Galaxy - Page 2
✔		Knowhere Vents	A steam vent cover from the Guardians of the Galaxy Play Set that opens and closes, providing platforms.	Platforming Toys	Custom	Toy Store Purchase (Guardians Landmark)	Guardians of the Galaxy - Page 2
✔		Knowhere Wall Fan	A Guardians of the Galaxy-themed decoration piece.	Platforming Toys	Custom	Toy Store Purchase (Guardians Landmark)	Guardians of the Galaxy - Page 2
✔		Knowhere Watchtower	A Guardians of the Galaxy-themed set piece.	Set Pieces	Static	Toy Store Purchase (Guardians Landmark)	Guardians of the Galaxy - Page 2
✔		Knowhere Winged Critter	An alien critter from the Guardians of the Galaxy Play Set.	Critters	Critter	Toy Store Purchase (Guardians Landmark)	Guardians of the Galaxy - Page 2
✔		Kree 1	An alien from the Guardians of the Galaxy Play Set.	Marvel Townspeople	Townspeople	Toy Store Purchase (Guardians Landmark)	Guardians of the Galaxy - Page 2
✔		Kree 2	An alien from the Guardians of the Galaxy Play Set.	Marvel Townspeople	Townspeople	Toy Store Purchase (Guardians Landmark)	Guardians of the Galaxy - Page 2
✔		Kree Shop Owner	A shop owner from the Guardians of the Galaxy Play Set.	Marvel Townspeople	Townspeople	Toy Store Purchase (Guardians Landmark)	Guardians of the Galaxy - Page 2
✔		Large Knowhere Container	A Guardians of the Galaxy-themed decoration piece.	Decorations	Static	Toy Store Purchase (Guardians Landmark)	Guardians of the Galaxy - Page 2
✔		Large Knowhere Fuel Tank	Large tank from the Guardians of the Galaxy Play Set used for climbing.	Decorations	Static	Toy Store Purchase (Guardians Landmark)	Guardians of the Galaxy - Page 2
✔		Large Knowhere Vent	A Guardians of the Galaxy-themed decoration piece.	Decorations	Custom	Toy Store Purchase (Guardians Landmark)	Guardians of the Galaxy - Page 2
✔		Male Scientist	A miner from the Guardians of the Galaxy Play Set.	Marvel Townspeople	Townspeople	Toy Store Purchase (Guardians Landmark)	Guardians of the Galaxy - Page 2
✔		Space Station Agent	An agent from the Guardians of the Galaxy Play Set.	Marvel Townspeople	Townspeople	Toy Store Purchase (Guardians Landmark)	Guardians of the Galaxy - Page 2
✔		Space Traveler	A traveler from the Guardians of the Galaxy Play Set.	Marvel Townspeople	Townspeople	Toy Store Purchase (Guardians Landmark)	Guardians of the Galaxy - Page 2

TOY BOX TOYS

Toy Box Toys

GOT IT?	ICON	TOY NAME	DESCRIPTION	CATEGORY	FUNCTION	UNLOCK	TOY STORE PAGE
✔		Aladdin Costume	A toy in an Aladdin costume from Aladdin.	Character Townspeople	Townspeople	Aladdin	Character Townspeople
✔		Baymax Costume	A toy in a Baymax costume from Big Hero Six.	Character Townspeople	Townspeople	Baymax	Character Townspeople
✔		Black Widow Costume	A toy in a Black Widow costume.	Character Townspeople	Townspeople	Black Widow	Character Townspeople
✔		Captain America Costume	A toy in a Captain America costume.	Character Townspeople	Townspeople	Captain America	Character Townspeople
✔		Donald Duck Costume	A toy in a Donald Duck costume.	Character Townspeople	Townspeople	Donald Duck	Character Townspeople

GOT IT?	ICON	TOY NAME	DESCRIPTION	CATEGORY	FUNCTION	UNLOCK	TOY STORE PAGE
			Toy Box Toys Continued				
✓		Drax Costume	A toy in a Drax costume.	Character Townspeople	Townspeople	Drax	Character Townspeople
✓		Falcon Costume	A toy in a Falcon costume.	Character Townspeople	Townspeople	Falcon	Character Townspeople
✓		Gamora Costume	A toy in a Gamora costume.	Character Townspeople	Townspeople	Gamora	Character Townspeople
✓		Groot Costume	A toy in a Groot costume.	Character Townspeople	Townspeople	Groot	Character Townspeople
✓		Hawkeye Costume	A toy in a Hawkeye costume.	Character Townspeople	Townspeople	Hawkeye	Character Townspeople
✓		Hiro Costume	A toy in a Hiro costume from Big Hero Six.	Character Townspeople	Townspeople	Hiro	Character Townspeople
✓		Hulk Costume	A toy in a Hulk costume.	Character Townspeople	Townspeople	Hulk	Character Townspeople
✓		Iron Fist Costume	A toy in an Iron Fist costume.	Character Townspeople	Townspeople	Iron Fist	Character Townspeople
✓		Iron Man Costume	A toy in an Iron Man costume.	Character Townspeople	Townspeople	Iron Man	Character Townspeople
✓		Maleficent Movie Costume	A toy in a Maleficent costume from Maleficent.	Character Townspeople	Townspeople	Maleficent	Character Townspeople
✓		Merida Costume	A toy in a Merida costume from Brave.	Character Townspeople	Townspeople	Merida	Character Townspeople
✓		Nick Fury Costume	A toy in a Nick Fury costume.	Character Townspeople	Townspeople	Nick Fury	Character Townspeople
✓		Nova Costume	A toy in a Nova costume.	Character Townspeople	Townspeople	Nova	Character Townspeople
✓		Princess Jasmine Costume	A toy in a Princess Jasmine costume from Aladdin.	Character Townspeople	Townspeople	Jasmine	Character Townspeople
✓		Rocket Raccoon Costume	A toy in a Rocket Raccoon costume.	Character Townspeople	Townspeople	Rocket Raccoon	Character Townspeople
✓		Spider-Man Costume	A toy in a Spider-Man costume.	Character Townspeople	Townspeople	Spider-Man	Character Townspeople
✓		Star-Lord Costume	A toy in a Star-Lord costume.	Character Townspeople	Townspeople	Star-Lord	Character Townspeople
✓		Stitch Costume	A toy in a Stitch costume from Lilo and Stitch.	Character Townspeople	Townspeople	Stitch	Character Townspeople
✓		Thor Costume	A toy in a Thor costume.	Character Townspeople	Townspeople	Thor	Character Townspeople
✓		Tinker Bell Costume	A toy in a Tinker Bell costume from Peter Pan.	Character Townspeople	Townspeople	Tinker Bell	Character Townspeople
✓		Venom Costume	A toy in a Venom costume.	Character Townspeople	Townspeople	Venom	Character Townspeople
✓		1st Place Podium	Celebrate a glorious victory with this 1st Place podium! Use the Challenge Maker to give the winning player the full hero treatment!	Creativi-Toys	Custom	Toy Store Purchase	Creativi-Toys
✓		2nd Place Podium	Celebrate a glorious victory with this 2nd Place podium! Use the Challenge Maker to give the winning player the full hero treatment!	Creativi-Toys	Custom	Toy Store Purchase	Creativi-Toys
✓		3rd Place Podium	Celebrate a glorious victory with this 3rd Place podium! Use the Challenge Maker to give the winning player the full hero treatment!	Creativi-Toys	Custom	Toy Store Purchase	Creativi-Toys
✓		4th Place Podium	Celebrate a glorious victory with this 4th Place podium! Use the Challenge Maker to give the winning player the full hero treatment!	Creativi-Toys	Custom	Toy Store Purchase	Creativi-Toys
✓		Ability Terminal	Use this tool to choose which character types can participate.	Creativi-Toys	Custom	Toy Store Purchase	Creativi-Toys
✓		Action Enforcer	You can have characters do a victory dance and other fun actions with this Action Enforcer!	Creativi-Toys	Custom	Toy Store Purchase	Creativi-Toys
✓		Angled Camera	Track Character movement from an overhead angle with this camera.	Creativi-Toys	Custom	Toy Store Purchase	Creativi-Toys
✓		Ballot Box	Indecisive? Vote on it! Use the settings in the Ballot Box to tally all the players' choices.	Creativi-Toys	Custom	Toy Store Purchase	Creativi-Toys
✓		Challenge Maker	Make up your own rules with the Challenge Maker! Scoreboards, countdowns, the start and finish, and even the title, can all be created by you.	Creativi-Toys	Custom	Toy Store Purchase	Creativi-Toys

			Toy Box Toys Continued				
GOT IT?	ICON	TOY NAME	DESCRIPTION	CATEGORY	FUNCTION	UNLOCK	TOY STORE PAGE
✓		Collectible Tracker	With the Collectible Tracker, you can keep stats on the various Collectibles you gather.	Creativi-Toys	Custom	Toy Store Purchase	Creativi-Toys
✓		Color-Changing Block	A Toy Box block that changes color.	Creativi-Toys	Custom	Toy Store Purchase	Creativi-Toys
✓		Confirmer	Ask the players in your game if they're sure about one of their actions with the Confirmer.	Creativi-Toys	Custom	Toy Store Purchase	Creativi-Toys
✓		Defeat Manager	Set the rules of losing with the Defeat Manager. Use the Properties menu to define how.	Creativi-Toys	Custom	Toy Store Purchase	Creativi-Toys
✓		Editor Manager	Choose when and how to use the Editor with the Editor Manager.	Creativi-Toys	Custom	Toy Store Purchase	Creativi-Toys
✓		Effects Generator	Want more explosions in your game? Use this toy to create special effects! You can even control how and where it goes off.	Creativi-Toys	Custom	Toy Store Purchase	Creativi-Toys
✓		Enemy Trail Guide	Your enemies will make their way toward the point of your choosing with the Enemy Trail Guide.	Creativi-Toys	Custom	Toy Store Purchase	Creativi-Toys
✓		Enemy Wave Generator	Create a flood of enemies with the Enemy Wave Generator! You can even choose who they are and who they'll fight.	Creativi-Toys	Custom	Toy Store Purchase	Creativi-Toys
✓		Friendly Wave Generator	Create a flood of friendly toys and mounts with the Friendly Wave Generator! You can even choose how many or who they are.	Creativi-Toys	Custom	Toy Store Purchase	Creativi-Toys
✓		Inventory Manager	Control the toys other players have and can use with the Inventory Manager.	Creativi-Toys	Custom	Toy Store Purchase	Creativi-Toys
✓		Level Starter	Reset your game with the Level Starter.	Creativi-Toys	Custom	Toy Store Purchase	Creativi-Toys
✓		Locator	Surprise other players with enemies, allies, or even new tools by connecting toys to the Locator!	Creativi-Toys	Custom	Toy Store Purchase	Creativi-Toys
✓		Logic Gate	An all-logic version of the Power Switch toy.	Creativi-Toys	Custom	Toy Store Purchase	Creativi-Toys
✓		Loot Chest	With the Loot Chest, you can make treasure chests with great toys inside for your friends.	Creativi-Toys	Custom	Toy Store Purchase	Creativi-Toys
✓		Loot Drop Manager	Decide how much and what kind of loot your enemies leave behind with the Loot Drop Manager.	Creativi-Toys	Custom	Toy Store Purchase	Creativi-Toys
✓		Money Manager	Manage the money that Characters gather and earn with this Money Manager.	Creativi-Toys	Custom	Toy Store Purchase	Creativi-Toys
✓		Packs and Tools Manager	Control the Packs and Tools other players have with the Packs and Tools Manager.	Creativi-Toys	Custom	Toy Store Purchase	Creativi-Toys
✓		Randomizer	Connect ten different toys to the Randomizer and watch them go off at random! Adjust the options in the Properties menu.	Creativi-Toys	Custom	Toy Store Purchase	Creativi-Toys
✓		Ready Up Checker	This checkpoint won't allow the game to proceed until everyone's in place and ready.	Creativi-Toys	Custom	Toy Store Purchase	Creativi-Toys
✓		Remote Controller	Remove your Character from the game and control objects instead with the Remote Controller.	Creativi-Toys	Custom	Toy Store Purchase	Creativi-Toys
✓		Satellite Receiver	Connect to other Toy Box Worlds with the Satellite Receiver! You can even open up secret rooms and Portal Doors in other worlds.	Creativi-Toys	Custom	Toy Store Purchase	Creativi-Toys
✓		Storefront	Sell specific toys to your players with the Storefront. You can control prices and quantities with the help of the Inventory and Money Managers.	Creativi-Toys	Custom	Toy Store Purchase	Creativi-Toys
✓		Target Camera	The Target Camera can be used to follow your friends through the game, or to keep watch on a certain location.	Creativi-Toys	Custom	Toy Store Purchase	Creativi-Toys
✓		Team Scoreboard	Rather than just individual scores, keep track of teams' scores with the Team Scoreboard. You can determine when and how it tallies.	Creativi-Toys	Custom	Toy Store Purchase	Creativi-Toys
✓		Text Creator	Create your own messages with the Text Creator! Type in your own words, save them, and see them displayed onscreen. Sign into a Disney Account to unlock this toy.	Creativi-Toys	Custom	Disney ID Reward	Creativi-Toys
✓		Text Displayer	Talk to your friends with the Text Displayer! Choose from over 80 different words and phrases.	Creativi-Toys	Custom	Toy Store Purchase	Creativi-Toys
✓		Toy Box Game Maker	Use this to save your current Toy Box as a Toy Box Game. You can also set the rules of the magic wand, the camera controls, the editor, and more.	Creativi-Toys	Custom	Toy Store Purchase	Creativi-Toys

			Toy Box Toys Continued				
GOT IT?	ICON	TOY NAME	DESCRIPTION	CATEGORY	FUNCTION	UNLOCK	TOY STORE PAGE
✓		Weather Vane	Create a wind with the Weather Vane! You can change the strength, direction, and other settings in the Properties menu.	Creativi-Toys	Custom	Toy Store Purchase	Creativi-Toys
✓		Whirlwind	This tiny whirlwind will blow you and your friends around!	Platforming Toys	Custom	Toy Store Purchase	Creativi-Toys
✓		Alice Costume	A toy in an Alice costume from Alice in Wonderland.	Disney Infinity Townspeople	Townspeople	Toy Store Purchase	Disney Townspeople - Page 1
✓		Baloo Costume	A toy in a Baloo costume from The Jungle Book.	Disney Infinity Townspeople	Townspeople	Toy Store Purchase	Disney Townspeople - Page 1
✓		Big Al Costume	A toy in a Big Al costume from the Magic Kingdom's Country Bear Jamboree.	Disney Infinity Townspeople	Townspeople	Toy Store Purchase	Disney Townspeople - Page 1
✓		Carl Fredricksen Costume	A toy in a Carl Fredricksen costume from Up.	Disney Infinity Townspeople	Townspeople	INterior Mission Reward	Disney Townspeople - Page 1
✓		Chernabog Costume	A toy in a Chernabog costume from Fantasia.	Disney Infinity Townspeople	Townspeople	Toy Store Purchase	Disney Townspeople - Page 1
✓		Cheshire Cat Costume	A toy in a Cheshire Cat costume from Alice in Wonderland.	Disney Infinity Townspeople	Townspeople	Toy Store Purchase	Disney Townspeople - Page 1
✓		Chip Costume	A toy in a Chip costume.	Disney Infinity Townspeople	Townspeople	Toy Store Purchase	Disney Townspeople - Page 1
✓		Cogsworth Costume	A toy in a Cogsworth costume from Beauty and the Beast.	Disney Infinity Townspeople	Townspeople	INterior Mission Reward	Disney Townspeople - Page 1
✓		Dale Costume	A toy in a Dale costume.	Disney Infinity Townspeople	Townspeople	Toy Store Purchase	Disney Townspeople - Page 1
✓		Darkwing Duck Costume	A toy in a Darkwing Duck costume.	Disney Infinity Townspeople	Townspeople	INterior Mission Reward	Disney Townspeople - Page 1
✓		Dipper Costume	A toy in a Dipper costume from Gravity Falls.	Disney Infinity Townspeople	Townspeople	Toy Store Purchase	Disney Townspeople - Page 1
✓		Duffy Costume	A toy in a Duffy the Disney Bear costume.	Disney Infinity Townspeople	Townspeople	Toy Store Purchase	Disney Townspeople - Page 1
✓		Dumbo Costume	A toy in a Dumbo costume.	Disney Infinity Townspeople	Townspeople	Toy Store Purchase	Disney Townspeople - Page 1
✓		Edna Mode Costume	A toy in an Edna Mode costume from The Incredibles.	Disney Infinity Townspeople	Townspeople	Toy Store Purchase	Disney Townspeople - Page 1
✓		Eeyore Costume	A toy in an Eeyore costume from Winnie the Pooh.	Disney Infinity Townspeople	Townspeople	Toy Store Purchase	Disney Townspeople - Page 1
✓		Flynt Costume	A toy in a Flynt costume from Tarzan.	Disney Infinity Townspeople	Townspeople	Toy Store Purchase	Disney Townspeople - Page 1
✓		Fozzie Bear Costume	A toy in a Fozzie Bear costume from the Muppets.	Disney Infinity Townspeople	Townspeople	Toy Store Purchase	Disney Townspeople - Page 1
✓		Giselle Costume	A toy in a Giselle costume from Enchanted.	Disney Infinity Townspeople	Townspeople	Toy Store Purchase	Disney Townspeople - Page 1
✓		Gonzo Costume	A toy in a Gonzo costume from the Muppets.	Disney Infinity Townspeople	Townspeople	Toy Store Purchase	Disney Townspeople - Page 1
✓		Goofy Costume	A toy in a Goofy costume.	Disney Infinity Townspeople	Townspeople	Toy Store Purchase	Disney Townspeople - Page 1
✓		Gus Costume	A toy in a Gus costume from Cinderella.	Disney Infinity Townspeople	Townspeople	Toy Store Purchase	Disney Townspeople - Page 1
✓		Happy Costume	A toy in a Happy costume from Snow White and the Seven Dwarfs.	Disney Infinity Townspeople	Townspeople	Toy Store Purchase	Disney Townspeople - Page 1
✓		Henry Costume	A toy in a Henry costume from the Magic Kingdom's Country Bear Jamboree.	Disney Infinity Townspeople	Townspeople	Toy Store Purchase	Disney Townspeople - Page 1
✓		Hercules Costume	A toy in a Hercules costume.	Disney Infinity Townspeople	Townspeople	Toy Store Purchase	Disney Townspeople - Page 1

GAME BASICS

CHARACTERS

POWER DISCS

MARVEL'S THE AVENGERS

SPIDER-MAN

GUARDIANS OF THE GALAXY

TOY BOX

TOY BOX COLLECTION

ACHIEVEMENTS

Toy Box Toys Continued

GOT IT?	ICON	TOY NAME	DESCRIPTION	CATEGORY	FUNCTION	UNLOCK	TOY STORE PAGE
✓		Jaq Costume	A toy in a Jaq costume from Cinderella.	Disney Infinity Townspeople	Townspeople	Toy Store Purchase	Disney Townspeople - Page 1
✓		King Louie Costume	A toy in a King Louie Costume from The Jungle Book.	Disney Infinity Townspeople	Townspeople	"Toy Box Introduction Mission Reward"	Disney Townspeople - Page 1
✓		Phil Costume	A toy in a Phil costume from Hercules.	Disney Infinity Townspeople	Townspeople	Toy Store Purchase	Disney Townspeople - Page 1
✓		Prisoner Hitchhiking Ghost Costume	A toy in a Prisoner Hitchhiking Ghost costume from Disney Parks' Haunted Mansion.	Disney Infinity Townspeople	Townspeople	Toy Store Purchase	Disney Townspeople - Page 1
✓		Skeleton Hitchhiking Ghost Costume	A toy in a Skeleton Hitchhiking Ghost costume from Disney Parks' Haunted Mansion.	Disney Infinity Townspeople	Townspeople	Toy Store Purchase	Disney Townspeople - Page 1
✓		Traveler Hitchhiking Ghost Costume	A toy in a Traveler Hitchhiking Ghost costume from Disney Parks' Haunted Mansion.	Disney Infinity Townspeople	Townspeople	Toy Store Purchase	Disney Townspeople - Page 1
✓		Eve Costume	A toy in an Eve costume from WALL-E.	Disney Infinity Townspeople	Townspeople	Toy Store Purchase	Disney Townspeople - Page 2
✓		Gnome	A little critter from Gravity Falls.	Critters	Critter	Toy Store Purchase	Disney Townspeople - Page 2
✓		Ice-Cream Man Costume	A toy in an Ice-Cream Man costume from Lilo and Stitch.	Disney Infinity Townspeople	Townspeople	Toy Store Purchase	Disney Townspeople - Page 2
✓		Kuzco Costume	A toy in a Kuzco costume from The Emperor's New Groove.	Disney Infinity Townspeople	Townspeople	INterior Mission Reward	Disney Townspeople - Page 2
✓		Lewis Costume	A toy in a Lewis costume from Meet the Robinsons.	Disney Infinity Townspeople	Townspeople	Toy Store Purchase	Disney Townspeople - Page 2
✓		Lilo Costume	A toy in a Lilo costume from Lilo and Stitch.	Disney Infinity Townspeople	Townspeople	Toy Store Purchase	Disney Townspeople - Page 2
✓		Luigi Costume	A toy in a Luigi costume from Cars.	Disney Infinity Townspeople	Townspeople	Toy Store Purchase	Disney Townspeople - Page 2
✓		Mabel Costume	A toy in a Mabel costume from Gravity Falls.	Disney Infinity Townspeople	Townspeople	Toy Store Purchase	Disney Townspeople - Page 2
✓		Mickey Mouse Costume	A toy in a Mickey Mouse costume.	Disney Infinity Townspeople	Townspeople	Toy Store Purchase	Disney Townspeople - Page 2
✓		Minnie Mouse Costume	A toy in a Minnie Mouse costume.	Disney Infinity Townspeople	Townspeople	Toy Store Purchase	Disney Townspeople - Page 2
✓		Mr. Gibbs Costume	A toy in a Mr. Gibbs costume from Pirates of the Caribbean.	Disney Infinity Townspeople	Townspeople	Toy Store Purchase	Disney Townspeople - Page 2
✓		Mr. Toad Costume	A toy in a Mr. Toad costume from The Wind in the Willows.	Disney Infinity Townspeople	Townspeople	INterior Mission Reward	Disney Townspeople - Page 2
✓		Mulan Costume	A toy in a Mulan costume.	Disney Infinity Townspeople	Townspeople	Toy Store Purchase	Disney Townspeople - Page 2
✓		Mushu Costume	A toy in a Mushu costume from Mulan.	Disney Infinity Townspeople	Townspeople	Toy Store Purchase	Disney Townspeople - Page 2
✓		Nani Costume	A toy in a Nani costume from Lilo and Stitch.	Disney Infinity Townspeople	Townspeople	Toy Store Purchase	Disney Townspeople - Page 2
✓		Oaken Costume	A toy in an Oaken costume.	Disney Infinity Townspeople	Townspeople	Toy Store Purchase	Disney Townspeople - Page 2
✓		Oswald Costume	A toy in an Oswald the Lucky Rabbit costume.	Disney Infinity Townspeople	Townspeople	Toy Store Purchase	Disney Townspeople - Page 2
✓		Periwinkle Costume	A toy in a Periwinkle costume from Secret of the Wings.	Disney Infinity Townspeople	Townspeople	Toy Store Purchase	Disney Townspeople - Page 2
✓		Pluto Costume	A toy in a Pluto costume.	Disney Infinity Townspeople	Townspeople	Toy Store Purchase	Disney Townspeople - Page 2
✓		Pumbaa Costume	A toy in a Pumbaa costume from The Lion King.	Disney Infinity Townspeople	Townspeople	Toy Store Purchase	Disney Townspeople - Page 2

			Toy Box Toys Continued			
GOT IT?	**ICON**	**TOY NAME**	**DESCRIPTION**	**CATEGORY**	**FUNCTION**	**UNLOCK**	**TOY STORE PAGE**

GOT IT?	**ICON**	**TOY NAME**	**DESCRIPTION**	**CATEGORY**	**FUNCTION**	**UNLOCK**	**TOY STORE PAGE**
✓		Queen of Hearts Costume	A toy in a Queen of Hearts costume from Alice in Wonderland.	Disney Infinity Townspeople	Townspeople	Toy Store Purchase	Disney Townspeople - Page 2
✓		Quorra Costume	A toy in a Quorra costume from Tron: Legacy.	Disney Infinity Townspeople	Townspeople	Toy Store Purchase	Disney Townspeople - Page 2
✓		Shmebulock	A little critter from Gravity Falls.	Critters	Critter	Toy Store Purchase	Disney Townspeople - Page 2
✓		Sleeping Beauty Costume	A toy in an Aurora costume from Sleeping Beauty.	Disney Infinity Townspeople	Townspeople	INterior Mission Reward	Disney Townspeople - Page 2
✓		Slightly Costume	A toy in a Slightly costume from Peter Pan.	Disney Infinity Townspeople	Townspeople	Toy Store Purchase	Disney Townspeople - Page 2
✓		Steamboat Willie Costume	A toy in a Steamboat Willie costume.	Disney Infinity Townspeople	Townspeople	Toy Store Purchase	Disney Townspeople - Page 2
✓		Sultan Costume	A toy in a Sultan costume from Aladdin.	Disney Infinity Townspeople	Townspeople	Toy Store Purchase	Disney Townspeople - Page 2
✓		Timon Costume	A toy in a Timon costume from The Lion King.	Disney Infinity Townspeople	Townspeople	Toy Store Purchase	Disney Townspeople - Page 2
✓		Vincent Costume	A toy in a Vincent costume from The Black Hole.	Disney Infinity Townspeople	Townspeople	Toy Store Purchase	Disney Townspeople - Page 2
✓		WALL-E Costume	A toy in a WALL-E costume.	Disney Infinity Townspeople	Townspeople	Toy Store Purchase	Disney Townspeople - Page 2
✓		Barrier Veer Left	A barrier piece for race tracks.	Race Track Pieces	Static	Toy Store Purchase	Invisible Walls
✓		Barrier Veer Right	A barrier piece for race tracks.	Race Track Pieces	Static	Toy Store Purchase	Invisible Walls
✓		Inside Barrier Bend	A barrier piece for race tracks.	Race Track Pieces	Static	Toy Store Purchase	Invisible Walls
✓		Inside Barrier Curve	A barrier piece for race tracks.	Race Track Pieces	Static	Toy Store Purchase	Invisible Walls
✓		Large Barrier Veer Left	A barrier piece for race tracks.	Race Track Pieces	Static	Toy Store Purchase	Invisible Walls
✓		Large Barrier Veer Right	A barrier piece for race tracks.	Race Track Pieces	Static	Toy Store Purchase	Invisible Walls
✓		Large Inside Barrier Bend	A barrier piece for race tracks.	Race Track Pieces	Static	Toy Store Purchase	Invisible Walls
✓		Large Inside Barrier Curve	A barrier piece for race tracks.	Race Track Pieces	Static	Toy Store Purchase	Invisible Walls
✓		Large Left Barrier Junction	A barrier piece for race tracks.	Race Track Pieces	Static	Toy Store Purchase	Invisible Walls
✓		Large Left Barrier Split	A barrier piece for race tracks.	Race Track Pieces	Static	Toy Store Purchase	Invisible Walls
✓		Large Outside Barrier Bend	A barrier piece for race tracks.	Race Track Pieces	Static	Toy Store Purchase	Invisible Walls
✓		Large Outside Barrier Curve	A barrier piece for race tracks.	Race Track Pieces	Static	Toy Store Purchase	Invisible Walls
✓		Large Right Barrier Junction	A barrier piece for race tracks.	Race Track Pieces	Static	Toy Store Purchase	Invisible Walls
✓		Large Right Barrier Split	A barrier piece for race tracks.	Race Track Pieces	Static	Toy Store Purchase	Invisible Walls
✓		Left Barrier Junction	A barrier piece for race tracks.	Race Track Pieces	Static	Toy Store Purchase	Invisible Walls
✓		Left Barrier Split	A barrier piece for race tracks.	Race Track Pieces	Static	Toy Store Purchase	Invisible Walls
✓		Outside Barrier Bend	A barrier piece for race tracks.	Race Track Pieces	Static	Toy Store Purchase	Invisible Walls
✓		Outside Barrier Curve	A barrier piece for race tracks.	Race Track Pieces	Static	Toy Store Purchase	Invisible Walls
✓		Right Barrier Junction	A barrier piece for race tracks.	Race Track Pieces	Static	Toy Store Purchase	Invisible Walls

GAME BASICS

CHARACTERS

POWER DISCS

MARVEL'S THE AVENGERS

SPIDER-MAN

GUARDIANS OF THE GALAXY

TOY BOX

TOY BOX COLLECTION

ACHIEVEMENTS

Toy Box Toys Continued

GOT IT?	ICON	TOY NAME	DESCRIPTION	CATEGORY	FUNCTION	UNLOCK	TOY STORE PAGE
✓		Right Barrier Split	A barrier piece for race tracks.	Race Track Pieces	Static	Toy Store Purchase	Invisible Walls
✓		Scalable Barrier Block	Create invisible barriers with this Barrier Block. You can also scale and stretch it to the size you want.	Platforming Toys	Static	Toy Store Purchase	Invisible Walls
✓		Corner Ledge Hang	A barrier piece with a ledge hang.	Platforming Toys	Ledge Hang	Toy Store Purchase	Ledge Hangs & Rails
✓		Diagonal Ledge Hang	A barrier piece with a ledge hang.	Platforming Toys	Ledge Hang	Toy Store Purchase	Ledge Hangs & Rails
✓		Diagonal Ledge Hang Inverse	A barrier piece with a ledge hang.	Platforming Toys	Ledge Hang	Toy Store Purchase	Ledge Hangs & Rails
✓		Double Corner Ledge Hang	A barrier piece with a ledge hang.	Platforming Toys	Ledge Hang	Toy Store Purchase	Ledge Hangs & Rails
✓		Double Inside Corner Ledge Hang	A barrier piece with a ledge hang.	Platforming Toys	Ledge Hang	Toy Store Purchase	Ledge Hangs & Rails
✓		Double Ledge Hang	A barrier piece with a ledge hang.	Platforming Toys	Ledge Hang	Toy Store Purchase	Ledge Hangs & Rails
✓		Flagpole Base	A climbable flagpole piece.	Platforming Toys	Static	Toy Store Purchase	Ledge Hangs & Rails
✓		Flagpole Middle	A climbable flagpole piece.	Platforming Toys	Static	Toy Store Purchase	Ledge Hangs & Rails
✓		Flagpole Top	A climbable flagpole piece.	Platforming Toys	Static	Toy Store Purchase	Ledge Hangs & Rails
✓		Horizontal Barrier Piece	A basic barrier piece.	Platforming Toys	Ledge Hang	Toy Store Purchase	Ledge Hangs & Rails
✓		Horizontal Rail Corner	A Toy Box-themed rail.	Platforming Toys	Rail Grind	Toy Store Purchase	Ledge Hangs & Rails
✓		Horizontal Sliding Ledge Hang	A barrier piece with a ledge hang.	Platforming Toys	Ledge Hang	Toy Store Purchase	Ledge Hangs & Rails
✓		Inside Corner Ledge Hang	A barrier piece with a ledge hang.	Platforming Toys	Ledge Hang	Toy Store Purchase	Ledge Hangs & Rails
✓		Ledge Hang	A barrier piece with a ledge hang.	Platforming Toys	Ledge Hang	Toy Store Purchase	Ledge Hangs & Rails
✓		Long Pipe Climb	A climbable pipe piece.	Platforming Toys	Static	Toy Store Purchase	Ledge Hangs & Rails
✓		Pipe Climb	A climbable pipe piece.	Platforming Toys	Static	Toy Store Purchase	Ledge Hangs & Rails
✓		Rail Combine Two	A Toy Box-themed rail.	Platforming Toys	Rail Grind	Toy Store Purchase	Ledge Hangs & Rails
✓		Rail Spiral	A Toy Box-themed rail.	Platforming Toys	Rail Grind	Toy Store Purchase	Ledge Hangs & Rails
✓		Rail Split Two	A Toy Box-themed rail.	Platforming Toys	Rail Grind	Toy Store Purchase	Ledge Hangs & Rails
✓		Rail Target Point	A holographic target that can be connected to other toys. It's especially useful in rail slide layouts.	Creativi-Toys	Custom	Toy Store Purchase	Ledge Hangs & Rails
✓		Rail Tri-Split	A Toy Box-themed rail.	Platforming Toys	Rail Grind	Toy Store Purchase	Ledge Hangs & Rails
✓		Rail Tri-Turnpike	A Toy Box-themed rail.	Platforming Toys	Rail Grind	Toy Store Purchase	Ledge Hangs & Rails
✓		Rail Turnpike Two	A Toy Box-themed rail.	Platforming Toys	Rail Grind	Toy Store Purchase	Ledge Hangs & Rails
✓		Rotating Double Ledge Hang	A barrier piece with a ledge hang.	Platforming Toys	Ledge Hang	Toy Store Purchase	Ledge Hangs & Rails
✓		Rotating Rail	A Toy Box-themed rail.	Platforming Toys	Rail Grind	Toy Store Purchase	Ledge Hangs & Rails
✓		Short Flagpole Middle	A climbable flagpole piece.	Platforming Toys	Static	Toy Store Purchase	Ledge Hangs & Rails
✓		Short Pipe Climb	A climbable pipe piece.	Platforming Toys	Static	Toy Store Purchase	Ledge Hangs & Rails
✓		Small Horizontal Barrier Piece	A barrier piece with a ledge hang.	Platforming Toys	Ledge Hang	Toy Store Purchase	Ledge Hangs & Rails
✓		Small Vertical Barrier Piece	A barrier piece with a ledge hang.	Platforming Toys	Ledge Hang	Toy Store Purchase	Ledge Hangs & Rails

GOT IT?	ICON	TOY NAME	DESCRIPTION	CATEGORY	FUNCTION	UNLOCK	TOY STORE PAGE
			Toy Box Toys Continued				
✓		Tall Vertical Sliding Ledge Hang	A barrier piece with a ledge hang.	Platforming Toys	Ledge Hang	Toy Store Purchase	Ledge Hangs & Rails
✓		Toy Box Rail Builder	This little toy will help you build a rail slide.	Builders and Creators	Builder	Toy Store Purchase	Ledge Hangs & Rails
✓		Toy Box Rail Creator	Place this Creator to quickly build a rail slide.	Builders and Creators	Creator	Toy Store Purchase	Ledge Hangs & Rails
✓		Vertical Barrier Piece	A barrier piece with a ledge hang.	Platforming Toys	Ledge Hang	Toy Store Purchase	Ledge Hangs & Rails
✓		Vertical Rail Corner	A Toy Box-themed rail.	Platforming Toys	Rail Grind	Toy Store Purchase	Ledge Hangs & Rails
✓		Vertical Sliding Ledge Hang	A barrier piece with a ledge hang.	Platforming Toys	Ledge Hang	Toy Store Purchase	Ledge Hangs & Rails
✓		Blue Ground !-Mark	Mark your game with these guiding signals.	Decorations	Static	Toy Store Purchase	Marker Toys
✓		Blue Ground ?-Mark	Mark your game with these guiding signals.	Decorations	Static	Toy Store Purchase	Marker Toys
✓		Blue Ground Check Mark	Mark your game with these guiding signals.	Decorations	Static	Toy Store Purchase	Marker Toys
✓		Blue Ground Danger Mark	Mark your game with these guiding signals.	Decorations	Static	Toy Store Purchase	Marker Toys
✓		Blue Ground Footprints	Mark your game with these guiding signals.	Decorations	Static	Toy Store Purchase	Marker Toys
✓		Blue Ground X-Mark	Mark your game with these guiding signals.	Decorations	Static	Toy Store Purchase	Marker Toys
✓		Blue Wall !-Mark	Mark your game with these guiding signals.	Decorations	Static	Toy Store Purchase	Marker Toys
✓		Blue Wall ?-Mark	Mark your game with these guiding signals.	Decorations	Static	Toy Store Purchase	Marker Toys
✓		Blue Wall Check Mark	Mark your game with these guiding signals.	Decorations	Static	Toy Store Purchase	Marker Toys
✓		Blue Wall Danger Mark	Mark your game with these guiding signals.	Decorations	Static	Toy Store Purchase	Marker Toys
✓		Blue Wall Footprints	Mark your game with these guiding signals.	Decorations	Static	Toy Store Purchase	Marker Toys
✓		Blue Wall X-Mark	Mark your game with these guiding signals.	Decorations	Static	Toy Store Purchase	Marker Toys
✓		Down Blue Arrow	Mark your game with these guiding signals.	Decorations	Static	Toy Store Purchase	Marker Toys
✓		Down Yellow Arrow	Mark your game with these guiding signals.	Decorations	Static	Toy Store Purchase	Marker Toys
✓		Ground Blue Arrow	Mark your game with these guiding signals.	Decorations	Static	Toy Store Purchase	Marker Toys
✓		Ground Yellow Arrow	Mark your game with these guiding signals.	Decorations	Static	Toy Store Purchase	Marker Toys
✓		Left Blue Arrow	Mark your game with these guiding signals.	Decorations	Static	Toy Store Purchase	Marker Toys
✓		Left Yellow Arrow	Mark your game with these guiding signals.	Decorations	Static	Toy Store Purchase	Marker Toys
✓		Right Blue Arrow	Mark your game with these guiding signals.	Decorations	Static	Toy Store Purchase	Marker Toys
✓		Right Yellow Arrow	Mark your game with these guiding signals.	Decorations	Static	Toy Store Purchase	Marker Toys
✓		Up Blue Arrow	Mark your game with these guiding signals.	Decorations	Static	Toy Store Purchase	Marker Toys
✓		Up Yellow Arrow	Mark your game with these guiding signals.	Decorations	Static	Toy Store Purchase	Marker Toys
✓		Yellow Ground !-Mark	Mark your game with these guiding signals.	Decorations	Static	Toy Store Purchase	Marker Toys
✓		Yellow Ground ?-Mark	Mark your game with these guiding signals.	Decorations	Static	Toy Store Purchase	Marker Toys
✓		Yellow Ground Check Mark	Mark your game with these guiding signals.	Decorations	Static	Toy Store Purchase	Marker Toys

GAME BASICS

CHARACTERS

POWER DISCS

MARVEL'S THE AVENGERS

SPIDER-MAN

GUARDIANS OF THE GALAXY

TOY BOX

TOY BOX COLLECTION

ACHIEVEMENTS

GOT IT?	ICON	TOY NAME	DESCRIPTION	CATEGORY	FUNCTION	UNLOCK	TOY STORE PAGE
✓		Yellow Ground Danger Mark	Mark your game with these guiding signals.	Decorations	Static	Toy Store Purchase	Marker Toys
✓		Yellow Ground Footprints	Mark your game with these guiding signals.	Decorations	Static	Toy Store Purchase	Marker Toys
✓		Yellow Ground X-Mark	Mark your game with these guiding signals.	Decorations	Static	Toy Store Purchase	Marker Toys
✓		Yellow Wall !-Mark	Mark your game with these guiding signals.	Decorations	Static	Toy Store Purchase	Marker Toys
✓		Yellow Wall ?-Mark	Mark your game with these guiding signals.	Decorations	Static	Toy Store Purchase	Marker Toys
✓		Yellow Wall Check Mark	Mark your game with these guiding signals.	Decorations	Static	Toy Store Purchase	Marker Toys
✓		Yellow Wall Danger Mark	Mark your game with these guiding signals.	Decorations	Static	Toy Store Purchase	Marker Toys
✓		Yellow Wall Footprints	Mark your game with these guiding signals.	Decorations	Static	Toy Store Purchase	Marker Toys
✓		Yellow Wall X-Mark	Mark your game with these guiding signals.	Decorations	Static	Toy Store Purchase	Marker Toys
✓		Adam Warlock Costume	A toy in an Adam Warlock costume.	Marvel Townspeople	Townspeople	Toy Store Purchase	Marvel Townspeople
✓		Agent Coulson Costume	A toy in an Agent Coulson costume.	Marvel Townspeople	Townspeople	INterior Mission Reward	Marvel Townspeople
✓		Ant-Man Costume	A toy in an Ant-Man costume.	Marvel Townspeople	Townspeople	Toy Store Purchase	Marvel Townspeople
✓		Aunt May Costume	A toy in an Aunt May costume.	Marvel Townspeople	Townspeople	Toy Store Purchase	Marvel Townspeople
✓		Beta Ray Bill Costume	A toy in a Beta Ray Bill costume.	Marvel Townspeople	Townspeople	Toy Store Purchase	Marvel Townspeople
✓		Black Panther Costume	A toy in a Black Panther costume.	Marvel Townspeople	Townspeople	Toy Store Purchase	Marvel Townspeople
✓		Captain Marvel Costume	A toy in a Captain Marvel costume.	Marvel Townspeople	Townspeople	Toy Store Purchase	Marvel Townspeople
✓		Cosmo Costume	A toy in a Cosmo costume.	Marvel Townspeople	Townspeople	Toy Store Purchase	Marvel Townspeople
✓		Deathlok Costume	A toy in a Deathlok costume.	Marvel Townspeople	Townspeople	Toy Store Purchase	Marvel Townspeople
✓		Destroyer Armor Costume	A toy in a Destroyer Armor costume.	Marvel Townspeople	Townspeople	Toy Store Purchase	Marvel Townspeople
✓		Doctor Octopus Costume	A toy in a Doctor Octopus costume.	Marvel Townspeople	Townspeople	Toy Store Purchase	Marvel Townspeople
✓		Ghost Rider Costume	A toy in a Ghost Rider costume.	Marvel Townspeople	Townspeople	Toy Store Purchase	Marvel Townspeople
✓		Green Goblin Costume	A toy in a Green Goblin costume.	Marvel Townspeople	Townspeople	Green Goblin	Marvel Townspeople
✓		Hydra Agent Costume	A toy in a Hydra Agent costume.	Marvel Townspeople	Townspeople	Toy Store Purchase	Marvel Townspeople
✓		Iron Patriot Costume	A toy in an Iron Patriot costume.	Marvel Townspeople	Townspeople	Toy Store Purchase	Marvel Townspeople
✓		Iron Spider Costume	A toy in an Iron Spider costume.	Marvel Townspeople	Townspeople	Toy Store Purchase	Marvel Townspeople
✓		J. Jonah Jameson Costume	A toy in a J. Jonah Jameson costume.	Marvel Townspeople	Townspeople	Toy Store Purchase	Marvel Townspeople
✓		Korath Costume	A toy in a Korath costume.	Marvel Townspeople	Townspeople	Toy Store Purchase	Marvel Townspeople
✓		Kraven the Hunter Costume	A toy in a Kraven the Hunter costume.	Marvel Townspeople	Townspeople	Toy Store Purchase	Marvel Townspeople
✓		Lizard Costume	A toy in a Lizard costume.	Marvel Townspeople	Townspeople	Toy Store Purchase	Marvel Townspeople
✓		Loki Costume	A toy in a Loki costume.	Marvel Townspeople	Townspeople	Loki	Marvel Townspeople
✓		Luke Cage Costume	A toy in a Luke Cage costume.	Marvel Townspeople	Townspeople	Toy Store Purchase	Marvel Townspeople

GOT IT?	ICON	TOY NAME	DESCRIPTION	CATEGORY	FUNCTION	UNLOCK	TOY STORE PAGE
			Toy Box Toys Continued				
✓		Nebula Costume	A toy in a Nebula costume.	Marvel Townspeople	Townspeople	Toy Store Purchase	Marvel Townspeople
✓		Pepper Potts Costume	A toy in a Pepper Potts costume.	Marvel Townspeople	Townspeople	Toy Store Purchase	Marvel Townspeople
✓		Potted Groot Costume	A toy in a Potted Groot costume.	Marvel Townspeople	Townspeople	Toy Store Purchase	Marvel Townspeople
✓		Quasar Costume	A toy in a Quasar costume.	Marvel Townspeople	Townspeople	Toy Store Purchase	Marvel Townspeople
✓		Red Skull Costume	A toy in a Red Skull costume.	Marvel Townspeople	Townspeople	Toy Store Purchase	Marvel Townspeople
✓		Rhino Costume	A toy in a Rhino costume.	Marvel Townspeople	Townspeople	Toy Store Purchase	Marvel Townspeople
✓		Rhomann Dey Costume	A toy in a Rhomann Dey costume.	Marvel Townspeople	Townspeople	Toy Store Purchase	Marvel Townspeople
✓		Ronan Costume	A toy in a Ronan costume.	Marvel Townspeople	Townspeople	Ronan	Marvel Townspeople
✓		S.H.I.E.L.D. Agent Costume	A toy in a S.H.I.E.L.D. Agent costume.	Marvel Townspeople	Townspeople	Toy Store Purchase	Marvel Townspeople
✓		Sandman Costume	A toy in a Sandman costume.	Marvel Townspeople	Townspeople	Toy Store Purchase	Marvel Townspeople
✓		Sif Costume	A toy in a Sif costume.	Marvel Townspeople	Townspeople	Toy Store Purchase	Marvel Townspeople
✓		The Collector Costume	A toy in The Collector costume.	Marvel Townspeople	Townspeople	Toy Store Purchase	Marvel Townspeople
✓		Titus Costume	A toy in a Titus costume.	Marvel Townspeople	Townspeople	Toy Store Purchase	Marvel Townspeople
✓		Vision Costume	A toy in a Vision costume.	Marvel Townspeople	Townspeople	Toy Store Purchase	Marvel Townspeople
✓		Wasp Costume	A toy in a Wasp costume.	Marvel Townspeople	Townspeople	Toy Store Purchase	Marvel Townspeople
✓		White Tiger Costume	A toy in a White Tiger costume.	Marvel Townspeople	Townspeople	Toy Store Purchase	Marvel Townspeople
✓		Winter Soldier Costume	A toy in a Winter Soldier costume.	Marvel Townspeople	Townspeople	Toy Store Purchase	Marvel Townspeople
✓		Wraith Costume	A toy in a Wraith costume.	Marvel Townspeople	Townspeople	Toy Store Purchase	Marvel Townspeople
✓		Banked Wide Track Curve	A Toy Box-themed race track piece.	Race Track Pieces	Track	Starting Toy	New Race Tracks
✓		Banked Wide Track Turn	A Toy Box-themed race track piece.	Race Track Pieces	Track	Starting Toy	New Race Tracks
✓		Large Short Curved Barrier	A Toy Box-themed race track barrier.	Race Track Pieces	Static	Toy Store Purchase	New Race Tracks
✓		Long Wide Track	A Toy Box-themed race track piece.	Race Track Pieces	Track	Starting Toy	New Race Tracks
✓		Medium Wide Track	A Toy Box-themed race track piece.	Race Track Pieces	Track	Starting Toy	New Race Tracks
✓		Narrow Short Barrier	A Toy Box-themed race track barrier.	Race Track Pieces	Static	Toy Store Purchase	New Race Tracks
✓		Sewer Manhole	A Toy Box-themed race track piece.	Race Track Pieces	Track	Toy Store Purchase	New Race Tracks
✓		Short Barrier Corner	A Toy Box-themed race track barrier.	Race Track Pieces	Static	Toy Store Purchase	New Race Tracks
✓		Short Curved Barrier	A Toy Box-themed race track barrier.	Race Track Pieces	Static	Toy Store Purchase	New Race Tracks
✓		Short Track Left	A Toy Box-themed race track piece.	Race Track Pieces	Track	Starting Toy	New Race Tracks
✓		Short Track Right	A Toy Box-themed race track piece.	Race Track Pieces	Track	Starting Toy	New Race Tracks
✓		Short Wide Track	A Toy Box-themed race track piece.	Race Track Pieces	Track	Starting Toy	New Race Tracks
✓		Short Wide Track Curve	A Toy Box-themed race track piece.	Race Track Pieces	Track	Starting Toy	New Race Tracks

			Toy Box Toys Continued				
GOT IT?	**ICON**	**TOY NAME**	**DESCRIPTION**	**CATEGORY**	**FUNCTION**	**UNLOCK**	**TOY STORE PAGE**
✓		Short Wide Track Left	A Toy Box-themed race track piece.	Race Track Pieces	Track	Starting Toy	New Race Tracks
✓		Short Wide Track Right	A Toy Box-themed race track piece.	Race Track Pieces	Track	Starting Toy	New Race Tracks
✓		Small Short Curved Barrier	A race track barrier from Disney Infinity.	Race Track Pieces	Static	Toy Store Purchase	New Race Tracks
✓		Steep Wide Track Ramp	A Toy Box-themed race track piece.	Race Track Pieces	Track	Starting Toy	New Race Tracks
✓		Steep Wide Track Ramp End	A Toy Box-themed race track piece.	Race Track Pieces	Track	Starting Toy	New Race Tracks
✓		Steep Wide Track Ramp Start	A Toy Box-themed race track piece.	Race Track Pieces	Track	Starting Toy	New Race Tracks
✓		Toy Box Wide Race Track Creator	Place this Creator to quickly build a wide race track.	Builders and Creators	Creator	Starting Toy	New Race Tracks
✓		Toy Box Wide Stunt Track Creator	Place this Creator to quickly build a wide race track with stunts.	Builders and Creators	Creator	Toy Store Purchase	New Race Tracks
✓		Toy Box Wide Track Creator	Place this Creator to quickly build a wide track.	Builders and Creators	Creator	Starting Toy	New Race Tracks
✓		Toy Box Wide Winding Track Creator	Place this Creator to quickly build a wide race track with lots of turns and hills.	Builders and Creators	Creator	Toy Store Purchase	New Race Tracks
✓		Track Ramp Curve Left	A Toy Box-themed race track piece.	Race Track Pieces	Track	Toy Store Purchase	New Race Tracks
✓		Track Ramp Curve Right	A Toy Box-themed race track piece.	Race Track Pieces	Track	Toy Store Purchase	New Race Tracks
✓		Very Short Wide Track	A Toy Box-themed race track piece.	Race Track Pieces	Track	Starting Toy	New Race Tracks
✓		Wide Track	A Toy Box-themed race track piece.	Race Track Pieces	Track	Starting Toy	New Race Tracks
✓		Wide Track Curve	A Toy Box-themed race track piece.	Race Track Pieces	Track	Starting Toy	New Race Tracks
✓		Wide Track Half Loop	A Toy Box-themed race track piece.	Race Track Pieces	Track	Toy Store Purchase	New Race Tracks
✓		Wide Track Intersect Left	A Toy Box-themed race track piece.	Race Track Pieces	Track	Toy Store Purchase	New Race Tracks
✓		Wide Track Intersect Right	A Toy Box-themed race track piece.	Race Track Pieces	Track	Toy Store Purchase	New Race Tracks
✓		Wide Track Intersection	A Toy Box-themed race track piece.	Race Track Pieces	Track	Toy Store Purchase	New Race Tracks
✓		Wide Track Junction Left	A Toy Box-themed race track piece.	Race Track Pieces	Track	Toy Store Purchase	New Race Tracks
✓		Wide Track Junction Right	A Toy Box-themed race track piece.	Race Track Pieces	Track	Toy Store Purchase	New Race Tracks
✓		Wide Track Left	A Toy Box-themed race track piece.	Race Track Pieces	Track	Starting Toy	New Race Tracks
✓		Wide Track Loop	A Toy Box-themed race track piece.	Race Track Pieces	Track	Toy Store Purchase	New Race Tracks
✓		Wide Track Ramp Curve Left	A Toy Box-themed race track piece.	Race Track Pieces	Track	Starting Toy	New Race Tracks
✓		Wide Track Ramp Curve Right	A Toy Box-themed race track piece.	Race Track Pieces	Track	Starting Toy	New Race Tracks
✓		Wide Track Ramp End	A Toy Box-themed race track piece.	Race Track Pieces	Track	Starting Toy	New Race Tracks
✓		Wide Track Ramp Small	A Toy Box-themed race track piece.	Race Track Pieces	Track	Starting Toy	New Race Tracks
✓		Wide Track Ramp Start	A Toy Box-themed race track piece.	Race Track Pieces	Creator	Starting Toy	New Race Tracks
✓		Wide Track Right	A Toy Box-themed race track piece.	Race Track Pieces	Track	Starting Toy	New Race Tracks
✓		Wide Track Split	A Toy Box-themed race track piece.	Race Track Pieces	Track	Toy Store Purchase	New Race Tracks
✓		Wide Track Starting Line	A Toy Box-themed race track piece.	Race Track Pieces	Track	Starting Toy	New Race Tracks

GOT IT?	ICON	TOY NAME	DESCRIPTION	CATEGORY	FUNCTION	UNLOCK	TOY STORE PAGE
					Toy Box Toys Continued		
✓		Aerial Detonator	This homing mine will seek out and destroy flying enemies.	Instant Fun	Custom	Toy Store Purchase	Special Toys
✓		Aladdin's Oasis	The desert oasis from Aladdin.	Set Pieces	Static	Toy Store Purchase	Special Toys
✓		Autopia Car (red)	A red car from Disney Parks' Autopia attraction.	Vehicles and Mounts	Vehicle	Toy Box Mission Reward	Special Toys
✓		Calico Motorcycle	Dr. Calico's motorcycle from Bolt.	Vehicles and Mounts	Motorcycle	Toy Store Purchase	Special Toys
✓		Communications Array	A radio tower with a large communications dish.	Set Pieces	Static	INterior Mission Reward	Special Toys
✓		Defense Survival Mode Door	A door that will transport the character to a specific Toy Box Game's Survival Mode.	Creativi-Toys	Custom	Defense Survival Mode Reward	Special Toys
✓		Disney Infinity Toy Stand	This toy will occasionally award bonus toys as you complete the Toy Box Hosts' missions.	Decorations	Static	"Toy Box Introduction Mission Reward"	Special Toys
✓		Enchanted Bed	The enchanted flying bed from Bedknobs and Broomsticks.	Vehicles and Mounts	Helicopter	Toy Store Purchase	Special Toys
✓		Exploration Survival Mode Door	A door that will transport the character to a specific Toy Box Game's Survival Mode.	Creativi-Toys	Custom	Exploration Survival Mode Reward	Special Toys
✓		Grandmother Willow Tree	The Grandmother Willow tree from Pocahontas.	Set Pieces	Static	Toy Store Purchase	Special Toys
✓		Gravity Falls Giant Footprint	A Gravity Falls building piece.	Set Pieces	Static	Toy Store Purchase	Special Toys
✓		Gravity Falls Gnome Stump	A Gravity Falls building piece.	Set Pieces	Static	Toy Store Purchase	Special Toys
✓		Gravity Falls Golf Cart	The golf cart Grunkle Stan drives in Gravity Falls.	Vehicles and Mounts	Vehicle	Toy Store Purchase	Special Toys
✓		Gravity Falls Mystery Shack	A Gravity Falls building piece.	Set Pieces	Static	Toy Store Purchase	Special Toys
✓		Gravity Falls Totem Pole	A Gravity Falls building piece.	Set Pieces	Static	Toy Store Purchase	Special Toys
✓		Gravity Falls Welcome Sign	A Gravity Falls building piece.	Set Pieces	Static	Toy Store Purchase	Special Toys
✓		Hall of Heroes Door	A Disney Infinity-themed door that leads to the Hall of Heroes.	Creativi-Toys	Custom	Toy Store Purchase -or- Toy Box Introduction Mission Reward	Special Toys
✓		Health Capsule	Collect this capsule to restore your character's health.	Instant Fun	Capsule	Toy Store Purchase	Special Toys
✓		Hero's Duty Bridge	A Hero's Duty-themed bridge from Wreck-It Ralph.	Set Pieces	Static	Toy Store Purchase	Special Toys
✓		INterior Door	A door that will transport the character to the host's INterior.	Creativi-Toys	Custom	Toy Store Purchase -or- Toy Box Introduction Mission Reward	Special Toys
✓		King Louie's Throne	King Louie's stone throne from The Jungle Book.	Set Pieces	Static	Toy Store Purchase	Special Toys
✓		Large Sand Dune	A large desert sand dune from Aladdin.	Disney Building Sets	Static	Toy Store Purchase	Special Toys
✓		Marvel's Hall of Super Heroes Door	A S.H.I.E.L.D.-themed door that leads to Marvel's Hall of Super Heroes.	Creativi-Toys	Custom	Toy Store Purchase -or- Toy Box Introduction Mission Reward	Special Toys
✓		Mine Toy	Watch your step! If you touch it, this Mine Toy will explode.	Instant Fun	Custom	Toy Store Purchase -or- Toy Box Introduction Mission Reward	Special Toys
✓		Mulan Fireworks Tower	The Imperial City fireworks tower from Mulan.	Set Pieces	Static	Toy Store Purchase	Special Toys
✓		Small World Façade	Disney Parks' it's a small world attraction façade.	Set Pieces	Static	Special Reward	Special Toys
✓		Space Mountain	Disney Parks' Space Mountain attraction.	Set Pieces	Static	Toy Store Purchase	Special Toys
✓		Special Move Capsule	Collect this capsule to fill your character's Special Move meter.	Instant Fun	Capsule	Toy Store Purchase	Special Toys
✓		Sven the Reindeer	Sven the reindeer from Frozen.	Vehicles and Mounts	Mount	Toy Store Purchase	Special Toys
✓		The Darling House	The London house from Peter Pan.	Set Pieces	Static	Toy Store Purchase	Special Toys

GAME BASICS

CHARACTERS

POWER DISCS

MARVEL'S THE AVENGERS

SPIDER-MAN

GUARDIANS OF THE GALAXY

TOY BOX

TOY BOX COLLECTION

ACHIEVEMENTS

			Toy Box Toys Continued				
GOT IT?	ICON	TOY NAME	DESCRIPTION	CATEGORY	FUNCTION	UNLOCK	TOY STORE PAGE
✓		Toy Box Door	A door that can be customized to lead to anywhere in your Toy Box.	Creativi-Toys	Custom	Toy Store Purchase -or- Toy Box Introduction Mission Reward	Special Toys
✓		2-Player Door Piece	You'll need a friend's help to open this 2-player door! This is a great toy for learning to work together with a friend.	Templates	Template	Prerequisite Unlock	Templates - Page 1
✓		Awards Podium Piece	Celebrate the winners by adding this Piece Template to your game.	Templates	Template	Prerequisite Unlock	Templates - Page 1
✓		Ballot Box Doors Piece	Which door, which door? Choose which door to open by popular vote!	Templates	Template	Prerequisite Unlock	Templates - Page 1
✓		Bouncy Bot Game	Try to see how long you can make Omnidroids fly with the Weather Vane in this single-player game!	Templates	Template	Prerequisite Unlock	Templates - Page 1
✓		Cauldron Gateway Piece	Destroy this cauldron and all the enemies it generates to open the connected door.	Templates	Template	Prerequisite Unlock	Templates - Page 1
✓		Cliffside Battle Arena Game	Battle with up to three other players in this customizable arena, and see if you can win in the allotted time!	Templates	Template	Prerequisite Unlock	Templates - Page 1
✓		Collector Challenge Kit	Move the Orbs in this Kit Template and have your friends race against the timer to collect as much as you can.	Templates	Template	Prerequisite Unlock	Templates - Page 1
✓		Color Plate Piece	Press these plates to match colors and open the connected door.	Templates	Template	Prerequisite Unlock	Templates - Page 1
✓		Easy Pinball Kit	Have yourself a ball with the Easy Pinball Kit Template! Customize where and what you add to the game.	Templates	Template	Prerequisite Unlock	Templates - Page 1
✓		Fireworks Plate Piece	Step on this trigger plate for your own mini celebration. Cake not included.	Templates	Template	Prerequisite Unlock	Templates - Page 1
✓		Flaming Hoops Piece	Fly through this hoop and set off fireworks!	Templates	Template	Prerequisite Unlock	Templates - Page 1
✓		Ledge Hang Layout A	Place this Template for an easy climb.	Templates	Template	Prerequisite Unlock	Templates - Page 1
✓		Ledge Hang Layout B	Place this Template for an easy climb.	Templates	Template	Prerequisite Unlock	Templates - Page 1
✓		Ledge Hang Layout C	Place this Template for an easy climb.	Templates	Template	Prerequisite Unlock	Templates - Page 1
✓		Limited Lives Piece	Use this to set and keep track of how often your characters get knocked out. If you are defeated three times, the game ends.	Templates	Template	Prerequisite Unlock	Templates - Page 1
✓		Mega Science Fair Piece	Trigger a volcanic eruption with this Mega Science Piece Template.	Templates	Template	Prerequisite Unlock	Templates - Page 1
✓		Money Bin Game	Protect the Money Bin from the Beagle Boys with the Money Bin Game Template!	Templates	Template	Prerequisite Unlock	Templates - Page 1
✓		Mountain Ledge Terrain	Scale the mountain wall with this pre-built Terrain Template.	Templates	Template	Prerequisite Unlock	Templates - Page 1
✓		Mountain Path Terrain	Climb up the mountain on a pre-built pathway with this Terrain Template.	Templates	Template	Prerequisite Unlock	Templates - Page 1
✓		Mountain Peak Terrain	Add a snowy mountain peak to your Toy Box with this pre-built Terrain Template.	Templates	Template	Prerequisite Unlock	Templates - Page 1
✓		One-Way Door Piece	Learn about gated play in puzzle and combat scenarios with the One-Way Door Piece Template.	Templates	Template	Prerequisite Unlock	Templates - Page 1
✓		Pinball Game	Have yourself a ball with the Pinball Template! Control the flippers and get points.	Templates	Template	Prerequisite Unlock	Templates - Page 1
✓		Pressure Plate Piece	Press these plates at the same time to open the connected door.	Templates	Template	Prerequisite Unlock	Templates - Page 1
✓		Racing Gate Kit	Move the racing gates in this Kit Template and race your friends three laps to the finish!	Templates	Template	Prerequisite Unlock	Templates - Page 1
✓		Rail Switch Piece	With the Rail Switch Template you can send your friend sliding in a different direction with the press of a button.	Templates	Template	Prerequisite Unlock	Templates - Page 1
✓		Rail Switch Target Piece	Shoot the target while sliding to switch the rails and end up heading in a different direction.	Templates	Template	Prerequisite Unlock	Templates - Page 1
✓		Rail Terrain	Add some sliding fun with this rail Terrain Template.	Templates	Template	Prerequisite Unlock	Templates - Page 1
✓		Replayer Piece	Learn how to replay, record, playback, and reset with this Replayer Piece Template.	Templates	Template	Prerequisite Unlock	Templates - Page 1

		Toy Box Toys Continued					
GOT IT?	**ICON**	**TOY NAME**	**DESCRIPTION**	**CATEGORY**	**FUNCTION**	**UNLOCK**	**TOY STORE PAGE**
✓		Smash and Bash Arena Kit	Battle with up to three other players in this customizable arena, and see if you can win in the allotted time!	Templates	Template	Prerequisite Unlock	Templates - Page 1
✓		Soccer Kit	Begin with this Soccer Kit Template, then add your own touches — enemies, timers, friends — for an unforgettable sports match!	Templates	Template	Prerequisite Unlock	Templates - Page 1
✓		Super Launch Piece	Set off the Weather Vane and get thrown off your feet with this Piece Template!	Templates	Template	Prerequisite Unlock	Templates - Page 1
✓		Switchback Hill	Place this terrain piece for a crazy mountain hike.	Templates	Template	Prerequisite Unlock	Templates - Page 1
✓		Target Camera Piece	Use this camera to follow a character or enemy through your game.	Templates	Template	Prerequisite Unlock	Templates - Page 1
✓		Terrain Top Battle Arena Game	Battle with up to three other players in this customizable arena, and see if you can win in the allotted time!	Templates	Template	Prerequisite Unlock	Templates - Page 1
✓		Time and Score Piece	How many points can you get in a certain amount of time? Find out with the Time and Score Template! This piece makes sports especially fun.	Templates	Template	Prerequisite Unlock	Templates - Page 1
✓		Timed Challenge Piece	Speed up your game with the Timed Challenge Piece Template! This piece makes races especially fun.	Templates	Template	Prerequisite Unlock	Templates - Page 1
✓		Townsperson Collection Kit	See if you can toss the townspeople into the Collection Pen in the allotted time!	Templates	Template	Prerequisite Unlock	Templates - Page 1
✓		Tunnel Battle Arena Game	Battle with up to three other players in this customizable arena, and see if you can win in the allotted time!	Templates	Template	Prerequisite Unlock	Templates - Page 1
✓		Twisty Rail Terrain	Add some twisty, sliding fun with this rail Terrain Template.	Templates	Template	Prerequisite Unlock	Templates - Page 1
✓		Ultimate Soccer Game	Have the ultimate soccer game with this Game Template!	Templates	Template	Prerequisite Unlock	Templates - Page 1
✓		Weather Vane Piece	Create things like a low-gravity room with this Weather Vane Piece Template!	Templates	Template	Prerequisite Unlock	Templates - Page 1
✓		Aerial Ring Collector Game	Fly through the Rings as fast as you can.	Templates	Template	Prerequisite Unlock	Templates - Page 2
✓		Angled Camera Piece	Watch characters from a set angle with this Angled Camera Piece Template.	Templates	Template	Prerequisite Unlock	Templates - Page 2
✓		Asgard Enemy Door Piece	This door template allows players to spawn enemies into your game.	Templates	Template	Prerequisite Unlock	Templates - Page 2
✓		Asgard Townsperson Door Piece	Let your townspeople and sidekicks search for treasure with this Piece Template. Careful, though...it may throw enemies your way!	Templates	Template	Prerequisite Unlock	Templates - Page 2
✓		Bird's Eye Camera Piece	Watch characters from above with this Bird's Eye Camera Piece Template.	Templates	Template	Prerequisite Unlock	Templates - Page 2
✓		Brave Enemy Closet Piece	This Brave-themed Piece Template will spawn enemies into your game.	Templates	Template	Prerequisite Unlock	Templates - Page 2
✓		Brave Sidekick Door B Piece	Let your townspeople and sidekicks search for treasure with this Piece Template. Careful, though...it may throw enemies your way!	Templates	Template	Prerequisite Unlock	Templates - Page 2
✓		Brave Sidekick Door Tree Piece	Let your townspeople and sidekicks search for treasure with this Piece Template. Careful, though...it may throw enemies your way!	Templates	Template	Prerequisite Unlock	Templates - Page 2
✓		Defeat Effects Piece	Defeat your enemies and set off a victory explosion effect at the same time!	Templates	Template	Prerequisite Unlock	Templates - Page 2
✓		Effects Creator Piece	Set off a burst of explosions and other special effects with this Piece Template!	Templates	Template	Prerequisite Unlock	Templates - Page 2
✓		End Game Sequence Piece	Have a grand finale! End your game by sending your characters to winning platforms, fanfares, and fireworks.	Templates	Template	Prerequisite Unlock	Templates - Page 2
✓		Enemy Wave Battle Kit	Defeat enemies as fast as you can in this customizable Kit Template.	Templates	Template	Prerequisite Unlock	Templates - Page 2
✓		King of the Hill Game	Destroy the other characters' blocks while keeping yourself safe from the lava.	Templates	Template	Prerequisite Unlock	Templates - Page 2
✓		Kyln Enemy Closet Piece	This Kyln-themed Piece Template will spawn enemies into your game.	Templates	Template	Prerequisite Unlock	Templates - Page 2
✓		Kyln Sidekick Door Piece	Let your townspeople and sidekicks search for treasure with this Piece Template. Careful, though...it may throw enemies your way!	Templates	Template	Prerequisite Unlock	Templates - Page 2

GAME BASICS

CHARACTERS

POWER DISCS

MARVEL'S THE AVENGERS

SPIDER-MAN

GUARDIANS OF THE GALAXY

TOY BOX

TOY BOX COLLECTION

ACHIEVEMENTS

Toy Box Toys Continued

GOT IT?	ICON	TOY NAME	DESCRIPTION	CATEGORY	FUNCTION	UNLOCK	TOY STORE PAGE
✓		Mount Race Game	Race an assortment of animals past checkpoints. Whoever completes three laps in the least amount of time wins!	Templates	Template	Prerequisite Unlock	Templates - Page 2
✓		Mounts Collector Game	Collect Orbs as fast as you can while riding on a mount.	Templates	Template	Prerequisite Unlock	Templates - Page 2
✓		Paintball Battle Game	Defeat enemies as fast as you can in this customizable Kit Template.	Templates	Template	Prerequisite Unlock	Templates - Page 2
✓		People Mover Corner A Piece	Shoot through a tube with this People Mover Piece Template.	Templates	Template	Prerequisite Unlock	Templates - Page 2
✓		People Mover Corner B Piece	Shoot through a tube with this People Mover Piece Template.	Templates	Template	Prerequisite Unlock	Templates - Page 2
✓		People Mover Corner C Piece	Shoot through a tube with this People Mover Piece Template.	Templates	Template	Prerequisite Unlock	Templates - Page 2
✓		People Mover Corner D Piece	Shoot through a tube with this People Mover Piece Template.	Templates	Template	Prerequisite Unlock	Templates - Page 2
✓		People Mover Horizontal Piece	Shoot through a tube with this People Mover Piece Template.	Templates	Template	Prerequisite Unlock	Templates - Page 2
✓		People Mover Vertical Down Piece	Shoot through a tube with this People Mover Piece Template.	Templates	Template	Prerequisite Unlock	Templates - Page 2
✓		People Mover Vertical Up Piece	Shoot through a tube with this People Mover Piece Template. Extra help about the Logic Connections in all People Mover Templates can be found in this one.	Templates	Template	Prerequisite Unlock	Templates - Page 2
✓		Random Platformer Game	This game creates different types of platform games and obstacle courses for you!	Templates	Template	Prerequisite Unlock	Templates - Page 2
✓		Red Light/Green Light Game	Race to the end without stepping on the red blocks in this Game Template.	Templates	Template	Prerequisite Unlock	Templates - Page 2
✓		Side-Step Camera Piece	Watch characters from the side with this Side-Step Camera Piece Template.	Templates	Template	Prerequisite Unlock	Templates - Page 2
✓		Stitch Enemy Door Piece	This door template allows players to spawn enemies into your game.	Templates	Template	Prerequisite Unlock	Templates - Page 2
✓		Stitch Townsperson Door Piece	Let your townspeople and sidekicks search for treasure with this Piece Template. Careful, though…it may throw enemies your way!	Templates	Template	Prerequisite Unlock	Templates - Page 2
✓		Stunt Park Game	Challenge your friends with this customizable stunt park full of tricks, toys, and games.	Templates	Template	Prerequisite Unlock	Templates - Page 2
✓		Stunt Park Kit	Challenge your friends with this customizable stunt park full of tricks, toys, and games.	Templates	Template	Prerequisite Unlock	Templates - Page 2
✓		Treasure Defense Kit	Protect the enemy target in this customizable Kit Template.	Templates	Template	Prerequisite Unlock	Templates - Page 2
✓		Vehicular Combat Game	Defeat enemies as fast as you can in this customizable Kit Template.	Templates	Template	Prerequisite Unlock	Templates - Page 2
✓		Western Wrangle Game	Race against the clock and use your mount to corral as many townspeople as you can.	Templates	Template	Prerequisite Unlock	Templates - Page 2
✓		3-Way Sewer with Ladder	A section of terrain with underground pipes and a ladder.	Terrain	Static	Toy Store Purchase	Terrain, Challenge, & Destruction Toys
✓		Blue Armored Orb	An Orb that can be collected by weapon impact.	Instant Fun	Collectible	Toy Store Purchase	Terrain, Challenge, & Destruction Toys
✓		Blue Challenge Orb	An Orb that can be collected by character contact.	Instant Fun	Collectible	Toy Store Purchase	Terrain, Challenge, & Destruction Toys
✓		Blue Challenge Ring	A Ring that can be collected by character contact.	Instant Fun	Collectible	Toy Store Purchase	Terrain, Challenge, & Destruction Toys
✓		Destructible Brick Wall	A breakable Toy Box block.	Instant Fun	Breakable	Toy Store Purchase	Terrain, Challenge, & Destruction Toys
✓		Destructible Concrete Wall	A breakable Toy Box block.	Instant Fun	Breakable	Toy Store Purchase	Terrain, Challenge, & Destruction Toys
✓		Destructible Wood Wall	A breakable Toy Box block.	Instant Fun	Breakable	Toy Store Purchase	Terrain, Challenge, & Destruction Toys
✓		Gold Armored Orb	An Orb that can be collected by weapon impact.	Instant Fun	Collectible	Toy Store Purchase	Terrain, Challenge, & Destruction Toys
✓		Gold Challenge Orb	An Orb that can be collected by character contact.	Instant Fun	Collectible	Starting Toy	Terrain, Challenge, & Destruction Toys
✓		Gold Challenge Ring	A Ring that can be collected by character contact.	Instant Fun	Collectible	Toy Store Purchase	Terrain, Challenge, & Destruction Toys

GOT IT?	ICON	TOY NAME	DESCRIPTION	CATEGORY	FUNCTION	UNLOCK	TOY STORE PAGE
			Toy Box Toys Continued				
✓		Green Armored Orb	An Orb that can be collected by weapon impact.	Instant Fun	Collectible	Toy Store Purchase	Terrain, Challenge, & Destruction Toys
✓		Green Challenge Orb	An Orb that can be collected by character contact.	Instant Fun	Collectible	Toy Store Purchase	Terrain, Challenge, & Destruction Toys
✓		Green Challenge Ring	A Ring that can be collected by character contact.	Instant Fun	Collectible	Toy Store Purchase	Terrain, Challenge, & Destruction Toys
✓		Large Mining Block	A breakable Toy Box block.	Instant Fun	Breakable	Toy Store Purchase	Terrain, Challenge, & Destruction Toys
✓		Large Terrain Corner	A Toy Box meadow-themed terrain piece.	Terrain	Static	Toy Store Purchase	Terrain, Challenge, & Destruction Toys
✓		Large Terrain Inverse Wedge	A Toy Box meadow-themed terrain piece.	Terrain	Static	Toy Store Purchase	Terrain, Challenge, & Destruction Toys
✓		Large Terrain Wedge	A Toy Box meadow-themed terrain piece.	Terrain	Static	Toy Store Purchase	Terrain, Challenge, & Destruction Toys
✓		Large WALL-E Garbage Block	A WALL-E breakable block.	Instant Fun	Breakable	Toy Store Purchase	Terrain, Challenge, & Destruction Toys
✓		Mining Block	A breakable Toy Box block.	Instant Fun	Breakable	Toy Store Purchase	Terrain, Challenge, & Destruction Toys
✓		Narrow Terrain Ramp	A Toy Box meadow-themed terrain piece.	Terrain	Static	Toy Store Purchase	Terrain, Challenge, & Destruction Toys
✓		Small Mining Block	A breakable Toy Box block.	Instant Fun	Breakable	Toy Store Purchase	Terrain, Challenge, & Destruction Toys
✓		Small Narrow Terrain Ramp	A Toy Box meadow-themed terrain piece.	Terrain	Static	Toy Store Purchase	Terrain, Challenge, & Destruction Toys
✓		Small Terrain Corner	A Toy Box meadow-themed terrain piece.	Terrain	Static	Toy Store Purchase	Terrain, Challenge, & Destruction Toys
✓		Small Terrain Inverse Wedge	A Toy Box meadow-themed terrain piece.	Terrain	Static	Toy Store Purchase	Terrain, Challenge, & Destruction Toys
✓		Small Terrain Ramp	A Toy Box meadow-themed terrain piece.	Terrain	Static	Toy Store Purchase	Terrain, Challenge, & Destruction Toys
✓		Small Terrain Ramp Corner	A Toy Box meadow-themed terrain piece.	Terrain	Static	Toy Store Purchase	Terrain, Challenge, & Destruction Toys
✓		Small Terrain Ramp Corner Hill	A Toy Box meadow-themed terrain piece.	Terrain	Static	Toy Store Purchase	Terrain, Challenge, & Destruction Toys
✓		Small Terrain Wedge	A Toy Box meadow-themed terrain piece.	Terrain	Static	Toy Store Purchase	Terrain, Challenge, & Destruction Toys
✓		Small WALL-E Garbage Block	A WALL-E breakable block.	Instant Fun	Breakable	Toy Store Purchase	Terrain, Challenge, & Destruction Toys
✓		Small Wide Terrain Ramp	A Toy Box meadow-themed terrain piece.	Terrain	Static	Toy Store Purchase	Terrain, Challenge, & Destruction Toys
✓		Terrain Block	A Toy Box meadow-themed terrain piece.	Terrain	Static	Toy Store Purchase	Terrain, Challenge, & Destruction Toys
✓		Terrain Prism	A Toy Box meadow-themed terrain piece.	Terrain	Static	Toy Store Purchase	Terrain, Challenge, & Destruction Toys
✓		Terrain Ramp	A Toy Box meadow-themed terrain piece.	Terrain	Static	Toy Store Purchase	Terrain, Challenge, & Destruction Toys
✓		Terrain Ramp Corner	A Toy Box meadow-themed terrain piece.	Terrain	Static	Toy Store Purchase	Terrain, Challenge, & Destruction Toys
✓		Terrain Ramp Corner Hill	A Toy Box meadow-themed terrain piece.	Terrain	Static	Toy Store Purchase	Terrain, Challenge, & Destruction Toys
✓		Tiny Mining Block	A breakable Toy Box block.	Instant Fun	Breakable	Toy Store Purchase	Terrain, Challenge, & Destruction Toys
✓		Tiny WALL-E Garbage Block	A WALL-E breakable block.	Instant Fun	Breakable	Toy Store Purchase	Terrain, Challenge, & Destruction Toys
✓		WALL-E Garbage Block	A WALL-E breakable block.	Instant Fun	Breakable	Toy Store Purchase	Terrain, Challenge, & Destruction Toys
✓		Wide Terrain Ramp	A Toy Box meadow-themed terrain piece.	Terrain	Static	Toy Store Purchase	Terrain, Challenge, & Destruction Toys

BUILDING SETS

GOT IT?	ICON	TOY NAME	DESCRIPTION	CATEGORY	FUNCTION	UNLOCK	TOY STORE PAGE
		Building Sets					
✓		Agrabah Archway	Part of the Agrabah Building Set from Aladdin.	Disney Building Sets	Static	Toy Store Purchase	Agrabah Bazaar Building Set
✓		Agrabah Booby Trapped Platform	Part of the Agrabah Building Set from Aladdin.	Disney Building Sets	Custom	Toy Store Purchase	Agrabah Bazaar Building Set
✓		Agrabah Canopy Awning	Part of the Agrabah Building Set from Aladdin.	Disney Building Sets	Static	Toy Store Purchase	Agrabah Bazaar Building Set
✓		Agrabah Canopy Balcony	Part of the Agrabah Building Set from Aladdin.	Disney Building Sets	Static	Toy Store Purchase	Agrabah Bazaar Building Set
✓		Agrabah Citadel	Part of the Agrabah Building Set from Aladdin.	Disney Building Sets	Static	Toy Store Purchase	Agrabah Bazaar Building Set
✓		Agrabah Citadel Archway	Part of the Agrabah Building Set from Aladdin.	Disney Building Sets	Static	Toy Store Purchase	Agrabah Bazaar Building Set
✓		Agrabah Citadel Corner	Part of the Agrabah Building Set from Aladdin.	Disney Building Sets	Static	Toy Store Purchase	Agrabah Bazaar Building Set
✓		Agrabah Corner Wall	Part of the Agrabah Building Set from Aladdin.	Disney Building Sets	Static	Toy Store Purchase	Agrabah Bazaar Building Set
✓		Agrabah Dome	Part of the Agrabah Building Set from Aladdin.	Disney Building Sets	Static	Toy Store Purchase	Agrabah Bazaar Building Set
✓		Agrabah Doorway Arch	Part of the Agrabah Building Set from Aladdin.	Disney Building Sets	Static	Toy Store Purchase	Agrabah Bazaar Building Set
✓		Agrabah Doorway Columns	Part of the Agrabah Building Set from Aladdin.	Disney Building Sets	Static	Toy Store Purchase	Agrabah Bazaar Building Set
✓		Agrabah Fence Corner	Part of the Agrabah Building Set from Aladdin.	Disney Building Sets	Static	Toy Store Purchase	Agrabah Bazaar Building Set
✓		Agrabah Market Canopy	Part of the Agrabah Building Set from Aladdin.	Disney Building Sets	Static	Toy Store Purchase	Agrabah Bazaar Building Set
✓		Agrabah Market Planks	Part of the Agrabah Building Set from Aladdin.	Disney Building Sets	Static	Toy Store Purchase	Agrabah Bazaar Building Set
✓		Agrabah Plank Awning	Part of the Agrabah Building Set from Aladdin.	Disney Building Sets	Static	Toy Store Purchase	Agrabah Bazaar Building Set
✓		Agrabah Plank Balcony	Part of the Agrabah Building Set from Aladdin.	Disney Building Sets	Static	Toy Store Purchase	Agrabah Bazaar Building Set
✓		Agrabah Plank Platform	Part of the Agrabah Building Set from Aladdin.	Disney Building Sets	Custom	Toy Store Purchase	Agrabah Bazaar Building Set
✓		Agrabah Reverse Sloping Fence	Part of the Agrabah Building Set from Aladdin.	Disney Building Sets	Static	Toy Store Purchase	Agrabah Bazaar Building Set
✓		Agrabah Rope Climb	Part of the Agrabah Building Set from Aladdin.	Disney Building Sets	Custom	Toy Store Purchase	Agrabah Bazaar Building Set
✓		Agrabah Sand Bank	Part of the Agrabah Building Set from Aladdin.	Disney Building Sets	Static	Toy Store Purchase	Agrabah Bazaar Building Set
✓		Agrabah Scaffold	Part of the Agrabah Building Set from Aladdin.	Disney Building Sets	Custom	Toy Store Purchase	Agrabah Bazaar Building Set
✓		Agrabah Sloping Fence	Part of the Agrabah Building Set from Aladdin.	Disney Building Sets	Static	Toy Store Purchase	Agrabah Bazaar Building Set
✓		Agrabah Spiral Staircase	Part of the Agrabah Building Set from Aladdin.	Disney Building Sets	Static	Toy Store Purchase	Agrabah Bazaar Building Set
✓		Agrabah Staircase	Part of the Agrabah Building Set from Aladdin.	Disney Building Sets	Static	Toy Store Purchase	Agrabah Bazaar Building Set
✓		Agrabah Stairs	Part of the Agrabah Building Set from Aladdin.	Disney Building Sets	Static	Toy Store Purchase	Agrabah Bazaar Building Set
✓		Agrabah Trampoline	Part of the Agrabah Building Set from Aladdin.	Disney Building Sets	Custom	Toy Store Purchase	Agrabah Bazaar Building Set
✓		Agrabah Wood Posts	Part of the Agrabah Building Set from Aladdin.	Disney Building Sets	Custom	Toy Store Purchase	Agrabah Bazaar Building Set
✓		Bridge Trap	Part of the Agrabah Building Set from Aladdin.	Disney Building Sets	Custom	Toy Store Purchase	Agrabah Bazaar Building Set
✓		Large Agrabah Citadel	Part of the Agrabah Building Set from Aladdin.	Disney Building Sets	Static	Toy Store Purchase	Agrabah Bazaar Building Set
✓		Large Agrabah Wall	Part of the Agrabah Building Set from Aladdin.	Disney Building Sets	Static	Toy Store Purchase	Agrabah Bazaar Building Set

		Building Sets Continued					
GOT IT?	ICON	TOY NAME	DESCRIPTION	CATEGORY	FUNCTION	UNLOCK	TOY STORE PAGE
✓		Long Agrabah Rope Climb	Part of the Agrabah Building Set from Aladdin.	Disney Building Sets	Custom	Toy Store Purchase	Agrabah Bazaar Building Set
✓		Massive Agrabah Citadel	Part of the Agrabah Building Set from Aladdin.	Disney Building Sets	Static	Toy Store Purchase	Agrabah Bazaar Building Set
✓		Short Agrabah Fence	Part of the Agrabah Building Set from Aladdin.	Disney Building Sets	Static	Toy Store Purchase	Agrabah Bazaar Building Set
✓		Short Agrabah Rope Climb	Part of the Agrabah Building Set from Aladdin.	Disney Building Sets	Custom	Toy Store Purchase	Agrabah Bazaar Building Set
✓		Small Agrabah Archway	Part of the Agrabah Building Set from Aladdin.	Disney Building Sets	Static	Toy Store Purchase	Agrabah Bazaar Building Set
✓		Small Agrabah Citadel	Part of the Agrabah Building Set from Aladdin.	Disney Building Sets	Static	Toy Store Purchase	Agrabah Bazaar Building Set
✓		Small Agrabah Wall	Part of the Agrabah Building Set from Aladdin.	Disney Building Sets	Static	Toy Store Purchase	Agrabah Bazaar Building Set
✓		Square Agrabah Citadel	Part of the Agrabah Building Set from Aladdin.	Disney Building Sets	Static	Toy Store Purchase	Agrabah Bazaar Building Set
✓		Toy Box Agrabah Builder	This little toy will help you build Agrabah.	Builders and Creators	Builder	Toy Store Purchase	Agrabah Bazaar Building Set
✓		Air Conditioning Unit	A decoration from the Incredibles Play Set.	Decorations	Static	Starting Toy	City Building Set - Page 1
✓		Awning	Part of the City Building Set.	City Building Set	Static	Starting Toy	City Building Set - Page 1
✓		Awning Roof	Part of the City Building Set.	City Building Set	Static	Starting Toy	City Building Set - Page 1
✓		Bench	A decoration from the Monsters University Play Set.	Decorations	Static	Starting Toy	City Building Set - Page 1
✓		Bistro Building	Part of the City Building Set.	City Building Set	Static	Starting Toy	City Building Set - Page 1
✓		Brick Skyscraper Piece	Part of the City Building Set.	City Building Set	Static	Starting Toy	City Building Set - Page 1
✓		Brownstone Building	Part of the City Building Set.	City Building Set	Static	Starting Toy	City Building Set - Page 1
✓		Business Building Corner	Part of the City Building Set.	City Building Set	Static	Starting Toy	City Building Set - Page 1
✓		Business Building Lobby	Part of the City Building Set.	City Building Set	Static	Starting Toy	City Building Set - Page 1
✓		Business Building Piece	Part of the City Building Set.	City Building Set	Static	Starting Toy	City Building Set - Page 1
✓		Cement Skyscraper Piece	Part of the City Building Set.	City Building Set	Static	Starting Toy	City Building Set - Page 1
✓		City Elevator	Part of the City Building Set.	City Building Set	Static	Starting Toy	City Building Set - Page 1
✓		Double Vertical Billboard	Part of the City Building Set.	City Building Set	Static	Starting Toy	City Building Set - Page 1
✓		Fire Hydrant	A decoration from the Incredibles Play Set.	Decorations	Breakable	Starting Toy	City Building Set - Page 1
✓		Glass Building Front	Part of the City Building Set.	City Building Set	Static	Starting Toy	City Building Set - Page 1
✓		Glass Skyscraper Piece	Part of the City Building Set.	City Building Set	Static	Starting Toy	City Building Set - Page 1
✓		Large Brick Skyscraper Piece	Part of the City Building Set.	City Building Set	Static	Starting Toy	City Building Set - Page 1
✓		Large Cement Skyscraper Piece	Part of the City Building Set.	City Building Set	Static	Starting Toy	City Building Set - Page 1
✓		Large Glass Skyscraper Piece	Part of the City Building Set.	City Building Set	Static	Starting Toy	City Building Set - Page 1
✓		Orange Billboard	Part of the City Building Set.	City Building Set	Static	Starting Toy	City Building Set - Page 1
✓		Quarter Office Skyscraper Piece	Part of the City Building Set.	City Building Set	Static	Starting Toy	City Building Set - Page 1
✓		Quarter Skyscraper Piece	Part of the City Building Set.	City Building Set	Static	Starting Toy	City Building Set - Page 1

			Building Sets Continued				
GOT IT?	ICON	TOY NAME	DESCRIPTION	CATEGORY	FUNCTION	UNLOCK	TOY STORE PAGE
✓		Rectangular Awning	Part of the City Building Set.	City Building Set	Static	Starting Toy	City Building Set - Page 1
✓		Retro Blue Billboard	Part of the City Building Set.	City Building Set	Static	Starting Toy	City Building Set - Page 1
✓		Retro Green Billboard	Part of the City Building Set.	City Building Set	Static	Starting Toy	City Building Set - Page 1
✓		Rounded Awning	Part of the City Building Set.	City Building Set	Static	Starting Toy	City Building Set - Page 1
✓		Sidewalk Corner Piece	A decoration from the Incredibles Play Set.	Decorations	Static	Starting Toy	City Building Set - Page 1
✓		Sidewalk Piece	A decoration from the Incredibles Play Set.	Decorations	Static	Starting Toy	City Building Set - Page 1
✓		Skyscraper	Part of the City Building Set.	City Building Set	Static	Starting Toy	City Building Set - Page 1
✓		Skyscraper Base	Part of the City Building Set.	City Building Set	Static	Starting Toy	City Building Set - Page 1
✓		Skyscraper Lobby	Part of the City Building Set.	City Building Set	Static	Starting Toy	City Building Set - Page 1
✓		Small Awning Dome	Part of the City Building Set.	City Building Set	Static	Starting Toy	City Building Set - Page 1
✓		Small Brick Skyscraper Piece	Part of the City Building Set.	City Building Set	Static	Starting Toy	City Building Set - Page 1
✓		Small Cement Skyscraper Piece	Part of the City Building Set.	City Building Set	Static	Starting Toy	City Building Set - Page 1
✓		Small Glass Skyscraper Piece	Part of the City Building Set.	City Building Set	Static	Starting Toy	City Building Set - Page 1
✓		Small Rounded Awning	Part of the City Building Set.	City Building Set	Static	Starting Toy	City Building Set - Page 1
✓		Small Stone Skyscraper Piece	Part of the City Building Set.	City Building Set	Static	Starting Toy	City Building Set - Page 1
✓		Stone Skyscraper Piece	Part of the City Building Set.	City Building Set	Static	Starting Toy	City Building Set - Page 1
✓		Striped Awning	Part of the City Building Set.	City Building Set	Static	Starting Toy	City Building Set - Page 1
✓		Striped Billboard	Part of the City Building Set.	City Building Set	Static	Starting Toy	City Building Set - Page 1
✓		Thin Skyscraper	Part of the City Building Set.	City Building Set	Static	Starting Toy	City Building Set - Page 1
✓		Toy Box City Builder	This little toy will help you build a city.	Builders and Creators	Builder	Starting Toy	City Building Set - Page 1
✓		Toy Box City Creator	Place this Creator to quickly build a city.	Builders and Creators	Creator	Starting Toy	City Building Set - Page 1
✓		Traffic Light	A decoration from the Incredibles Play Set.	Decorations	Static	Starting Toy	City Building Set - Page 1
✓		Trash Receptacle	A decoration from the Incredibles Play Set.	Decorations	Breakable	Starting Toy	City Building Set - Page 1
✓		Vacation Billboard A	Part of the City Building Set.	City Building Set	Static	Starting Toy	City Building Set - Page 1
✓		Vacation Billboard B	Part of the City Building Set.	City Building Set	Static	Starting Toy	City Building Set - Page 1
✓		Building Frame	Part of the City Building Set.	City Building Set	Static	Toy Store Purchase	City Building Set - Page 2
✓		Building Wood Frame	Part of the City Building Set.	City Building Set	Static	Toy Store Purchase	City Building Set - Page 2
✓		City Flag	Part of the City Building Set.	City Building Set	Static	Toy Store Purchase	City Building Set - Page 2
✓		City Helipad	Part of the City Building Set.	City Building Set	Static	Toy Store Purchase	City Building Set - Page 2
✓		City Park Terrace	Part of the City Building Set.	City Building Set	Static	Toy Store Purchase	City Building Set - Page 2
✓		City Railing	Part of the City Building Set.	City Building Set	Static	Toy Store Purchase	City Building Set - Page 2

			Building Sets Continued				
GOT IT?	ICON	TOY NAME	DESCRIPTION	CATEGORY	FUNCTION	UNLOCK	TOY STORE PAGE
✓		City Railing Corner	Part of the City Building Set.	City Building Set	Static	Toy Store Purchase	City Building Set - Page 2
✓		City Railing Inner Corner	Part of the City Building Set.	City Building Set	Static	Toy Store Purchase	City Building Set - Page 2
✓		City Rooftop	Part of the City Building Set.	City Building Set	Static	Toy Store Purchase	City Building Set - Page 2
✓		City Swimming Pool	Part of the City Building Set.	City Building Set	Static	Toy Store Purchase	City Building Set - Page 2
✓		City Tennis Court	Part of the City Building Set.	City Building Set	Static	Toy Store Purchase	City Building Set - Page 2
✓		Climbing Pipe	Part of the City Building Set.	City Building Set	Static	Toy Store Purchase	City Building Set - Page 2
✓		Corner Grated Platform	Part of the City Building Set.	City Building Set	Static	Toy Store Purchase	City Building Set - Page 2
✓		Edge City Rooftop	Part of the City Building Set.	City Building Set	Static	Toy Store Purchase	City Building Set - Page 2
✓		Florist Building	Part of the City Building Set.	City Building Set	Static	Toy Store Purchase	City Building Set - Page 2
✓		Gas Station	Part of the City Building Set.	City Building Set	Static	Toy Store Purchase	City Building Set - Page 2
✓		Grated Platform	Part of the City Building Set.	City Building Set	Static	Toy Store Purchase	City Building Set - Page 2
✓		Gusteau's Sign	Part of the City Building Set.	City Building Set	Static	Toy Store Purchase	City Building Set - Page 2
✓		Hamburger Sign	Part of the City Building Set.	City Building Set	Static	Toy Store Purchase	City Building Set - Page 2
✓		Ice Cream Shoppe Sign	Part of the City Building Set.	City Building Set	Static	Toy Store Purchase	City Building Set - Page 2
✓		Inside Corner Grated Platform	Part of the City Building Set.	City Building Set	Static	Toy Store Purchase	City Building Set - Page 2
✓		Large Climbing Pipe	Part of the City Building Set.	City Building Set	Static	Toy Store Purchase	City Building Set - Page 2
✓		Large Flower Bed	Part of the City Building Set.	Plants	Static	Toy Store Purchase	City Building Set - Page 2
✓		Mounted City Flag	Part of the City Building Set.	City Building Set	Static	Toy Store Purchase	City Building Set - Page 2
✓		Orange Maple Tree	Part of the City Building Set.	Plants	Static	Toy Store Purchase	City Building Set - Page 2
✓		Orange Street Barrier	Part of the City Building Set.	City Building Set	Static	Toy Store Purchase	City Building Set - Page 2
✓		Quarter City Rooftop	Part of the City Building Set.	City Building Set	Static	Toy Store Purchase	City Building Set - Page 2
✓		Red Maple Tree	Part of the City Building Set.	Plants	Static	Toy Store Purchase	City Building Set - Page 2
✓		Rooftop AC Unit	Part of the City Building Set.	City Building Set	Static	Toy Store Purchase	City Building Set - Page 2
✓		Rooftop Pigeon Coop	Part of the City Building Set.	City Building Set	Static	Toy Store Purchase	City Building Set - Page 2
✓		Short City Railing	Part of the City Building Set.	City Building Set	Static	Toy Store Purchase	City Building Set - Page 2
✓		Single Story Parking Garage	Part of the City Building Set.	City Building Set	Static	Toy Store Purchase	City Building Set - Page 2
✓		Small Climbing Pipe	Part of the City Building Set.	City Building Set	Static	Toy Store Purchase	City Building Set - Page 2
✓		Small Flower Bed	Part of the City Building Set.	Plants	Static	Toy Store Purchase	City Building Set - Page 2
✓		Street Barrier	Part of the City Building Set.	City Building Set	Static	Toy Store Purchase	City Building Set - Page 2
✓		Theater Marquee	Part of the City Building Set.	City Building Set	Static	Toy Store Purchase	City Building Set - Page 2
✓		Theater Piece	Part of the City Building Set.	City Building Set	Static	Toy Store Purchase	City Building Set - Page 2

GAME BASICS

CHARACTERS

POWER DISCS

MARVEL'S THE AVENGERS

SPIDER-MAN

GUARDIANS OF THE GALAXY

TOY BOX

TOY BOX COLLECTION

ACHIEVEMENTS

			Building Sets Continued				
GOT IT?	ICON	TOY NAME	DESCRIPTION	CATEGORY	FUNCTION	UNLOCK	TOY STORE PAGE
✔		Two Story Parking Garage	Part of the City Building Set.	City Building Set	Static	Toy Store Purchase	City Building Set - Page 2
✔		Yellow Aspen Tree	Part of the City Building Set.	Plants	Static	Toy Store Purchase	City Building Set - Page 2
✔		Art Nouveau Billboard	Part of the City Building Set.	City Building Set	Static	Toy Store Purchase	City Building Set - Page 3
✔		Artsy Billboard	Part of the City Building Set.	City Building Set	Static	Toy Store Purchase	City Building Set - Page 3
✔		Bubble Pink Billboard	Part of the City Building Set.	City Building Set	Static	Toy Store Purchase	City Building Set - Page 3
✔		City Cul-De-Sac	A Toy Box city building piece.	Decorations	Static	Toy Store Purchase	City Building Set - Page 3
✔		Curved Sidewalk	A Toy Box city building piece.	Decorations	Static	Toy Store Purchase	City Building Set - Page 3
✔		Electric Billboard	Part of the City Building Set.	City Building Set	Static	Toy Store Purchase	City Building Set - Page 3
✔		Fin Billboard	Part of the City Building Set.	City Building Set	Static	Toy Store Purchase	City Building Set - Page 3
✔		Green Square Billboard	Part of the City Building Set.	City Building Set	Static	Toy Store Purchase	City Building Set - Page 3
✔		Horizontal Billboard	Part of the City Building Set.	City Building Set	Static	Toy Store Purchase	City Building Set - Page 3
✔		Minimalist Billboard	Part of the City Building Set.	City Building Set	Static	Toy Store Purchase	City Building Set - Page 3
✔		Pink Sunrise Billboard	Part of the City Building Set.	City Building Set	Static	Toy Store Purchase	City Building Set - Page 3
✔		Red Electric Billboard	Part of the City Building Set.	City Building Set	Static	Toy Store Purchase	City Building Set - Page 3
✔		Red Pillar Billboard	Part of the City Building Set.	City Building Set	Static	Toy Store Purchase	City Building Set - Page 3
✔		Retro Mondrian Billboard	Part of the City Building Set.	City Building Set	Static	Toy Store Purchase	City Building Set - Page 3
✔		Rounded Retro Billboard	Part of the City Building Set.	City Building Set	Static	Toy Store Purchase	City Building Set - Page 3
✔		Sidewalk	A Toy Box city building piece.	Decorations	Static	Toy Store Purchase	City Building Set - Page 3
✔		Sidewalk Junction	A Toy Box city building piece.	Decorations	Static	Toy Store Purchase	City Building Set - Page 3
✔		Street Lamp	A Toy Box city building piece.	Decorations	Static	Toy Store Purchase	City Building Set - Page 3
✔		Stylin' Billboard	Part of the City Building Set.	City Building Set	Static	Toy Store Purchase	City Building Set - Page 3
✔		Sunburst Billboard	Part of the City Building Set.	City Building Set	Static	Toy Store Purchase	City Building Set - Page 3
✔		Tall Blue Billboard	Part of the City Building Set.	City Building Set	Static	Toy Store Purchase	City Building Set - Page 3
✔		Fantasyland Awning	Part of the Fantasyland Building Set.	Disney Building Sets	Static	Toy Store Purchase	Cottage Building Set
✔		Fantasyland Awning Corner	Part of the Fantasyland Building Set.	Disney Building Sets	Static	Toy Store Purchase	Cottage Building Set
✔		Fantasyland Balcony	Part of the Fantasyland Building Set.	Disney Building Sets	Static	Toy Store Purchase	Cottage Building Set
✔		Fantasyland Base	Part of the Fantasyland Building Set.	Disney Building Sets	Static	Toy Store Purchase	Cottage Building Set
✔		Fantasyland Base Corner	Part of the Fantasyland Building Set.	Disney Building Sets	Static	Toy Store Purchase	Cottage Building Set
✔		Fantasyland Bench	Part of the Fantasyland Building Set.	Disney Building Sets	Static	Toy Store Purchase	Cottage Building Set
✔		Fantasyland Building Window	Part of the Fantasyland Building Set.	Disney Building Sets	Static	Toy Store Purchase	Cottage Building Set
✔		Fantasyland Canopy	Part of the Fantasyland Building Set.	Disney Building Sets	Static	Toy Store Purchase	Cottage Building Set

				Building Sets Continued			
GOT IT?	ICON	TOY NAME	DESCRIPTION	CATEGORY	FUNCTION	UNLOCK	TOY STORE PAGE
✓		Fantasyland Canopy Corner	Part of the Fantasyland Building Set.	Disney Building Sets	Static	Toy Store Purchase	Cottage Building Set
✓		Fantasyland Cottage Entry	Part of the Fantasyland Building Set.	Disney Building Sets	Static	Toy Store Purchase	Cottage Building Set
✓		Fantasyland Cottage Portico	Part of the Fantasyland Building Set.	Disney Building Sets	Static	Toy Store Purchase	Cottage Building Set
✓		Fantasyland Cupola	Part of the Fantasyland Building Set.	Disney Building Sets	Static	Toy Store Purchase	Cottage Building Set
✓		Fantasyland Gable Roof	Part of the Fantasyland Building Set.	Disney Building Sets	Static	Toy Store Purchase	Cottage Building Set
✓		Fantasyland Gablet Roof	Part of the Fantasyland Building Set.	Disney Building Sets	Static	Toy Store Purchase	Cottage Building Set
✓		Fantasyland Hall	Part of the Fantasyland Building Set.	Disney Building Sets	Static	Toy Store Purchase	Cottage Building Set
✓		Fantasyland Narrow Base	Part of the Fantasyland Building Set.	Disney Building Sets	Static	Toy Store Purchase	Cottage Building Set
✓		Fantasyland Platform	Part of the Fantasyland Building Set.	Disney Building Sets	Static	Toy Store Purchase	Cottage Building Set
✓		Fantasyland Pointed Roof	Part of the Fantasyland Building Set.	Disney Building Sets	Static	Toy Store Purchase	Cottage Building Set
✓		Fantasyland Pyramid Roof	Part of the Fantasyland Building Set.	Disney Building Sets	Static	Toy Store Purchase	Cottage Building Set
✓		Fantasyland Rock Base	Part of the Fantasyland Building Set.	Disney Building Sets	Static	Toy Store Purchase	Cottage Building Set
✓		Fantasyland Roof	Part of the Fantasyland Building Set.	Disney Building Sets	Static	Toy Store Purchase	Cottage Building Set
✓		Fantasyland Roof Corner	Part of the Fantasyland Building Set.	Disney Building Sets	Static	Toy Store Purchase	Cottage Building Set
✓		Fantasyland Small Base	Part of the Fantasyland Building Set.	Disney Building Sets	Static	Toy Store Purchase	Cottage Building Set
✓		Fantasyland Spiral Stairs	Part of the Fantasyland Building Set.	Disney Building Sets	Static	Toy Store Purchase	Cottage Building Set
✓		Fantasyland Stairs	Part of the Fantasyland Building Set.	Disney Building Sets	Static	Toy Store Purchase	Cottage Building Set
✓		Fantasyland Stone Base	Part of the Fantasyland Building Set.	Disney Building Sets	Static	Toy Store Purchase	Cottage Building Set
✓		Fantasyland Stone Frame Base	Part of the Fantasyland Building Set.	Disney Building Sets	Static	Toy Store Purchase	Cottage Building Set
✓		Fantasyland Straw Roof	Part of the Fantasyland Building Set.	Disney Building Sets	Static	Toy Store Purchase	Cottage Building Set
✓		Fantasyland Straw Roof Corner	Part of the Fantasyland Building Set.	Disney Building Sets	Static	Toy Store Purchase	Cottage Building Set
✓		Fantasyland Tall Base	Part of the Fantasyland Building Set.	Disney Building Sets	Static	Toy Store Purchase	Cottage Building Set
✓		Fantasyland Timber Frame Base	Part of the Fantasyland Building Set.	Disney Building Sets	Static	Toy Store Purchase	Cottage Building Set
✓		Fantasyland Tower Corner	Part of the Fantasyland Building Set.	Disney Building Sets	Static	Toy Store Purchase	Cottage Building Set
✓		Fantasyland Tower Half	Part of the Fantasyland Building Set.	Disney Building Sets	Static	Toy Store Purchase	Cottage Building Set
✓		Fantasyland Tower Top	Part of the Fantasyland Building Set.	Disney Building Sets	Static	Toy Store Purchase	Cottage Building Set
✓		Fantasyland Turret	Part of the Fantasyland Building Set.	Disney Building Sets	Static	Toy Store Purchase	Cottage Building Set
✓		Fantasyland Water Wheel	Part of the Fantasyland Building Set.	Disney Building Sets	Static	Toy Store Purchase	Cottage Building Set
✓		Fantasyland Well	Part of the Fantasyland Building Set.	Disney Building Sets	Static	Toy Store Purchase	Cottage Building Set
✓		Large Fantasyland Base	Part of the Fantasyland Building Set.	Disney Building Sets	Static	Toy Store Purchase	Cottage Building Set
✓		Large Fantasyland Chimney	Part of the Fantasyland Building Set.	Disney Building Sets	Static	Toy Store Purchase	Cottage Building Set

GAME BASICS

CHARACTERS

POWER DISCS

MARVEL'S THE AVENGERS

SPIDER-MAN

GUARDIANS OF THE GALAXY

TOY BOX

TOY BOX COLLECTION

ACHIEVEMENTS

			Building Sets Continued				
GOT IT?	ICON	TOY NAME	DESCRIPTION	CATEGORY	FUNCTION	UNLOCK	TOY STORE PAGE
✓		Medium Fantasyland Chimney	Part of the Fantasyland Building Set.	Disney Building Sets	Static	Toy Store Purchase	Cottage Building Set
✓		Round Fantasyland Tower	Part of the Fantasyland Building Set.	Disney Building Sets	Static	Toy Store Purchase	Cottage Building Set
✓		Small Fantasyland Balcony	Part of the Fantasyland Building Set.	Disney Building Sets	Static	Toy Store Purchase	Cottage Building Set
✓		Small Fantasyland Chimney	Part of the Fantasyland Building Set.	Disney Building Sets	Static	Toy Store Purchase	Cottage Building Set
✓		Small Fantasyland Roof	Part of the Fantasyland Building Set.	Disney Building Sets	Static	Toy Store Purchase	Cottage Building Set
✓		Tall Fantasyland Tower	Part of the Fantasyland Building Set.	Disney Building Sets	Static	Toy Store Purchase	Cottage Building Set
✓		Toy Box Cottage Builder	This little toy will help you build a fantasy cottage.	Builders and Creators	Builder	Toy Store Purchase	Cottage Building Set
✓		Toy Box Cottage Creator	Place this Creator to quickly build a fantasy cottage.	Builders and Creators	Creator	Toy Store Purchase	Cottage Building Set
✓		Wide Fantasyland Balcony	Part of the Fantasyland Building Set.	Disney Building Sets	Static	Toy Store Purchase	Cottage Building Set
✓		Wide Fantasyland Roof	Part of the Fantasyland Building Set.	Disney Building Sets	Static	Toy Store Purchase	Cottage Building Set
✓		DunBroch Castle Armory	A castle piece from Brave's DunBroch Kingdom.	Disney Building Sets	Static	Toy Store Purchase	DunBroch Building Set
✓		DunBroch Castle Block	A castle piece from Brave's DunBroch Kingdom.	Disney Building Sets	Static	Toy Store Purchase	DunBroch Building Set
✓		DunBroch Castle Chapel	A castle piece from Brave's DunBroch Kingdom.	Disney Building Sets	Static	Toy Store Purchase	DunBroch Building Set
✓		DunBroch Castle Gate	A castle piece from Brave's DunBroch Kingdom.	Disney Building Sets	Static	Toy Store Purchase	DunBroch Building Set
✓		DunBroch Castle Stable	A castle piece from Brave's DunBroch Kingdom.	Disney Building Sets	Static	Toy Store Purchase	DunBroch Building Set
✓		DunBroch Castle Stairs	A castle piece from Brave's DunBroch Kingdom.	Disney Building Sets	Static	Toy Store Purchase	DunBroch Building Set
✓		DunBroch Castle Turret	A castle piece from Brave's DunBroch Kingdom.	Disney Building Sets	Static	Toy Store Purchase	DunBroch Building Set
✓		DunBroch Castle Wall	A castle piece from Brave's DunBroch Kingdom.	Disney Building Sets	Static	Toy Store Purchase	DunBroch Building Set
✓		DunBroch Corner Crenellation	A castle piece from Brave's DunBroch Kingdom.	Disney Building Sets	Static	Toy Store Purchase	DunBroch Building Set
✓		DunBroch Corner Tower Piece	A castle piece from Brave's DunBroch Kingdom.	Disney Building Sets	Static	Toy Store Purchase	DunBroch Building Set
✓		DunBroch Courtyard Tent	A castle piece from Brave's DunBroch Kingdom.	Disney Building Sets	Static	Toy Store Purchase	DunBroch Building Set
✓		DunBroch Ladder	A castle piece from Brave's DunBroch Kingdom.	Disney Building Sets	Static	Toy Store Purchase	DunBroch Building Set
✓		DunBroch Long Crenellation	A castle piece from Brave's DunBroch Kingdom.	Disney Building Sets	Static	Toy Store Purchase	DunBroch Building Set
✓		DunBroch Short Crenellation	A castle piece from Brave's DunBroch Kingdom.	Disney Building Sets	Static	Toy Store Purchase	DunBroch Building Set
✓		DunBroch Tower	A castle piece from Brave's DunBroch Kingdom.	Disney Building Sets	Static	Toy Store Purchase	DunBroch Building Set
✓		DunBroch Tower Piece	A castle piece from Brave's DunBroch Kingdom.	Disney Building Sets	Static	Toy Store Purchase	DunBroch Building Set
✓		DunBroch Tower Top	A castle piece from Brave's DunBroch Kingdom.	Disney Building Sets	Static	Toy Store Purchase	DunBroch Building Set
✓		Short DunBroch Ladder	A castle piece from Brave's DunBroch Kingdom.	Disney Building Sets	Static	Toy Store Purchase	DunBroch Building Set
✓		Tall DunBroch Ladder	A castle piece from Brave's DunBroch Kingdom.	Disney Building Sets	Static	Toy Store Purchase	DunBroch Building Set
✓		Toy Box Castle Builder	This little toy will help you build a castle.	Builders and Creators	Builder	Toy Store Purchase	DunBroch Building Set
✓		Toy Box Castle Creator	Place this Creator to quickly build a castle.	Builders and Creators	Creator	Toy Store Purchase	DunBroch Building Set

		Building Sets Continued					
GOT IT?	ICON	TOY NAME	DESCRIPTION	CATEGORY	FUNCTION	UNLOCK	TOY STORE PAGE
✓		Long Mountain Saddle Corner	A Toy Box mountain-themed terrain piece.	Terrain	Static	Toy Store Purchase	Mountain Building Set
✓		Mountain Corner Ledge	A Toy Box mountain-themed terrain piece.	Terrain	Static	Toy Store Purchase	Mountain Building Set
✓		Mountain Corner Ridge	A Toy Box mountain-themed terrain piece.	Terrain	Static	Toy Store Purchase	Mountain Building Set
✓		Mountain Corner Slope	A Toy Box mountain-themed terrain piece.	Terrain	Static	Toy Store Purchase	Mountain Building Set
✓		Mountain Corner Wedge	A Toy Box mountain-themed terrain piece.	Terrain	Static	Toy Store Purchase	Mountain Building Set
✓		Mountain Craggy Corner	A Toy Box mountain-themed terrain piece.	Terrain	Static	Toy Store Purchase	Mountain Building Set
✓		Mountain Middle	A Toy Box mountain-themed terrain piece.	Terrain	Static	Toy Store Purchase	Mountain Building Set
✓		Mountain Middle Path	A Toy Box mountain-themed terrain piece.	Terrain	Static	Toy Store Purchase	Mountain Building Set
✓		Mountain Middle Ridge	A Toy Box mountain-themed terrain piece.	Terrain	Static	Toy Store Purchase	Mountain Building Set
✓		Mountain Middle Tunnel	A Toy Box mountain-themed terrain piece.	Terrain	Static	Toy Store Purchase	Mountain Building Set
✓		Mountain Middle Wedge	A Toy Box mountain-themed terrain piece.	Terrain	Static	Toy Store Purchase	Mountain Building Set
✓		Mountain Saddle	A Toy Box mountain-themed terrain piece.	Terrain	Static	Toy Store Purchase	Mountain Building Set
✓		Mountain Saddle Corner	A Toy Box mountain-themed terrain piece.	Terrain	Static	Toy Store Purchase	Mountain Building Set
✓		Mountain with Cave	A Toy Box mountain-themed terrain piece.	Terrain	Static	Toy Store Purchase	Mountain Building Set
✓		Mountain with Tunnel	A Toy Box mountain-themed terrain piece.	Terrain	Static	Toy Store Purchase	Mountain Building Set
✓		Small Mountain Corner	A Toy Box mountain-themed terrain piece.	Terrain	Static	Toy Store Purchase	Mountain Building Set
✓		Small Mountain Middle	A Toy Box mountain-themed terrain piece.	Terrain	Static	Toy Store Purchase	Mountain Building Set
✓		Small Mountaintop	A Toy Box mountain-themed terrain piece.	Terrain	Static	Toy Store Purchase	Mountain Building Set
✓		Small Mountaintop Peak	A Toy Box mountain-themed terrain piece.	Terrain	Static	Toy Store Purchase	Mountain Building Set
✓		Small Mountaintop Wedge	A Toy Box mountain-themed terrain piece.	Terrain	Static	Toy Store Purchase	Mountain Building Set
✓		Snowy Mountaintop	A Toy Box mountain-themed terrain piece.	Terrain	Static	Toy Store Purchase	Mountain Building Set
✓		Volcano	A Toy Box mountain-themed terrain piece.	Terrain	Static	Toy Store Purchase	Mountain Building Set
✓		Black San Fransokyo Eaves	A piece of the Big Hero 6 Building Set.	City Building Set	Static	Toy Store Purchase	San Fransokyo Set
✓		Blue San Fransokyo Eaves	A piece of the Big Hero 6 Building Set.	City Building Set	Static	Toy Store Purchase	San Fransokyo Set
✓		Blue San Fransokyo Roof	A piece of the Big Hero 6 Building Set.	City Building Set	Static	Toy Store Purchase	San Fransokyo Set
✓		Brown San Fransokyo Eaves	A piece of the Big Hero 6 Building Set.	City Building Set	Static	Toy Store Purchase	San Fransokyo Set
✓		Brown San Fransokyo Roof	A piece of the Big Hero 6 Building Set.	City Building Set	Static	Toy Store Purchase	San Fransokyo Set
✓		Flat Blue San Fransokyo Roof	A piece of the Big Hero 6 Building Set.	City Building Set	Static	Toy Store Purchase	San Fransokyo Set
✓		Flat Brown San Fransokyo Roof	A piece of the Big Hero 6 Building Set.	City Building Set	Static	Toy Store Purchase	San Fransokyo Set
✓		Flat Red San Fransokyo Roof	A piece of the Big Hero 6 Building Set.	City Building Set	Static	Toy Store Purchase	San Fransokyo Set
✓		Long Black San Fransokyo Roof	A piece of the Big Hero 6 Building Set.	City Building Set	Static	Toy Store Purchase	San Fransokyo Set

GAME BASICS

CHARACTERS

POWER DISCS

MARVEL'S THE AVENGERS

SPIDER-MAN

GUARDIANS OF THE GALAXY

TOY BOX

TOY BOX COLLECTION

ACHIEVEMENTS

			Building Sets Continued				
GOT IT?	**ICON**	**TOY NAME**	**DESCRIPTION**	**CATEGORY**	**FUNCTION**	**UNLOCK**	**TOY STORE PAGE**
✓		Red San Fransokyo Eaves	A piece of the Big Hero 6 Building Set.	City Building Set	Static	Toy Store Purchase	San Fransokyo Set
✓		Red San Fransokyo Roof	A piece of the Big Hero 6 Building Set.	City Building Set	Static	Toy Store Purchase	San Fransokyo Set
✓		San Fransokyo Bridge	A piece of the Big Hero 6 Building Set.	City Building Set	Static	Toy Store Purchase	San Fransokyo Set
✓		San Fransokyo Flying Green Turbine	A piece of the Big Hero 6 Building Set.	City Building Set	Static	Toy Store Purchase	San Fransokyo Set
✓		San Fransokyo Flying Orange Turbine	A piece of the Big Hero 6 Building Set.	City Building Set	Static	Toy Store Purchase	San Fransokyo Set
✓		San Fransokyo Flying Pink Turbine	A piece of the Big Hero 6 Building Set.	City Building Set	Static	Toy Store Purchase	San Fransokyo Set
✓		San Fransokyo Sign A	A piece of the Big Hero 6 Building Set.	City Building Set	Static	Toy Store Purchase	San Fransokyo Set
✓		San Fransokyo Sign B	A piece of the Big Hero 6 Building Set.	City Building Set	Static	Toy Store Purchase	San Fransokyo Set
✓		San Fransokyo Sign C	A piece of the Big Hero 6 Building Set.	City Building Set	Static	Toy Store Purchase	San Fransokyo Set
✓		San Fransokyo Sign D	A piece of the Big Hero 6 Building Set.	City Building Set	Static	Toy Store Purchase	San Fransokyo Set
✓		San Fransokyo Sign E	A piece of the Big Hero 6 Building Set.	City Building Set	Static	Toy Store Purchase	San Fransokyo Set
✓		San Fransokyo Tower	A piece of the Big Hero 6 Building Set.	City Building Set	Static	Toy Store Purchase	San Fransokyo Set
✓		Small Blue San Fransokyo Roof	A piece of the Big Hero 6 Building Set.	City Building Set	Static	Toy Store Purchase	San Fransokyo Set
✓		Small Brown San Fransokyo Roof	A piece of the Big Hero 6 Building Set.	City Building Set	Static	Toy Store Purchase	San Fransokyo Set
✓		Small Red San Fransokyo Roof	A piece of the Big Hero 6 Building Set.	City Building Set	Static	Toy Store Purchase	San Fransokyo Set
✓		Garage	Part of the Suburb Building Set.	City Building Set	Static	Toy Store Purchase	Suburbs Building Set
✓		Garage Door	Part of the Suburb Building Set.	City Building Set	Static	Toy Store Purchase	Suburbs Building Set
✓		Hot Tub	Part of the Suburb Building Set.	City Building Set	Static	Toy Store Purchase	Suburbs Building Set
✓		Large Suburb Home	Part of the Suburb Building Set.	City Building Set	Static	Toy Store Purchase	Suburbs Building Set
✓		Medium Suburb Home	Part of the Suburb Building Set.	City Building Set	Static	Toy Store Purchase	Suburbs Building Set
✓		Narrow Suburb Roof	Part of the Suburb Building Set.	City Building Set	Static	Toy Store Purchase	Suburbs Building Set
✓		Small Suburb Home	Part of the Suburb Building Set.	City Building Set	Static	Toy Store Purchase	Suburbs Building Set
✓		Small Suburb Roof	Part of the Suburb Building Set.	City Building Set	Static	Toy Store Purchase	Suburbs Building Set
✓		Suburb Balcony Support	Part of the Suburb Building Set.	City Building Set	Static	Toy Store Purchase	Suburbs Building Set
✓		Suburb Deck	Part of the Suburb Building Set.	City Building Set	Static	Toy Store Purchase	Suburbs Building Set
✓		Suburb Deck Corner	Part of the Suburb Building Set.	City Building Set	Static	Toy Store Purchase	Suburbs Building Set
✓		Suburb Dormer Roof	Part of the Suburb Building Set.	City Building Set	Static	Toy Store Purchase	Suburbs Building Set
✓		Suburb Fence	Part of the Suburb Building Set.	City Building Set	Static	Toy Store Purchase	Suburbs Building Set
✓		Suburb Half Roof	Part of the Suburb Building Set.	City Building Set	Static	Toy Store Purchase	Suburbs Building Set
✓		Suburb Lattice Roof	Part of the Suburb Building Set.	City Building Set	Static	Toy Store Purchase	Suburbs Building Set
✓		Suburb Patio	Part of the Suburb Building Set.	City Building Set	Static	Toy Store Purchase	Suburbs Building Set

Building Sets Continued

GOT IT?	ICON	TOY NAME	DESCRIPTION	CATEGORY	FUNCTION	UNLOCK	TOY STORE PAGE
✓		Suburb Patio Concrete	Part of the Suburb Building Set.	City Building Set	Static	Toy Store Purchase	Suburbs Building Set
✓		Corner Treehouse Branch	Part of the Treehouse Building Set.	Disney Building Sets	Static	Toy Store Purchase	Treehouse Building Set
✓		Large Treehouse Branch	Part of the Treehouse Building Set.	Disney Building Sets	Static	Starting Toy	Treehouse Building Set
✓		Small Treehouse Branch	Part of the Treehouse Building Set.	Disney Building Sets	Static	Starting Toy	Treehouse Building Set
✓		Straight Treehouse Branch	Part of the Treehouse Building Set.	Disney Building Sets	Static	Toy Store Purchase	Treehouse Building Set
✓		Tall Treehouse Roof	Part of the Treehouse Building Set.	Disney Building Sets	Static	Toy Store Purchase	Treehouse Building Set
✓		Thatched Treehouse Roof	Part of the Treehouse Building Set.	Disney Building Sets	Static	Toy Store Purchase	Treehouse Building Set
✓		Toy Box Treehouse Builder	This little toy will help you build a treehouse.	Builders and Creators	Builder	Starting Toy	Treehouse Building Set
✓		Toy Box Treehouse Creator	Place this Creator to quickly build a treehouse.	Builders and Creators	Creator	Toy Store Purchase	Treehouse Building Set
✓		Treehouse Balcony	Part of the Treehouse Building Set.	Disney Building Sets	Static	Toy Store Purchase	Treehouse Building Set
✓		Treehouse Branch	Part of the Treehouse Building Set.	Disney Building Sets	Static	Starting Toy	Treehouse Building Set
✓		Treehouse Branch Step	Part of the Treehouse Building Set.	Disney Building Sets	Static	Starting Toy	Treehouse Building Set
✓		Treehouse Closed Room	Part of the Treehouse Building Set.	Disney Building Sets	Static	Toy Store Purchase	Treehouse Building Set
✓		Treehouse Corner Platform	Part of the Treehouse Building Set.	Disney Building Sets	Static	Toy Store Purchase	Treehouse Building Set
✓		Treehouse Covered Platform	Part of the Treehouse Building Set.	Disney Building Sets	Static	Toy Store Purchase	Treehouse Building Set
✓		Treehouse Crow's Nest	Part of the Treehouse Building Set.	Disney Building Sets	Static	Toy Store Purchase	Treehouse Building Set
✓		Treehouse Curved Platform	Part of the Treehouse Building Set.	Disney Building Sets	Static	Toy Store Purchase	Treehouse Building Set
✓		Treehouse Forecastle Balcony	Part of the Treehouse Building Set.	Disney Building Sets	Static	Toy Store Purchase	Treehouse Building Set
✓		Treehouse Half Trunk	Part of the Treehouse Building Set.	Disney Building Sets	Static	Toy Store Purchase	Treehouse Building Set
✓		Treehouse Hanging Bridge	Part of the Treehouse Building Set.	Disney Building Sets	Static	Toy Store Purchase	Treehouse Building Set
✓		Treehouse Hidden Door	Part of the Treehouse Building Set.	Disney Building Sets	Static	Toy Store Purchase	Treehouse Building Set
✓		Treehouse Lamp	Part of the Treehouse Building Set.	Disney Building Sets	Static	Toy Store Purchase	Treehouse Building Set
✓		Treehouse Lantern	Part of the Treehouse Building Set.	Disney Building Sets	Static	Toy Store Purchase	Treehouse Building Set
✓		Treehouse Large Canopy	Part of the Treehouse Building Set.	Disney Building Sets	Static	Starting Toy	Treehouse Building Set
✓		Treehouse Medium Canopy	Part of the Treehouse Building Set.	Disney Building Sets	Static	Toy Store Purchase	Treehouse Building Set
✓		Treehouse Open Room	Part of the Treehouse Building Set.	Disney Building Sets	Static	Toy Store Purchase	Treehouse Building Set
✓		Treehouse Platform	Part of the Treehouse Building Set.	Disney Building Sets	Static	Starting Toy	Treehouse Building Set
✓		Treehouse Platform	Part of the Treehouse Building Set.	Disney Building Sets	Static	Starting Toy	Treehouse Building Set
✓		Treehouse Quarter Trunk	Part of the Treehouse Building Set.	Disney Building Sets	Static	Starting Toy	Treehouse Building Set
✓		Treehouse Roots	Part of the Treehouse Building Set.	Disney Building Sets	Static	Starting Toy	Treehouse Building Set
✓		Treehouse Rope Climb	Part of the Treehouse Building Set.	Disney Building Sets	Static	Toy Store Purchase	Treehouse Building Set

GAME BASICS

CHARACTERS

POWER DISCS

MARVEL'S THE AVENGERS

SPIDER-MAN

GUARDIANS OF THE GALAXY

TOY BOX

TOY BOX COLLECTION

ACHIEVEMENTS

Building Sets Continued

GOT IT?	ICON	TOY NAME	DESCRIPTION	CATEGORY	FUNCTION	UNLOCK	TOY STORE PAGE
✓		Treehouse Rope Climb Canopy	Part of the Treehouse Building Set.	Disney Building Sets	Static	Toy Store Purchase	Treehouse Building Set
✓		Treehouse Small Canopy	Part of the Treehouse Building Set.	Disney Building Sets	Static	Starting Toy	Treehouse Building Set
✓		Treehouse Spiral Staircase	Part of the Treehouse Building Set.	Disney Building Sets	Static	Toy Store Purchase	Treehouse Building Set
✓		Treehouse Staircase	Part of the Treehouse Building Set.	Disney Building Sets	Static	Toy Store Purchase	Treehouse Building Set
✓		Treehouse Stump	Part of the Treehouse Building Set.	Disney Building Sets	Static	Starting Toy	Treehouse Building Set
✓		Treehouse Trunk	Part of the Treehouse Building Set.	Disney Building Sets	Static	Toy Store Purchase	Treehouse Building Set
✓		Treehouse Windows	Part of the Treehouse Building Set.	Disney Building Sets	Static	Toy Store Purchase	Treehouse Building Set

INTERIOR DECORATIONS

Interior Decorations

GOT IT?	ICON	TOY NAME	DESCRIPTION	CATEGORY	FUNCTION	UNLOCK	TOY STORE PAGE
✓		Bathtub	A squeaky clean piece of furniture, well-suited for a bathroom.	INterior (Floor Decoration)	Static	Toy Store Purchase	Basic Decorations - Page 1
✓		Bed	A comfortable bed where you can catch some Z's.	INterior (Floor Decoration)	Static	Toy Store Purchase	Basic Decorations - Page 1
✓		Chair	A charming, wooden chair, appropriate for just sitting around.	INterior (Floor Decoration)	Static	INterior Mission Reward	Basic Decorations - Page 1
✓		Coat Rack	A hospitable coat rack like this one will be a fine welcome for any guest.	INterior (Floor Decoration)	Static	Toy Store Purchase	Basic Decorations - Page 1
✓		Corner Counter	Doll up a corner of your kitchen with this corner tiled counter.	INterior (Floor Decoration)	Static	Toy Store Purchase	Basic Decorations - Page 1
✓		Counter Sink	Your kitchen has everything but this!	INterior (Floor Decoration)	Static	Toy Store Purchase	Basic Decorations - Page 1
✓		Cupboard	Pots, pans, cookie jars... they have all found a home within this cupboard.	INterior (Wall Decoration)	Static	Toy Store Purchase	Basic Decorations - Page 1
✓		Disney Infinity Painting	A fine piece of art displaying your fine sense of culture.	INterior (Wall Decoration)	Static	Toy Store Purchase	Basic Decorations - Page 1
✓		Floor Lamp	Add some style and light with this floor lamp.	INterior (Floor Decoration)	Static	INterior Mission Reward	Basic Decorations - Page 1
✓		Fridge	No kitchen is complete without this cool refrigerator.	INterior (Floor Decoration)	Static	Toy Store Purchase	Basic Decorations - Page 1
✓		Grand Piano	This musical instrument will convey your fine musical tastes.	INterior (Floor Decoration)	Static	Toy Store Purchase	Basic Decorations - Page 1
✓		Green Chair	Relax on this comfortable, overstuffed, green chair.	INterior (Floor Decoration)	Static	INterior Mission Reward	Basic Decorations - Page 1
✓		Green Couch	An overstuffed, comfortable, green sofa like this one is both relaxing and welcoming.	INterior (Floor Decoration)	Static	INterior Mission Reward	Basic Decorations - Page 1
✓		Guest Gatherer	A statue that attracts townspeople and guests.	INterior (Floor Decoration)	Custom	INterior Mission Reward	Basic Decorations - Page 1
✓		Large Corner Counter	This large, corner counter will make your kitchen feel homey.	INterior (Floor Decoration)	Static	Toy Store Purchase	Basic Decorations - Page 1
✓		Long Counter	Add charm to your kitchen with this long, tiled counter.	INterior (Floor Decoration)	Static	Toy Store Purchase	Basic Decorations - Page 1
✓		Nightstand	A bedside table like this one will complement any bedroom with style.	INterior (Floor Decoration)	Static	Toy Store Purchase	Basic Decorations - Page 1
✓		Oven	Every kitchen needs this cooking appliance.	INterior (Floor Decoration)	Static	Toy Store Purchase	Basic Decorations - Page 1
✓		Potted Fern	Foliage like this potted fern will give your home a fresh, earthy feel.	INterior (Floor Decoration)	Static	INterior Mission Reward	Basic Decorations - Page 1
✓		Potted Vine	A lovely, potted vine can add a touch of earthy sweetness to any room.	INterior (Floor Decoration)	Static	INterior Mission Reward	Basic Decorations - Page 1
✓		Red Chair	An overstuffed red chair for someone who likes both comfort and style.	INterior (Floor Decoration)	Static	Toy Store Purchase	Basic Decorations - Page 1

			Interior Decorations Continued				
GOT IT?	ICON	TOY NAME	DESCRIPTION	CATEGORY	FUNCTION	UNLOCK	TOY STORE PAGE
✓		Red Couch	Relax on this stylish, overstuffed, red chair.	INterior (Floor Decoration)	Static	Toy Store Purchase	Basic Decorations - Page 1
✓		Round Blue Rug	A round, blue rug like this one can be a lovely accent to a room.	INterior (Floor Decoration)	Static	Toy Store Purchase	Basic Decorations - Page 1
✓		Round Ornate Rug	A decorative rug that will add just the right touch to a fancy room.	INterior (Floor Decoration)	Static	INterior Mission Reward	Basic Decorations - Page 1
✓		Short Counter	A short, tiled counter like this one will add flair to your kitchen.	INterior (Floor Decoration)	Static	Toy Store Purchase	Basic Decorations - Page 1
✓		Shower	Keep it clean with this shower and shower curtain.	INterior (Floor Decoration)	Static	Toy Store Purchase	Basic Decorations - Page 1
✓		Small Dresser	A small dresser to accent a room.	INterior (Floor Decoration)	Static	Toy Store Purchase	Basic Decorations - Page 1
✓		Table	This small, wooden table with a vase of flowers will brighten up your home.	INterior (Floor Decoration)	Static	Toy Store Purchase	Basic Decorations - Page 1
✓		Tall Dresser	This tall dresser is good for stowing all the clothes you've wanted to wear.	INterior (Floor Decoration)	Static	Toy Store Purchase	Basic Decorations - Page 1
✓		Toilet	A restroom furniture necessity in any home.	INterior (Floor Decoration)	Static	Toy Store Purchase	Basic Decorations - Page 1
✓		Toon Window	A lovely window like this one will add a friendly light to any wall.	INterior (Wall Decoration)	Static	INterior Mission Reward	Basic Decorations - Page 1
✓		1-Door Room	A customizable area for your Toy Box INterior.	INterior (Rooms)	Room	INterior Mission Reward	Basic Decorations - Page 2
✓		2-Door Room A	A customizable area for your Toy Box INterior.	INterior (Rooms)	Room	INterior Mission Reward	Basic Decorations - Page 2
✓		2-Door Room B	A customizable area for your Toy Box INterior.	INterior (Rooms)	Room	INterior Mission Reward	Basic Decorations - Page 2
✓		3-Door Room A	A customizable area for your Toy Box INterior.	INterior (Rooms)	Room	INterior Mission Reward	Basic Decorations - Page 2
✓		3-Door Room B	A customizable area for your Toy Box INterior.	INterior (Rooms)	Room	INterior Mission Reward	Basic Decorations - Page 2
✓		4-Door Room A	A customizable area for your Toy Box INterior.	INterior (Rooms)	Room	INterior Mission Reward	Basic Decorations - Page 2
✓		4-Door Room B	A customizable area for your Toy Box INterior.	INterior (Rooms)	Room	INterior Mission Reward	Basic Decorations - Page 2
✓		All-Star Trophy	A Toy Box-themed decorative trophy.	INterior (Floor Decoration)	Static	Feat Reward	Basic Decorations - Page 2
✓		Basin Trophy	A Toy Box-themed decorative trophy.	INterior (Floor Decoration)	Static	Feat Reward	Basic Decorations - Page 2
✓		Corner Fantasyland Counter	An old-fashioned, stone, corner counter.	INterior (Floor Decoration)	Static	Toy Store Purchase	Basic Decorations - Page 2
✓		Corner Tomorrowland Counter	A corner, futuristic counter.	INterior (Floor Decoration)	Static	Toy Store Purchase	Basic Decorations - Page 2
✓		Elegant Trophy	A Toy Box-themed decorative trophy.	INterior (Floor Decoration)	Static	Feat Reward	Basic Decorations - Page 2
✓		Elevator Room	A customizable, two-story area with a lift for your Toy Box INterior.	INterior (Rooms)	Room	INterior Mission Reward	Basic Decorations - Page 2
✓		First Place Trophy	A Toy Box-themed decorative trophy.	INterior (Floor Decoration)	Static	Feat Reward	Basic Decorations - Page 2
✓		Hallway Turn	A hall to connect your Toy Box INterior rooms.	INterior (Rooms)	Room	INterior Mission Reward	Basic Decorations - Page 2
✓		Large Tomorrowland Counter	A futuristic counter.	INterior (Floor Decoration)	Static	Toy Store Purchase	Basic Decorations - Page 2
✓		Long Fantasyland Counter	A long, old-fashioned, stone counter.	INterior (Floor Decoration)	Static	Toy Store Purchase	Basic Decorations - Page 2
✓		Long Hall	A hall to connect your Toy Box INterior rooms.	INterior (Rooms)	Room	INterior Mission Reward	Basic Decorations - Page 2
✓		Mug Trophy	A Toy Box-themed decorative trophy.	INterior (Floor Decoration)	Static	Feat Reward	Basic Decorations - Page 2
✓		Pipe Climb Room	A customizable area for your Toy Box INterior.	INterior (Rooms)	Room	INterior Mission Reward	Basic Decorations - Page 2
✓		Rug of the Future	A futuristic rug.	INterior (Floor Decoration)	Static	Toy Store Purchase	Basic Decorations - Page 2

GAME BASICS

CHARACTERS

POWER DISCS

MARVEL'S THE AVENGERS

SPIDER-MAN

GUARDIANS OF THE GALAXY

TOY BOX

TOY BOX COLLECTION

ACHIEVEMENTS

			Interior Decorations Continued				
GOT IT?	ICON	TOY NAME	DESCRIPTION	CATEGORY	FUNCTION	UNLOCK	TOY STORE PAGE
✓		Short Fantasyland Counter	A short, old-fashioned, stone counter.	INterior (Floor Decoration)	Static	Toy Store Purchase	Basic Decorations - Page 2
✓		Short Hall	A hall to connect your Toy Box INterior rooms.	INterior (Rooms)	Room	INterior Mission Reward	Basic Decorations - Page 2
✓		Short Tomorrowland Counter	A short, futuristic counter.	INterior (Floor Decoration)	Static	Toy Store Purchase	Basic Decorations - Page 2
✓		Starred Trophy	A Toy Box-themed decorative trophy.	INterior (Floor Decoration)	Static	Feat Reward	Basic Decorations - Page 2
✓		Superstar Trophy	A Toy Box-themed decorative trophy.	INterior (Floor Decoration)	Static	Feat Reward	Basic Decorations - Page 2
✓		Vessel Trophy	A Toy Box-themed decorative trophy.	INterior (Floor Decoration)	Static	Feat Reward	Basic Decorations - Page 2
✓		Aladdin Portrait	A framed picture of your favorite character to decorate your wall.	INterior (Wall Decoration)	Static	Aladdin	Character Portraits
✓		Baymax Portrait	A framed picture of your favorite character to decorate your wall.	INterior (Wall Decoration)	Static	Baymax	Character Portraits
✓		Black Widow Portrait	A framed picture of your favorite character to decorate your wall.	INterior (Wall Decoration)	Static	Black Widow	Character Portraits
✓		Captain America Portrait	A framed picture of your favorite character to decorate your wall.	INterior (Wall Decoration)	Static	Captain America	Character Portraits
✓		Donald Duck Portrait	A framed picture of your favorite character to decorate your wall.	INterior (Wall Decoration)	Static	Donald Duck	Character Portraits
✓		Drax Portrait	A framed picture of your favorite character to decorate your wall.	INterior (Wall Decoration)	Static	Drax	Character Portraits
✓		Falcon Portrait	A framed picture of your favorite character to decorate your wall.	INterior (Wall Decoration)	Static	Falcon	Character Portraits
✓		Gamora Portrait	A framed picture of your favorite character to decorate your wall.	INterior (Wall Decoration)	Static	Gamora	Character Portraits
✓		Green Goblin Portrait	A framed picture of your favorite character to decorate your wall.	INterior (Wall Decoration)	Static	Green Goblin	Character Portraits
✓		Groot Portrait	A framed picture of your favorite character to decorate your wall.	INterior (Wall Decoration)	Static	Groot	Character Portraits
✓		Hawkeye Portrait	A framed picture of your favorite character to decorate your wall.	INterior (Wall Decoration)	Static	Hawkeye	Character Portraits
✓		Hiro Portrait	A framed picture of your favorite character to decorate your wall.	INterior (Wall Decoration)	Static	Hiro	Character Portraits
✓		Hulk Portrait	A framed picture of your favorite character to decorate your wall.	INterior (Wall Decoration)	Static	Hulk	Character Portraits
✓		Iron Fist Portrait	A framed picture of your favorite character to decorate your wall.	INterior (Wall Decoration)	Static	Iron Fist	Character Portraits
✓		Iron Man Portrait	A framed picture of your favorite character to decorate your wall.	INterior (Wall Decoration)	Static	Iron Man	Character Portraits
✓		Jasmine Portrait	A framed picture of your favorite character to decorate your wall.	INterior (Wall Decoration)	Static	Jasmine	Character Portraits
✓		Loki Portrait	A framed picture of your favorite character to decorate your wall.	INterior (Wall Decoration)	Static	Loki	Character Portraits
✓		Maleficent Portrait	A framed picture of your favorite character to decorate your wall.	INterior (Wall Decoration)	Static	Maleficent	Character Portraits
✓		Merida Portrait	A framed picture of your favorite character to decorate your wall.	INterior (Wall Decoration)	Static	Merida	Character Portraits
✓		Nick Fury Portrait	A framed picture of your favorite character to decorate your wall.	INterior (Wall Decoration)	Static	Nick Fury	Character Portraits
✓		Nova Portrait	A framed picture of your favorite character to decorate your wall.	INterior (Wall Decoration)	Static	Nova	Character Portraits
✓		Rocket Raccoon Portrait	A framed picture of your favorite character to decorate your wall.	INterior (Wall Decoration)	Static	Rocket Raccoon	Character Portraits
✓		Ronan Portrait	A framed picture of your favorite character to decorate your wall.	INterior (Wall Decoration)	Static	Ronan	Character Portraits
✓		Spider-Man Portrait	A framed picture of your favorite character to decorate your wall.	INterior (Wall Decoration)	Static	Spider-Man	Character Portraits
✓		Star-Lord Portrait	A framed picture of your favorite character to decorate your wall.	INterior (Wall Decoration)	Static	Star-Lord	Character Portraits

	**Interior Decorations Continued**
GOT IT?	**ICON**	**TOY NAME**	**DESCRIPTION**	**CATEGORY**	**FUNCTION**	**UNLOCK**	**TOY STORE PAGE**
✓		Stitch Portrait	A framed picture of your favorite character to decorate your wall.	INterior (Wall Decoration)	Static	Stitch	Character Portraits
✓		Thor Portrait	A framed picture of your favorite character to decorate your wall.	INterior (Wall Decoration)	Static	Thor	Character Portraits
✓		Tinker Bell Portrait	A framed picture of your favorite character to decorate your wall.	INterior (Wall Decoration)	Static	Tinker Bell	Character Portraits
✓		Venom Portrait	A framed picture of your favorite character to decorate your wall.	INterior (Wall Decoration)	Static	Venom	Character Portraits
✓		Yondu Portrait	A framed picture of your favorite character to decorate your wall.	INterior (Wall Decoration)	Static	Yondu	Character Portraits
✓		Dipper's Book	A rustic piece of furniture from Gravity Falls.	INterior (Floor Decoration)	Static	Toy Store Purchase	Disney Channel Decorations
✓		Doofenshmirtz's Badly-Forged Fine Art	A piece of furniture from Phineas and Ferb.	INterior (Wall Decoration)	Static	Toy Store Purchase	Disney Channel Decorations
✓		Doofenshmirtz's Chair	A piece of furniture from Phineas and Ferb.	INterior (Floor Decoration)	Static	Toy Store Purchase	Disney Channel Decorations
✓		Doofenshmirtz's Fine Art	A piece of furniture from Phineas and Ferb.	INterior (Wall Decoration)	Static	Toy Store Purchase	Disney Channel Decorations
✓		Doofenshmirtz's Fireplace	A piece of furniture from Phineas and Ferb.	INterior (Wall Decoration)	Static	Toy Store Purchase	Disney Channel Decorations
✓		Doofenshmirtz's Telephone	A piece of furniture from Phineas and Ferb.	INterior (Floor Decoration)	Static	Toy Store Purchase	Disney Channel Decorations
✓		Doofenshmirtz's Television	A piece of furniture from Phineas and Ferb.	INterior (Floor Decoration)	Static	Toy Store Purchase	Disney Channel Decorations
✓		Ferb's Bed	A piece of furniture from Phineas and Ferb.	INterior (Floor Decoration)	Static	Toy Store Purchase	Disney Channel Decorations
✓		Gimmelshtump Gnome	A fashionable piece of décor from Phineas and Ferb.	INterior (Floor Decoration)	Static	Toy Store Purchase	Disney Channel Decorations
✓		Gravity Falls Window	A stained glass window from Gravity Falls.	INterior (Wall Decoration)	Static	Toy Store Purchase	Disney Channel Decorations
✓		Gruncle Stan's Chair	An overstuffed chair from Gravity Falls.	INterior (Floor Decoration)	Static	Toy Store Purchase	Disney Channel Decorations
✓		Mabel and Waddles Portrait	A rustic wall hanging from Gravity Falls.	INterior (Wall Decoration)	Static	Toy Store Purchase	Disney Channel Decorations
✓		Mabel Posters	A rustic wall hanging from Gravity Falls.	INterior (Wall Decoration)	Static	Toy Store Purchase	Disney Channel Decorations
✓		Mabel's Bed	A rustic piece of furniture from Gravity Falls.	INterior (Floor Decoration)	Static	Toy Store Purchase	Disney Channel Decorations
✓		Mystery Shack Aquarium Exhibit	A rustic piece of furniture from Gravity Falls.	INterior (Floor Decoration)	Static	Toy Store Purchase	Disney Channel Decorations
✓		Mystery Shack Chess Board	A rustic piece of furniture from Gravity Falls.	INterior (Floor Decoration)	Static	Toy Store Purchase	Disney Channel Decorations
✓		Mystery Shack Curiosity Exhibit	A rustic piece of furniture from Gravity Falls.	INterior (Floor Decoration)	Static	Toy Store Purchase	Disney Channel Decorations
✓		Mystery Shack Fortune Teller Machine	A piece of nostalgic furniture from Gravity Falls.	INterior (Floor Decoration)	Static	Toy Store Purchase	Disney Channel Decorations
✓		Mystery Shack Fur Trout Exhibit	An unusual, mounted wall decoration from Gravity Falls.	INterior (Wall Decoration)	Static	Toy Store Purchase	Disney Channel Decorations
✓		Mystery Shack Jackalope Exhibit	A rustic piece of furniture from Gravity Falls.	INterior (Floor Decoration)	Static	Feat Reward	Disney Channel Decorations
✓		Mystery Shack Portrait	A rustic wall hanging from Gravity Falls.	INterior (Wall Decoration)	Static	Toy Store Purchase	Disney Channel Decorations
✓		Mystery Shack Rug	A rustic rug from Gravity Falls.	INterior (Floor Decoration)	Static	Toy Store Purchase	Disney Channel Decorations
✓		Mystery Shack TV	A rustic piece of furniture from Gravity Falls.	INterior (Floor Decoration)	Static	Toy Store Purchase	Disney Channel Decorations
✓		Mystery Shack Unicorn Bear Exhibit	A mounted animal head decoration from Gravity Falls.	INterior (Wall Decoration)	Static	Toy Store Purchase	Disney Channel Decorations
✓		Mystery Shack Vending Machine	A rustic piece of furniture from Gravity Falls.	INterior (Floor Decoration)	Static	Toy Store Purchase	Disney Channel Decorations
✓		Mystery Shack Waterfall Box	A rustic piece of furniture from Gravity Falls.	INterior (Wall Decoration)	Static	Toy Store Purchase	Disney Channel Decorations

GAME BASICS

CHARACTERS

POWER DISCS

MARVEL'S THE AVENGERS

SPIDER-MAN

GUARDIANS OF THE GALAXY

TOY BOX

TOY BOX COLLECTION

ACHIEVEMENTS

Interior Decorations Continued

GOT IT?	ICON	TOY NAME	DESCRIPTION	CATEGORY	FUNCTION	UNLOCK	TOY STORE PAGE
✓		Phineas' Bed	A piece of furniture from Phineas and Ferb.	INterior (Floor Decoration)	Static	Toy Store Purchase	Disney Channel Decorations
✓		Agrabah Palace Corner	A marble corner from the Sultan's palace.	INterior (Floor Decoration)	Static	Toy Store Purchase	Disney Decorations - Page 1
✓		Agrabah Palace Pillar	A marble pillar from the Sultan's palace.	INterior (Floor Decoration)	Static	Toy Store Purchase	Disney Decorations - Page 1
✓		Agrabah Palace Sconce	A wall panel with embellishment from the Sultan's palace.	INterior (Wall Decoration)	Static	Toy Store Purchase	Disney Decorations - Page 1
✓		Agrabah Palace Throne	The massive, gold elephant throne from the Sultan's palace.	INterior (Floor Decoration)	Static	Toy Store Purchase	Disney Decorations - Page 1
✓		Agrabah Palace Window	An Arabian, mullioned window ensconced between two marble pillars.	INterior (Wall Decoration)	Static	Toy Store Purchase	Disney Decorations - Page 1
✓		Belle's Bookshelf	Belle's bookshelf of her favorite books, from Beauty and the Beast.	INterior (Floor Decoration)	Static	Toy Store Purchase	Disney Decorations - Page 1
✓		Belle's Large Bookshelf	A large bookshelf from Beauty and the Beast.	INterior (Floor Decoration)	Static	Toy Store Purchase	Disney Decorations - Page 1
✓		Cave of Wonders Large Treasure	A large pile of forbidden treasure from the Cave of Wonders.	INterior (Floor Decoration)	Static	Toy Store Purchase	Disney Decorations - Page 1
✓		Cave of Wonders Statue	The cursed gem, held between the carved hands of the Cave of Wonders' monkey statue.	INterior (Floor Decoration)	Static	Toy Store Purchase	Disney Decorations - Page 1
✓		Cave of Wonders Treasure	A small pile of forbidden treasure from the Cave of Wonders.	INterior (Floor Decoration)	Static	Toy Store Purchase	Disney Decorations - Page 1
✓		Enchanted Rose	The enchanted rose from Beauty and the Beast.	INterior (Floor Decoration)	Static	Toy Store Purchase	Disney Decorations - Page 1
✓		Gaston's Chair	Gaston's antler-bedecked chair from the tavern in Beauty and the Beast.	INterior (Floor Decoration)	Static	Toy Store Purchase	Disney Decorations - Page 1
✓		Gaston's Portrait	Gaston's antler-bedecked, heroic portrait from Beauty and the Beast.	INterior (Wall Decoration)	Static	Feat Reward	Disney Decorations - Page 1
✓		Jafar's Hourglass	Give someone the time of day with this Arabian hourglass.	INterior (Floor Decoration)	Static	Toy Store Purchase	Disney Decorations - Page 1
✓		Jasmine's Footstool	Jasmine keeps this in her room for when she wants to put her feet up.	INterior (Floor Decoration)	Static	Toy Store Purchase	Disney Decorations - Page 1
✓		Jasmine's Settee	Jasmine's favorite Arabian lounge chair.	INterior (Floor Decoration)	Static	Toy Store Purchase	Disney Decorations - Page 1
✓		Jasmine's Vanity	Every princess needs a mirror like Jasmine's to get ready for the day.	INterior (Floor Decoration)	Static	Toy Store Purchase	Disney Decorations - Page 1
✓		Prince Eric Statue	Eric's fine-carved birthday present statue, from The Little Mermaid.	INterior (Floor Decoration)	Static	Toy Store Purchase	Disney Decorations - Page 1
✓		The Beast's Ballroom Sconce	A candle sconce decoration from the ballroom in Beauty and the Beast.	INterior (Wall Decoration)	Static	Toy Store Purchase	Disney Decorations - Page 1
✓		The Beast's Ballroom Window	A grand, mullioned ballroom window from Beauty and the Beast.	INterior (Wall Decoration)	Static	Toy Store Purchase	Disney Decorations - Page 1
✓		The Beast's Castle Window	The enchanted, stained glass window from Beauty and the Beast.	INterior (Wall Decoration)	Static	Toy Store Purchase	Disney Decorations - Page 1
✓		The Beast's Chair	The Beast's favorite chair from Beauty and the Beast.	INterior (Floor Decoration)	Static	Toy Store Purchase	Disney Decorations - Page 1
✓		The Beast's Fireplace	The castle fireplace from Beauty and the Beast.	INterior (Wall Decoration)	Static	Feat Reward	Disney Decorations - Page 1
✓		The Beast's Rug	A square rug with rose embroidery from Beauty and the Beast.	INterior (Floor Decoration)	Static	Toy Store Purchase	Disney Decorations - Page 1
✓		The Beast's Suit of Armor	A suit of armor from Beauty and the Beast.	INterior (Floor Decoration)	Static	Toy Store Purchase	Disney Decorations - Page 1
✓		The Great Stone Dragon	The Fa Family's ancestral dragon statue from Mulan.	INterior (Floor Decoration)	Static	Toy Store Purchase	Disney Decorations - Page 1
✓		The Magic Lamp	Genie's lamp, set on a rock pedestal.	INterior (Floor Decoration)	Static	Feat Reward	Disney Decorations - Page 1
✓		The Prince's Portrait	A torn and abandoned portrait of the prince from Beauty and the Beast.	INterior (Wall Decoration)	Static	Toy Store Purchase	Disney Decorations - Page 1
✓		Aurora's Birthday Cake	Briar Rose's 16th birthday cake, almost baked for her by Fauna.	INterior (Floor Decoration)	Static	Toy Store Purchase	Disney Decorations - Page 2
✓		Aurora's Cottage Chair	A small, wooden chair from the cottage in Sleeping Beauty.	INterior (Floor Decoration)	Static	Toy Store Purchase	Disney Decorations - Page 2

		Interior Decorations Continued				
GOT IT?	ICON	TOY NAME	DESCRIPTION	CATEGORY	FUNCTION	UNLOCK	TOY STORE PAGE
✔		Aurora's Cottage Chest	A chest from the cottage in Sleeping Beauty.	INterior (Floor Decoration)	Static	Toy Store Purchase	Disney Decorations - Page 2
✔		Aurora's Cottage Fireplace	A warm cottage fireplace from Sleeping Beauty.	INterior (Wall Decoration)	Static	Toy Store Purchase	Disney Decorations - Page 2
✔		Aurora's Cottage Log Chair	A small, log bench from the cottage in Sleeping Beauty.	INterior (Floor Decoration)	Static	Toy Store Purchase	Disney Decorations - Page 2
✔		Aurora's Cottage Rug	A fairy tale rug with floral designs, from the cottage in Sleeping Beauty.	INterior (Floor Decoration)	Static	Toy Store Purchase	Disney Decorations - Page 2
✔		Aurora's Cottage Seat	A charming little chair made from a tree stump, from the cottage in Sleeping Beauty.	INterior (Floor Decoration)	Static	Toy Store Purchase	Disney Decorations - Page 2
✔		Aurora's Cottage Shelf	A wooden shelf with pot and plate, from the cottage in Sleeping Beauty.	INterior (Wall Decoration)	Static	Toy Store Purchase	Disney Decorations - Page 2
✔		Aurora's Cottage Small Window	A carved, wooden window from the cottage in Sleeping Beauty.	INterior (Wall Decoration)	Static	Toy Store Purchase	Disney Decorations - Page 2
✔		Aurora's Cottage Window	The cottage window ensconced in tree branches, from Sleeping Beauty.	INterior (Wall Decoration)	Static	Toy Store Purchase	Disney Decorations - Page 2
✔		Cinderella Castle Carpet	An ornate, round rug with floral designs, from the castle in Cinderella.	INterior (Floor Decoration)	Static	Toy Store Purchase	Disney Decorations - Page 2
✔		Cinderella Castle Drapes	A wall-hanging drapery from Cinderella, excellent for dressing up a wall or hanging between rooms.	INterior (Wall Decoration)	Static	Toy Store Purchase	Disney Decorations - Page 2
✔		Cinderella Castle Fern	A smaller shrubbery accent from the castle gardens in Cinderella.	INterior (Floor Decoration)	Static	Feat Reward	Disney Decorations - Page 2
✔		Cinderella Castle Pillar	A draped, marble pillar from the castle in Cinderella.	INterior (Floor Decoration)	Static	Toy Store Purchase	Disney Decorations - Page 2
✔		Cinderella Castle Shrub	A beautiful perennial accent from the castle gardens in Cinderella.	INterior (Floor Decoration)	Static	Feat Reward	Disney Decorations - Page 2
✔		Cinderella Castle Window	A tall, mullioned window from Cinderella Castle, ensconced in marble pillars.	INterior (Wall Decoration)	Static	Toy Store Purchase	Disney Decorations - Page 2
✔		Cinderella's Pink Dress	Cinderella's mouse-made dress on display.	INterior (Floor Decoration)	Static	Feat Reward	Disney Decorations - Page 2
✔		Cinderella's Slipper	The glass slipper from Cinderella.	INterior (Floor Decoration)	Static	Feat Reward	Disney Decorations - Page 2
✔		Maleficent Couch	A dragon sofa and rug inspired by Sleeping Beauty, complementing any evil lair.	INterior (Floor Decoration)	Static	Toy Store Purchase	Disney Decorations - Page 2
✔		Maleficent's Spinning Wheel	The cursed spinning wheel from Sleeping Beauty.	INterior (Floor Decoration)	Static	Toy Store Purchase	Disney Decorations - Page 2
✔		Maleficent's Stone Raven	The stone raven, Diablo, from Maleficent's castle in the Forbidden Mountains.	INterior (Floor Decoration)	Static	Toy Store Purchase	Disney Decorations - Page 2
✔		Maleficent's Throne	Maleficent's raven-shaped throne, from her castle in the Forbidden Mountains.	INterior (Floor Decoration)	Static	Toy Store Purchase	Disney Decorations - Page 2
✔		Sleeping Beauty Corner Tree	A corner tree trunk from Sleeping Beauty.	INterior (Floor Decoration)	Static	Toy Store Purchase	Disney Decorations - Page 2
✔		Sleeping Beauty Tree	A tree trunk that will add a quaint forest feel to any room, from Sleeping Beauty.	INterior (Floor Decoration)	Static	Toy Store Purchase	Disney Decorations - Page 2
✔		Sleeping Beauty's Bed	Princess Aurora's Castle Bed.	INterior (Floor Decoration)	Static	Toy Store Purchase	Disney Decorations - Page 2
✔		Darling Nursery Chair	A comfortable place to sit in the nursery from Peter Pan.	INterior (Floor Decoration)	Static	Toy Store Purchase	Disney Decorations - Page 3
✔		Darling Nursery Dresser	A globe and dresser in the nursery from Peter Pan.	INterior (Floor Decoration)	Static	Toy Store Purchase	Disney Decorations - Page 3
✔		Darling Nursery Nightstand	The little nightstand in the nursery from Peter Pan.	INterior (Floor Decoration)	Static	Toy Store Purchase	Disney Decorations - Page 3
✔		Darling Nursery Pictures 1	An arrangement of pictures in the nursery from Peter Pan.	INterior (Wall Decoration)	Static	Toy Store Purchase	Disney Decorations - Page 3
✔		Darling Nursery Pictures 2	An arrangement of pictures in the nursery from Peter Pan.	INterior (Wall Decoration)	Static	Toy Store Purchase	Disney Decorations - Page 3
✔		Darling Nursery Pictures 3	An arrangement of pictures in the nursery from Peter Pan.	INterior (Wall Decoration)	Static	Toy Store Purchase	Disney Decorations - Page 3
✔		Darling Nursery Rug	A round blue rug in the nursery from Peter Pan.	INterior (Floor Decoration)	Static	Toy Store Purchase	Disney Decorations - Page 3

GAME BASICS

CHARACTERS

POWER DISCS

MARVEL'S THE AVENGERS

SPIDER-MAN

GUARDIANS OF THE GALAXY

TOY BOX

TOY BOX COLLECTION

ACHIEVEMENTS

			Interior Decorations Continued				
GOT IT?	ICON	TOY NAME	DESCRIPTION	CATEGORY	FUNCTION	UNLOCK	TOY STORE PAGE
✓		Darling Nursery Toy Chest	The toy chest in the nursery from Peter Pan.	INterior (Floor Decoration)	Static	Toy Store Purchase	Disney Decorations - Page 3
✓		Darling Nursery Toy Pile	A pile of toys in the nursery from Peter Pan.	INterior (Floor Decoration)	Static	Toy Store Purchase	Disney Decorations - Page 3
✓		Darling Nursery Wall Lamp	A wall lighting fixture in the nursery from Peter Pan.	INterior (Wall Decoration)	Static	Toy Store Purchase	Disney Decorations - Page 3
✓		Darling Nursery Window	The window and window seat in the nursery from Peter Pan.	INterior (Wall Decoration)	Static	Toy Store Purchase	Disney Decorations - Page 3
✓		Dwarf's Bed	A quilted bed from the cottage in Snow White and the Seven Dwarfs.	INterior (Floor Decoration)	Static	Toy Store Purchase	Disney Decorations - Page 3
✓		Dwarfs' Chair	A charming, carved chair from the cottage in Snow White and the Seven Dwarfs.	INterior (Floor Decoration)	Static	Toy Store Purchase	Disney Decorations - Page 3
✓		Dwarfs' Cottage Rug	A simple oval rug from the cottage in Snow White and the Seven Dwarfs.	INterior (Floor Decoration)	Static	Toy Store Purchase	Disney Decorations - Page 3
✓		Dwarfs' Cottage Window	A pleasant little window with carved jambs, from the cottage in Snow White and the Seven Dwarfs.	INterior (Wall Decoration)	Static	Toy Store Purchase	Disney Decorations - Page 3
✓		Dwarfs' Kitchen Table	A quaint table with settings, from the cottage in Snow White and the Seven Dwarfs.	INterior (Floor Decoration)	Static	Toy Store Purchase	Disney Decorations - Page 3
✓		Dwarfs' Large Cottage Window	A large, carved window from the cottage in Snow White and the Seven Dwarfs.	INterior (Wall Decoration)	Static	Toy Store Purchase	Disney Decorations - Page 3
✓		Dwarfs' Large Treasure	A larger piles of gems from the mines in Snow White and the Seven Dwarfs.	INterior (Floor Decoration)	Static	Toy Store Purchase	Disney Decorations - Page 3
✓		Dwarfs' Mine Cart	A mining cart with gems, from the dwarfs' mine in Snow White and the Seven Dwarfs.	INterior (Floor Decoration)	Static	Toy Store Purchase	Disney Decorations - Page 3
✓		Dwarfs' Pipe Organ	Make beautiful music with this carved musical instrument from the cottage in Snow White and the Seven Dwarfs.	INterior (Floor Decoration)	Static	Feat Reward	Disney Decorations - Page 3
✓		Dwarfs' Treasure	Dig for these gems from the mines in Snow White and the Seven Dwarfs.	INterior (Floor Decoration)	Static	Toy Store Purchase	Disney Decorations - Page 3
✓		Evil Queen's Cauldron	Trouble is brewing with the Evil Queen's dungeon cauldron.	INterior (Floor Decoration)	Static	Toy Store Purchase	Disney Decorations - Page 3
✓		Evil Queen's Pedestal	A pedestal featuring a basket of apples from Snow White and the Seven Dwarfs.	INterior (Floor Decoration)	Static	Toy Store Purchase	Disney Decorations - Page 3
✓		Hunter's Heart Box	The Evil Queen's dungeon shelf, showcasing her evil spell books, potions, and the hunter's heart box.	INterior (Floor Decoration)	Static	Toy Store Purchase	Disney Decorations - Page 3
✓		John Darling's Bed	John's ship-bedecked bed in the nursery from Peter Pan.	INterior (Floor Decoration)	Static	Toy Store Purchase	Disney Decorations - Page 3
✓		Magic Golden Flower	The magical, rejuvenating flower from Tangled.	INterior (Floor Decoration)	Static	Toy Store Purchase	Disney Decorations - Page 3
✓		Michael Darling's Bed	Michael's bed in the nursery from Peter Pan.	INterior (Floor Decoration)	Static	Toy Store Purchase	Disney Decorations - Page 3
✓		Neverland Map	Captain Hook's map from Peter Pan.	INterior (Wall Decoration)	Static	Toy Store Purchase	Disney Decorations - Page 3
✓		Rapunzel's Bed	Rapunzel's draped, four-poster bed, from her loft tower room.	INterior (Floor Decoration)	Static	Toy Store Purchase	Disney Decorations - Page 3
✓		Rapunzel's Flower Pots	Rapunzel's arrangement of potted foliage.	INterior (Floor Decoration)	Static	Toy Store Purchase	Disney Decorations - Page 3
✓		Rapunzel's Mirror	Rapunzel's mirror and stand from her tower room.	INterior (Floor Decoration)	Static	Toy Store Purchase	Disney Decorations - Page 3
✓		Rapunzel's Royal Banners	A string of pennants featuring the kingdom's symbol.	INterior (Wall Decoration)	Static	Toy Store Purchase	Disney Decorations - Page 3
✓		Rapunzel's Rug	Rapunzel's round rug featuring the kingdom's sun symbol.	INterior (Floor Decoration)	Static	Toy Store Purchase	Disney Decorations - Page 3
✓		Rapunzel's Tower Hearth	The painted fireplace from the tower in Tangled.	INterior (Wall Decoration)	Static	Toy Store Purchase	Disney Decorations - Page 3
✓		Rapunzel's Tower Window	The mullioned window from the tower in Tangled.	INterior (Wall Decoration)	Static	Toy Store Purchase	Disney Decorations - Page 3
✓		Rapunzel's Wardrobe	This lovely wardrobe from the tower in Tangled is good for storing paints or stowing miscreants.	INterior (Floor Decoration)	Static	Toy Store Purchase	Disney Decorations - Page 3

			Interior Decorations Continued				
GOT IT?	ICON	TOY NAME	DESCRIPTION	CATEGORY	FUNCTION	UNLOCK	TOY STORE PAGE
✓		Wendy Darling's Bed	Wendy's four-poster bed in the nursery from Peter Pan.	INterior (Floor Decoration)	Static	Toy Store Purchase	Disney Decorations - Page 3
✓		Wendy Darling's Nursery Rug	A round feminine rug in the nursery from Peter Pan.	INterior (Floor Decoration)	Static	Toy Store Purchase	Disney Decorations - Page 3
✓		Christmas Town Tree	The bedraggled Christmas tree from The Nightmare Before Christmas.	INterior (Floor Decoration)	Static	Toy Store Purchase	Disney Decorations - Page 4
✓		Game Grid Chair	An electronic-style chair inspired by Tron.	INterior (Floor Decoration)	Static	Toy Store Purchase	Disney Decorations - Page 4
✓		Game Grid Corner Counter	An electronic-style corner counter inspired by Tron.	INterior (Floor Decoration)	Static	Toy Store Purchase	Disney Decorations - Page 4
✓		Game Grid Couch	An electronic-style sofa inspired by Tron.	INterior (Floor Decoration)	Static	Toy Store Purchase	Disney Decorations - Page 4
✓		Game Grid Counter	An electronic-style counter inspired by Tron.	INterior (Floor Decoration)	Static	Toy Store Purchase	Disney Decorations - Page 4
✓		Game Grid Decorative Map	An electronic-style piece of fine art inspired by Tron.	INterior (Wall Decoration)	Static	Toy Store Purchase	Disney Decorations - Page 4
✓		Game Grid Floor Cover	An electronic-style rug inspired by Tron.	INterior (Floor Decoration)	Static	Toy Store Purchase	Disney Decorations - Page 4
✓		Game Grid Floor Lamp	An electronic-style floor lamp inspired by Tron.	INterior (Floor Decoration)	Static	Toy Store Purchase	Disney Decorations - Page 4
✓		Game Grid Fridge	An electronic-style refrigerator inspired by Tron.	INterior (Floor Decoration)	Static	Toy Store Purchase	Disney Decorations - Page 4
✓		Game Grid Identity Disc	An electronic-style wall hanging inspired by Tron.	INterior (Wall Decoration)	Static	Toy Store Purchase	Disney Decorations - Page 4
✓		Game Grid Table	An electronic-style table inspired by Tron.	INterior (Floor Decoration)	Static	Toy Store Purchase	Disney Decorations - Page 4
✓		Game Grid TV	An electronic-style television inspired by Tron.	INterior (Floor Decoration)	Static	Toy Store Purchase	Disney Decorations - Page 4
✓		Game Grid Window	An electronic-style window inspired by Tron.	INterior (Wall Decoration)	Static	Toy Store Purchase	Disney Decorations - Page 4
✓		Halloween Town Gargoyle Wreath	A festively decorated, stone gargoyle from The Nightmare Before Christmas.	INterior (Wall Decoration)	Static	Toy Store Purchase	Disney Decorations - Page 4
✓		Halloween Town Man-Eating Wreath	A hungry wreath from The Nightmare Before Christmas.	INterior (Wall Decoration)	Static	Toy Store Purchase	Disney Decorations - Page 4
✓		Halloween Town Snowflake	A spider snowflake from The Nightmare Before Christmas.	INterior (Wall Decoration)	Static	Toy Store Purchase	Disney Decorations - Page 4
✓		Jack Skellington's Bed	Jack Skellington's bed from The Nightmare Before Christmas.	INterior (Floor Decoration)	Static	Toy Store Purchase	Disney Decorations - Page 4
✓		Jack Skellington's Candelabra	A set of candlesticks from The Nightmare Before Christmas.	INterior (Floor Decoration)	Static	Toy Store Purchase	Disney Decorations - Page 4
✓		Jack Skellington's Chalkboard	A festooned chalkboard from The Nightmare Before Christmas.	INterior (Wall Decoration)	Static	Toy Store Purchase	Disney Decorations - Page 4
✓		Jack Skellington's Rug	A patchwork rug from The Nightmare Before Christmas.	INterior (Floor Decoration)	Static	Toy Store Purchase	Disney Decorations - Page 4
✓		Jack Skellington's Window	A dark, shrouded window from The Nightmare Before Christmas.	INterior (Wall Decoration)	Static	Toy Store Purchase	Disney Decorations - Page 4
✓		Jack's Sandy Claws Portrait	Jack Skellington's Sandy Claws portrait from The Nightmare Before Christmas.	INterior (Wall Decoration)	Static	Toy Store Purchase	Disney Decorations - Page 4
✓		Lock, Shock, and Barrel's Tub	A clawed-foot bathtub from The Nightmare Before Christmas.	INterior (Floor Decoration)	Static	Toy Store Purchase	Disney Decorations - Page 4
✓		Sandy Claws Fireplace	A black brick fireplace from The Nightmare Before Christmas.	INterior (Wall Decoration)	Static	Toy Store Purchase	Disney Decorations - Page 4
✓		Snake Christmas Tree	A festive decoration from The Nightmare Before Christmas.	INterior (Floor Decoration)	Static	Toy Store Purchase	Disney Decorations - Page 4
✓		Tron Arcade Game	The arcade game cabinet from Tron.	INterior (Floor Decoration)	Static	Toy Store Purchase	Disney Decorations - Page 4
✓		Adventureland Tiki Masks	A piece of furniture inspired by Disney Parks' Enchanted Tiki Room.	INterior (Floor Decoration)	Static	Toy Store Purchase	Disney Decorations - Page 5
✓		Dr. Facilier's Voodoo Table	An assortment of Voodoo charms and curse tokens belonging to Dr. Facilier, from The Princess and the Frog.	INterior (Floor Decoration)	Static	Toy Store Purchase	Disney Decorations - Page 5
✓		Fix-It Felix Jr. Arcade Game	The standing arcade cabinet of Fix-It Felix, from Wreck-It Ralph.	INterior (Floor Decoration)	Static	Toy Store Purchase	Disney Decorations - Page 5

GAME BASICS
CHARACTERS
POWER DISCS
MARVEL'S THE AVENGERS
SPIDER-MAN
GUARDIANS OF THE GALAXY
TOY BOX
TOY BOX COLLECTION
ACHIEVEMENTS

Interior Decorations Continued

GOT IT?	ICON	TOY NAME	DESCRIPTION	CATEGORY	FUNCTION	UNLOCK	TOY STORE PAGE
✓		Hawaiian Surfboards	A tropical decoration from Lilo and Stitch.	INterior (Wall Decoration)	Static	Toy Store Purchase	Disney Decorations - Page 5
✓		Hercules Star Chart	A framed picture of Hercules, written in the stars.	INterior (Wall Decoration)	Static	Toy Store Purchase	Disney Decorations - Page 5
✓		Hero's Duty Arcade Game	The arcade game cabinet of Hero's Duty, from Wreck-It Ralph.	INterior (Floor Decoration)	Static	Feat Reward	Disney Decorations - Page 5
✓		Honeypots	A delicious pot full of honey for Winnie the Pooh.	INterior (Floor Decoration)	Static	Toy Store Purchase	Disney Decorations - Page 5
✓		King Louie's Throne	A jungle-themed royal seat.	INterior (Floor Decoration)	Static	Toy Store Purchase	Disney Decorations - Page 5
✓		Lilo's Hammock	A tropical place to rest from Lilo and Stitch.	INterior (Floor Decoration)	Static	Toy Store Purchase	Disney Decorations - Page 5
✓		Lilo's Wagon	A wagon full of toys and Elvis records from Lilo and Stitch.	INterior (Floor Decoration)	Static	Toy Store Purchase	Disney Decorations - Page 5
✓		Mama Odie's Gumbo Cauldron	Mama Odie's cauldron full of steamin' hot gumbo, from The Princess and the Frog.	INterior (Floor Decoration)	Static	Toy Store Purchase	Disney Decorations - Page 5
✓		Mickey Mouse Club Sign	A vintage wall hanging for the true Disney aficionado.	INterior (Wall Decoration)	Static	Toy Store Purchase	Disney Decorations - Page 5
✓		Pooh-Coo Clock	Winnie the Pooh's cuckoo clock.	INterior (Wall Decoration)	Static	Toy Store Purchase	Disney Decorations - Page 5
✓		Scrooge McDuck's Money Pile	Scrooge McDuck's pile of hard-earned gold coins.	INterior (Floor Decoration)	Static	Feat Reward	Disney Decorations - Page 5
✓		Small World Arched Window	A piece of furniture inspired by Disney Parks' it's a small world Attraction.	INterior (Wall Decoration)	Static	Toy Store Purchase	Disney Decorations - Page 5
✓		Small World Bed	A piece of furniture inspired by Disney Parks' it's a small world Attraction.	INterior (Floor Decoration)	Static	Toy Store Purchase	Disney Decorations - Page 5
✓		Small World Chair	A piece of furniture inspired by Disney Parks' it's a small world Attraction.	INterior (Floor Decoration)	Static	Toy Store Purchase	Disney Decorations - Page 5
✓		Small World Clock	The happy clock face from Disney Parks' it's a small world Attraction.	INterior (Wall Decoration)	Static	Toy Store Purchase	Disney Decorations - Page 5
✓		Small World Fireplace	A piece of furniture inspired by Disney Parks' it's a small world Attraction.	INterior (Wall Decoration)	Static	Toy Store Purchase	Disney Decorations - Page 5
✓		Small World Mask	A piece of furniture inspired by Disney Parks' it's a small world Attraction.	INterior (Wall Decoration)	Static	Toy Store Purchase	Disney Decorations - Page 5
✓		Small World Nightstand	A piece of furniture inspired by Disney Parks' it's a small world Attraction.	INterior (Floor Decoration)	Static	Toy Store Purchase	Disney Decorations - Page 5
✓		Small World Plant	A piece of furniture inspired by Disney Parks' it's a small world Attraction.	INterior (Floor Decoration)	Static	Toy Store Purchase	Disney Decorations - Page 5
✓		Small World Rug	A piece of furniture inspired by Disney Parks' it's a small world Attraction.	INterior (Floor Decoration)	Static	Toy Store Purchase	Disney Decorations - Page 5
✓		Small World Sofa	A piece of furniture inspired by Disney Parks' it's a small world Attraction.	INterior (Floor Decoration)	Static	Toy Store Purchase	Disney Decorations - Page 5
✓		Small World Table	A piece of furniture inspired by Disney Parks' it's a small world Attraction.	INterior (Floor Decoration)	Static	Toy Store Purchase	Disney Decorations - Page 5
✓		Small World Window	A piece of furniture inspired by Disney Parks' it's a small world Attraction.	INterior (Wall Decoration)	Static	Toy Store Purchase	Disney Decorations - Page 5
✓		Stitch's Sand Castle	A sandy piece of décor from Lilo and Stitch.	INterior (Floor Decoration)	Static	Toy Store Purchase	Disney Decorations - Page 5
✓		Sugar Rush Arcade Game	The racing arcade cabinet of Sugar Rush, from Wreck-It Ralph.	INterior (Floor Decoration)	Static	Toy Store Purchase	Disney Decorations - Page 5
✓		The Devil's Eye	The bayou pirate's treasure hidden in a skull, from The Rescuers.	INterior (Floor Decoration)	Static	Toy Store Purchase	Disney Decorations - Page 5
✓		The Golden Harp	Happy Valley's singing harp from Mickey and the Beanstalk.	INterior (Floor Decoration)	Static	Toy Store Purchase	Disney Decorations - Page 5
✓		Tiki Head Table	A small Tiki table from Lilo and Stitch.	INterior (Floor Decoration)	Static	Toy Store Purchase	Disney Decorations - Page 5
✓		Tiki Room Birds	A piece of furniture inspired by Disney Parks' Enchanted Tiki Room.	INterior (Floor Decoration)	Static	Toy Store Purchase	Disney Decorations - Page 5
✓		Tiki Torches	A tropical-style lamp from Lilo and Stitch.	INterior (Floor Decoration)	Static	Toy Store Purchase	Disney Decorations - Page 5
✓		Toad Hall Portrait	A painting of Mr. Toad from The Wind in the Willows.	INterior (Wall Decoration)	Static	Toy Store Purchase	Disney Decorations - Page 5

GOT IT?	ICON	TOY NAME	DESCRIPTION	CATEGORY	FUNCTION	UNLOCK	TOY STORE PAGE
			Interior Decorations Continued				
✓		Tony's Restaurant Dinner Table	A table set with Tony's specialty: spaghetti and meatballs, from Lady and the Tramp.	INterior (Floor Decoration)	Static	Toy Store Purchase	Disney Decorations - Page 5
✓		Tropical Table	A tropical table from Lilo and Stitch.	INterior (Floor Decoration)	Static	Toy Store Purchase	Disney Decorations - Page 5
✓		Avengers Logo	An Avengers-themed furniture piece.	INterior (Wall Decoration)	Static	Toy Store Purchase	Marvel Decorations - Page 1
✓		Avengers Tower Monitor	A tech furniture piece from Avengers Tower.	INterior (Wall Decoration)	Static	Toy Store Purchase	Marvel Decorations - Page 1
✓		Avengers Tower Pillar	An Avengers-themed furniture piece.	INterior (Floor Decoration)	Static	Toy Store Purchase	Marvel Decorations - Page 1
✓		Captain America Couch	A piece of furniture from Captain America.	INterior (Floor Decoration)	Static	Toy Store Purchase	Marvel Decorations - Page 1
✓		Captain America Poster	A Captain America-themed poster.	INterior (Wall Decoration)	Static	Toy Store Purchase	Marvel Decorations - Page 1
✓		Captain America Rug	A Captain America-themed rug.	INterior (Floor Decoration)	Static	Toy Store Purchase	Marvel Decorations - Page 1
✓		Captain America Table	A piece of furniture from Captain America.	INterior (Floor Decoration)	Static	Toy Store Purchase	Marvel Decorations - Page 1
✓		Captain America Wall Shield	A Captain America-themed wall hanging.	INterior (Wall Decoration)	Static	Toy Store Purchase	Marvel Decorations - Page 1
✓		Captain America Window	A Captain America-themed window.	INterior (Wall Decoration)	Static	Toy Store Purchase	Marvel Decorations - Page 1
✓		Captain America's Shield	A piece of furniture from Captain America.	INterior (Wall Decoration)	Static	Toy Store Purchase	Marvel Decorations - Page 1
✓		Command Chair	An Avengers-themed furniture piece.	INterior (Floor Decoration)	Static	Toy Store Purchase	Marvel Decorations - Page 1
✓		Command Console	An Avengers-themed furniture piece.	INterior (Floor Decoration)	Static	Toy Store Purchase	Marvel Decorations - Page 1
✓		Command Desk	An Avengers-themed furniture piece.	INterior (Floor Decoration)	Static	Toy Store Purchase	Marvel Decorations - Page 1
✓		Computer Console	An Avengers-themed furniture piece.	INterior (Floor Decoration)	Static	Toy Store Purchase	Marvel Decorations - Page 1
✓		Earth Hologram	The Avengers' aircraft piece of furniture.	INterior (Floor Decoration)	Static	Feat Reward	Marvel Decorations - Page 1
✓		Hail Hydra!	A Hydra flag from Captain America.	INterior (Wall Decoration)	Static	Toy Store Purchase	Marvel Decorations - Page 1
✓		Helicarrier Computer	The Avengers' aircraft industrial-style computer.	INterior (Floor Decoration)	Static	Toy Store Purchase	Marvel Decorations - Page 1
✓		Helicarrier Consoles	The Avengers' aircraft industrial-style piece of furniture.	INterior (Floor Decoration)	Static	Feat Reward	Marvel Decorations - Page 1
✓		Helicarrier Pillar	The Avengers' aircraft industrial-style piece of furniture.	INterior (Floor Decoration)	Static	Toy Store Purchase	Marvel Decorations - Page 1
✓		Helicarrier Table	The Avengers' aircraft industrial-style table.	INterior (Floor Decoration)	Static	Toy Store Purchase	Marvel Decorations - Page 1
✓		Helicarrier Window	The Avengers' aircraft industrial-style window.	INterior (Wall Decoration)	Static	Toy Store Purchase	Marvel Decorations - Page 1
✓		JARVIS Console	An Avengers-themed furniture piece.	INterior (Floor Decoration)	Static	Toy Store Purchase	Marvel Decorations - Page 1
✓		Loki's Staff	The Avengers' aircraft Chitauri Scepter furniture piece.	INterior (Floor Decoration)	Static	Feat Reward	Marvel Decorations - Page 1
✓		Power Center	An Avengers-themed furniture piece.	INterior (Floor Decoration)	Static	Toy Store Purchase	Marvel Decorations - Page 1
✓		S.H.I.E.L.D. Logo	The Avengers' aircraft industrial-style wall hanging.	INterior (Wall Decoration)	Static	Toy Store Purchase	Marvel Decorations - Page 1
✓		S.H.I.E.L.D. Wall Panel	A decorative Avengers-themed wall hanging.	INterior (Wall Decoration)	Static	Toy Store Purchase	Marvel Decorations - Page 1
✓		Shawarma	A table of delicious food from The Avengers.	INterior (Floor Decoration)	Static	Feat Reward	Marvel Decorations - Page 1
✓		Steve Rogers' Army Cot	A piece of furniture from Captain America.	INterior (Floor Decoration)	Static	Toy Store Purchase	Marvel Decorations - Page 1
✓		Steve Rogers' Punching Bag	A piece of furniture from Captain America.	INterior (Floor Decoration)	Static	Toy Store Purchase	Marvel Decorations - Page 1

GAME BASICS

CHARACTERS

POWER DISCS

MARVEL'S THE AVENGERS

SPIDER-MAN

GUARDIANS OF THE GALAXY

TOY BOX

TOY BOX COLLECTION

ACHIEVEMENTS

			Interior Decorations Continued				
GOT IT?	ICON	TOY NAME	DESCRIPTION	CATEGORY	FUNCTION	UNLOCK	TOY STORE PAGE
✓		Super Soldier Serum	A piece of furniture from Captain America.	INterior (Floor Decoration)	Static	Toy Store Purchase	Marvel Decorations - Page 1
✓		Arc Reactor Decorations	A piece of furniture from Iron Man.	INterior (Wall Decoration)	Static	Toy Store Purchase	Marvel Decorations - Page 2
✓		Captain America Shield Clock	A piece of furniture from Iron Man.	INterior (Wall Decoration)	Static	Toy Store Purchase	Marvel Decorations - Page 2
✓		Crushed Construction Cones	A pile of Hulk-smashed traffic equipment to add to your décor.	INterior (Floor Decoration)	Static	Toy Store Purchase	Marvel Decorations - Page 2
✓		Dark Aster Rug	A Guardians of the Galaxy-themed piece of décor.	INterior (Floor Decoration)	Static	Toy Store Purchase	Marvel Decorations - Page 2
✓		Giant Bunny	A piece of furniture from Iron Man.	INterior (Floor Decoration)	Static	Toy Store Purchase	Marvel Decorations - Page 2
✓		Hulk Bed	A Hulk-inspired piece of furniture.	INterior (Floor Decoration)	Static	Toy Store Purchase	Marvel Decorations - Page 2
✓		Hulk Coffee Table	A Hulk-inspired piece of furniture.	INterior (Floor Decoration)	Static	Toy Store Purchase	Marvel Decorations - Page 2
✓		Hulk Couch	A Hulk-inspired sofa.	INterior (Floor Decoration)	Static	Toy Store Purchase	Marvel Decorations - Page 2
✓		Hulk Damage	A Hulk-inspired wall and floor decoration.	INterior (Wall Decoration)	Static	Toy Store Purchase	Marvel Decorations - Page 2
✓		Hulk Lamp	A Hulk-inspired piece of light fixture.	INterior (Floor Decoration)	Static	Toy Store Purchase	Marvel Decorations - Page 2
✓		Hulk Rug	A Hulk-inspired piece of furniture.	INterior (Floor Decoration)	Static	Toy Store Purchase	Marvel Decorations - Page 2
✓		Hulk Stop Sign	A Hulk-inspired piece of furniture.	INterior (Wall Decoration)	Static	Toy Store Purchase	Marvel Decorations - Page 2
✓		Hulk Window	A Hulk-inspired window.	INterior (Wall Decoration)	Static	Toy Store Purchase	Marvel Decorations - Page 2
✓		Iron Man Armored Sofa	A piece of furniture from Iron Man.	INterior (Floor Decoration)	Static	Toy Store Purchase	Marvel Decorations - Page 2
✓		Iron Man Rug	A piece of furniture from Iron Man.	INterior (Floor Decoration)	Static	Toy Store Purchase	Marvel Decorations - Page 2
✓		Iron Man Suit: Mark 1	A wardrobe featuring one of Iron Man's suits.	INterior (Floor Decoration)	Static	Toy Store Purchase	Marvel Decorations - Page 2
✓		Iron Man Suit: Mark 7	A wardrobe featuring one of Iron Man's suits.	INterior (Floor Decoration)	Static	Toy Store Purchase	Marvel Decorations - Page 2
✓		Iron Man Window	A piece of furniture from Iron Man.	INterior (Wall Decoration)	Static	Toy Store Purchase	Marvel Decorations - Page 2
✓		Knowhere Shrub	A Guardians of the Galaxy-themed piece of furniture.	INterior (Floor Decoration)	Static	Feat Reward	Marvel Decorations - Page 2
✓		Peter Quill's Audio Player	A Guardians of the Galaxy-themed piece of nostalgic décor.	INterior (Floor Decoration)	Static	Feat Reward	Marvel Decorations - Page 2
✓		Star-Lord Air Vents	A Guardians of the Galaxy-themed piece of décor.	INterior (Wall Decoration)	Static	Toy Store Purchase	Marvel Decorations - Page 2
✓		Star-Lord Bioscanner	A Guardians of the Galaxy-themed piece of décor.	INterior (Floor Decoration)	Static	Toy Store Purchase	Marvel Decorations - Page 2
✓		Star-Lord Blue Sign	A Guardians of the Galaxy-themed piece of décor.	INterior (Wall Decoration)	Static	Toy Store Purchase	Marvel Decorations - Page 2
✓		Star-Lord Brazier	A Guardians of the Galaxy-themed piece of décor.	INterior (Floor Decoration)	Static	Toy Store Purchase	Marvel Decorations - Page 2
✓		Star-Lord Cyan Sign	A Guardians of the Galaxy-themed piece of décor.	INterior (Wall Decoration)	Static	Toy Store Purchase	Marvel Decorations - Page 2
✓		Star-Lord Fan	A Guardians of the Galaxy-themed piece of décor.	INterior (Wall Decoration)	Static	Toy Store Purchase	Marvel Decorations - Page 2
✓		Star-Lord Fine Art	A Guardians of the Galaxy-themed piece of décor.	INterior (Floor Decoration)	Static	Toy Store Purchase	Marvel Decorations - Page 2
✓		Star-Lord Light	A Guardians of the Galaxy-themed piece of décor.	INterior (Wall Decoration)	Static	Toy Store Purchase	Marvel Decorations - Page 2
✓		Star-Lord Light Pillar	A Guardians of the Galaxy-themed piece of décor.	INterior (Floor Decoration)	Static	Toy Store Purchase	Marvel Decorations - Page 2
✓		Star-Lord Purple Sign	A Guardians of the Galaxy-themed piece of décor.	INterior (Wall Decoration)	Static	Toy Store Purchase	Marvel Decorations - Page 2

			Interior Decorations Continued				
GOT IT?	ICON	TOY NAME	DESCRIPTION	CATEGORY	FUNCTION	UNLOCK	TOY STORE PAGE
✓		Star-Lord Security Camera	A Guardians of the Galaxy-themed piece of décor.	INterior (Wall Decoration)	Static	Toy Store Purchase	Marvel Decorations - Page 2
✓		Star-Lord Wall Canister	A Guardians of the Galaxy-themed piece of décor.	INterior (Wall Decoration)	Static	Toy Store Purchase	Marvel Decorations - Page 2
✓		Star-Lord Wall Piece	A Guardians of the Galaxy-themed piece of décor.	INterior (Wall Decoration)	Static	Toy Store Purchase	Marvel Decorations - Page 2
✓		Daily Bugle Billboard	A Spider-Man-themed piece of furniture.	INterior (Wall Decoration)	Static	Toy Store Purchase	Marvel Decorations - Page 3
✓		J. Jonah Jameson Ranting TV	A Spider-Man-themed piece of furniture.	INterior (Floor Decoration)	Static	Feat Reward	Marvel Decorations - Page 3
✓		Laboratory Canister	A Spider-Man-themed piece of furniture.	INterior (Floor Decoration)	Static	Toy Store Purchase	Marvel Decorations - Page 3
✓		Laboratory Chair	A Spider-Man-themed piece of furniture.	INterior (Floor Decoration)	Static	Toy Store Purchase	Marvel Decorations - Page 3
✓		Laboratory Command Center A	A Spider-Man-themed piece of furniture.	INterior (Floor Decoration)	Static	Toy Store Purchase	Marvel Decorations - Page 3
✓		Laboratory Command Center B	A Spider-Man-themed piece of furniture.	INterior (Floor Decoration)	Static	Toy Store Purchase	Marvel Decorations - Page 3
✓		Laboratory Cryo Tube	A Spider-Man-themed piece of furniture.	INterior (Floor Decoration)	Static	Toy Store Purchase	Marvel Decorations - Page 3
✓		Laboratory Curved Command Center	A Spider-Man-themed piece of furniture.	INterior (Floor Decoration)	Static	Toy Store Purchase	Marvel Decorations - Page 3
✓		Laboratory Security Center A	A Spider-Man-themed piece of furniture.	INterior (Floor Decoration)	Static	Toy Store Purchase	Marvel Decorations - Page 3
✓		Laboratory Security Center B	A Spider-Man-themed piece of furniture.	INterior (Floor Decoration)	Static	Toy Store Purchase	Marvel Decorations - Page 3
✓		Laboratory Security Center C	A Spider-Man-themed piece of furniture.	INterior (Floor Decoration)	Static	Toy Store Purchase	Marvel Decorations - Page 3
✓		Laboratory Stool	A Spider-Man-themed piece of furniture.	INterior (Floor Decoration)	Static	Toy Store Purchase	Marvel Decorations - Page 3
✓		Large Laboratory Canister	A Spider-Man-themed piece of furniture.	INterior (Floor Decoration)	Static	Toy Store Purchase	Marvel Decorations - Page 3
✓		Large Oscorp Desk	A Spider-Man-themed piece of furniture.	INterior (Floor Decoration)	Static	Toy Store Purchase	Marvel Decorations - Page 3
✓		Medium Oscorp Desk	A Spider-Man-themed piece of furniture.	INterior (Floor Decoration)	Static	Toy Store Purchase	Marvel Decorations - Page 3
✓		Newspaper Coffee Table	A Spider-Man-themed piece of furniture.	INterior (Floor Decoration)	Static	Toy Store Purchase	Marvel Decorations - Page 3
✓		Oscorp Work Area	A Spider-Man-themed piece of furniture.	INterior (Floor Decoration)	Static	Toy Store Purchase	Marvel Decorations - Page 3
✓		Radioactive Spider Nightstand	A Spider-Man-themed piece of furniture.	INterior (Floor Decoration)	Static	Feat Reward	Marvel Decorations - Page 3
✓		Small Laboratory Canisters	A Spider-Man-themed piece of furniture.	INterior (Floor Decoration)	Static	Toy Store Purchase	Marvel Decorations - Page 3
✓		Small Oscorp Desk	A Spider-Man-themed piece of furniture.	INterior (Floor Decoration)	Static	Toy Store Purchase	Marvel Decorations - Page 3
✓		Spider-Man Bean Bag	A Spider-Man-themed piece of furniture.	INterior (Floor Decoration)	Static	Toy Store Purchase	Marvel Decorations - Page 3
✓		Spider-Man Bed	A Spider-Man-themed piece of furniture.	INterior (Floor Decoration)	Static	Toy Store Purchase	Marvel Decorations - Page 3
✓		Spider-Man No More	A Spider-Man-themed piece of furniture.	INterior (Floor Decoration)	Static	Toy Store Purchase	Marvel Decorations - Page 3
✓		Spider-Man Rug	A Spider-Man-themed piece of furniture.	INterior (Floor Decoration)	Static	Toy Store Purchase	Marvel Decorations - Page 3
✓		Spider-Man Window	A Spider-Man-themed piece of furniture.	INterior (Wall Decoration)	Static	Toy Store Purchase	Marvel Decorations - Page 3
✓		Spidey's Front Page News	A Spider-Man-themed piece of furniture.	INterior (Wall Decoration)	Static	Toy Store Purchase	Marvel Decorations - Page 3
✓		The Spider's Web	A Spider-Man-themed piece of furniture.	INterior (Wall Decoration)	Static	Toy Store Purchase	Marvel Decorations - Page 3
✓		Venom Chair	A Spider-Man-themed piece of furniture.	INterior (Floor Decoration)	Static	Feat Reward	Marvel Decorations - Page 3

Interior Decorations Continued

GOT IT?	ICON	TOY NAME	DESCRIPTION	CATEGORY	FUNCTION	UNLOCK	TOY STORE PAGE
✓		Ant-Man's Helmet	Ant-Man's protective head covering.	INterior (Floor Decoration)	Static	Toy Store Purchase	Marvel Decorations - Page 4
✓		Asgard Torch Lamp	An Asgardian piece of furniture.	INterior (Floor Decoration)	Static	Toy Store Purchase	Marvel Decorations - Page 4
✓		Book of the Vishanti	Doctor Strange's white magic grimoire.	INterior (Floor Decoration)	Static	Toy Store Purchase	Marvel Decorations - Page 4
✓		Casket of Ancient Winters	An Asgardian piece of furniture.	INterior (Floor Decoration)	Static	Toy Store Purchase	Marvel Decorations - Page 4
✓		Doctor Strange's Sanctum Window	An oculus window from The Avengers.	INterior (Wall Decoration)	Static	Toy Store Purchase	Marvel Decorations - Page 4
✓		Elektra's Sai	An Elektra-themed wall hanging with sai crossed.	INterior (Wall Decoration)	Static	Toy Store Purchase	Marvel Decorations - Page 4
✓		Eye of Agamotto	A mystical piece of furniture from Doctor Strange's collection.	INterior (Floor Decoration)	Static	Feat Reward	Marvel Decorations - Page 4
✓		Frog Thor Statue	A statue of a frog-shaped Thor.	INterior (Floor Decoration)	Static	Toy Store Purchase	Marvel Decorations - Page 4
✓		Ghost Rider Fireplace	A black industrial-style fireplace.	INterior (Wall Decoration)	Static	Toy Store Purchase	Marvel Decorations - Page 4
✓		Ghost Rider Medallion	A Ghost Rider wall hanging.	INterior (Wall Decoration)	Static	Toy Store Purchase	Marvel Decorations - Page 4
✓		Infinity Gauntlet	A Guardians of the Galaxy-themed piece of furniture.	INterior (Floor Decoration)	Static	Feat Reward	Marvel Decorations - Page 4
✓		Odin's Bed	An Asgardian piece of furniture.	INterior (Floor Decoration)	Static	Assault on Asgard Reward	Marvel Decorations - Page 4
✓		Stormbreaker	Beta Ray Bill's Hammer.	INterior (Floor Decoration)	Static	Toy Store Purchase	Marvel Decorations - Page 4
✓		The Darkhold	An excellent furniture piece featuring a tome written by Chthon.	INterior (Floor Decoration)	Static	Toy Store Purchase	Marvel Decorations - Page 4
✓		The Tesseract	A cosmic cube furniture piece from the Avengers.	INterior (Floor Decoration)	Static	Feat Reward	Marvel Decorations - Page 4
✓		Throne of Thanos	A futuristic throne from Guardians of the Galaxy.	INterior (Floor Decoration)	Static	Toy Store Purchase	Marvel Decorations - Page 4
✓		Andy's Bed	Andy's Buzz Lightyear bed from Toy Story.	INterior (Floor Decoration)	Static	Feat Reward	Pixar Decorations
✓		Andy's Rug	Andy's oval rug from Toy Story.	INterior (Floor Decoration)	Static	Toy Store Purchase	Pixar Decorations
✓		Andy's Toy Chest	Andy's covered wagon toy chest from Toy Story.	INterior (Floor Decoration)	Static	Toy Store Purchase	Pixar Decorations
✓		Andy's Window	Andy's bedroom window from Toy Story.	INterior (Wall Decoration)	Static	Toy Store Purchase	Pixar Decorations
✓		Buy 'n' Large Poster	A wall hanging from WALL-E.	INterior (Wall Decoration)	Static	Toy Store Purchase	Pixar Decorations
✓		Clan DunBroch Tapestry	Merida's family tapestry from Brave.	INterior (Wall Decoration)	Static	Toy Store Purchase	Pixar Decorations
✓		M.U. Fraternity Pennants	A Monster University pennant from Monsters University.	INterior (Wall Decoration)	Static	Toy Store Purchase	Pixar Decorations
✓		M.U. Refrigerator	A monster-style refrigerator from Monsters University.	INterior (Floor Decoration)	Static	Toy Store Purchase	Pixar Decorations
✓		M.U. Sofa	A stylish, purple sofa from Monsters University.	INterior (Floor Decoration)	Static	Toy Store Purchase	Pixar Decorations
✓		Monsters, Inc. Door Station	A Scare Floor door station from Monsters, Inc.	INterior (Floor Decoration)	Static	Feat Reward	Pixar Decorations
✓		Space Crane Game	A Claw Game from Toy Story's Pizza Planet.	INterior (Floor Decoration)	Static	Toy Store Purchase	Pixar Decorations
✓		WALL-E Cube Sprout	A sprouting cube of compacted trash from WALL-E.	INterior (Floor Decoration)	Static	Toy Store Purchase	Pixar Decorations
✓		WALL-E Garbage Cube	A block of compacted trash from WALL-E.	INterior (Floor Decoration)	Static	Toy Store Purchase	Pixar Decorations

STARTING TOYS

GOT IT?	ICON	TOY NAME	DESCRIPTION	CATEGORY	FUNCTION	UNLOCK	TOY STORE PAGE
✓		Agrabah Guard	The Sultan's guard from Aladdin.	Enemies	Enemy	Starting Toy	Starting Toys - Page 1
✓		Attack Copter	Take to the skies in this combat-ready copter!	Vehicles and Mounts	Air Vehicle	Starting Toy	Starting Toys - Page 1
✓		Autopia Car (blue)	The attraction vehicle from Disney Parks' Autopia	Vehicles and Mounts	Vehicle	Starting Toy	Starting Toys - Page 1
✓		Beach Ball	A beach ball from Disney Infinity.	Instant Fun	Physics Ball	Starting Toy	Starting Toys - Page 1
✓		Bluff	A section of terrain with a grassy ramp.	Terrain	Static	Starting Toy	Starting Toys - Page 1
✓		Capsule Creator	When this beacon is activated, breakable objects will be randomly placed in your Toy Box from time to time.	Instant Fun	Custom	Starting Toy	Starting Toys - Page 1
✓		Cinderella Castle	The iconic symbol of Walt Disney World's Magic Kingdom park.	Set Pieces	Static	Starting Toy	Starting Toys - Page 1
✓		Corner Block with Ramps	A section of terrain that includes switchback ramps.	Terrain	Static	Starting Toy	Starting Toys - Page 1
✓		Crate	A breakable object from Disney Infinity.	Decorations	Breakable	Starting Toy	Starting Toys - Page 1
✓		Disney Infinity Spruce Tree	A Disney Infinity tree.	Plants	Breakable	Starting Toy	Starting Toys - Page 1
✓		Enemy Creator	When this beacon is activated, enemies will be randomly introduced into your Toy Box from time to time.	Instant Fun	Custom	Starting Toy	Starting Toys - Page 1
✓		Floating Rope Cliff	A floating cliff with a rope for climbing.	Terrain	Static	Starting Toy	Starting Toys - Page 1
✓		Floating Waterfall	A jutting section of terrain with a small waterfall pouring over the side.	Terrain	Static	Starting Toy	Starting Toys - Page 1
✓		Frog	A woodland critter from Disney Infinity.	Critters	Critter	Starting Toy	Starting Toys - Page 1
✓		Lamp Post	Fantasy landscape from Disney Infinity.	Decorations	Static	Starting Toy	Starting Toys - Page 1
✓		Large Corner Hill	A section of terrain that is raised in one corner.	Terrain	Static	Starting Toy	Starting Toys - Page 1
✓		Large Corner Slope	A section of terrain that sinks in one corner.	Terrain	Static	Starting Toy	Starting Toys - Page 1
✓		Large Rounded Cliff	A section of rounded cliff terrain.	Terrain	Static	Starting Toy	Starting Toys - Page 1
✓		Large Terrain Block	A large, square terrain block.	Terrain	Static	Starting Toy	Starting Toys - Page 1
✓		Log	Paul Bunyan aficionados will love this log!	Decorations	Static	Starting Toy	Starting Toys - Page 1
✓		Massive Rounded Cliff	A section of rounded cliff terrain.	Terrain	Static	Starting Toy	Starting Toys - Page 1
✓		Narrow Floating Cliff	An outer edge of terrain.	Terrain	Static	Starting Toy	Starting Toys - Page 1
✓		Pond	A section of terrain that includes a pond.	Terrain	Static	Starting Toy	Starting Toys - Page 1
✓		Rhino Guard	Prince John's henchman from Robin Hood.	Enemies	Enemy	Starting Toy	Starting Toys - Page 1
✓		River	A section of terrain that includes a river.	Terrain	Static	Starting Toy	Starting Toys - Page 1
✓		River Gazebo	A gazebo surrounded by a flowing river.	Terrain	Static	Starting Toy	Starting Toys - Page 1
✓		Rocky Layered Block	A section of rocky terrain for climbing.	Terrain	Static	Starting Toy	Starting Toys - Page 1
✓		Rocky Terrain Block	A section of rocky terrain for climbing.	Terrain	Static	Starting Toy	Starting Toys - Page 1
✓		Sky Changer	Change your sky with a mere push of a button.	Instant Fun	Custom	Starting Toy	Starting Toys - Page 1
✓		Slope	A section of terrain that includes a large slope.	Terrain	Static	Starting Toy	Starting Toys - Page 1

GAME BASICS

CHARACTERS

POWER DISCS

MARVEL'S THE AVENGERS

SPIDER-MAN

GUARDIANS OF THE GALAXY

TOY BOX

TOY BOX COLLECTION

ACHIEVEMENTS

			Starting Toys Continued				
GOT IT?	ICON	TOY NAME	DESCRIPTION	CATEGORY	FUNCTION	UNLOCK	TOY STORE PAGE
✓		Small Bridge Cliff	A section of terrain with a small bridge.	Terrain	Static	Starting Toy	Starting Toys - Page 1
✓		Small Disney Infinity Spruce Tree	A Disney Infinity tree.	Plants	Breakable	Starting Toy	Starting Toys - Page 1
✓		Small Rocky Terrain Block 1	A small section of rocky terrain for climbing.	Terrain	Static	Starting Toy	Starting Toys - Page 1
✓		Soldier of Clubs Costume	A combat toy in a Soldier Card costume from Alice in Wonderland.	Enemies	Enemy	Starting Toy	Starting Toys - Page 1
✓		Soldier of Hearts Costume	A combat toy in a Soldier Card costume from Alice in Wonderland.	Enemies	Enemy	Starting Toy	Starting Toys - Page 1
✓		Step Cliff	A section of terrain with climbing cliff steps.	Terrain	Static	Starting Toy	Starting Toys - Page 1
✓		Stepped Grassy Corner	A corner section of stepped terrain.	Terrain	Static	Starting Toy	Starting Toys - Page 1
✓		Stunt Buggy	The perfect buggy for stunts and off-road racing.	Vehicles and Mounts	Vehicle	Starting Toy	Starting Toys - Page 1
✓		Terrain Block	A square terrain block.	Terrain	Static	Starting Toy	Starting Toys - Page 1
✓		The King's Guard	The King's guard from Tangled.	Enemies	Enemy	Starting Toy	Starting Toys - Page 1
✓		Tiny Terrain Block	A tiny, square terrain block.	Terrain	Static	Starting Toy	Starting Toys - Page 1
✓		Toy Box Blaster	The Toy Box's most basic, reliable blaster.	Tool/Pack	Tool	Starting Toy	Starting Toys - Page 1
✓		Toy Box Terrain Creator	Place this Creator to quickly build some terrain.	Builders and Creators	Creator	Starting Toy	Starting Toys - Page 1
✓		Wide Floating Cliff	An outer edge of terrain.	Terrain	Static	Starting Toy	Starting Toys - Page 1
✓		Arched Race Track Ramp	A race track ramp from Disney Infinity.	Race Track Pieces	Track	Starting Toy	Starting Toys - Page 2
✓		Banked Race Track Curve	A banked section of race track from Disney Infinity.	Race Track Pieces	Track	Starting Toy	Starting Toys - Page 2
✓		Banked Race Track Turn	A banked section of race track from Disney Infinity.	Race Track Pieces	Track	Starting Toy	Starting Toys - Page 2
✓		Bowed Race Track Ramp	A race track ramp from Disney Infinity.	Race Track Pieces	Track	Starting Toy	Starting Toys - Page 2
✓		Disney Infinity Flowers 1	Disney Infinity flowers.	Plants	Static	Starting Toy	Starting Toys - Page 2
✓		Disney Infinity Flowers 2	Disney Infinity flowers.	Plants	Static	Starting Toy	Starting Toys - Page 2
✓		Disney Infinity Flowers 3	Disney Infinity flowers.	Plants	Static	Starting Toy	Starting Toys - Page 2
✓		Disney Infinity Leaf Patch	A Disney Infinity plant.	Plants	Static	Starting Toy	Starting Toys - Page 2
✓		Disney Infinity Pine Tree	A Disney Infinity pine tree.	Plants	Static	Starting Toy	Starting Toys - Page 2
✓		Fantasy Terrain 1	Fantasy landscape from Disney Infinity.	Plants	Customization Cluster	Starting Toy	Starting Toys - Page 2
✓		Fantasy Terrain 2	Fantasy landscape from Disney Infinity.	Plants	Customization Cluster	Starting Toy	Starting Toys - Page 2
✓		Fantasy Terrain 3	Fantasy landscape from Disney Infinity.	Plants	Customization Cluster	Starting Toy	Starting Toys - Page 2
✓		Fantasy Terrain 4	Fantasy landscape from Disney Infinity.	Plants	Customization Cluster	Starting Toy	Starting Toys - Page 2
✓		Fantasy Terrain 5	Fantasy landscape from Disney Infinity.	Plants	Customization Cluster	Starting Toy	Starting Toys - Page 2
✓		Fantasy Terrain Corner 1	Fantasy landscape from Disney Infinity.	Plants	Customization Cluster	Starting Toy	Starting Toys - Page 2
✓		Fantasy Terrain Corner 2	Fantasy landscape from Disney Infinity.	Plants	Customization Cluster	Starting Toy	Starting Toys - Page 2
✓		Fantasy Terrain Strip 1	Fantasy landscape from Disney Infinity.	Plants	Customization Cluster	Starting Toy	Starting Toys - Page 2

			Starting Toys Continued				
GOT IT?	ICON	TOY NAME	DESCRIPTION	CATEGORY	FUNCTION	UNLOCK	TOY STORE PAGE
✓		Fantasy Terrain Strip 2	Fantasy landscape from Disney Infinity.	Plants	Customization Cluster	Starting Toy	Starting Toys - Page 2
✓		Flat Race Track Ramp	A race track ramp from Disney Infinity.	Race Track Pieces	Track	Starting Toy	Starting Toys - Page 2
✓		Large Disney Infinity Pine Tree	A Disney Infinity pine tree.	Plants	Static	Starting Toy	Starting Toys - Page 2
✓		Long Race Track	A straight section of race track from Disney Infinity.	Race Track Pieces	Track	Starting Toy	Starting Toys - Page 2
✓		Long Race Track Ramp	A race track ramp from Disney Infinity.	Race Track Pieces	Track	Starting Toy	Starting Toys - Page 2
✓		Medium Race Track	A straight section of race track from Disney Infinity.	Race Track Pieces	Track	Starting Toy	Starting Toys - Page 2
✓		Race Track	A straight section of race track from Disney Infinity.	Race Track Pieces	Track	Starting Toy	Starting Toys - Page 2
✓		Race Track Curve	A curved section of race track from Disney Infinity.	Race Track Pieces	Track	Starting Toy	Starting Toys - Page 2
✓		Race Track Intersection	A race track intersection from Disney Infinity.	Race Track Pieces	Track	Starting Toy	Starting Toys - Page 2
✓		Race Track Left	A veering section of race track from Disney Infinity.	Race Track Pieces	Track	Starting Toy	Starting Toys - Page 2
✓		Race Track Right	A veering section of race track from Disney Infinity.	Race Track Pieces	Track	Starting Toy	Starting Toys - Page 2
✓		Race Track Start	A race track starting line from Disney Infinity.	Race Track Pieces	Track	Starting Toy	Starting Toys - Page 2
✓		Short Race Track	A straight section of race track from Disney Infinity.	Race Track Pieces	Track	Starting Toy	Starting Toys - Page 2
✓		Short Race Track Curve	A curved section of race track from Disney Infinity.	Race Track Pieces	Track	Starting Toy	Starting Toys - Page 2
✓		Small Disney Infinity Pine Tree	A Disney Infinity pine tree.	Plants	Static	Starting Toy	Starting Toys - Page 2
✓		Steep Arched Race Track Ramp	A steep race track ramp from Disney Infinity.	Race Track Pieces	Track	Starting Toy	Starting Toys - Page 2
✓		Steep Bowed Race Track Ramp	A steep race track ramp from Disney Infinity.	Race Track Pieces	Track	Starting Toy	Starting Toys - Page 2
✓		Steep Flat Race Track Ramp	A steep race track ramp from Disney Infinity.	Race Track Pieces	Track	Starting Toy	Starting Toys - Page 2
✓		Toy Box Race Track Creator	Place this Creator to quickly build a race track.	Builders and Creators	Creator	Starting Toy	Starting Toys - Page 2
✓		Toy Box Stunt Track Creator	Place this Creator to quickly build a race track with stunts.	Builders and Creators	Creator	Toy Store Purchase	Starting Toys - Page 2
✓		Toy Box Track Creator	Place this Creator to quickly build a track.	Builders and Creators	Creator	Starting Toy	Starting Toys - Page 2
✓		Toy Box Winding Track Creator	Place this Creator to quickly build a race track with lots of turns and hills.	Builders and Creators	Creator	Toy Store Purchase	Starting Toys - Page 2
✓		Very Long Race Track	A straight section of race track from Disney Infinity.	Race Track Pieces	Track	Starting Toy	Starting Toys - Page 2
✓		Very Short Race Track	A straight section of race track from Disney Infinity.	Race Track Pieces	Track	Starting Toy	Starting Toys - Page 2
✓		Cliff Ledge	An outer edge of terrain.	Terrain	Static	Starting Toy	Starting Toys - Page 3
✓		Cliff Slope 1	A section of terrain with a sloping cliff.	Terrain	Static	Starting Toy	Starting Toys - Page 3
✓		Cliff Slope 2	A section of terrain with a sloping cliff.	Terrain	Static	Starting Toy	Starting Toys - Page 3
✓		Curved Floating Bridge	A section of terrain with a curving bridge.	Terrain	Static	Starting Toy	Starting Toys - Page 3
✓		Flat Terrain Block	A square terrain block.	Terrain	Static	Starting Toy	Starting Toys - Page 3
✓		Floating Bridge Hill	A section of terrain with an arched bridge.	Terrain	Static	Starting Toy	Starting Toys - Page 3
✓		Grassy Bridge	A section of terrain that includes a grassy bridge.	Terrain	Static	Starting Toy	Starting Toys - Page 3

GAME BASICS

CHARACTERS

POWER DISCS

MARVEL'S THE AVENGERS

SPIDER-MAN

GUARDIANS OF THE GALAXY

TOY BOX

TOY BOX COLLECTION

ACHIEVEMENTS

Starting Toys Continued

GOT IT?	ICON	TOY NAME	DESCRIPTION	CATEGORY	FUNCTION	UNLOCK	TOY STORE PAGE
✓		Jutting Ledge	A section of terrain that includes a grassy perch.	Terrain	Static	Starting Toy	Starting Toys - Page 3
✓		Large Cliff Ledge	A jutting edge of terrain.	Terrain	Static	Starting Toy	Starting Toys - Page 3
✓		Large Flat Terrain Block	A large, square terrain block.	Terrain	Static	Starting Toy	Starting Toys - Page 3
✓		Large Slope	A section of terrain that includes a slope.	Terrain	Static	Starting Toy	Starting Toys - Page 3
✓		Long Flat Terrain Block	A long, flat terrain block.	Terrain	Static	Starting Toy	Starting Toys - Page 3
✓		Long Tiny Terrain Block	A long, tiny terrain block.	Terrain	Static	Starting Toy	Starting Toys - Page 3
✓		Massive Terrain Block	A large, square terrain block.	Terrain	Static	Starting Toy	Starting Toys - Page 3
✓		Medium Cliff Ledge	A small, jutting edge of terrain.	Terrain	Static	Starting Toy	Starting Toys - Page 3
✓		Overhanging Corner	A rocky, overhanging ledge corner.	Terrain	Static	Starting Toy	Starting Toys - Page 3
✓		Overhanging Ledge	A rocky, overhanging ledge.	Terrain	Static	Starting Toy	Starting Toys - Page 3
✓		Sloping Hill	A small section of sloping terrain.	Terrain	Static	Starting Toy	Starting Toys - Page 3
✓		Small Cliff Ledge	A corner edge of terrain.	Terrain	Static	Starting Toy	Starting Toys - Page 3
✓		Small Flat Terrain Block	A small, square terrain block.	Terrain	Static	Starting Toy	Starting Toys - Page 3
✓		Small Floating Cliff	An outer edge of terrain.	Terrain	Static	Starting Toy	Starting Toys - Page 3
✓		Small Jutting Ledge	An outer edge of terrain.	Terrain	Static	Starting Toy	Starting Toys - Page 3
✓		Small Ramp Cliff	A section of terrain that includes a short ramp.	Terrain	Static	Starting Toy	Starting Toys - Page 3
✓		Small Slope	A section of terrain that includes a small slope.	Terrain	Static	Starting Toy	Starting Toys - Page 3
✓		Small Terrain Block	A small, square terrain block.	Terrain	Static	Starting Toy	Starting Toys - Page 3
✓		Tall Narrow Terrain Block	A tall, narrow terrain block.	Terrain	Static	Starting Toy	Starting Toys - Page 3
✓		Tall Terrain Block	A tiny, square terrain block.	Terrain	Static	Starting Toy	Starting Toys - Page 3
✓		Tiny Slope	A tiny section of sloping terrain.	Terrain	Static	Starting Toy	Starting Toys - Page 3
✓		Tiny Tall Terrain Block	A tiny, square terrain block.	Terrain	Static	Starting Toy	Starting Toys - Page 3
✓		Wide Floating Bridge Hill	A section of terrain with a wide bridge.	Terrain	Static	Starting Toy	Starting Toys - Page 3
✓		Winding Floating Bridge 1	A winding section of terrain.	Terrain	Static	Starting Toy	Starting Toys - Page 3
✓		Winding Floating Bridge 2	A winding section of terrain.	Terrain	Static	Starting Toy	Starting Toys - Page 3
✓		Arch Block	A building block that can be used as a doorway or path.	Basic Blocks	Static	Starting Toy	Starting Toys - Page 4
✓		Balcony	An overhanging building block ledge.	Basic Blocks	Static	Starting Toy	Starting Toys - Page 4
✓		Block Wall	A building block wall.	Basic Blocks	Static	Starting Toy	Starting Toys - Page 4
✓		Block Wall Corner	A building block wall corner.	Basic Blocks	Static	Starting Toy	Starting Toys - Page 4
✓		Column	A building block column.	Basic Blocks	Static	Starting Toy	Starting Toys - Page 4
✓		Curved Block	This building block with a rounded top can cap your block structure.	Basic Blocks	Static	Starting Toy	Starting Toys - Page 4

			Starting Toys Continued					
GOT IT?	ICON	TOY NAME	DESCRIPTION	CATEGORY	FUNCTION	UNLOCK	TOY STORE PAGE	
✓		Dip Beam	A recessed building block beam.	Basic Blocks	Static	Starting Toy	Starting Toys - Page 4	
✓		Full Dome	A complete building block dome.	Basic Blocks	Static	Starting Toy	Starting Toys - Page 4	
✓		Half Dome	Half of a building block dome.	Basic Blocks	Static	Starting Toy	Starting Toys - Page 4	
✓		Large Block Wall	A large building block wall.	Basic Blocks	Static	Starting Toy	Starting Toys - Page 4	
✓		Large Floor	A large building block floor.	Basic Blocks	Static	Starting Toy	Starting Toys - Page 4	
✓		Ledge Block	A building block with a ledge for climbing.	Basic Blocks	Static	Starting Toy	Starting Toys - Page 4	
✓		Long Block	A long building block.	Basic Blocks	Static	Starting Toy	Starting Toys - Page 4	
✓		Long Support Arch	A long building block for arch construction.	Basic Blocks	Static	Starting Toy	Starting Toys - Page 4	
✓		Long Wedge Block	A long, wedge-shaped building block that can be used as a ramp or a jump.	Basic Blocks	Static	Starting Toy	Starting Toys - Page 4	
✓		Obelisk	A decorative obelisk building block.	Basic Blocks	Static	Starting Toy	Starting Toys - Page 4	
✓		Onion Dome	An onion-shaped building block dome.	Basic Blocks	Static	Starting Toy	Starting Toys - Page 4	
✓		Pillar Block	A building block pillar.	Basic Blocks	Static	Starting Toy	Starting Toys - Page 4	
✓		Ramp Block	A wedge-shaped building block that can be used as a ramp or jump.	Basic Blocks	Static	Starting Toy	Starting Toys - Page 4	
✓		Ramp Vertical	A tall, vertical wedge-shaped block that can be used as a ramp or a jump.	Basic Blocks	Static	Starting Toy	Starting Toys - Page 4	
✓		Rounded Ledge Block	A rounded building block with a ledge for climbing.	Basic Blocks	Static	Starting Toy	Starting Toys - Page 4	
✓		Short Block Wall	A building block wall.	Basic Blocks	Static	Starting Toy	Starting Toys - Page 4	
✓		Short Support Arch	A short building block for arch construction.	Basic Blocks	Static	Starting Toy	Starting Toys - Page 4	
✓		Small Floor	A building block floor.	Basic Blocks	Static	Starting Toy	Starting Toys - Page 4	
✓		Square Block	A square building block.	Basic Blocks	Static	Starting Toy	Starting Toys - Page 4	
✓		Stairs	A building block with built-in stairs.	Basic Blocks	Static	Starting Toy	Starting Toys - Page 4	
✓		Tall Block	A tall building block.	Basic Blocks	Static	Starting Toy	Starting Toys - Page 4	
✓		Tall Vaulted Platform	A tall, vaulted building block platform.	Basic Blocks	Static	Starting Toy	Starting Toys - Page 4	
✓		Triangle Block	A decorative, pyramid-shaped building block.	Basic Blocks	Static	Starting Toy	Starting Toys - Page 4	
✓		Trim	A building block with decorative trim.	Basic Blocks	Static	Starting Toy	Starting Toys - Page 4	
✓		Upside-Down Curved Block	An upside-down rounded building block.	Basic Blocks	Static	Starting Toy	Starting Toys - Page 4	
✓		Upside-Down Full Dome	An upside-down building block dome.	Basic Blocks	Static	Starting Toy	Starting Toys - Page 4	
✓		Upside-Down Half Dome	An upside-down building block half dome.	Basic Blocks	Static	Starting Toy	Starting Toys - Page 4	
✓		Upside-Down Triangle Block	An upside-down pyramid-shaped building block.	Basic Blocks	Static	Starting Toy	Starting Toys - Page 4	
✓		Vaulted Platform	A vaulted building block platform.	Basic Blocks	Static	Starting Toy	Starting Toys - Page 4	
✓		Wedge Block	A wedge-shaped building block that can be used as a ramp or a jump.	Basic Blocks	Static	Starting Toy	Starting Toys - Page 4	
✓		Bear	A woodland critter from Disney Infinity.	Critters	Critter	Starting Toy	Starting Toys - Page 5	

Starting Toys Continued

GOT IT?	ICON	TOY NAME	DESCRIPTION	CATEGORY	FUNCTION	UNLOCK	TOY STORE PAGE
✓		Bending Rail	Connect rails together from end to end, then hop on for the ride of your life!	Platforming Toys	Rail Grind	Starting Toy	Starting Toys - Page 5
✓		Bird	A woodland critter from Disney Infinity.	Critters	Critter	Starting Toy	Starting Toys - Page 5
✓		Buck	A woodland critter from Disney Infinity.	Critters	Critter	Starting Toy	Starting Toys - Page 5
✓		Bump Rail	Connect rails together from end to end, then hop on for the ride of your life!	Platforming Toys	Rail Grind	Starting Toy	Starting Toys - Page 5
✓		Curved Rail	Connect rails together from end to end, then hop on for the ride of your life!	Platforming Toys	Rail Grind	Starting Toy	Starting Toys - Page 5
✓		Deer	A woodland critter from Disney Infinity.	Critters	Critter	Starting Toy	Starting Toys - Page 5
✓		Dipped Rail	Connect rails together from end to end, then hop on for the ride of your life!	Platforming Toys	Rail Grind	Starting Toy	Starting Toys - Page 5
✓		Gopher	A woodland critter from Disney Infinity.	Critters	Critter	Starting Toy	Starting Toys - Page 5
✓		Left Rail	Connect rails together from end to end, then hop on for the ride of your life!	Platforming Toys	Rail Grind	Starting Toy	Starting Toys - Page 5
✓		Left Upward Curving Rail	Connect rails together from end to end, then hop on for the ride of your life!	Platforming Toys	Rail Grind	Starting Toy	Starting Toys - Page 5
✓		Rabbit	A woodland critter from Disney Infinity.	Critters	Critter	Starting Toy	Starting Toys - Page 5
✓		Ramp Rail	Connect rails together from end to end, then hop on for the ride of your life!	Platforming Toys	Rail Grind	Starting Toy	Starting Toys - Page 5
✓		Rat	A woodland critter from Disney Infinity.	Critters	Critter	Starting Toy	Starting Toys - Page 5
✓		Right Rail	Connect rails together from end to end, then hop on for the ride of your life!	Platforming Toys	Rail Grind	Starting Toy	Starting Toys - Page 5
✓		Right Upward Curving Rail	Connect rails together from end to end, then hop on for the ride of your life!	Platforming Toys	Rail Grind	Starting Toy	Starting Toys - Page 5
✓		Short Straight Rail	Connect rails together from end to end, then hop on for the ride of your life!	Platforming Toys	Rail Grind	Starting Toy	Starting Toys - Page 5
✓		Steep Bending Rail	Connect rails together from end to end, then hop on for the ride of your life!	Platforming Toys	Rail Grind	Starting Toy	Starting Toys - Page 5
✓		Steep Ramp Rail	Connect rails together from end to end, then hop on for the ride of your life!	Platforming Toys	Rail Grind	Starting Toy	Starting Toys - Page 5
✓		Straight Rail	Connect rails together from end to end, then hop on for the ride of your life!	Platforming Toys	Rail Grind	Starting Toy	Starting Toys - Page 5
✓		Wolf	A woodland critter from Disney Infinity.	Critters	Critter	Starting Toy	Starting Toys - Page 5

TOY BOX GAMES

ASSAULT ON ASGARD

GOT IT?	ICON	TOY NAME	DESCRIPTION	CATEGORY	FUNCTION	UNLOCK	TOY STORE PAGE
✓		Asgard Enemy Door	Contain your enemies with this toy and the Enemy Wave Generator! You can even control when to open and close the doors.	Creativi-Toys	Custom	Assault on Asgard Reward	Asgard Toys - Page 1
✓		Asgard Townsperson Door	Throw a townsperson or sidekick into this door to activate other toys that have been connected to it.	Creativi-Toys	Custom	Assault on Asgard Reward	Asgard Toys - Page 1
✓		Asgardian	Odin's Guard.	Marvel Townspeople	Townspeople	Assault on Asgard Reward	Asgard Toys - Page 1
✓		Asgardian Barrier	This barrier can stave off enemy assaults for a short period of time.	Instant Fun	Custom	Assault on Asgard Reward	Asgard Toys - Page 1
✓		Asgardian Battle Wedge	Crafted from magical uru metal, this vehicle decimates any foolish enough to stand in its way.	Instant Fun	Vehicle	Assault on Asgard Reward	Asgard Toys - Page 1

			Assault On Asgard Continued				
GOT IT?	ICON	TOY NAME	DESCRIPTION	CATEGORY	FUNCTION	UNLOCK	TOY STORE PAGE
✓		Asgardian Catapult Trap	Enemies foolish enough to trigger this trap are nearly launched back to Midgard.	Instant Fun	Custom	Assault on Asgard Reward	Asgard Toys - Page 1
✓		Asgardian Conveyor Belt	A golden Asgardian building piece with a horizontal moving surface.	Platforming Toys	Custom	Assault on Asgard Reward	Asgard Toys - Page 1
✓		Asgardian Decoy	Dim-witted enemies are lured to this decoy so Thor can utilize his hammer and battle prowess.	Instant Fun	Custom	Assault on Asgard Reward	Asgard Toys - Page 1
✓		Asgardian Energy Shield	Thor uses this device to provide protection from missiles and projectiles.	Instant Fun	Custom	Assault on Asgard Reward	Asgard Toys - Page 1
✓		Asgardian Focus Turret	Channeling the raw power of Lightning, Thor empowers this turret to protect an area.	Instant Fun	Custom	Assault on Asgard Reward	Asgard Toys - Page 1
✓		Asgardian Freeze Mine	Foes that trigger this trap momentarily become colder than the most frigid Frost Giant.	Instant Fun	Custom	Assault on Asgard Reward	Asgard Toys - Page 1
✓		Asgardian Healing Rune	Should a foe somehow slow the Thunder God, Thor can revitalize next to this Healing Rune.	Instant Fun	Custom	Assault on Asgard Reward	Asgard Toys - Page 1
✓		Asgardian Implosion Mine	Making use of the blackest Dark Elf magic, Thor can pulverize his foes with this trap.	Instant Fun	Custom	Assault on Asgard Reward	Asgard Toys - Page 1
✓		Asgardian Lava Terrain	A dangerous lava block.	Platforming Toys	Custom	Assault on Asgard Reward	Asgard Toys - Page 1
✓		Asgardian Mine Deployer	Dwarven allies crafted this explosive trap on behalf of the Asgardian heroes.	Instant Fun	Custom	Assault on Asgard Reward	Asgard Toys - Page 1
✓		Asgardian Spread Turret	Thor uses this turret to use its reduced firepower to protect a wider area.	Instant Fun	Custom	Assault on Asgard Reward	Asgard Toys - Page 1
✓		Large Asgardian Lava Terrain	A dangerous lava block.	Platforming Toys	Custom	Assault on Asgard Reward	Asgard Toys - Page 1
✓		Massive Asgardian Lava Terrain	A dangerous lava block.	Platforming Toys	Custom	Assault on Asgard Reward	Asgard Toys - Page 1
✓		Odin's Bed	This object attracts enemies and can be used as the goal of defense missions. Set it to a team in the Properties menu.	Creativi-Toys	Custom	Assault on Asgard Reward	Asgard Toys - Page 1
✓		Odin's Treasure	This object attracts enemies and can be used as the goal of defense missions. Set it to a team in the Properties menu.	Creativi-Toys	Custom	Assault on Asgard Reward	Asgard Toys - Page 1
✓		Small Asgardian Lava Terrain	A dangerous lava block.	Platforming Toys	Custom	Assault on Asgard Reward	Asgard Toys - Page 1
✓		Asgardian Centerpiece Foliage	An Asgardian-themed building piece.	Plants	Static	Toy Store Purchase (Assault on Asgard)	Asgard Toys - Page 2
✓		Asgardian Corner Foliage Railing	An Asgardian-themed building piece.	Plants	Static	Toy Store Purchase (Assault on Asgard)	Asgard Toys - Page 2
✓		Asgardian Foliage Railing	An Asgardian-themed building piece.	Plants	Static	Toy Store Purchase (Assault on Asgard)	Asgard Toys - Page 2
✓		Asgardian Planter	An Asgardian-themed building piece.	Plants	Static	Toy Store Purchase (Assault on Asgard)	Asgard Toys - Page 2
✓		Asgardian Railing	An Asgardian-themed building piece.	Decorations	Static	Toy Store Purchase (Assault on Asgard)	Asgard Toys - Page 2
✓		Asgardian Railing End	An Asgardian-themed building piece.	Decorations	Static	Toy Store Purchase (Assault on Asgard)	Asgard Toys - Page 2
✓		Asgardian Railing Inner Corner	An Asgardian-themed building piece.	Decorations	Static	Toy Store Purchase (Assault on Asgard)	Asgard Toys - Page 2
✓		Asgardian Railing Outer Corner	An Asgardian-themed building piece.	Decorations	Static	Toy Store Purchase (Assault on Asgard)	Asgard Toys - Page 2
✓		Asgardian Trim Piece	An Asgardian-themed building piece.	Decorations	Static	Toy Store Purchase (Assault on Asgard)	Asgard Toys - Page 2
✓		Long Asgardian Railing	An Asgardian-themed building piece.	Decorations	Static	Toy Store Purchase (Assault on Asgard)	Asgard Toys - Page 2
✓		Short Asgardian Railing	An Asgardian-themed building piece.	Decorations	Static	Toy Store Purchase (Assault on Asgard)	Asgard Toys - Page 2
✓		Small Asgardian Brazier	An Asgardian-themed building piece.	Decorations	Static	Toy Store Purchase (Assault on Asgard)	Asgard Toys - Page 2
✓		Very Short Asgardian Railing	An Asgardian-themed building piece.	Decorations	Static	Toy Store Purchase (Assault on Asgard)	Asgard Toys - Page 2

GAME BASICS
CHARACTERS
POWER DISCS
MARVEL'S THE AVENGERS
SPIDER-MAN
GUARDIANS OF THE GALAXY
TOY BOX
TOY BOX COLLECTION
ACHIEVEMENTS

ESCAPE FROM THE KYLN

GOT IT?	ICON	TOY NAME	DESCRIPTION	CATEGORY	FUNCTION	UNLOCK	TOY STORE PAGE
✓		Kyln Barrier	A Kyln-themed building piece.	Decorations	Static	Toy Store Purchase (Escape from the Kyln)	Kyln Toys - Page 1
✓		Kyln Boiler	A Kyln-themed building piece.	Decorations	Static	Toy Store Purchase (Escape from the Kyln)	Kyln Toys - Page 1
✓		Kyln Boiler Room Cloister	A Kyln-themed building piece.	Decorations	Static	Toy Store Purchase (Escape from the Kyln)	Kyln Toys - Page 1
✓		Kyln Bridge End	A Kyln-themed building piece.	Platforming Toys	Decoration	Toy Store Purchase (Escape from the Kyln)	Kyln Toys - Page 1
✓		Kyln Bridge End 2	A Kyln-themed building piece.	Platforming Toys	Decoration	Toy Store Purchase (Escape from the Kyln)	Kyln Toys - Page 1
✓		Kyln Bridge End 3	A Kyln-themed building piece.	Platforming Toys	Decoration	Toy Store Purchase (Escape from the Kyln)	Kyln Toys - Page 1
✓		Kyln Bridge End 4	A Kyln-themed building piece.	Platforming Toys	Decoration	Toy Store Purchase (Escape from the Kyln)	Kyln Toys - Page 1
✓		Kyln Bridge Piece	A Kyln-themed building piece.	Platforming Toys	Decoration	Toy Store Purchase (Escape from the Kyln)	Kyln Toys - Page 1
✓		Kyln Engine	A Kyln-themed building piece.	Decorations	Static	Toy Store Purchase (Escape from the Kyln)	Kyln Toys - Page 1
✓		Kyln Machine Post	A Kyln-themed building piece.	Decorations	Static	Toy Store Purchase (Escape from the Kyln)	Kyln Toys - Page 1
✓		Kyln Machinery	A Kyln-themed building piece.	Decorations	Static	Toy Store Purchase (Escape from the Kyln)	Kyln Toys - Page 1
✓		Kyln Pylon	A Kyln-themed building piece.	Decorations	Static	Toy Store Purchase (Escape from the Kyln)	Kyln Toys - Page 1
✓		Kyln Railing	A Kyln-themed building piece.	Decorations	Static	Toy Store Purchase (Escape from the Kyln)	Kyln Toys - Page 1
✓		Kyln Railing End	A Kyln-themed building piece.	Decorations	Static	Toy Store Purchase (Escape from the Kyln)	Kyln Toys - Page 1
✓		Kyln Railing Inner Corner	A Kyln-themed building piece.	Decorations	Static	Toy Store Purchase (Escape from the Kyln)	Kyln Toys - Page 1
✓		Kyln Railing Outer Corner	A Kyln-themed building piece.	Decorations	Static	Toy Store Purchase (Escape from the Kyln)	Kyln Toys - Page 1
✓		Kyln Wall Lighting	A Kyln-themed building piece.	Decorations	Static	Toy Store Purchase (Escape from the Kyln)	Kyln Toys - Page 1
✓		Long Kyln Railing	A Kyln-themed building piece.	Decorations	Static	Toy Store Purchase (Escape from the Kyln)	Kyln Toys - Page 1
✓		Short Kyln Railing	A Kyln-themed building piece.	Decorations	Static	Toy Store Purchase (Escape from the Kyln)	Kyln Toys - Page 1
✓		Very Short Kyln Railing	A Kyln-themed building piece.	Decorations	Static	Toy Store Purchase (Escape from the Kyln)	Kyln Toys - Page 1
✓		Anarchy	Don't go alone! Take a Kyln sidekick to help you in your adventure.	Sidekicks	Sidekick	Escape from the Kyln Reward	Kyln Toys - Page 2
✓		Bedlam	Don't go alone! Take a Kyln sidekick to help you in your adventure.	Sidekicks	Sidekick	Escape from the Kyln Reward	Kyln Toys - Page 2
✓		Brawler	Don't go alone! Take a Kyln sidekick to help you in your adventure.	Sidekicks	Sidekick	Escape from the Kyln Reward	Kyln Toys - Page 2
✓		Chaos	Don't go alone! Take a Kyln sidekick to help you in your adventure.	Sidekicks	Sidekick	Escape from the Kyln Reward	Kyln Toys - Page 2
✓		Combatant	Don't go alone! Take a Kyln sidekick to help you in your adventure.	Sidekicks	Sidekick	Escape from the Kyln Reward	Kyln Toys - Page 2
✓		Destruction	Don't go alone! Take a Kyln sidekick to help you in your adventure.	Sidekicks	Sidekick	Escape from the Kyln Reward	Kyln Toys - Page 2
✓		Disorder	Don't go alone! Take a Kyln sidekick to help you in your adventure.	Sidekicks	Sidekick	Escape from the Kyln Reward	Kyln Toys - Page 2
✓		Disturbance	Don't go alone! Take a Kyln sidekick to help you in your adventure.	Sidekicks	Sidekick	Escape from the Kyln Reward	Kyln Toys - Page 2
✓		Growler	Don't go alone! Take a Kyln sidekick to help you in your adventure.	Sidekicks	Sidekick	Escape from the Kyln Reward	Kyln Toys - Page 2
✓		Havoc	Don't go alone! Take a Kyln sidekick to help you in your adventure.	Sidekicks	Sidekick	Escape from the Kyln Reward	Kyln Toys - Page 2

Escape From The Kyln Continued

GOT IT?	ICON	TOY NAME	DESCRIPTION	CATEGORY	FUNCTION	UNLOCK	TOY STORE PAGE
✓		Mayhem	Don't go alone! Take a Kyln sidekick to help you in your adventure.	Sidekicks	Sidekick	Escape from the Kyln Reward	Kyln Toys - Page 2
✓		Rebel	Don't go alone! Take a Kyln sidekick to help you in your adventure.	Sidekicks	Sidekick	Escape from the Kyln Reward	Kyln Toys - Page 2
✓		Trouble	Don't go alone! Take a Kyln sidekick to help you in your adventure.	Sidekicks	Sidekick	Escape from the Kyln Reward	Kyln Toys - Page 2
✓		Turmoil	Don't go alone! Take a Kyln sidekick to help you in your adventure.	Sidekicks	Sidekick	Escape from the Kyln Reward	Kyln Toys - Page 2
✓		Uproar	Don't go alone! Take a Kyln sidekick to help you in your adventure.	Sidekicks	Sidekick	Escape from the Kyln Reward	Kyln Toys - Page 2
✓		Empty Kyln Cell Block	An empty Kyln prison piece.	Decorations	Static	Escape from the Kyln Reward	Kyln Toys - Page 6
✓		Empty Large Kyln Cell Block	An empty Kyln prison piece.	Decorations	Static	Escape from the Kyln Reward	Kyln Toys - Page 6
✓		Kyln Brazier	A Kyln-themed light.	Decorations	Static	Escape from the Kyln Reward	Kyln Toys - Page 6
✓		Kyln Cell Block	A Kyln prison piece with enemies inside.	Decorations	Static	Escape from the Kyln Reward	Kyln Toys - Page 6
✓		Kyln Chest	A Kyln-themed treasure chest.	Creativi-Toys	Custom	Escape from the Kyln Reward	Kyln Toys - Page 6
✓		Kyln Color Pressure Plate	Press this Pressure Plate and it will change color—as well as trigger things you set through the Logic menu. You can even have certain colors trigger certain things.	Creativi-Toys	Custom	Escape from the Kyln Reward	Kyln Toys - Page 6
✓		Kyln Crate	A Kyln-themed breakable building piece.	Decorations	Breakable	Escape from the Kyln Reward	Kyln Toys - Page 6
✓		Kyln Enemy-Spawning Chamber	A breakable Kyln enemy generator.	Creativi-Toys	Custom	Escape from the Kyln Reward	Kyln Toys - Page 6
✓		Kyln Key Card	A Guardians of the Galaxy collectible.	Creativi-Toys	Custom	Escape from the Kyln Reward	Kyln Toys - Page 6
✓		Kyln Liftable Block	A weighted block that can be heaved, thrown, and dropped.	Creativi-Toys	Custom	Escape from the Kyln Reward	Kyln Toys - Page 6
✓		Kyln Loot Piece	A Kyln-themed piece of loot.	Creativi-Toys	Custom	Escape from the Kyln Reward	Kyln Toys - Page 6
✓		Kyln Passage Gate	A Kyln gateway.	Creativi-Toys	Custom	Escape from the Kyln Reward	Kyln Toys - Page 6
✓		Kyln Pressure Plate	Press this Pressure Plate to trigger events that you set through the Logic menu.	Creativi-Toys	Custom	Escape from the Kyln Reward	Kyln Toys - Page 6
✓		Kyln Sidekick Outfitter	Access and customize your sidekicks with the Sidekick Outfitter.	Creativi-Toys	Custom	Escape from the Kyln Reward	Kyln Toys - Page 6
✓		Kyln Sidekick Wall Door	Throw a townsperson or sidekick into this door to activate other toys that have been connected to it.	Creativi-Toys	Custom	Escape from the Kyln Reward	Kyln Toys - Page 6
✓		Kyln Stack of Crates	A Kyln-themed breakable building piece.	Decorations	Breakable	Escape from the Kyln Reward	Kyln Toys - Page 6
✓		Large Kyln Cell Block	A Kyln prison piece with enemies inside.	Decorations	Static	Escape from the Kyln Reward	Kyln Toys - Page 6
✓		Large Kyln Passage Gate	A Kyln gateway that allows the player to go between areas.	Creativi-Toys	Custom	Escape from the Kyln Reward	Kyln Toys - Page 6
✓		Large Rubbish Block	A Kyln-themed breakable building piece.	Instant Fun	Breakable	Escape from the Kyln Reward	Kyln Toys - Page 6
✓		Rubbish Block	A Kyln-themed breakable building piece.	Instant Fun	Breakable	Escape from the Kyln Reward	Kyln Toys - Page 6
✓		Small Rubbish Block	A Kyln-themed breakable building piece.	Instant Fun	Breakable	Escape from the Kyln Reward	Kyln Toys - Page 6
✓		Tiny Rubbish Block	A Kyln-themed breakable building piece.	Instant Fun	Breakable	Escape from the Kyln Reward	Kyln Toys - Page 6

GAME BASICS

CHARACTERS

POWER DISCS

MARVEL'S THE AVENGERS

SPIDER-MAN

GUARDIANS OF THE GALAXY

TOY BOX

TOY BOX COLLECTION

ACHIEVEMENTS

ACHIEVEMENTS AND TROPHIES

	Achievements and Trophies				
GOT IT?	#	NAME	LOCATION	CRITERIA	XBOX 360 AND XBOX ONE ACHIEVEMENTS	PS3 AND PS4 TROPHIES
✔	1	On the Level	Global	Level up one character to Level 20.	20	Silver
✔	2	Level With You	Global	Level up two characters to Level 20.	50	Gold
✔	3	You Got Skills	Global	Unlock 30 character skills.	30	Silver
✔	4	The Long Hall	Global	Visit the Hall of Heroes.	20	Bronze
✔	5	Seasoned Traveler	Global	Ride a mount and a motorcycle, drive a car, and pilot a flying vehicle.	20	Bronze
✔	6	World Traveler	Global	Download five user-generated games.	20	Bronze
✔	7	Door to Door	Global	Link five Toy Boxes together with Toy Box Doors.	20	Bronze
✔	8	Toy Box Maker	Global	Publish your own Toy Box Game.	20	Bronze
✔	9	Enemy Combatant	Global	Defeat 100 enemies.	20	Bronze
✔	10	Enemy Onslaught	Global	Defeat 500 enemies.	50	Gold
✔	11	Save It for Later	Toy Box	Save four Toy Boxes.	20	Bronze
✔	12	All Four One	Toy Box	Play a four-player game.	20	Silver
✔	13	Friendly Fire	Toy Box	Defeat another player's character.	20	Bronze
✔	14	With Friends Like These...	Toy Box	Defeat another player's character 40 times.	20	Silver
✔	15	Feat First	Toy Box	Complete 10 Feats.	30	Silver
✔	16	Get on Your Feat	Toy Box	Complete 25 Feats.	30	Silver
✔	17	Put Your Feat Up	Toy Box	Complete 50 Feats.	30	Silver
✔	18	The World at Your Feat	Toy Box	Complete 90 Feats.	100	Gold
✔	19	Good Buy	Toy Box	Purchase a full page of toys from the Toy Store.	20	Bronze
✔	20	Shopping Spree	Toy Box	Purchase 100 toys.	50	Gold
✔	21	Double Trouble	Toy Box Games	Play a Toy Box Game with two players.	30	Silver
✔	22	Sidekickin' It into Gear	Toy Box Games	Unlock five sidekicks.	30	Silver
✔	23	Super Sidekick	Toy Box Games	Collect 50 pieces of equipment for your sidekicks.	50	Silver
✔	24	Trap Master	Toy Box Games	Place 50 traps in Assault on Asgard or Stitch's Tropical Rescue.	30	Silver
✔	25	Survival of the Fittest	Toy Box Games	Complete Exploration Survival Mode.	100	Gold
✔	26	INterior Specialist	Toy Box INteriors	Complete all INterior tutorials.	20	Bronze
✔	27	Room for Expansion	Toy Box INteriors	Build a 10-room INterior.	50	Silver
✔	28	INterior Decorator	Toy Box INteriors	Purchase 25 INterior decorations from the Toy Store.	20	Bronze
✔	29	Master Decorator	Toy Box INteriors	Purchase 50 INterior decorations from the Toy Store.	40	Silver
✔		Platinum Hero	Global (PS3 and PS4 only)	Collect every Trophy.	N/A	Platinum

2.0 EDITION

MARVEL
SUPER HEROES
ACCESSORIES

POWER DISC BINDER

MARVEL SUPER HEROES

PLAYZONE

ARMOR BAG

POWER DISC CAPSULE

TECH ZONE

Disney INFINITY

2.0 EDITION

MARVEL
SUPER HEROES

WRITTEN BY

MICHAEL KNIGHT & MICHAEL SEARLE

PRIMA OFFICIAL GAME GUIDE

PRIMA GAMES

AN IMPRINT OF RANDOM HOUSE, INC.

3000 LAVA RIDGE COURT, SUITE 100

ROSEVILLE, CA 95661

WWW.PRIMAGAMES.COM/DISNEYINFINITYMARVEL

The Prima Games logo is a registered trademark of Random House LLC, registered in the United States and other countries. Primagames.com is a registered trademark of Random House LLC, registered in the United States.

Prima Games is an imprint of Random House LLC, New York, a Penguin Random House Company.

© MARVEL © Disney

Managing Editor: **DONATO TICA**
Design and Layout: **IN COLOR DESIGN**
Copyeditor: **JULIA MASCARDO**
Gameplay Support: **JOSEF FRECH**

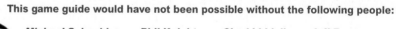

This game guide would have not been possible without the following people:

Michael Schneider	Phil Knight	Chad Liddell	Jeff Byers
Kristie Crawford	Bob Lowe	Andrew Hayes	Greg Hayes
Amber Anderson	Troy Johnson	David White	Cyril Bornette
Jessica B. Klein			

IMPORTANT:

Prima Games has made every effort to determine that the information contained in this book is accurate. However, the publisher makes no warranty, either expressed or implied, as to the accuracy, effectiveness, or completeness of the material in this book; nor does the publisher assume liability for damages, either incidental or consequential, that may result from using the information in this book. The publisher cannot provide any additional information or support regarding gameplay, hints and strategies, or problems with hardware or software. Such questions should be directed to the support numbers provided by the game and/or device manufacturers as set forth in their documentation. Some game tricks require precise timing and may require repeated attempts before the desired result is achieved.

ISBN: 978-0804-16363-7 | Printed in the United States of America